D0946056

# TRAVELER'S GUIDE TO

# ALASKAN CAMPING

## Explore Alaska And The Yukon With RV Or Tent

*Mike and Terri Church*

*ROLLING HOMES PRESS*

Copyright © 1998 by Mike and Terri Church

All Rights reserved. No part of this book may be reproduced in any form except brief extracts for the purpose of review, without permission in writing from the publisher. All inquiries should be addresed to Rolling Homes Press.

Published by
Rolling Homes Press
P.O. Box 2099
Kirkland, WA  98083-2099


Printed in the United States of America
First Printing 1998



**Publisher's Cataloging in Publication**


Church, Mike 1951-
  Traveler's Guide To Alaskan Camping : explore Alaska and the Yukon with RV or tent / Mike and Terri Church
    p.cm.
    Includes index.
  Preassigned LCCN: 98-91216
    ISBN 0-9652968-2-2



  1. Alaska--Guidebooks. 2. Camping--Alaska--Guidebooks.  I. Church, Terri. II. Title.

F902.3.C48 1998                     917.9804/51--dc21

*This book is dedicated*
*to the memory of our grandparents,*

**MURIEL AND CARL JOHNSON**

Muriel and Carl lived most of their lives in Fairbanks, Alaska. They fished, hunted, dug clams, and picked wild berries every year and enjoyed Alaska to its fullest. Our love of Alaska, the outdoors, and camping came from them.

**Other Books by Mike and Terri Church**
**and**
**Rolling Homes Press**

*Traveler's Guide To Mexican Camping*
*Traveler's Guide To European Camping*

A brief summary of the above books is provided on pages 414 and 415

# WARNING, DISCLOSURE, AND COMMUNICATION WITH THE AUTHORS AND PUBLISHERS

Half the fun of travel is the unexpected, and self-guided camping travel can produce much in the way of unexpected pleasures, and alternately, complications and problems. This book is designed to increase the pleasures of Alaskan camping and reduce the number of unexpected problems you may encounter. You can help ensure a smooth trip by doing additional advance research, planning ahead, and exercising caution when appropriate. There can be no guarantee that your trip will be trouble free.

Although the authors and publisher have done their best to ensure that the information presented in this book was correct at the time of publication they do not assume and hereby disclaim any liability to any party for any loss or damage caused by errors, omissions, or any other cause.

In a book like this it is inevitable that there will be omissions or mistakes, especially as things do change over time. If you find inaccuracies we would like to hear about them so that they can be corrected in future editions. We would also like to hear about your enjoyable experiences. If you come upon an outstanding campground or destination please let us know, those kinds of things may also find their way to future versions of the guide. You can reach us by mail at:

Rolling Homes Press
P.O. Box 2099
Kirkland, WA  98083-2099

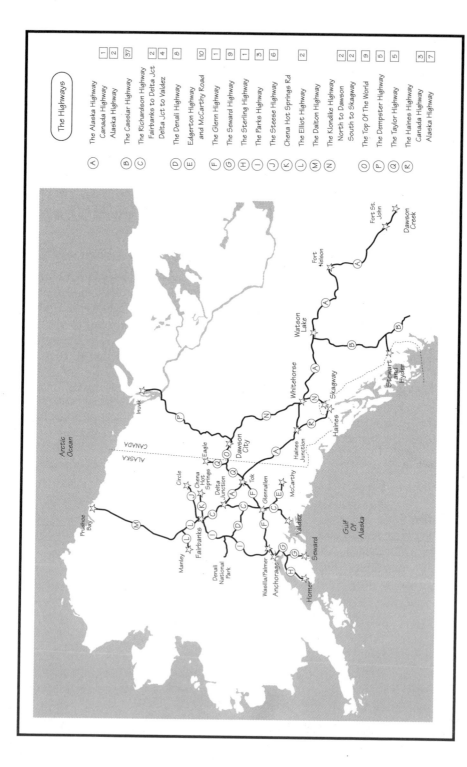

The Highways

| | | |
|---|---|---|
| (A) | The Alaska Highway | ☐ 1 |
| | Canada Highway | ☐ 2 |
| | Alaska Highway | ☐ 37 |
| (B) | The Cassiar Highway | ☐ 2 |
| (C) | The Richardson Highway | |
| | Fairbanks to Delta Jct | ☐ 2 |
| | Delta Jct to Valdez | ☐ 4 |
| (D) | The Denali Highway | ☐ 8 |
| (E) | Edgerton Highway | |
| | and McCarthy Road | ☐ 10 |
| (F) | The Glenn Highway | ☐ 1 |
| (G) | The Seward Highway | ☐ 9 |
| (H) | The Sterling Highway | ☐ 1 |
| (I) | The Parks Highway | ☐ 3 |
| (J) | The Steese Highway | ☐ 6 |
| (K) | Chena Hot Springs Rd | |
| (L) | The Elliot Highway | ☐ 2 |
| (M) | The Dalton Highway | |
| (N) | The Klondike Highway | |
| | North to Dawson | ☐ 2 |
| | South to Skagway | ☐ 2 |
| (O) | The Top Of The World | ☐ 9 |
| (P) | The Dempster Highway | ☐ 5 |
| (Q) | The Taylor Highway | ☐ 5 |
| (R) | The Haines Highway | |
| | Canada Highway | ☐ 3 |
| | Alaska Highway | ☐ 7 |

# TABLE OF CONTENTS

# INTRODUCTION

For most people Alaska is the dream camping destination. No wonder! There is just no other destination with the same combination of accessibility, scenery, wildlife, outdoor activities, history, facilities, and support. Any camping trip to Alaska, whether in an RV or on foot, along the road system or a remote river, for sightseeing or for fishing, is bound to be the trip of a lifetime.

We've been traveling extensively in an RV for several years now. We've camped around the U.S., Europe, and Mexico. There are lots of places to go and lots to see, but it seems that each year finds us back in Alaska.

We do have a few more Alaska connections than most people. One of us, Mike, was born and raised in Fairbanks. His family arrived there in 1906, fresh from Dawson City and the gold rush there—his grandmother was one of the few children born in Dawson City during the gold rush. There's an Alcan connection too—his mother first came to Alaska in 1947 over the highway, a year before it officially opened to civilian traffic. He's lived in Fairbanks, Anchorage, Cooper Landing, Kenai, Homer, Nenana, Tok, and even Denali Park. Terri arrived in Alaska the day after she graduated from college and lived and worked in Fairbanks, Kenai, and Anchorage for over ten years. We're based in Seattle now, but the state continues to draw us back.

Mike was introduced to camping by his grandparents, both true sourdoughs. His earliest camping experiences were travels along the Richardson between Fairbanks and Anchorage in the fifties, the campground most nights was a gravel pit and dinner was a grayling from a nearby stream. Very few summers since then have gone by without at least one camping vacation somewhere in the state.

*Traveler's Guide to Alaskan Camping* is our third guidebook. The first two are very similar in some ways to this one. They are *Traveler's Guide to European Camping* and *Traveler's Guide to Mexican Camping*. The three volumes are the key to a world of travel fun! We hope you will join us.

| A L A S K A |

Top Row Left:  On the road between Soldotna and Homer
Top Row Right:  Tent camping at Portage Cove State
Campground in Haines
Bottom Row Left:  Glacier near Portage on the Kenai Peninsula
Bottom Row Right:  Beautiful scenery on the Tok Cutoff

# CHAPTER

. . . . . . . . . 1

# WHY CAMP ALASKA?

Each year tens of thousands of people head out to camp in Alaska. Some are RVers who drive their rigs up the Alaska Highway. Some are Alaska residents who have waited through the long winter for breakup and summer days of fishing, hiking, floating rivers and enjoying the great outdoors. Others are nature lovers and adventure campers from around the world drawn to some of the most spectacular wilderness anywhere.

There are probably as many reasons to camp Alaska as there are people who do it, but here are a few.

## The Attractions

The State of Alaska holds so much wilderness that it is difficult to even grasp its immensity. There are 587,878 square miles in Alaska and about 600,000 residents. That works out to 1 square mile for each person. That's a lot of country with few people, especially when you realize that most of the people are in the cities. As you drive Alaska's highways you'll often cover miles and miles without sighting another person. Leave the road system and you're really alone. The pure solitude is sometimes almost overwhelming, but it's an experience to be treasured in today's world.

Scenery-wise Alaska is unbeatable. Southeast Alaska has deep blue fjords surrounded by steep mountains and glaciers. The interior's tree-covered hills march into the distance bathed by the light of the midnight sun. Icy Mt. McKinley looms above you as it rises to 20,320 feet from its nearly-sea level base. Beauty is everywhere you look.

Want to see wildlife? Alaska has big animals like grizzly bears, caribou, and moose and small ones like beavers and porcupines. Along the coast you can spot whales and sea otters. Each spring millions of birds migrate to Alaska for your viewing pleasure, over 300 species are present. Most appreciated by novice birdwatchers seem to be bald eagles, which are actually common in some areas, or perhaps the puffins that can easily be seen from the tour boats that visit nesting islands from Seward and Homer.

Outdoor sports enthusiasts go crazy in Alaska. The fishing is world class and much of it can be accessed from the road system. Ocean kayakers can explore Southeast Alaska, Prince William Sound, Kodiak Island, and the fjords of the Kenai Peninsula. If you prefer rivers you should be aware that Alaska is home to over twenty designated National Wild and Scenic Rivers, and most are truly wild and scenic. There is an extensive system of hiking trails on the Kenai Peninsula and there are many other trails north of Fairbanks and in Southeast Alaska. You can also hike where there are nothing but animal trails in places like Gates of the Arctic National Park and Lake Clark National Park.

Speaking of National Parks-Alaska has nine of them plus two Historical National Parks. And that's just the beginning. There are National Parks, National Monuments, National Preserves, National Forests, and Wildlife Refuges. And the State of Alaska has its own huge State Parks. Almost all of this land is easily accessible to outdoors enthusiasts although they may have to hitch a ride on a boat or airplane to get there.

The wilderness isn't the only attraction in Alaska. There's history too. Gold has played an important part in the history of the state; you can hike the Chilkoot Trail, float the Yukon, or visit famous gold-mining areas like Dawson City, Nome, Circle, or the Fortymile Country.

The Alcan Highway was one of the greatest engineering and construction projects of its time, a drive along it is the best way to appreciate the accomplishment. All along the highway you'll find museums and historical markers. It would be fun even if there weren't hundreds of fishing steams, lots of opportunities to spot wildlife, and gobs of beautiful scenery.

There's another huge engineering project in Alaska that has been in the news over the last 20 years—the Trans-Alaska Oil Pipeline. The arguments over oil in Alaska are still hot. During your visit you can see for yourself if the oil facilities on the North Slope seem to be scaring the caribou, whether the 800-mile pipeline is really an eyesore, and walk the previously oil-soaked beaches of Prince William Sound to assess the visible damage.

The truth is that there is enough to do and see in Alaska to bring you back each year for many years. The few things we've described above are just the beginning, you need to come and see for yourself.

## Why Camp?

It is hard to understand how anyone would visit Alaska and not camp. Along the highways and in the wilderness there is no better way to appreciate the country. If you spend your time riding a tour bus and staying in hotels you'll soon find yourself wondering what all the excitement is about. After all, most people really don't come to Alaska for its restaurants, hotels, and souvenir shops. An important part of the Alaska experience has always been the freedom to do your own thing, and a guided tour doesn't really give you that.

Camping doesn't really mean roughing it. Modern RVs provide a lot of comfort. Screens on the windows mean that you aren't at the mercy of mosquitoes while you cook, eat, relax and sleep. Furnaces and comfortable beds mean you'll sleep well and wake to a warm rig. Sophisticated plumbing systems mean you can take a hot shower every day. Uncrowded roads make driving an RV a snap, and there's no better wildlife-viewing platform than the high seats of an RV. If you don't have your own RV or if you don't want to drive it up the Alaska Highway you can easily rent an RV in Alaska and spend a week or two exploring the state.

You don't really even need an RV to enjoy the camping along Alaska's road system. It's easy to pack a tent, sleeping bags, and camping equipment into the trunk of a car and hit the road. Most of the state is plenty warm enough for you to be comfortable during June, July, and August. Just make sure you have a good tent that is rain and bug proof, and sleeping bags that will keep you warm down to 40° F or so if you run into an unusually cold night.

If you want to visit the country away from the road system camping is really your only viable alternative. Oh sure, you could stay in one of those $4,000 per week fishing lodges, but how much fun could that be? Most of the state is accessible using either aircraft or boats, and the only real costs for a camper are equipment, food and transportation. There really is one additional alternative, the state and federal government own many small cabins scattered around the state, and they rent them out for a very reasonable fee. They're nothing fancy, really just a high-class form of camping, so we don't feel guilty about covering them in this book about camping. See Chapter 14 - Camping Away From the Road System for more information.

## The Alaska Grand Tour

One of the best ways to show you what Alaska has to offer is to outline an itinerary for an RV trip to Alaska. This is the Full Monty, the mother of all road trips, a drive to Alaska on the Alaska Highway. It is a full tour of most of the roads of Alaska and much of the Yukon, and a return by Alaska State Ferry through Southeast Alaska.

Set aside as much time as possible for this tour, we wouldn't even attempt it in less than two months. Below we lay it out in 50 days, but you'll add some days for relaxing or choose some interesting side trips. Timing is essential, you want to do this between May 15 and September 15. Just one of the suggested week-long side trip additions would make this a two-month trip.

If you have only a week or two for a vacation in Alaska there is no problem. Just fly into Anchorage, Kenai, or Whitehorse; rent a car or RV, and head for the Kenai Peninsula or Denali National Park. Rental vehicles are also available in other towns including Fairbanks and Whitehorse. See Chapter 2 for information about RV rental outfits.

You also don't need much time to visit off the road destinations in Alaska. Visiting most of them involves only doing your research by mail, flying a commercial carrier to a departure city or town, and then using a charter airplane or boat to get into the bush. All of this can be easily arranged by telephone and you can probably be camping on your first day in Alaska. See Chapter 14 for more information.

You will notice that much of the time in the itinerary below is actually spent getting to and returning from Alaska. We allow a full two weeks just for getting to the beginning of the Alaska Highway and returning home from Prince Rupert. This isn't unreasonable, take a good look at a map.

The itinerary below can be modified, a couple of ideas suggest themselves. Many visitors do not venture south to Anchorage and the Kenai Peninsula. They limit the Alaska portion of their visit to Fairbanks, Denali Park, and perhaps Valdez. This would cut about a week off our itinerary. We wouldn't do it, but you can.

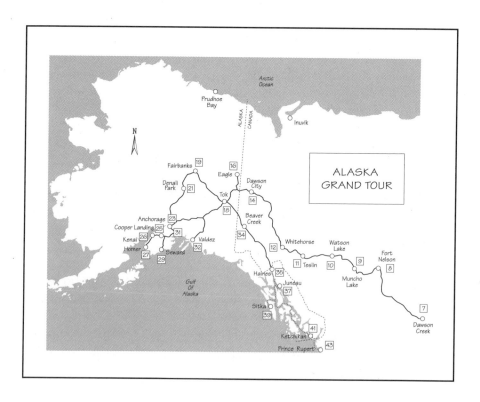

Another possible change is to drive both ways and not use the ferry system for your return. If you return on the Cassiar Highway you won't have to drive the same highway both ways and will see some new country.

A word of warning here. It will be necessary to plan ahead and make reservations for the Alaska State Ferry portion of this trip long before you leave home. See Chapter 13 for more information about the ferries. It might also be worthwhile to make camping and bus reservations at Denali Park before leaving home, see Chapter 9 for information about this.

As you read through the itinerary you can refer to the Table of Contents in the front of this book and the Index at the back to find more detailed information about routes, destinations, activities, and campgrounds.

**Days 1 to 7 - Getting to Dawson Creek** - You're on your own getting to Dawson Creek. For some folks from the southern U.S. it will probably take more than a week. Figure three days from Seattle (817 miles) if you've come up the west coast and three days from Great Falls in northern Montana (875 miles) if you come from east of the Rockies. You'll probably wish you had more time for both of these routes, there are lots of interesting stops and side trips. In Dawson Creek stock up on groceries and make sure your rig is in tip-top condition.

**Day 8 - Dawson Creek to Fort Nelson - 283 miles, 6 hours** - The road is excellent between Dawson Creek and Fort Nelson, good fast paved two-lane road. Be sure to start watching for wildlife, there are both bears and moose in the area. You have a choice between two excellent RV parks in Fort Nelson. Take a look at the museum and attend the show at the Phoenix Theater.

**Day 9 - Fort Nelson to Muncho Lake - 153 miles, 5 hours** - Between Fort Nelson and Muncho Lake the highway climbs into the mountains. The road is fine, you just won't be able to make great time because it is narrower and has more curves and hills than the road farther south. At Muncho Lake take a cruise on the lake or perhaps do a little fishing for lake trout. In the evening make the short hike to the nearby mineral lick to see if any stone sheep are there.

**Day 10 - Muncho Lake to Watson Lake - 177 miles, 6 hours** - Get an early start for the best chance to see animals along the road. Stop at Liard Hot Springs for a dip and stay to fix a nice relaxed lunch. It's only another 136 miles in to Watson Lake. In Watson Lake visit the signpost forest and the visitor center's Alcan exhibit, you might also attend a show at the new Northern Lights Centre.

**Day 11 - Watson Lake to Teslin - 163 miles, 4 hours** - This is a short day's drive, but get an early start anyway. Spend some time in Teslin, shop at the Nisutlin Trading Post and visit the George Johnson Museum. Then drive on another 8 miles to Mukluk Annie's Salmon Bake. Dry camp for free along the lake shore and enjoy the salmon bake in the evening. Top things off by joining your fellow campers for a houseboat ride on Teslin Lake.

**Day 12 and 13 - Teslin to Whitehorse - 100 miles, 2 hours -** Another short day's drive will bring you to Whitehorse. You have many campgrounds to choose from and you might as well spend two days here in the capital of the Yukon Territory. There's lots to see and do. See the sternwheeler *Klondike* and cruise through Miles Canyon. Don't forget to stock up on groceries here, you won't be seeing big stores again for a while.

**Day 14 and 15 - Whitehorse to Dawson City - 327 miles, 7 hours -** The road to Dawson City is excellent so you can easily drive through in one day if you get an early start. Don't forget to stop at the overlook for the view of Five Finger Rapids. With the long days this far north you'll probably have lots of energy left when you get to Dawson, so make an evening of it and see the Gaslight Follies at the Palace Theater. That should put you in the proper mood to spend the following day exploring Dawson and the creeks. In the evening of your second day in Dawson you can visit Diamond Tooth Gerties gambling hall.

If you have an extra week you can use it here. Drive the Dempster Highway up across the Arctic Circle to Inuvik. Driving out and back on this 456-mile gravel road will let you visit some of the most remote country you've ever seen.

**Day 16 and 17 - Dawson City to Eagle - 144 miles, 5 hours -** This trip over the Top of the World Highway and then up to Eagle on the Taylor Highway is your first real taste of gravel unless you drove the Dempster. It also finally brings you to Alaska!

ALASKA

The Taylor portion of the route is a small road so take it easy. Enjoy the wilderness. Spend a day relaxing in little laid-back Eagle (population 150) and take the historic tour, it's one of Alaska's most enjoyable.

**Day 18 - Eagle to Tok - 173 miles, 6 hours -** You'll return to the Alaska Highway today after a long day on the gravel. Tok has the highest per capita number of RV spaces in the state, it's the first Alaskan town most Alaska Highway travelers reach. The most important thing to do here is visit the Tok Visitor's Center.

**Day 19 and 20 - Tok to Fairbanks - 206 miles, 5 hours -** Today you'll follow the Tanana River downstream to Alaska's second-largest city. We've allotted two days, it probably won't be enough. Don't miss everyone's Fairbanks favorite—a cruise on the riverboat *Discovery*. Visit the gold fields near Fox or Ester where you'll find the Malemut Saloon. In a quieter vein, the University's Otto Geist Museum is one of the best in the state.

Here's another place you can easily add a week to your trip, or even two weeks. Several roads lead north from Fairbanks including the Dalton Highway to the North Slope and Prudhoe Bay. The Steese, Chena Hot Springs, and Elliott Highways are all worth a look-see, they each have a rustic hot spring resort at the end of the trail. This is also excellent hiking and canoeing country.

**Day 21 and 22 - Fairbanks to Denali Park - 121 miles, 2.5 hours -** If you've made reservations you can camp in the park. Otherwise you'll probably be perfectly happy in one of the many campsites outside the park entrance. The thing you must do here is take a shuttle-bus trip into the park at least as far as Eielson Visitor's Center. Denali Park is probably the best place you will ever visit for observing grizzly bears up close. Cross your fingers for a clear day to see the mountain.

**Day 23 and 24 - Denali Park to Anchorage - 237 miles, 5 hours -** Today's trip is a cruiser, down through Broad Pass and across the Mat-Su Valley on Alaska's best roads. You'll actually have some four-lane freeway going into Anchorage. Anchorage is the best place in the state to get any maintenance problems fixed and stock up on supplies. During your layover check the sporting good stores to see which spots are hot on the Kenai Peninsula and pick up some fishing tackle.

Anchorage is one of the most livable cities anywhere. This is your chance to visit a good restaurant and explore the town. Wander around Town Square and 4th Avenue, all decked out with flowers, and perhaps catch a performance in the Alaska Center for the Performing Arts or of the Alaska Native Performance Series. Treat yourself to a night out at an outstanding restaurant and a visit to Mr. Whitekeys' *Whale Fat Follies* at the Fly By Night Club.

**Day 25 - Anchorage to Cooper Landing - 101 miles, 3 hours -** Drive down scenic Turnagain Arm and make sure you stop at Portage Glacier. In Cooper Landing if you've timed it right you can "combat fish" at the mouth of the Russian River and fill your icebox with red salmon. If not just enjoy some of Alaska's best scenery. Hikers will find what may be the finest trails in the state leading into the mountains nearby. There's also an excellent float trip down the Upper Kenai.

**Day 26 - Cooper Landing to Kenai - 57 miles, 1.5 hours -** Avoid the Soldotna fishing crowds and stay in Kenai. Visit the historic Russian church and perhaps see some beluga whales chasing salmon below the bluff. Ask at your campground or the information center about clam tides, you might have arrived at the perfect time for a clamming expedition.

**Day 27 and 28 - Kenai to Homer - 97 miles, 2.5 hours -** Today's drive brings you to another scenic highlight, Homer. You can camp in town or out on the bustling spit. Either way consider a halibut fishing trip or a bird-watching cruise out to Gull Island and Halibut Cove or Seldovia.

**Day 29 and 30 - Homer to Seward - 173 miles, 4 hours -** A day of backtracking and a chance to see the things you missed on the way down to Homer. Perhaps a visit to Ninilchik or a pause to wet a line in one of the many world-famous fishing rivers along the route. In Seward the silver salmon may be running or you might take a cruise into the Kenai Fjords National Park to see whales, sea otters, puffins, and glaciers.

**Day 31- Seward to Anchorage - 126 miles,  3 hours -** Back to Anchorage to stock up and prepare for the drive south.

Here's something to consider. The Alaska State Ferry runs from Seward to Valdez most Thursday mornings. You can save yourself two days and about 430 miles of driving by taking this ferry. It will cost more than making the road trip but it's a lot easier and just as scenic.

**Day 32 and 33 - Anchorage to Valdez - 304 miles, 7 hours -** A long day of driving through beautiful country will bring you to Valdez. Tour the Trans-Alaska Pipeline's terminal, see the huge tankers, fish for salmon or take a scenic cruise across Prince William Sound to Columbia Glacier.

**Day 34 - Valdez to Beaver Creek - 399 miles, 9 hours -** Another very long day of driving. To shorten it a bit you could stay at any of the campgrounds between Tok and Beaver Creek. On the other hand, like a horse heading home you may want to spend a long day on the road.

**Day 35 and 36 - Beaver Creek to Haines - 336 miles, 8 hours -** You drive south along Kluane Lake, through Haines Junction, and then across the Chilkat Pass to tidewater at the head of the Inside Passage. This is the last day on the road for a week, you'll let the ferry captain do the driving as far as Prince Rupert. During your layover day in Haines take the water taxi up the Lynn Canal to Skagway and spend the day touring this gold rush town.

**Day 37 and 38 - Ferry to Juneau, 4.5 hours -** Use your time in Juneau to explore Alaska's capital. If you have the time consider a cruise to Glacier Bay National Park or Tracy Arm or a helicopter flight to the top of the nearby ice field.

**Day 39 and 40 - Ferry to Sitka, 9 hours -** You've seen Alaska's present capital, now wander around the former capital of Russian America. Don't miss the Sheldon Jackson Museum.

**Day 41 and 42 - Ferry to Ketchikan, 19 hours cruising time plus possible time in port in Petersburg and Wrangell -** Consider booking a stateroom for this segment of your ferry trip. Ketchikan is Alaska's totem pole center. You also might take a cruise or sightseeing flight to Misty Fjords National Monument, your last chance to visit really pristine wilderness before leaving the state.

**Day 43 - Ferry to Prince Rupert, 6 hours -** You'll save yourself a bundle by leaving Alaska through Prince Rupert rather than riding the ferry all the way to Bellingham.

**Day 44 to 50 - Drive home -** From Prince Rupert to Seattle is 1,035 miles, Prince Rupert to Great Falls is 1,235 miles. Both routes are paved all the way.

Once you reach home you can start planning next-year's trip.

# DETAILS, DETAILS, DETAILS

## Animals (Wildlife)

For most visitors to Alaska the wildlife is a huge attraction. During even a road trip to the state you are likely to see grizzly bears, black bears, moose, caribou, stone and Dall sheep, mountain goats, and perhaps even a musk ox. In addition to these large mammals Alaska has some of the best bird watching opportunities anywhere, over 350 species are present. Marine mammals including whales, sea otters, and seals are common in many salt water areas easily accessible on short sightseeing cruises. You can even watch fish at the many salmon-spawning viewing sites.

Be sure to bring along a set of binoculars and perhaps a spotting scope. These are particularly useful for birders but will also help you spot and enjoy watching larger animals.

You can see more wildlife while driving if you: 1. Watch closely and don't drive too fast, 2. Plan to be on the road in the early morning and late evening when animals are most active, 3. Get away from the road system by hiking or using air or water transportation.

As you drive along make sure to keep an eye on the brush line along the road. During the spring (May, June) and during berry season (July and August) there are often bears feeding in the wide cleared open areas next to the highways. RVers have an advantage over those driving passenger cars since they have an elevated seating position. Stop often to check likely habitats. Moose are often browsing along the shores of lakes along the road. Bears are sometimes seen on gravel bars along rivers. It is often possible to see bears, sheep and goats on grassy mountainsides with a pair of binoculars. If you aren't proactive in your wildlife watching you'll only see the few animals that cross directly in front of your vehicle.

You'll see more animals if you schedule your driving in the early morning and late evening. That's when animals are most active. With the long daylight hours during June and July it would actually be possible to see wildlife during the entire night, but a night time driving schedule would probably be going a little overboard. Perhaps early starts and late stops with an afternoon nap thrown in makes more sense.

There are some outstanding places to see wildlife in the state and on the routes north, here are a few. In both **Stone Mountain Park** and **Muncho Lake Park** along the Alaska Highway both stone sheep and caribou are often spotted. Just outside Hyder, Alaska near the Cassiar Highway is **Fish Creek** where you can see both brown and black bears as well as bald eagles during the August salmon runs. **Haines, Alaska** is world famous for its congregation of bald eagles during the late fall along the Chilkat River. On a bus ride into **Denali Park** it would be unusual not to see several grizzlies as well as assorted caribou, sheep, and smaller animals. A boat tour from Seward into the **Kenai Fjords National Park** or from Juneau into **Glacier Bay** in Southeast Alaska will probably net you a whale spotting or two, not to mention sea otters, puffins, sea lions, dolphins, and perhaps seals. Even as you just drive the highways, you're bound to see a moose or two and even the occasional bear.

A CARIBOU ALONG THE ALASKA HIGHWAY

There's another side to the wildlife in the North. Some of it presents a certain amount of danger, particularly large animals like bears and moose. Bears are attracted by food so proper food and garbage handling procedures are important when camping. Tent campers will want to keep food in vehicles or suspended from trees. In the tundra country where this isn't possible make sure to cache your food far from your tent. Garbage containers in campgrounds are now often bear proof, if they aren't you should consider the location of garbage containers when choosing your camp site.

Many people consider the presence of grizzlies an indicator of true wilderness. They are widespread in Alaska and quite common in many places. Grizzlies can be extremely dangerous since they are big, fast, and sometimes aggressive. On the other hand, fishermen often share streams with grizzlies and hikers in some places often find themselves with bears as visitors in camp. You'll find pamphlets about the proper way to handle yourself in bear country at many information offices. Thousands of people spend time in the northern wilderness with no problems, you just have to take care and do things properly. See Chapter 14 for a more thorough discussion of bear safety.

## Border Crossings

It is very possible that your Alaska camping trip will involve several border crossings. These are generally uneventful but there are a few things you should bear in mind.

No visa or passport is required for US or Canadian citizens crossing either way across Canadian or U.S. borders but proof of citizenship must be carried. This means a passport, certified birth certificate, or voters registration card, along with a photo I.D. like your drivers license. A drivers license alone is not enough. If you have children along it is very important to have certified copies of their birth certificates and permission letters from parents if they are not yours.

For your vehicle you'll want the following: registration, up to date license tags, and proof of insurance. Make sure you have your vehicle registration with you and if you are not the legal owner a signed statement that it is OK to take it out of the country. You can get a Canadian Nonresident Interprovince Motor Vehicle Liability Insurance Card from your insurance company. It is likely that you will not have to show any of these documents but having them on hand is definitely nice if you are asked for them.

Guns are always a problem going into Canada. Rifles and shotguns are sometimes allowed, pistols never are. Border agents are allowed some discretion so it is important that you show the proper image and attitude if you want to cross the border with a weapon. Self defense is definitely not considered a proper reason to carry a weapon in Canada. We've been turned back at the border when en route to Alaska during hunting season, and we're definitely clean cut and non-threatening. Never fib about weapons, vehicles are often searched at the border and penalties are steep. The best policy is to forget about taking a gun through Canada.

Many people like to carry pepper spray for defense against bears. This often presents a problem at the border. Several different laws are involved, if your spray wasn't manufactured in Canada it probably isn't legal. Spays designed for defense against people definitely aren't allowed. With bear spray, as with guns, the border agent has quite a bit of discretion so be polite.

Dogs, cats, or small animals need a recent rabies vaccination and a certificate stating so from a veterinarian. Your veterinarian will probably know about this.

Make sure your automobile insurance is good in Canada (or the U.S. if you are Canadian). Check into the deductible for your windows since you are almost certain to get at least a ding in them (and probably more than one) during your trip.

Both Canada and the U.S. have regulations about importing certain things (like souvenirs) made of restricted animal parts like ivory and hides. Unfortunately the regulations are not the same so some things purchased in Canada can't come into the U.S. and vice versa. Check this if possible before purchase.

Finally, you must theoretically have enough money on hand to get where you are going and back out of Canada. There are no hard and fast rules. We've never had problems carrying bank cards that allow us to get cash along the way. You probably won't even be asked unless you look to the customs officer like you might not have enough cash to get by.

For more information about border crossings you can use these addresses: Canadian Customs, Connaught Building, Sussex Drive, Ottawa, Ontario K1A 0L5, Canada or Customs Office, 333 Dunsmuir Street, Suite 503, Vancouver, B.C. V6B 5R4, Canada; 604 666-0545 and United States Customs, P.O. Box 7407, Washington, D.C. 20044; 202 566-8195.

## Budget

Each person has his own idea of an acceptable standard of living so there is no one budget for every person. On the other hand, if you are camping you are not at the mercy of the local tourist economy like a traveler staying in hotels. In Alaska, you'll save a lot of money by camping. Here are some guidelines that should help.

The Canadian dollar has devalued against the U.S. Dollar in recent years. This has helped keep prices in Canada a little more reasonable for those from the U.S. Campgrounds, in particular, seem to be reasonably priced. A Canadian dollar coverted to about $.70 U.S in early 1998.

In general, transportation is a big part of the price of things along the highways and in Alaska. Gasoline, groceries, and services get more expensive as you get farther into the bush. This applies along the Alcan too. Expect prices on remote sections of the roads to be much higher than in Dawson Creek or Whitehorse. Fill your tanks and buy your groceries in the larger towns. See also the Gasoline Prices section in this chapter. Prices in Canada have been converted to U.S. dollars.

Alaskan prices are much more reasonable in larger towns than in years past. Much of the gasoline is refined in the state and prices are comparable to the Lower 48 in the big cities. Groceries too are reasonable. Although most are shipped from the Lower 48 there is lots of competition in the big cities like Anchorage, Fairbanks, Kenai and Juneau. In other places prices are higher, transportation and lack of competition become more important.

## Campfires

A campfire is a big part of a cheerful and enjoyable campsite. Fortunately, you'll have lots of opportunities to have a campfire while camping in the North. Virtually all governmental campgrounds in both Alaska and Canada have fire pits or rings. Many privately operated campgrounds outside towns have them too. We've included information about whether a campground has fire pits in the individual descriptions.

A very nice feature of the government campgrounds in both the Yukon and British Columbia is free firewood. It is usually dry but seldom split, bring along an axe. In Alaska free firewood is no longer provided. Many campgrounds, however, have it for sale. Use of downed trees near the campgrounds is usually allowed, but you may have to travel some distance from the more popular ones to find it.

Wilderness campers will find that the forested areas of south-central and central Alaska have lots of dry downed wood, the best is usually in the form of dead spruce. Campfires are perfectly acceptable in these areas if extreme care is taken not to start a wild fire. Stoves sill work best for cooking. Make sure your fire is on mineral, not vegetable soil. Gravel bars in rivers are the best place for fires, they are generally scoured clean by the high water each spring.

In southeast Alaska there may be plenty of wood but it is often too wet to burn. In the far west and north there are often no trees so firewood is scarce. Campers in these areas will have to rely on portable stoves.

## Campgrounds

Throughout the areas covered in this book you will have a choice: government or privately-operated campgrounds. In general you can expect government campgrounds to have more scenic locations with more land per camper. They also almost always provide picnic tables and fire pits. On the other hand, toilets are almost always outhouses (pit toilets) and there are never hookups or showers.

In Alaska you will find that government campgrounds are run by either the State of Alaska, the United States Forest Service (USFS), the United States Fish and Wildlife Service (USF&W), the National Parks Service (NPS), or one of the local governments. Information about all of the Alaskan governmental campgrounds run by all of these organizations and their related public lands are available from four Alaska Public Lands Information Centers located in Anchorage (Anchorage APLIC, 605 W. 4th

Ave., Suite 105, Anchorage, AK 99501; 907 271-2737), Fairbanks (Fairbanks APLIC, 250 Cushman St., Suite 1A, Fairbanks, AK 99701; 907 456-0527), Tok (Tok APLIC, P.O. Box 359, Tok, AK 99780; 907 883-5667), and Ketchikan (Ketchikan APLIC, 50 Main St., Ketchikan, AK 99901; 907 228-6219). While similar, there are some differences between these government campgrounds. Note that the Campground Index at the back of the book identifies the campground type.

State of Alaska campgrounds are scattered throughout the state virtually wherever there are highways. In recent years they have begun charging a fee, most commonly between $6 and $10 per night, per party. It is also possible to purchase an annual pass which costs $75 for residents and $200 for nonresidents. Remember, these passes are only good in state campgrounds, not those run by the federal government, and at $10 per night you would have to stay in state campgrounds for a minimum of 20 days to break even. The passes are windshield stickers that are nontransferable and they can be purchased at the Alaska Public Lands Information Centers mentioned above.

The United States Forest Service (USFS) operates the second highest number of campgrounds in Alaska. These are in Chugach National Forest on the Kenai Peninsula near Anchorage and in the Tongass National Forest in Southeast Alaska. They vary in quality, a few have been upgraded recently with paved roads and handicapped facilities—Russian River near Cooper Landing and Williwaw near Portage Glacier are two of the upgraded ones. Some also accept reservations including Williwaw, Ptarmigan Creek, Trail River, Cooper Creek, and Russian River. Call 800 280-CAMP for reservations. Daily camping fees are usually under $10 and there is usually a 14 day limit. Wilderness tent camping outside the developed campground areas is also allowed in these forests.

The National Park Service (NPS) has more parkland in Alaska than in all of the rest of the country, but they have very few developed campgrounds. The only ones connected to the road system are those in Denali National Park, one tent-camping area at the Exit Glacier near Seward, and one near Skagway at the foot of the Chilkoot Trail. There are also walk-in tent campgrounds in Glacier Bay National Park & Preserve and Katmai National Park & Preserve. The National Park Service also manages the Klondike Gold Rush National Park which has campgrounds along the Chilkoot Trail and the Sitka National Historical Park which has no camping at all. Wilderness camping is allowed throughout the national parks, monuments, preserves and national wild rivers throughout the state with some restrictions.

The Bureau of Land Management manages campgrounds on Federal Lands not controlled by other agencies. In Alaska these include campgrounds along the Dalton Highway Pipeline Corridor and those along National Wild Rivers like the Gulkana and the Fortymile. BLM campgrounds are usually small with limited facilities but the Paxson Campground on the Gulkana River off the Richardson is large with handicapped facilities and a dump station.

The U.S. Fish and Wildlife Service (USF&W) manages 16 national wildlife refuges with 77 million acres in Alaska. Their campgrounds are small and there aren't many. They are usually free. You'll find two of them along the Alaska Highway just inside the Alaska border.

The Yukon Territory maintains many campgrounds along roads throughout the territory. They are usually fairly large and located near water. The usual facilities include outhouses, picnic tables, fire pits and free firewood. There are also often picnic shelters and children's playgrounds.

British Columbian Provincial Parks are located along the roads throughout the Province. They usually provide about the same amenities as the campgrounds in the Yukon Territory although many are upgraded with paved roads and parking pads.

There are many excellent commercial campgrounds in Alaska. Most have electricity, sewer, and water hookups as well as modern restrooms with flush toilets and hot showers. When you are visiting one of the urban areas in the North, private campgrounds are usually much more conveniently located than government ones.

Private campgrounds in both Canada and Alaska are in competition primarily with the government which has free land and can impose hard-to-meet and expensive restrictions upon private owners. Among these are dump station requirements, charges for signage, and just plain taxes. We suggest that you give the private campground operator a break whenever possible. Here's an example. Don't dump your holding tanks at a rural campground when you could just as conveniently do so later in the day at a campground or dump station hooked up to a municipal sewage system. Holding tank discharge is difficult and expensive for a remote campground using a septic system to handle.

## Camping Reservations

We generally do not bother with reservations for a campground in the evening. On the other hand, we're generally happy with almost any campsite at the end of a long day and we usually travel in a small rig. If you want the best campsites (like along the water) or if you are planning to visit one of the most popular destinations during a busy part of the season (like when the salmon are running) you can call ahead to make a reservation. In the campground section we make a note when campground reservations are a good idea. You will also find campground telephone numbers and addresses there. As you travel along you'll quickly realize whether you need reservations or not, it just depends upon how many people are traveling at the same time you are.

## Camping Vehicles and Tents

You can camp in Alaska, the Yukon, and British Columbia in any kind of rig, or without one if you like.

If you are planning to camp in the back country away from the roads you will be tent camping. You can also comfortably tent camp from the trunk of a car or when bicycling. A tent with a floor and good bug screens is essential. Have some kind of waterproof fly for rainy periods, they can last for many days. A plastic sheet with poles and guy ropes is very useful around the campsite during long rainy periods. A dark-colored tent is nice to block out the light during those summer periods when it never really gets dark. You may be surprised at how hard it is to sleep in the daylight. Consider bringing some kind of blindfold for sleeping. A large water container is useful in campgrounds. Bring an axe if you plan to burn wood, that in the campgrounds is often not split. If you are tough it is possible to tent camp all year, but the best months are June, July, and August.

Pickup campers and vans are very popular with Alaska residents. They let you use all of the campgrounds and also find good free camping spots. Their small size and maneuverability is a big plus when you get a little off the beaten track. An additional thing to keep in mind - charges on the ferries are based upon length.

Motorhomes, trailers, and fifth wheels have to be the most comfortable camping vehicles. If you are driving the highway just to visit don't buy a special rig for Alaska camping since virtually anything will work as long as it is durable and in good condition. Most major roads are paved and high mountain passes are actually uncommon. If you want to travel the few long gravel highways you probably won't want to be pulling a trailer since flying gravel can be hard on them. If you have a trailer or fifth wheel consider bringing along a tent for use while exploring the gravel roads like the Dalton Highway, Dempster Highway, or the roads north of Fairbanks. Any kind of rig provides big advantages in bug protection and extends the comfortable season for camping.

## Caravans

RV caravan tours to Alaska are very popular. They generally start in the U.S. or perhaps Dawson Creek and spend many weeks driving up the Alaska Highway or the Cassiar, exploring the state, and then returning by either road or ferry. There are lots of variations.

A typical caravan tour is composed of about 20 rigs. The price paid generally includes a knowledgeable caravan leader in his own RV, a tail-gunner or caboose RV with an experienced mechanic, campground fees, many meals and tours at stops along the way, and lots of camaraderie. Many people love RV tours because someone else does all the planning, there is security in numbers, and a good caravan can be a very memorable experience. They aren't for everyone, however.

Remember that there will be a lot of costs in addition to those covered by the fee paid to the caravan company including fuel, insurance, maintenance, ferry charges, and groceries. We hear a lot of good things about caravans, but also many complaints. Common problems include caravans that do not spend enough time at interesting places, delays due to mechanical problems with other rigs in the caravan, and poor caravan leaders who do not really know the territory. A badly run caravan can be a disaster.

We've given the names, addresses and phone numbers below of some of the leading caravan companies. Give them a call or write a letter to get information about the tours they will be offering for the coming year. Once you have received the information do not hesitate to call back and ask questions. Ask for the names and phone numbers of people who have recently taken tours with the same caravan leader scheduled to be in charge of the tour you are considering. Call these references and find out what they liked and what they didn't like. They are likely to have some strong feelings about these things.

Adventure Caravans, 101 Rainbow Dr., Suite # 2434, Livingston, TX 77351-9300 (800 872-7897) and (409) 646-6768.

ElDorado Tours, P.O. Box 1145, Alma, AR 72921-1145 (800 852-2500).

Fantasy Caravans, P.O. Box 95605, Las Vegas, NV 89193-5605 (800) 952-8496.

Point South RV Tours, 11313 Edmonson Ave., Moreno Valley, CA 92555 (800 421-1394).

Tracks to Adventure, 2811 Jackson Ave., El Paso, TX 79930 (800 351-6053).

## Cash and Credit Cards

There are really only two currency problems that you are likely to run into during a trip to Alaska. The first is that cash and perhaps credit cards are the preferred tender in the cities and along highways. Cash machines are easy to find in larger towns but not available in all of the small ones. Credit cards (Master Card and Visa) are almost always accepted for gas and in restaurants. You should probably keep a cash stash (say $200) available for emergencies. Checks are unlikely to be accepted anywhere.

The second challenge is Canadian currency, and it isn't really much of a challenge. Don't convert on a transaction-by-transaction basis, it will cost you a lot. Instead, stop at a bank or cash machine when you reach a sizeable town after crossing the border to get a Canadian cash fund. Cash machines will accept your U.S. card and they give a good exchange rate. Check with your bank card issuer before leaving home to make sure it will work in Canada, sometimes special PIN numbers (personal identification numbers) are needed for international use.

## CB Radio

A CB radio can be useful for emergencies and for communication between rigs if you are traveling as part of a group. No standard frequency is used for communications in Alaska but channel 9 and 11 are used for emergencies. If those don't work try 14 and 19. Channel 19 is the frequency used by truckers on the Dalton Highway.

## Children

One of the nice things about an Alaska outdoors trip is that the summer visitors season coincides with the summer school recess. An outdoors vacation is perfect for children of all ages and present opportunities for all types of activities.

On thing to keep in mind is that distances can be long and the driving sometimes a little boring. Remember, the Alaska Highway was originally described as miles and miles of miles and miles. The scenery is sometimes spectacular but there will also be many driving hours to fill with activities.

## Clothing

For RV campers it is important to bring warm clothing like sweaters, jackets, and long underwear so that you are comfortable outdoors on cloudy days and in the evening. Otherwise you will spend little time outside and miss the pleasures of the evening campfire or stroll. A really heavy coat probably isn't necessary, instead have things you can layer to suit your activities and the temperature. You don't want to spend all of your time indoors while visiting this premier wilderness area. There are also some more specific things you should bring along.

Don't forget your bathing suit for Liard Hot Springs, and others. Also some lakes. People commonly swim at Big Lake in the Mat-Su and at Harding and Birch Lakes

ROAD CONSTRUCTION ON THE ALASKA HIGHWAY

near Fairbanks. Shorts can be useful when the temperatures rise over 70° F and the mosquitoes are temporarily somewhere else.

Rain gear is a necessity. Southcentral and Southeast sometimes have long periods of rainy weather and you'll have to get out in it if you want to be active.

Bring hiking boots. Also consider rubber break-up boots or some kind of waterproof hiking boots for hiking in wet areas. Trails in much of Alaska are very wet. Fishermen will want hip boots or waders.

Hikers and bikers have special requirements. See Chapter 14 for more about this.

## Distances

As you plan your camping trip to Alaska and as you drive the highways you have to remember that the distances can make for some long driving days. It is difficult to cover over 300 miles in a reasonable day of driving. We've included a mileage chart nearby so that you can find the mileage information you need in one place.

## Driving and Road Conditions

Most of your driving in Northern Canada and Alaska will be on two-lane roads. For safety's sake you should leave your headlights on at all times to enhance the visibility of your rig to traffic approaching from the other direction. Canadians in the North leave their headlights on most of the time, Alaskans aren't quite so good about it. Experiments have shown that the use of headlights on two-lane roads does reduce the accident rate substantially.

In both Alaska and Canada the use of seatbelts is mandatory. Radar detectors are illegal in the Yukon Territory.

Frost heaves are a unique road hazard in Alaska and the Yukon. They are caused by both permafrost and the constant freezing and thawing of water in the gravel underlying the pavement. After being bounced off the ceiling by the first couple you hit you'll learn to keep a sharp lookout for them. We've seen them so bad that we had to unhook our tow car and drive it separately to save the hitch.

## Dump Stations

There are plenty of dump stations to fill your needs while visiting the North Country but in remote areas they are not as common as you might sometimes wish. In Canada you'll find them marked as sani-dumps. It is important to plan ahead so you don't find yourself with a full holding tank miles from the nearest place to empty it.

In general, remember to always empty your tanks when you are in a town. More heavily populated areas have sewage treatment plants and can deal with sewage more easily than can operators in remote areas who either depend upon cesspools and drainage

## DISTANCE TABLE

Miles

*A large triangular road-distance matrix between Alaska/Western-Canada cities. The diagonal cells carry the city names; the upper-right triangle gives distances in miles and the lower-left triangle gives the same distances in kilometers. The readable values are transcribed below.*

Cities along the diagonal (in order): Anchorage, Calgary, Chicken Hot Springs, Circle, Dawson City, Dawson Creek, Delta Junction, Denali Park, Eagle, Fairbanks, Fort Nelson, Fort St. John, Glennallen, Haines, Haines Junction, Homer, Hyder, Prince George, Prince Rupert, Seattle, Skagway, Stewart, Tok, Valdez, Watson Lake, Whitehorse.

**Anchorage row — distances in miles (to each successive city):**
2160, 419, 520, 515, 1610, 340, 237, 501, 358, 1327, 1657, 189, 775, 625, 226, 996, 1605, 847, 2435, 126, 832, 147, 1387, 328, 997, 304, 724

**Anchorage row — distances in kilometers:**
3478, 675, 837, 829, 2592, 547, 382, 807, 576, 2136, 2668, 304, 1248, 1006, 364, 1604, 2584, 1364, 3920, 203, 1340, 237, 2233, 528, 1604, 489, 1166

**Further miles values appearing across the table (by band, left to right):**
1436, 2086, 1161, 1832, 937, 2307, 1544, 2286, 738, 2527, 950, 2178, 2386, 1526, 1687, 1967, 595, 831, 2038, 1907, 2159, 1940, 548, 1747, 2220, 2099

663, 425, 936, 267, 1326, 566, 771, 545, 2574, 540, 1544, 935, 645, 564, 714, 310, 1502, 1266, 61, 440, 182, 159, 1549, 454, 214

764, 526, 1037, 368, 1427, 667, 872, 646, 2475, 1972, 1645, 1036, 746, 665, 815, 411, 1603, 1367, 162, 541, 283, 260, 1650, 555

327, 441, 609, 187, 985, 662, 435, 641, 2022, 882, 1192, 481, 741, 417, 578, 322, 1175, 939, 144, 395

895, 1536, 613, 1282, 693, 1757, 993, 1736, 817, 1977, 706, 1653, 1836, 985, 1137, 1417, 47, 283, 1468

495, 777, 270, 108, 1167, 487, 603, 466, 2215, 587, 1385, 776, 566, 405, 555, 151, 1343, 1107, 98

723, 996, 475, 327, 1386, 384, 831, 363, 2434, 610, 1604, 995, 463, 622, 774, 356, 1562, 1326, 121

471, 753, 427, 173, 1252, 384, 579, 627, 2166, 868, 1336, 625, 727, 460, 620, 308, 1319, 1083, 500

602, 875, 364, 206, 1129, 505, 710, 484, 2513, 1453, 874, 653, 584, 505, 249, 1441, 1205, 379

531, 804, 119, 701, 989, 336, 639, 359, 2242, 738, 1412, 803, 415, 432, 582, 1090

251, 533, 372, 447, 135, 989, 922, 901, 315, 1962, 1132, 1009, 1001, 152

90, 1430, 549, 297, 446, 772, 207, 559, 749, 1810, 1142, 857

950, 1123, 530, 554, 734, 85, 1058, 710, 946, 990, 851

758, 370, 922, 668, 740, 1143, 866, 1689, 753, 1930

861, 1144, 1040, 1277, 1235, 1416, 1122, 315, 1605

531, 404, 609, 1531, 135, 285, 989, 639

251, 658, 804, 1091, 1373, 1752, 994

396, 660, 650, 1842, 974, 1199

650, 923, 1220, 726, 765, 958

282, 454, 174, 811, 979, 94

fields or pay high charges for pumping services.

Few government campgrounds have dump stations. Private campgrounds allow visitors to dump, usually for a fee. This is a reasonable charge, in remote areas operators often have to pay high pump-out fees on a per gallon basis. If you aren't staying in the campground you should help pay the fee.

In our campground descriptions we mention dump stations located in campgrounds or alternatives nearby if there are any. Campgrounds with dump stations on site or nearby are marked with a special symbol. We also include information about additional dump stations at the end of each campground chapter.

## Fishing

Everyone knows that Alaska offers a wide selection of fishing opportunities. Along the Alaska Highway and throughout the interior rivers, streams, and lakes have grayling, lake trout, and even salmon. Southcentral Alaska offers many river fishing hot spots, especially along the Parks Highway near Wasilla and on the Kenai Peninsula in the Soldotna area. Both Seward and Valdez are known for their salt water salmon fishing and Homer is a big halibut charter center. Every Southeast destination mentioned in this book offers at least salt water fishing possibilities.

The best fishing tends not to be right along the highways, especially if you are not fishing for salmon. A fly-out fishing trip should be a part of any fisherman's trip to Alaska. A time-honored technique for catching fish along streams crossing the highways is to walk some distance up or downstream from the road to reach less easily accessed waters. On the other hand, I can remember many occasions when I've hooked a fish on the first cast into a pool directly under the highway bridge.

Fishermen from outside Alaska will find that trout and salmon fishing may require a new assortment of tackle. Local knowledge is essential and tackle is available almost everywhere since fishing is such a popular recreational pursuit. The best prices, however, are in the larger cities. It would be worth your time to pick up one of the readily available Alaska fishing guides before leaving home to make sure you bring the right poles, reels, and more expensive equipment. See the Travel Library section of this chapter for some suggestions. You can buy terminal tackle once you reach the area where you plan to fish. A small boat or canoe can be very useful, particularly if you enjoy lake fishing.

British Columbia, the Yukon, and Alaska all require non-resident fishing licenses. Additional licenses are required in some parks. Licenses can usually be issued by tackle stores, a good excuse to go in and ask questions. The State of Alaska Fish and Game Department has a web site: http://www.state.ak.us/local/akpages/FISH.GAME/ adfghome.htm. For general information about Alaska sportfishing write to Alaska Department of Fish & Game, P.O. Box 25526, Juneau, AK 99802.

## Free Camping

Many people love to find a free campsite. The thrill of spending the night parked without paying anyone a fee is hard to deny. If you love to free camp and successfully find good parking spots in the Lower 48 there is no doubt you'll love Alaska. Many Alaska campers never use a formal campground.

On the other hand, we prefer formal campgrounds for many reasons. They are safer because there are usually many fellow campers around. You never have to get up in the middle of the night to answer a trooper's knock and be told to move on. Garbage is usually properly handled so that it won't attract bears. Alaska's campgrounds don't cost much, particularly the government ones, and they are often in a much more attractive and scenic location than any free pull-off. Campgrounds also provide picnic

A PLEASANT FREE CAMPING SPOT

tables, toilets, firewood, fire pits, and sometimes showers.

It is probably a fact of life that if you spend a night camping outside a campground you are breaking some kind of law. It may be a trespass law, it may be a vagrancy law, it may be something else. That doesn't necessarily mean that anyone will care. We often see people camping on city streets, in parking lots, or on pull-offs along the road. The key is to be low profile, don't make a pest of yourself, and don't obstruct traffic.

In general, the farther you are from civilization the easier it is to find free camping spots. In the less populated areas of the state no one is likely to care if you pull off the road at a good looking spot next to a river or on an abandoned section of road. Just make sure not to park in places where there are no parking signs, don't block access, and avoid private property.

There are a couple of unusual free camping possibilities in the cities of Anchorage and Kenai. In 1997 the Seward Highway Wal-Mart in Anchorage allowed self-contained RVers to camp in their huge parking lot. In Kenai the Fred Meyer store actually encourages RVers to park in their lot, they have even installed dump stations. The situation at these stores could change at any time due to political pressure from RV park owners or a change of heart of store management.

## Gasoline Cost

| City | Regular Unleaded | Premium Unleaded | Diesel |
|---|---|---|---|
| Anchorage, Alaska | 1.32 | 1.42 | - |
| Cooper Landing, Alaska | 1.57 | - | - |
| Dawson Creek, Canada | 1.59 | 1.80 | 1.40 |
| Fairbanks, Alaska | 1.42 | - | 1.40 |
| Fort Nelson, Canada | 1.78 | 1.86 | 1.41 |
| Haines Junction, Canada | 1.77 | 2.07 | 1.59 |
| Haines, Alaska | 1.64 | 1.78 | 1.65 |
| Nenana, Alaska | 1.47 | - | 1.38 |
| Prince Rupert, Canada | 1.67 | - | - |
| Seward, Alaska | 1.53 | 1.63 | 1.57 |
| Skagway, Alaska | 1.69 | 1.83 | 1.70 |
| Soldotna, Alaska | 1.40 | 1.55 | 1.43 |
| Stewart, Canada | 1.72 | 1.96 | - |
| Tok, Alaska | 1.60 | 1.75 | 1.49 |
| Valdez, Alaska | 1.57 | - | 1.57 |
| Wasilla, Alaska | 1.34 | 1.50 | - |
| Watson Lake, Canada | 1.88 | 1.93 | 1.59 |
| Whitehorse, Canada | 1.80 | - | 1.56 |

Gasoline is readily available throughout Alaska and the Yukon but prices vary widely and change often. The following prices for normal grade unleaded were observed during the summer of 1997. They're bound to change but will give you an idea what to expect. We've converted Candadian dollars to U.S. dollars and liters to gallons for comparison purposes. Several of the locations either did not sell all three types of fuel or we were unable to obtain the prices. Keep in mind that worldwide gas prices have dropped significantly since these prices were recorded in the summer of 1997.

## How Much Time is Required for a Visit to Alaska

The time you'll need for an Alaska trip depends upon your starting point, of course. For an Alaska resident a weekend is plenty of time for a visit to a salmon stream or hiking trail. For an RVer from the lower 48 much more time is required. Remember, just getting to Dawson Creek is quite a journey from most parts of the U.S. Dawson Creek is 817 miles north of Seattle, Washington and 875 miles north of Great Falls, Montana.

If you are planning to drive the Alaska Highway and want to see at least part of the state give yourself at least three weeks from the time you reach Dawson Creek. It takes most people about a week to drive the highway to Anchorage or Fairbanks. After driving that far you deserve to have some time to explore and relax. Most cara-van companies allow at least 5 weeks for their guided trips and they don't visit all areas of the state. Our itinerary in Chapter 1 requires a good two months if you don't want to exhaust yourself.

The quickest and most relaxing way for a non-resident to visit Alaska is to rent an RV in one of the major towns. Take a look at the Motorhome and RV Rentals section in this chapter for more information. With a rental you can have an enjoyable trip even if you only have a week available for your visit.

## Information by Mail or Phone - Prepare for Your Trip

It is always a good idea to know as much as you can about a destination before you go. Knowing what to expect makes planning easier and increases your appreciation of the new places you see and the things there are to do.

There is a great deal of information available about Alaska, the Yukon, and British Columbia. See the Internet Addresses section of this chapter for some places to start an internet research project. Addresses for visitor centers and information centers are given throughout this book in almost every section. To easily find them go to the index and look for entries under the following headings: Visitor Information, local; Alaska Public Lands Information Center; BLM addresses; NPS addresses; State of Alaska addresses; USF&W Service addresses; and USFS addresses. Finally, the Travel Library section of this chapter contains information about an excellent selection of books about many aspects of visiting Alaska and the Yukon.

Here are some places to write for general information about the state and the roads north:

Alaska Division of Tourism, P.O. Box 110801, Juneau, Alaska 99811; 907 465-2010, Fax 907 465-2287.

Alaska Native Tourism Council, 1577 C Street, Suite 304, Anchorage, Alaska; Fax 907 263-9971.

Alaska Natural History Association, 401 W. 1st Avenue, Anchorage, Alaska 99501; 907 274-8440.

Alaska Public Lands Information Center, 605 W. 4th Avenue, #105, Anchorage, Alaska 99501; 907 271-2737.

Alaska Wilderness Recreation and Tourism Association, P.O. Box 22827, Juneau, Alaska 99802; 907 463-3038, Fax 907 463-3280.

Klondike Visitors Association, P.O. Box 389, Dawson City, Y.T. Y0B 1G0, Canada; 867 993-5575, Fax 867 993-6415.

Northern British Columbia Tourism Association, Box 1030, Smithers, B.C. V0J 2N0, Canada; 800 663-8843, 250 847-5227, Fax 250 847-7585.

Tourism British Columbia, P.O. Box 9830, Stn. Prov. Govt., 1117 Wharf Street, Victoria, B.C. V8W 9W5, Canada; 800 663-6000.

Tourism North, Dept. 811, P.O. Box 110801, Juneau, Alaska 99811.

Tourism Yukon, Dept. 8308, P.O. Box 2745, Whitehorse, Y.T. Y1A 5B9, Canada.

## Insects and Other Pests (like bears)

Alaska and the Yukon are famous for their mosquitoes. They also both are home to two other northland pests—white sox and no-see-ums. On the positive side, there are no poisonous snakes. Bears, both blacks and browns, often fall into the pest category, particularly around campgrounds, dumps, and fishing streams. Even the shy and slow-witted moose can sometimes be a problem.

Mosquitoes, white sox and no-see-ums are not present in all locations and at all times. Many variables including the amount of standing water, the severity of the winter, the time of the season, and the strength of the breeze make a big difference. When you pick a campsite it pays to stay away from puddles and swampy areas and pick a site with at least the possibility of a breeze.

Mosquitoes are present throughout the summer. They appear as soon as the weather begins to get warm in May and last until the hard freezes in September. They are at their worst in the early season just after breakup. Scientists say that only the females will attack you, but it seems to us that they must all be females. It actually takes a mosquito about a minute to poke into you, inject the saliva that keeps your blood from being too thick to suck, and begin drawing blood. It is the saliva that causes the mosquito prick to itch afterwards.

White sox are also known as black flies in other places, the ones in Alaska have white on their legs. They are present from mid summer until freezing. Their bite is actually worse than that of a mosquito.

No-see-ums are very small and travel in swarms. They tend to land and then crawl under your clothing. Any breeze at all will keep them down, and you can probably out-run them at even a walking pace since they are slow fliers. Their bite is every bit as bad as a white sox and they are present during about the same period.

If you use the proper techniques these flying pests can be dealt with and you can enjoy the outdoors. When they are present you should wear clothing that covers your arms and legs. Some people think that dark colored clothing attracts them.

Anti-insect products containing DEET (diethyl-meta-toluamide) or citronella work best. There is some question about DEET's safety, it is pretty powerful stuff. Be aware that DEET is a solvent and will soften and damage things like plastic fishing lines and plastic watches. Citronella isn't as effective but does not have these problems. We use DEET. Some folks also swear by Skin-So-Soft, an Avon skin cream which wasn't even designed to repel insects but has a cult following.

Another essential product to have along is an anti-itch product, often these are combined with an antiseptic. Once you receive the inevitable bite an anti-itch cream will help you forget about it and reduce the scratching and swelling that results.

It is very important to have good insect screens on your rig and on your tent. You must have some retreat to get away from the bugs when they are really bad, and they will occasionally be very bad. Tent campers should have a head net. They may look funny but when you need them they are priceless and allow you to lead an almost normal life while setting up camp, preparing food, or even while hiking.

Bears can be a problem in camp, particularly if you don't take the proper precautions. They are attracted by food so there are two rules that you should always follow. Do not feed them and keep a very clean camp. All food items must be inside a rig or hung out of reach away from the tent and campsite. Cook away from your tent, never cook in your tent. Make sure your tent is clean if you have done so in the past. Dispose of trash well away from tent. Camp away from trash barrels. In the wilderness watch for bear trails, especially along streams and beaches and do not set up your tent near them. Dogs seem to attract bears so it is best not to have one along in bear country.

Moose can be dangerous. They seem slow-moving and stolid but they are huge, can cover ground quickly, and when riled sometimes protect themselves by trying to stomp their foe. Don't get too close when taking pictures and be careful around mothers and calves. They often stomp dogs and bears, they can do the same to you. Dogs and moose don't mix well, dogs often harass moose and cause real problems, don't let your dog run loose.

## Internet Sites

Every day there are more and more internet sites devoted to Alaska, the Yukon, and B.C. They are a great way to familiarize yourself with the North Country before leaving home. There's no way to tell how long a site will last but here are some that may have some staying power. Once you start looking you will find lots of links to other sites.

The Alaska Marine Highway site is at **http://www.dot.state.ak.us/external/amhs/home.html**.

The British Columbia Ferries web site is at **http://bcferries.bc.ca/ferries**.

The Yukon Territory has information about road conditions at **http://www.gov.yk.ca/depts/cts/highways/report.html**.

The Alaska Department of Transportation reports information about road construction at **http://www.dot.state.ak.us**.

The Milepost has new owners in 1998 and they have set up a new site. The address is **http://www.themilepost.com**.

Visitor centers and visitor's organizations in many town have net sites. Here are a few:

| | |
|---|---|
| Anchorage, Alaska | **http://www.alaska.net/~acvb** |
| Dawson City, Canada | **http://www.DawsonCity.com** |
| Fairbanks, Alaska | **http://fairbanks.polarnet.com** |
| also | **http://www.polarnet.com/users/fcvb** |
| Haines, Alaska | **http://www.haines.ak.us** |
| Homer, Alaska | **http://alaska.net/~hnews** |
| Juneau, Alaska | **http://www.juneau.lib.ak.us/jcvb/jcvb.html** |
| Kenai, Alaska | **http://www.ptialaska.net/~kenai** |
| Ketchikan, Alaska | **http://www.ktn.net** |
| Kodiak, Alaska | **http://kodiak.org** |
| Nome, Alaska | **htp://www.alaska.net/~nome** |
| Petersburg, Alaska | **http://www.petersburg.org** |
| Sitka, Alaska | **http://www.sitka.com** |
| Skagway, Alaska | **http://www.skagway.org** |

| Soldotna, Alaska | **http://www.ptialaska.net/~solchmbr** |
| Tok, Alaska | **http://www.tokalaska.com** |
| Watson Lake, Canada | **http://www.yukon.net/northernlights** |
| Whitehorse, Canada | **http://www.parallel.ca/Yukon** |
| Wrangell, Alaska | **http://www.wrangell.com** |

There is a lot of information available about the North's wilderness parks and other public lands. Try some of these sites.

**http://www.nps.gov/parks.html**

**http://www.nps.gov/aplic/center/index.html**

**http://www.gorp.com/gorp/location/ak/ak.html**

**http://www.pch/gc/ca**

**http://www.dnr.state.ak.us/parks/directry.htm**

There are also many general sites with lots of items of interest. Your list of sites will rapidly increase as one link leads to another.

**http://alaska.edu/info/general.html**

**http://www.klondike.org**

**http://touryukon.com**

**http://www.north-to-alaska.com**

**http://www.gold.rush.org**

**http://www.AlaskaOne.com/Travel**

**http://ptialaska.net/~tripod**

**http://www.alaska.net.com**

**http://www.interax.~com/~huntfishalaska/Home.shtml**

**http://www.netcasting.net/alaska/index.whtml**

**http://www.kenaipeninsula.com**

**http://www.allurealaska.com/akmag**

**http://www.iditarod.com**

**http://www.juneau.com/guide**

**http://www.alaska.com**

## Laundry

Finding a place to do your laundry won't be a problem in Alaska and the Yukon. Almost all privately-owned RV parks have coin operated clothes washing equipment. If you are camping in government campgrounds you will be able to find a public laundromat with little problem. Even the smallest communities usually have a laundromat since many locals don't have running water or electricity. Laundromats also often have shower facilities, this is good to know if you frequent government campgrounds or free camp.

## Mail

Alaska, the Yukon, and British Columbia all have excellent mail service. Outlying areas have slightly slower service than you may be accustomed to, add a couple of days for towns along the highways. Even outlying villages off the road system often have frequent air mail service since aircraft are their only link to the outside world.

In the U.S. just have your mail sent to General Delivery of a town you expect to visit. Some of the important zip codes are as follows: Anchorage 99510, Fairbanks 99701, Juneau 99801, Ketchikan 99901, Kenai 99611, Homer 99603, Seward 99664, Valdez 99686, Tok 99780, Denali National Park 99755.

## Motorhome and RV Rentals

If you don't have your own rig for an Alaska trip you can always rent one. This is an extremely popular way to visit Alaska. Here are some of the rental outfits. Note that some are located in Alaska while others are in British Columbia or the Yukon Territory. Reserve your rental RV as early as possible, many companies are fully booked by the time the camping season arrives. Often there is an early booking discount. The rental company listing below is only a starting point. All of these companies will send you an information pack if you request information. When you receive the packages take a look at the following items to compare them.

- Types of rigs
- Rates
- Mileage charges
- Required deposits
- Insurance coverage and related extra charges
- Pick up and drop off procedures, times, and locations
- Availability of one-way rentals
- Extra charges for housekeeping and linen packages
- Limitations on where you can take the rig, and extra charges for gravel roads
- Pets allowed?
- State of Alaska campground sticker included?

**ABC Motorhome & Car Rentals**, 2360 Commercial Dr., Anchorage, AK 99501; (800) 421-7456, fax (907) 243-6363, internet site http://www.alaskan.com/abcmotorhomes/. Rental pick ups/drop offs in Anchorage, Skagway, Haines, Seattle, Elkhart (Indiana) and Phoenix (Arizona). Also pick ups in other cities in the Lower 48. They offer pickup trucks with campers and motorhomes from 20 feet to 30 feet.

**Affordable RV Rental**, 3101 S. Cushman Street, Fairbanks, AK 99701; (800) 471-3101, (907) 452-7341, fax (907) 451-6371. Rental vehicle pick ups/drop offs in

Fairbanks and Anchorage. They offer 21 foot and 28 foot motorhomes.

**Alaska Economy RVs**, 4517 Old Seward Highway, Anchorage, AK 99503; (907) 561-7723, (800) 764-4625, fax (907) 561-2093, internet address http://www.goalaska.com. Non smoking units only. Rental vehicle pick up/drop off is in Anchorage. They offer small economy 4 wheel drive pickups with folding campers, full-size four wheel drive pickups with campers, and motorhomes from 21 feet to 29 feet.

**Alaskan Adventures RV Rentals**, P.O. Box 230427, Anchorage, AK 99523; (907) 333-7997, (800) 676-8911, fax (907) 337-8632. Pick up/drop off is in Anchorage. They offer pickup campers, van conversions, and motorhomes from 21 feet to 31 feet.

**Alaska Panorama R.V. Rentals, Inc.**, 712 West Potter Drive, Anchorage, AK 99518; (907) 562-1401, (800) 478-1401, fax (907) 561-8762. Pick up/drop off is in Anchorage with drop offs also possible in Fairbanks, Haines, Skagway, and Whitehorse. They offer motorhomes from 20 feet to 33 feet.

**Alaska Recreational Rentals**, P.O. Box 592, Soldotna, Alaska 99669; (907) 262-2700, internet site http://alaskamall.com/ARR/. Rental vehicle pick ups/ drop offs in Soldotna/Kenai, Anchorage, or Seward. They offer motorhomes from 21 feet to 29 feet.

**Alldrive Canada Inc.**, 1908 - 10$^{th}$ Avenue S.W., Calgary, Alberta T3C 0J8, Canada; (403) 245-2935, (888) 736-8787, fax (403) 245-2959, internet site at http://www.alldrive.com. Rental pick ups/drop offs are in Calgary and Vancouver. They offer pickups with campers, conversion vans, trucks with 5$^{th}$ wheel campers, and motorhomes from 21 feet to 31 feet.

**Alutiiq RV Adventures**, 550 W. 54$^{th}$ St., Anchorage, Alaska 99518; (907) 561-8747, fax (907) 561-7788, web page http://www.alaska.net/~alutiiq. Rental vehicle pick up/ drop off in Anchorage. Drop offs also available in Haines, Skagway, and Fairbanks. They offer four-wheel-drive pickups with campers and motorhomes to 29 feet.

**C.C. Canada Camper R.V. Rentals Ltd.**, 1080 Millcarch St., Richmond, B.C. V6V 2H4, Canada; (604) 327-3003, fax (604) 324-1044. Web page at http://www.canada-camper.com. Rental vehicle pick ups/drop offs in Vancouver, B.C. area and Calgary. They offer jeep rentals, conversion vans, pickup-style campers, and motorhomes to 29 feet.

**Candan RV Rentals**, 20257 Langley Bypass, Langley, B.C. V3A 6K9, Canada; (604) 530-3645, fax (604) 530-1696, web site at http://www.candan.com. Rental vehicle pick ups/drop offs in the Vancouver, B.C. area and Calgary. They offer a wide variety of RVs including van conversions, 5$^{th}$ wheels with pickups, and motorhomes to 34 feet.

**Clippership Motorhome Rentals**, 5401 Old Seward Highway, Anchorage, AK 99518; (800) 421-3456 or (907) 562-7051, fax (907) 562-7053. Web page at http://

www.customcpu.com/commercial/clippership. Rental pick up/drop off in Anchorage, drop offs available in Fairbanks, Haines, Homer, Kenai, Denali Park, Seward, Skagway, Soldotna, Valdez or Whitehorse. They offer motorhomes from 20 to 27 feet.

**Compact RV Rental**, P.O. Box 91246, Anchorage, AK 99509; (907) 333-7368, (800) 841-0687, fax (907) 333-7358. Rental pick up/drop off is in Anchorage. They offer Ford Explorer SUV's and a range of pickups with campers from sub compacts to large 4x4's.

**Go West Motorhome Rentals**, 1577 Lloyd Avenue, North Vancouver, B.C. V7P 3K8 Canada; (604) 987-5288, (800) 661-8813, internet address http://www.go-west.com. Rental pick ups/drop offs are in Vancouver and Calgary. They offer pick-ups with campers, van conversions, and motorhomes from 19 to 31 feet.

**Great Alaskan Holidays**, 3901 W. International Airport Road, Anchorage, AK 99502; (907) 248-7777, (888) 225-2752, fax (907) 248-7878. Rental pick up/drop off is in Anchorage. They offer motorhomes from 20 feet to 29 feet.

**Holiday Rentals & Sales Ltd.**, #5 - 26004 Fraser Highway, Aldergrove, B.C. V4W 3V7, Canada; (604) 857-9889, fax (604) 857-9839. Rental pick ups/drop off in Aldergrover, B.C. which is near the U.S.- Canada border east of Vancouver. They offer van conversions, pickups with campers, trucks with 5th wheel trailers, and motorhomes to 30 feet.

**Klondike Recreational Rentals Ltd.**, Box 5156, Whitehorse, Yukon Y1A 4S3, Canada; (867) 668-2200, fax (867) 668-6567. Rental pick up/drop off in Whitehorse with limited pick up/drop off in Kamloops (British Columbia). They offer touring vans, pickups with campers, and motorhomes from 24 feet to 30 feet.

**Murphy's RV Inc.**, P.O. Box 202063, Anchorage, AK 99520; (907) 276-0688, (907) 243-6058 eves, (800) 582-5123, fax (907) 258-4510. Rental pick up/drop off is in Anchorage. They offer motorhomes from 21 feet to 31 feet.

**Rocky Mountain Campers**, P.O. Box 48115, Midlake P.O., 40 Midlake Boulevard S.E., Calgary, Alberta T2X 3C9, Canada; (403) 291-0711, (800) 757-0444 in Canada, fax (403) 264-9329. Rental pick ups/drop offs in Calgary, Vancouver, and Whitehorse. They offer pickups and campers, van conversions, and motorhomes.

**Sourdough R.V. Rentals**, 5011 Jewel Lake Rd., Anchorage, AK 99502; (907) 243-0006, (800) 770-3268, fax (907) 248-4902, internet address http://www.alaskaone.com/sourdough. Rental pick up/drop off is in Anchorage. They offer pickup trucks with pop-up tents in the beds, pickup campers, conversion vans, and motorhomes from 22 feet to 28 feet.

**Sweet Retreat Motorhome Rentals**, 6820 Arctic Blvd., Anchorage, AK 99518; (800) 759-4861, fax (907) 344-8279, web site at http://www.custom-cpu/commercial/sweet. Rental pick up/drop off is in Anchorage. They offer motorhomes from 21 feet to 33 feet.

**Tanana Motorhome Rentals**, P.O. Box 82446, Fairbanks, AK 99708; (907) 488-7564, fax (907) 488-7564. Rental pick up/drop off in Fairbanks with the possibility of other locations in Alaska. They offer motorhomes from 21 feet to 34 feet.

**Westcoast Mountain Campers Ltd.**, 150 11800 Voyageur Way, Richmond, B.C. V6X 3N8, Canada; (604) 279-0550, fax (604) 279-0527. Rental pick ups/drop offs in Vancouver and Calgary. They offer pickups with campers, Volkswagen campers, van conversions, and motorhomes from 23 feet to 27 feet.

Some rental outfits have an extra charge for gravel roads or restrict driving on them. Check on this if you plan to drive on them. Dropping the rig off at another location tends to be very expensive.

## Northern Lights and the Midnight Sun

One of the reasons that Alaska has a special ambiance is the far northern location. The midnight sun and the northern lights are manifestations of this.

During June and July the days are very long. Baseball games are played at midnight, people are full of energy and work and play until all hours of the night. Most Alaskans love this, for them it helps make up for the long, dark winter. You'll probably like it too, but many people have trouble sleeping in broad daylight. Either take along something to cover your eyes when you are sleeping or cover the windows of your rig with something to keep out the light, many people use aluminum foil. Tenters may find that a dark-colored tent helps.

The longest day of the year is June 20 or 21. It is known as the summer solstice. On that day a person standing on the arctic circle would be able to see the sun all night long if the terrain were perfectly flat. As a practical matter, people from Fairbanks go to the summits north of town where they have some altitude and are guaranteed the sun for their summer solstice celebration even though they really aren't as far north as the Arctic Circle.

One reason to plan a late trip to Alaska is the northern lights. You won't be able to see them unless it is dark at night, and for campers that means September.

There's a great exhibit on northern lights at the University of Alaska museum in Fairbanks. There's also a new theater devoted to shows about the northern lights in Watson Lake, Y.T. Either of them provides a good introduction.

To see the northern lights you'll need a clear dark night. They do not appear every night but if you keep an eye open you'll eventually have a good sighting. They'll be toward the north and are usually best after midnight.

## Photography

Wildlife, scenery, and outdoor sports, all make great photography subjects. If you're traveling by RV bring your gear. If you have to carry it in a backpack you'll have to pack lighter, but don't forget a camera.

Definitely bring along a telephoto. Also fast film so that you can take advantage of it. A tripod is very useful for telephoto photography. You'll also want a medium length lens that can be hand held since wildlife often won't stick around while you set up your tripod. For dark blue skies use a polarizing filter.

## Propane

You'll have no problem finding propane throughout the North Country. All larger towns have several sources and virtually every smaller town also has some place where you can fill up. Just ask at the campground for advice. Plan ahead so that you don't run out while far from civilization.

## Public Transportation

There's a variety of public transportation in the North. Many of the larger towns have bus systems that work great for getting around while staying at a campground on the outskirts of town. A limited number of busses ply the highways. State ferries connect the towns of southeast Alaska and also run to Kodiak, Cordova and out the Aleutian Chain. And in the bush you might find that public transportation will take the form of a small airplane.

The cities of Anchorage, Whitehorse, and Juneau all have public bus systems. Many of the city campgrounds are on or near a bus route.

While intercity busses are infrequent in Alaska and the Yukon it is possible for travelers without their own wheels to get around. In places where there is enough demand service is available, although often in the form of vans able to carry only a few passengers. Bus service offerings tend to change frequently, just as airline service offerings do, but here are some places to begin your search for transportation. Greyhound Lines of Canada (867 667-2223) offers bus service from Vancouver, B.C. and other Canadian towns and U.S./Canada border crossings on a route along the Alaska Highway as far as Whitehorse. Connections on to Alaska are available from there. Alaska Direct (867 668-4833 or 800 770-6652) runs busses from Anchorage to Denali Park, Fairbanks, Dawson City, Whitehorse, and Skagway. Grey Line's Alaskan Express (800 544-2206) has similar routes. Grey Line also has an extensive list of bus and bus-air or bus-boat tours including Anchorage - Kenai Fjords, Anchorage - Portage Glacier, Anchorage - Valdez - Whittier - Anchorage, Anchorage - Whittier - Valdez - Denali National Park - Fairbanks - Anchorage, Anchorage - Denali National Park, Fairbanks - Denali National Park, Fairbanks - Prudhoe Bay along the Dalton Highway, Fairbanks - Dawson City - Whitehorse - Skagway, and Fairbanks - Eagle - Dawson City by boat on the Yukon - Fairbanks. In fact, Gray Line offers tours to do almost anything you would like to do including fly-in fishing, charter-boat salt-water fishing, rafting, city tours, railroad trips, and airline tours to remote locations like Nome, Kotzebue and the Pribilof Islands. Call 800 628-2449 for a mouth-watering brochure.

Also check the web site at http://www.yukonweb.com/tourism/westours.

Small vans provide service along several routes. Probably the most interesting are runs from Anchorage and Fairbanks to Denali National Park, from Fairbanks up the Dalton Highway, and from Glennallen to McCarthy. You will be able to find information about these and other van operations locally.

The Alaska Railroad offers some interesting transportation options. The railroad is very tourist-friendly, they have excellent schedules for sightseeing and also can arrange tours at the destinations. Trains run between Anchorage and Fairbanks with stops in Talkeetna and at Denali National Park. They also run to Seward and to Whittier from Anchorage. Contact the railroad at P.O. Box 107500, Anchorage, AK 99510: (800) 544-0552, (907) 265-2494, internet site at http://www.alaska.net/~akrr/. They have a good brochure outlining their services.

Another service provided by the Alaska Railroad is the Portage/Whittier shuttle. Whittier is a ferry port on Prince William Sound. It has no road access. To get there you load your car (or walk aboard) on a shuttle train at Portage for a 35-minute ride through a tunnel to Whittier. The shuttle makes several trips daily, no reservations are taken. Call (907) 265-2607 for recorded schedule information.

Air transportation in Alaska is widespread and easy to find. Airlines flying modern jets provide scheduled service between larger cities. From the larger cities smaller operators flying light aircraft provide both scheduled and charter flights to any village with a safe airstrip and to a huge selection of lakes and rivers large enough for a float-equipped airplane. If you are bound for a remote campsite it is generally more economical to fly a scheduled operator to a hub town or village near your eventual destination and then charter a small aircraft for a short flight. More information about access to remote locations is included in Chapter 14 of this book.

## Telephones

The good news is that phones in Alaska and Canada use much the same system that is used in the Lower 48. You can direct dial in and out of Canada and Alaska using the normal area code and seven-digit number format. It is not necessary to use an international country code when calling Canada from the U.S. or the U.S. from Canada. The area code for all of Alaska is 907, for all of the Yukon it has recently been changed to 867, and for all of British Columbia except the Vancouver area it is 250.

Telephone rates are more expensive than those in the Lower 48. Sometimes, especially in remote areas you will notice an echo or delay because telephone signals are bounced off a satellite.

We have found that some U.S. calling cards will not work in Canada. Before entering Canada you should call your service provider and make sure it will work in Canada, and particularly in remote areas of the Yukon along the highway. Otherwise you may find yourself out of touch with home.

## Time Zones

All of Alaska except the very western islands of the Aleutian Chain are in one time zone and use Alaska Time. This is one hour earlier than Pacific time as used on the West Coast of the U.S. and Canada. The Yukon is on Pacific Time also. British Columbia has two time zones, Pacific time is used in most areas but the far eastern area of the Province including the part of the Alaska Highway from Dawson Creek north to Fort Nelson is on Mountain Time. Alaska, the Yukon, and British Columbia all observe daylight saving time.

## Tourist Information Offices

Tourist information is very easy to find throughout Alaska, the Yukon, and British Columbian. Any town of even moderate size seems to have a tourist office, we've tried to give their locations, addresses, and phone numbers in the city descriptions included in the campground chapters of this book. The U.S. government and the Alaska government also have information offices in various locations, usually related to government-owned lands like National Forests and State and National Parks. You'll find addresses and phone numbers throughout the book. To easily find them go to the index and look for entries under the following headings: Visitor Information, local; Alaska Public Lands Information Center; BLM addresses; NPS addresses; State of Alaska addresses; USF&W Service addresses; and USFS addresses.

## Travel Library

One of the best things about traveling in your own vehicle is that you have plenty of room for a library. Your appreciation of the country will be much improved by a little background reading and the availability of a few reference books as you travel.

*The Milepost* (Morris Communications Corporation, 1998, ISBN 1878425307) is the bible of Alaska highway travel. It contains a wealth of information about services, history, sights, and just about everything else. It also has mile-by-mile logs of all of the routes to and in Alaska. The one drawback to the Milepost is that almost all commercial facilities mentioned are advertisers who write their own descriptions. Enough said.

Off-highway campers have their own Milepost, *The Alaska Wilderness Guide* by the Milepost editors (Vernon Publications, Inc.; Bellevue, WA; 1993; ISBN 1878425501).

Another Milepost-type book you may see is *Bell's Mile By Mile Alaska, Yukon, and British Columbia Travel Guide*(Bell's Alaska Travel Guide; Kelowna, British Columbia; ISBN 1880840057). This is a more compact book than the Milepost, it also contains a lot less information and is much cheaper. Backpackers might appreciate its size.

Probably the best history of the Klondike gold rush readily available is *The Klondike Fever: The Life and Death of the Last Great Gold Rush* by Pierre Berton (Carroll &

Graf, New York, N.Y.; 1985; ISBN 0881841390). First published in 1958 this book continues in print today, which is a real testimony to it's quality. The author grew up in Dawson City.

As you sit beside your campfire in the evening you'll probably find you have lots of light for reading. Make sure to have a copy of the poems of Robert Service on hand. His ballads of the gold rush days have a special resonance when you visit the far North.

In a place like Alaska, especially away from the roads, you'll need maps. A good place to start is DeLorme Mapping's *Alaska Atlas & Gazetteer* (ISBN 0899332013) which has 1:300,000 and 1:1,400,000 scale topographic maps covering the entire state. Later you'll want to get maps that show more detail for hiking or when you get away from the highway.

Your interest in the construction of the Alcan is bound to be piqued when you drive it. Heath Twichell's *Northwest Epic: The Building of the Alaska Highway* (St. Martin's Press; New York, N.Y.; 1992; ISBN 0312077548) will help. You should actually read it before driving the route.

If you find yourself intrigued by the GPS navigation system and want more in-depth information there's a new book that will help. It is *GPS Land Navigation: A Complete Guidebook for Backcountry Users of the Navstar Satellite System* by Michael Ferguson (Glassford Publishing; Boise, Idaho; 1997, ISBN 0965220257).

There are two excellent guides to hiking in Alaska. The classic is *55 Ways to the Wilderness in Southcentral* Alaska by Helen Nienhueser and Nancy Simmerman (The Mountaineers; Seattle, Washington; 1994; ISBN 0898863899). *Hiking Alaska* by Dean Littlepage (Falcon Press Publishing Co., Inc.; Helena, Montana; 1997; ISBN: 1560445513) is a new favorite and covers the entire state.

A good guide to floatable Alaska rivers is *The Alaska River Guide: Canoeing, Kayaking, and Rafting in the Last Frontier* by Karen Jettmar (Alaska Northwest Books; Seattle, Washington; 1998; ISBN 0882404970.

Fishermen will need a guide showing techniques and other information about Alaskan fishing. Readily available is *Fishing Alaska* by Evan & Margaret Swensen (Falcon Press; Helena and Billings, Montana; 1997; ISBN 1560445238.

The ultimate guide to Alaska's government lands is the encyclopedic *Alaska's Parklands* by Nancy Lange Simmerman (The Mountaineers; Seattle, Washington; 1991; ISBN 0898860539).

## Units of Measurement

Alaska uses the same measurement systems as the lower 48 - miles, gallons, and degrees Fahrenheit. Canada does not, there you have to deal with kilometers, liters, and degrees Celsius.

Here are a few conversion factors and tricks to help you cope.

One kilometer is about .62 miles (actually .6124). For converting miles to kilometers divide the number of miles by .62. For converting kilometers to miles multiply the kilometers by .62. Since kilometers are shorter than miles the number of kilometers after converting will always be more than the number of miles, if they aren't you divided when you should have multiplied or multiplied when you should have divided.

For liquid measurement it is usually enough to know that a liter is about the same as a quart. When you need more accuracy, like when you are trying to make some sense out of your miles per gallon calculations, there are 3.79 liters in a U.S. gallon.

Here are a few useful conversion factors:

> 1 km = .62 mile
> 1 mile = 1.61 km
> 1 meter = 3.28 feet
> 1 foot = .3 meters
> 1 liter = .26 U.S. gallon
> 1 U.S. gallon = 3.79 liters
> 1 kilogram = 2.21 pounds
> 1 pound = .45 kilograms
> Convert from °F to °C by subtracting 32 and multiplying by 5/9
> Convert from °C to °F by multiplying by 1.8 and adding 32

## Vehicle Preparation and Breakdowns

Vehicle preparation for the trip north runs the gamut. Some people do nothing more than change the oil . Others definitely go overboard. We tend to take the middle road. It is important to have a rig that will not go haywire on you and force you to make expensive repairs (not to mention incur an expensive tow bill) in an isolated location.

Make sure that your tires are in very good shape and that you have a spare. Consider carrying two spares if you plan to spend a lot of time on gravel roads like the Dalton Highway (Prudhoe Bay Haul Road) or the Dempster. Make sure that you have a good jack and tire wrench that will work on your rig, some new motorhomes do not come with either. Even if you can't manage to change a tire on one of the huge rigs yourself you should at least have the tools to let someone help you.

Do a complete systems check before you leave home. If you have a nagging problem with something in your vehicle, say a balky refrigerator or a leak of some kind make sure to fix it before heading north. It is bound to get worse during a long trip and repairs are definitely not cheaper up north.

Bring jumper cables and small tool kit. Spares are usually not necessary but if you know of some filter or essential part that is particularly difficult to find you might want to bring an extra along so that you are not faced with a long delay in a remote location. If a part isn't essential you can sometimes get your rig to a place where parts are available, we once drove over 500 miles in second gear to reach Whitehorse when an electronic part in our motorhome's transmission went south near Muncho Lake.

Emergency road service insurance is well worth while even if it is only for the peace of mind. Towing charges can be very high, especially in remote areas. Make sure your plan will cover you in northern Canada and Alaska and on remote roads.

Gravel roads are probably the hazard requiring the most vehicle preparation. Fortunately, you're really likely to run into few of them if you keep to the main highways. The Alaska Highway is paved for the entire distance although there are likely to be some unpaved sections where upgrades and road repairs are underway. The Cassiar Highway now has under 100 miles of unpaved road. The only other gravel most people are likely to encounter is the Klondike Loop between Dawson City and Tok. More aggressive travelers will see gravel if they drive the Taylor Highway north to Eagle, the Denali Highway between the Tangle Lakes and the Parks Highway, the Nabesna Road, the McCarthy road to McCarthy, the Dalton Highway to Prudhoe Bay, the Dempster Highway from Dawson City to Inuvik, and the roads north of Fairbanks to Circle and Manley Hot Springs. Read on if you plan to travel these roads.

Many people feel that a slight reduction in tire pressure while on gravel roads will reduce the incidence of blowouts. This should only be done while on gravel roads and at slow speeds. We don't do it because it is sometimes difficult to find air once you are ready to drive on pavement, especially if you need lots of pressure for big truck tires.

There are a few things that can easily be done to cope with dust on gravel roads. You may already know the spots where dust leaks into your RV. Consider using duct tape to seal leaky storage compartments and doors while underway. It also helps to have a positive air pressure inside your vehicle, turn on your heater or air conditioner fan and close your windows to do this.

Flying rocks can do a lot of damage and are difficult to avoid. Even if you drive carefully you are likely to get hit by rocks thrown up by people passing you in both directions. The large front windshields of RV's are particularly vulnerable. They are virtually impossible to protect so just make sure you have insurance. We make sure that we get small dings repaired when we reach Anchorage or Fairbanks so cracks won't spread. Forward facing windows on trailers, campers and motorhomes (not windshields) can be protected with cardboard and tape. This must be done or you will probably get a broken window The cardboard covering may also help you sleep in the midnight sun.

Rocks will also hit your headlights. You can buy inexpensive protectors in auto shops that will save your headlights. Radiators also sometimes get hit by rocks, you can protect them with metal bug screening. This has always seemed like overkill to us but many people do it. We've had no radiator problems due to leaving ours unprotected.

Plumbing and dump fixtures on RVs are often made of plastic and hang down where flying rocks from the tires will easily hit and break them. Consider carrying extras or building rock deflectors. We find that wrapping them with fiberglass insulation and duct tape is effective and easy, but not very pretty. Don't forget the copper pipes and valves of your propane system. They can be covered with insulation or a rubber hose that has been split for installation and then taped.

Vehicles that are being towed are particularly vulnerable to rocks thrown up by the towing vehicle. Use cardboard or plywood shields on the front of trailers and fifth wheels. Fit your tow vehicle with good mud flaps and cover the nose of a towed car with something to protect it from flying rocks. Don't worry about how it looks, you'll save it from a lot of damage. If you don't want to do this consider unhooking and driving the car separately when you reach a stretch of gravel.

Gravel sections of the Alaska Highway are often treated with chemicals to keep the dust down. You should wash your RV after traversing these areas because the chemicals are corrosive, many campgrounds provide washing facilities. Don't forget the underside of the vehicle.

In "the old days" travelers on the Alaska Highway seemed to often get leaks in their gas tanks from flying rocks. This isn't likely today since there are so few miles of gravel. A quick fix used then was to rub the outside of the puncture with a bar of soap, it often worked until you could reach a repair shop.

## Water

It is easy to fall into the trap of thinking that drinking water in a place as huge and unspoiled as Alaska must be safe. This is not exactly the case, you must be just as careful about your drinking water in the North as you would be in the Lower 48.

Giardia (causes beaver fever) and other contaminants are wide-spread in Alaska, even in places far from the nearest settlement. Use a filter or water treatment on all surface water. This is likely to be a problem only if you are camping away from the road system since good pure water is available at almost all private campgrounds and many government ones. We have noted, however, that Yukon Government campgrounds often post a notice that their water must be purified. You should do so if posted.

Campgrounds may have good water but getting the water into your rig at a government campground may be difficult. Many have hand pumps or faucets that can not be used with a hose. Your only solution may be to pump water into a container and then fill your vehicle's water tank using a funnel. If you plan to camp solely at government campgrounds you will probably want to add a bucket and funnel to your equipment list. For more about water treatment see Chapter 14.

## When to Camp - The Weather

This book is primarily aimed at the summer camper. Most camping facilities are open from break-up in the middle of May until freeze-up sometime in September or early

October. Many government campgrounds close in September but many others stay open until the snow flies. Actually, most of the RVing traffic from warmer climes disappears during the first part of September and only local hunters are in the campgrounds until snow and cold force them to close.

June, July, and August are the most popular camping months, the high season. There are few mosquitoes in May but things haven't really dried out from break-up in many areas. The end of the month is often OK. Things start to turn green in June and in many areas this month has the least rain. July is the warmest month, the Fairbanks area can see 90° F, Anchorage residents are happy with 70°. August sees the days start to grown shorter and the temperature fall just a litle. September is the fall, trees quickly turn yellow and "termination dust", snow begins to appear on the hills. By the end of the month in the interior the leaves are gone and the hard freezes have started.

**Southcentral** - The best weather in the Anchorage area including the Susitna Valley and the Kenai Peninsula is June—July and August have a little more rain. Expect 50° to 70° F in Anchorage, slightly warmer on the Kenai Peninsula and in the Mat-Su Valley. The Anchorage bowl can sock in for long periods, if it does just head for the Kenai or the Interior.

**Interior** - The weather is pretty good in the interior during all three high-season months. Fairbanks often has temperatures in the 70° to 80° F range. There's more rain in the summer than snow in the winter but the interior is fairly dry. Expect a few rainy periods but many days of clear or partly-clear weather with perhaps a rain shower or two. September is our favorite month in the interior. Temperatures start to fall but aren't bad if you have a heated RV for waking up in the morning, campgrounds are virtually empty, the northern lights are out at night, and the trees are beautiful.

**Southeast** - Expect rain in Southeast. If you get lucky and have a few days of sunshine consider yourself blessed. The scenery is spectacular when the sun shines. Temperatures in southeast are mild, say 45° to 60° F during most of the summer. Rainfall patterns are important. June is the driest month with rainfall increasing through the summer until October, which is the wettest month. Also note that rainfall is heaviest in the south and lightest in the north.

# CHAPTER

............ 3

# HOW TO USE THE DESTINATION CHAPTERS

Chapters 4 through 14 of this book contain information about the many camping destinations available to you in Alaska and along the Alaska and Cassiar Highways. Chapters 4 through 12 covering campgrounds along the highways, are all similarly arranged. Each covers the campgrounds along a major highway route. Chapter 13 on Southeast Alaska and Chapter 14 on Camping Away from the Road System follow different self-explanatory formats, this chapter does not apply to them.

## Introductory Road Map

Each of the campground chapters begins with a road map. The map shows a lot of information that will allow you to use it as an index to find campgrounds as you travel. The map shows the route covered in the chapter and also the most important towns. Many towns along the route, shown as stars, have their own maps which are placed later in the chapter and show in-town campground locations. Dotted lines outline areas outside towns that have their own campground location maps. These two types of maps together cover all areas along the road system. An index on the map page shows the names of all route and town descriptions in the chapter and the page number where each starts.

## Introductory Text

Each chapter starts with an **Introduction** giving important information about the route or routes covered in the chapter. Usually there is something of the history of the route and the area, a description of the lay of the land, and a summary of the highlights. These might be important towns, unusual geographical or physical features, or out-standing destinations of one kind or another.

In Alaska outdoor activities are a primary attraction. We have discovered, however, that it is very easy to miss an area's outdoor attractions if you don't have a handy guide. For this reason we've included information about four different kinds of outdoor activities that we think will be popular with our readers: Fishing; Boating Rafting, Canoeing, and Kayaking; Hiking and Mountain Biking; and Wildlife Viewing. Our intention is not to try to replace the many individual guides that are published about each of these activities, we just want you to be aware of each area's attractions. If you are interested you can look farther for more detailed information. We've included references in many places to help you do just that. Some of the books listed in Chapter 2 will also be helpful.

## Route and Town Descriptions

Following the introductory material in each chapter is the **Routes, Towns, and Campgrounds** section. In addition to the campground overview maps described below this section has a few paragraphs of text describing each route or town. We've described the local attractions and also included information about the location and phone number of the visitor center in each town if there happens to be one.

Our descriptions of the destinations and routes in this book are intended to give you an idea of what the city or region has to offer. They are by no means complete, you will undoubtedly need additional guides during your visit. Local visitor centers in Alaska and along the roads north are essential stops, they have lots of interesting materials and usually are staffed by knowledgeable locals.

We have given population and altitude information for each major town. These are our estimates. Population figures are constantly changing and sometimes they reflect artificial political boundaries, we've just tried to give you some idea ahead of time of what you can expect by giving you our best estimate based upon many different sources. The altitudes are also estimates, some are based upon the local airport altitude which may be somewhat different than the altitude of the central business district, we've tried to correct for this.

We've also included many mileage figures. Mileages are the best way to fix locations along the roads in the north but they are often not 100% accurate for several reasons. Most northern roads have mileposts placed along them and these mileposts are used to determine location. It would be prohibitively expensive to change them all each time a road is straightened and shortened. You will find that many older establishments along the Alaska Highway list addresses based upon historical mileposts that are twenty or more miles different than today's mileposts, which are really kilometer posts. Another problem is that many of the mileposts are missing for one reason or another.

If you examine guidebooks to rural Alaska and the roads north you will see that each has slightly different mileage numbers as each tries in its own way to cope with the problems. We've done the same and no doubt you will find some of our figures that do not quite agree with your own odometer. This may be because we usually round to the nearest mile or kilometer. None of this should cause you any big problems, the north is pretty empty and if you are close to a destination you will usually have no problem finding it.

As everyone knows the U.S. uses miles and Canada uses kilometers. We've tried to use miles when we are writing about Alaska and kilometers when we are writing about Canada. Canadians will no doubt notice our bias—we also translate the kilometers into miles when we use them. Our excuse is that most Canadians are accustomed to both kilometers and miles while most of us folks from the states haven't yet learned to deal with kilometers.

## Campground Overview Maps

Each important city or town and each region between the towns has its own campground overview maps. These maps are designed to do two things: they quickly show you the lay of the land and the campgrounds that are available, and if you examine them more carefully they will help you drive right to the campground you have decided to use.

There are two different types of campground overview maps. The first is a city map. Each city map is associated with a written description of the city and a listing of the campgrounds in that city. The second type is an area map. These usually show the road between two cities and each is associated with a description of that road and also a listing of the campgrounds on that road. Campgrounds are never shown on two different maps. In some cases a campground that might be shown along the road between towns is instead shown on a town map. This happens when we think the campground is a good place to stay for a visit to the town even though it might be located a short distance down the road.

While the maps are for the most part self-explanatory here is a key.

## Campground Descriptions

Each campground section begins with address and telephone number. While it is not generally necessary to obtain campground reservations in Alaska you may want to do so for some very popular campgrounds. This is particularly true in areas where people congregate to wait for ferries or where weekend crowds from nearby cities are likely to plug the campgrounds.

One thing you will not find in our campground descriptions is a rating with some kind of system of stars, checks, or tree icons. Hopefully we've included enough information in our campground descriptions to let you make your own analysis.

We've included limited information about campground prices. The price you pay depends upon the type of rig you drive, the number in your party, your use of hookups, and sometimes even the time of year.

Generally you can expect that tent campers will pay the least. Throughout the north the prices charged by commercial campgrounds for both tenters and dry sites are heavily influenced by the prices charged in the many government campgrounds. Usually the commercial price is a dollar or two more than local government campgrounds because commercial campgrounds generally have additional amenities (like showers).

RV charges depend more upon the hookups used than the size of the rig. Expect dry sites to cost a few dollars more than a space in a government campground, electricity will add a few dollars, and a sewer hookup a few more.

There is one more important factor. In remote locations hookups and dump station use can be more expensive than in a city. Electricity is sometimes generated on site, this can be a costly proposition. Dump stations in remote areas are often septic systems, sometimes everything you dump must be pumped out by the operator and trucked away. This also is an expensive operation. We always try to dump our tanks in a town with a city sewer system, it's better for the environment and it saves everyone a lot of trouble and money.

We've grouped the campground fees into the following categories in our campground descriptions:

| | |
|---|---|
| Free | |
| Low | Up to $10 |
| Medium | Over $10 and up to $20 |
| High | Over $20 |

All of these prices are summer prices for an RV with 2 people using full hookups if available. In government campgrounds the prices are for an RV. Note that in most government campgrounds there is only one price, all pay the same price.

Campground icons can be useful for a quick overview of campground facilities or if you are quickly looking for a particular feature.

Most of the campgrounds in this book accept both RVs and tents. If the campground is for tents only we say so in the text. If an RV campground does not accept tents or we feel that it is not suitable for tents we show the no tents symbol.

A few campgrounds listed provide no drinking water and we use a no water symbol for them. If water is provided, even if it is posted as non-potable, we do not use the symbol. Most water provided at campgrounds is fine, we don't purify water from pumps or taps unless it is posted as non-potable.

We show the dump station symbol only if there is a dump station. If sewer drains are available we say so in the text. Note that in the far north drains can be a real maintenance problem due to very cold winter temperatures and permafrost, many campgrounds do not have them.

We show a toilet symbol if a campground has flush toilets. If there are no toilets of any kind we say so in the text. The rest of the campgrounds listed have what we've always called outhouses, some call them pit toilets, dry toilets, or vault toilets. They don't flush.

We show a campfire symbol if there are fire pits or if a central campfire area is provided. Many commercial campgrounds do not allow campfires at the individual spaces but do have a central campfire area. Almost all government campgrounds have fire pits or grills.

We show a restaurant symbol if there is one at the campground or if one is within easy walking distance.

We show a fishing symbol if fishing is possible within easy walking distance.

We show a hiking symbol is there are hiking trails near the campground. This could mean there is a short nature trail or it could mean that a long cross-country trail starts nearby. Generally we try to say which it is.

The swimming symbol is used if any swimming is available. Since few campgrounds have swimming pools (usually just the few hot springs) this probably means lake swimming. The lakes in Alaska are usually only warm enough for swimming in July and early August, and even then only if you're young or very tough.

We use the handicapped symbol if a campground advertises that it has handicapped facilities. Provisions provided for the handicapped vary considerably. We advise that you check with the campground operator directly before your visit to determine exactly what the situation is and whether you should reserve a particular space.

 Finally, many campgrounds give a Good Sam discount. We note them if they advertise that they do.

You'll find that this book has a much larger campground description than most guidebooks. We've tried to include more information so you can make a more informed decision about which one you want to pick for your stay.

## GPS (Global Positioning System) Coordinates

You will note that for some of the campgrounds we have provided a GPS Location. GPS is a new navigation tool that uses signals from satellites. For less than $150 you can now buy a hand-held receiver that will give you your latitude, longitude, and approximate altitude anywhere in the world. You can also enter the coordinates we have given for the campgrounds in this book into the receiver and it will tell you exactly where the campground lies in relation to your position. If our maps and descriptions just don't lead you to the campground you can fall back on the GPS information.

We have not provided this information for all of the campgrounds. That may be because we visited before we acquired the GPS receiver, it also might be because we forgot to take a reading or because we could not pick up the satellites for one reason or another. Nearby mountains or tree cover sometimes block satellite signals.

If you don't have a GPS receiver already you certainly don't need to go out and buy one to use this book. On the other hand, if you do have one bring it along. We expect that GPS will actually be installed in many vehicles during the next few years so we thought we'd get a jump on things. If you are finding that our readings are not entirely accurate you should check to see which Map Datum your machine is set to use. The coordinates in this book are based upon the World Geodetic System 1984 (WGS 84) datum.

Finally, if you are going to go on a hike from the campground and use the GPS as a tool to help you return **do not use** our readings. Take your own reading before leaving the campground to ensure accuracy. Our readings  in some cases were taken using too few satellites for complete (3D) accuracy. Some authorities now feel that that can induce significant errors. We have not rechecked the readings. For more information about GPS you might want to check out the book we recommend in Chapter 2.

## Dump Stations

At the end of each chapter we have included a listing of dump stations that are not located in campgrounds. The information comes from information provided from government organizations and from lists obtained from gasoline distributors.

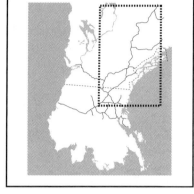

THE ALASKA HIGHWAY

# CHAPTER
. . . . . . . . . 4
# THE ALASKA HIGHWAY

## INTRODUCTION

For many years the Alaska Highway (the Alcan) has held a special place in the hearts of adventurous highway travelers. This major highway was constructed through almost unexplored wilderness during World War II. It opened a huge and fascination territory—Alaska, the Yukon, and Northern British Columbia—to anyone who could climb into a vehicle and drive north.

The Alaska Highway begins at Dawson Creek in British Columbia. Just getting to Dawson Creek is an adventure. From Seattle the driving distance to Dawson Creek is 815 miles, from Great Falls, Montana it is 867 miles. Information about the routes to Dawson Creek could form the basis for several guidebooks, unfortunately there is not room for it here. For the most part you can be confident that the roads leading north to Dawson Creek are paved and services easy to find.

We'll start our coverage at Dawson Creek. Some folks may decide to follow one of the other routes north: the Cassiar Highway (Chapter 5 in this book) or the ferry routes through the Inside Passage (Chapter 13 in this book).

### Highlights

The Alcan (Alaska-Canada Highway), now called the **Alaska Highway**, is itself an interesting destination. Construction of the highway from Dawson Creek to Tok, Alaska was undertaken during World War II to provide a supply route to Alaska in case the Japanese gained control of water routes. Construction was begun in 1942 with little prior exploration of some remote portions of the route chosen. Planned routings were only approximations and construction techniques to

deal with permafrost and swampy terrain had not been developed. U.S. Army con-
structions crews punched a narrow, rough, and almost impassible road through the
mountains and tundra from Dawson Creek to Delta, Alaska in eight months. Since
that time crews have been continuously upgrading the road. Anyone planning to drive
the Alaska Highway should read one of the many books that have been written about
the project. We recommend one in the Travel Library section in Chapter 2.

As you travel along the highway you will find many information boards commemo-
rating events during road construction. You'll also see many Historic Signposts with
original Alcan mileages on them. They are of little use today for navigation since road
mileage has changed, but they designate important spots along the road. There are
also several museums covering the highway construction along the route, including
ones in Dawson Creek, Fort Nelson, Watson Lake, and Whitehorse.

There are seven small towns along the Alaska Highway. These are **Dawson Creek,
Fort St. John/Taylor, Fort Nelson, Watson Lake, Whitehorse, Tok**, and **Delta
Junction**. These towns are the best place to buy provisions and get repair work done
if you need it. They also have interesting histories, museums, and good campgrounds.
Each is covered in more detail later in this chapter.

You'll find miles and miles of virtually empty country along the highway but the
section of road through Rocky Mountains between Fort Nelson and Watson Lake
stands out. There are two British Columbia Provincial Parks along this segment of
road: **Stone Mountain Provincial Park** and **Muncho Lake Provincial Park**. Both
have campgrounds and offer opportunities to view wildlife including caribou and
stone sheep.

At Km 765 (Mile 478) of the highway, about 132 miles south of Watson Lake is
**Liard Hotsprings**. Liard has two pools where you can soak in the hot spring water
(no sulfur) with changing rooms and benches in the natural pools. The lower pool is
particularly nice with a pebbled bottom and benches in the water. There's also a provincial campground and several commercial campgrounds nearby. Seems like everyone
traveling the highway stops here for at least a quick dip.

As you travel along the highway keep an eye peeled for wildlife. Moose are likely to
burst from the underbrush and cross in front of you and bears often feed on berries in
the cleared areas along the road. This isn't a zoo so animals aren't guaranteed, but if
you keep your eyes open you will see them.

### The Road

The Alaska Highway stretches 1,300 miles from Dawson Creek in British Columbia to Delta Junction in Alaska. Along the way it crosses the
Rocky Mountains and passes through the province of British Columbia the Yukon
Territory and the state of Alaska. The road is without a doubt one of the most interesting in North America. It is also very long.

The entire length of the Alaska Highway is now paved. This doesn't mean you won't find stretches of gravel, however. The road is constantly being upgraded and repaired and you are bound to run into patches of dirt and gravel. All road work has to be done during the summer when temperatures are above freezing so road work follows the same pattern each year. As early as possible in the spring (May) sections of road are torn up and work commences. By fall the road has to be ready for winter so by late August and September many of the places that were bad in the early summer have been finished or temporarily surfaced. We think that early September is the best time for campers to travel the highway.

Mileage markings along the highway can be confusing. The road was originally marked in miles. It was longer then, between Dawson Creek and the Alaska border the road was originally 1,221.8 miles long, now it is about 30 miles shorter. Many establishments along the road still use their original milepost locations as an address and there are occasional historical milepost monuments along the road for tourism purposes.

Today the entire Canadian portion of the road has been re-posted with kilometer markers. In some sections these kilometer markings have been updated to reflect actual distances on the shortened road, in others they are simply a conversion of the original mileage. We use these kilometer posts to designate locations of campgrounds in this chapter. We also give a number in miles. In Canada the mile figure is an approximation of the actual distance from Dawson Creek and is similar to the number used in many guides to the highway, it lets you calculate the distance between two locations.

At the Alaska border things change. Alaska uses miles, of course. They also use the original Alcan mileage as a starting point at the border. Although the border is now about 1,190 miles from Dawson Creek mileposts at the Alaska border start at 1,222. We use mile markings that conform to those you will find along the road, they may not reflect the actual driving distance in some cases.

As a practical matter you'll find that all of this makes little difference. When you are on the road it is easy to find things you are watching for, a few kilometers or miles one way or another will make less difference than you might think.

 ## Fishing

One of the joys of traveling on the Alaska Highway is the many opportunities to wet a line at the many rivers and streams that cross the highway. Often fishing isn't great near the road but a little hike will change your luck.

Between Dawson Creek and Fort Nelson try the **Peace River** (Km 55, Mile 34) for grayling and Dollies; **Charlie Lake** (Km 81, Mile 51) for walleye, northern pike, and perch; the **Sikanni Chief River** (Km 256, Mile 159) for grayling, northern pike, and Dollies; the **Buckinghorse River** (Km 279, Mile 173) for grayling; **Beaver Creek** (Km 328, Mile 204); and the **Prophet River** (Km 349, Mile 217) for Dollies and grayling.

From Fort Nelson to Watson Lake try the **Tetsa River** (Km 554, Mile 346) for grayling and Dollies; **Summit Lake** (Km 598, Mile 374) for lake trout, rainbows, and grayling; **115 Creek** and **MacDonald Creek** (Km 615, Mile 384) for grayling and Dollies; **MacDonald River** (Km 628, Mile 393) for grayling and Dollies; **Racing River** (Km 641, Mile 401) for Dollies and grayling; **Toad River** (Km 672, Mile 420) for grayling and Dollies; **Muncho Lake** (Km 701, Mile 438) for lake trout, rainbows, Dollies, and grayling; the **Trout River** (Km 733, Mile 458) for grayling; the **Liard River** (Km 763, Mile 477) for northern pike, grayling and Dollies; **Iron Creek Lake** (Km 922, Mile 576) for stocked rainbows; **Hyland River** (Km 937, Mile 585) for lake trout, grayling and Dollies; and finally, **Watson Lake** for lake trout and grayling.

From Watson Lake to Whitehorse are the **Upper Liard River** (Km 1,033, Mile 620) for grayling and Dollies; the **Rancheria River** (Km 1,106, Mile 664) for grayling and Dollies; the **Swift River** (Km 1,180, Mile 710) for grayling; **Morley Lake and River** (Km 1,251, Mile 752) for lake trout, northern pike, and grayling; **Teslin Lake** (Km 1,294, Mile 776) for lake trout, grayling and northern pike; the **Teslin River at Johnson's Crossing** (Km 1,346, Mile 809) for lake trout, northern pike, and grayling; **Squanga Lake** (Km 1,366, Mile 821) for northern pike, grayling, and lake trout; **Marsh Lake** (Km 1,432, Mile 860) for lake trout, northern pike, and grayling; and **Wolf Creek** (Km 1,459, Mile 877) for grayling.

Between Whitehorse and Tok try huge **Kluane Lake** (from Km 1,712, Mile 1,032 to Km 1,760, Mile 1,062) for lake trout, grayling, and northern pike; **Edith Creek** (Km 1,844, Mile 1,114) for grayling; **Pickhandle Lake** (Km 1,865, Mile 1,126) for lake trout, grayling, and Dollies; **Deadman Lake** (Mile 1,249) for northern pike; and **Moose Creek and the Chisana River** on the Northway Road (from Mile 1,264) for northern pike.

### Hiking and Mountain Biking

We think that the best hiking along the Alaska Highway is in Canada's **Kluane National Park** near Haines Junction. The Kluane National Park Visitor's Center (P.O. Box 5339K, Haines Junction, Yukon Y0B 1L0, Canada; (867) 634-2293) is in Haines Junction and has maps and information as well as hiking guidebooks. There's also a visitor's center farther north at Sheep Mountain (Km 1,707, Mile 1,029) at the south end of Kluane Lake. You must sign in and out at a visitor center or by phone when hiking at Kluane so the rangers know who is out in the park. Some good trails are the 85-km **Cottonwood Trail** from the Kathleen Lake Campground (See Chapter 12 - Skagway and Haines) back to the road at Dezadeash Lodge near Dezadeash Lake; the 15-km **Auriol Loop Trail** from 6 km south of Haines Junction on the Haines Highway (Km 239, Mile 147); the 24-km **Alsek Pass Trail** from near the Mackintosh Lodge at Km 1,646 (Mile 992) of the Alaska Highway, and the **Slim River Trails** near Kluane Lake that start near the Sheep Mountain Visitor Center at Km 1,707 (Mile 1,029) of the Alaska Highway. Many of these trails are mining trails or roads leading to old remote mining sites.

### Wildlife Viewing

 As you head north from Dawson Creek on the highway you should begin to get into the habit of actively watching for wildlife. Most of the north is not a zoo or park with large numbers of animals waiting near the roadside for you to happen by and see them. On the other hand, there are many more animals than most people see, it is quite easy to drive right by and miss them.

You may have a chance to try your spotting skills early in the trip. If it is July watch the bushes in the cleared area back to the tree line along the road. Between Fort St. John and Fort Nelson there are often bears, sometimes grizzlies, feeding there. Most people don't notice them.

In **Stone Mountain Provincial Park** near Summit Lake at Km 598 (Mile 374) caribou and stone sheep are often present.

Near **Muncho Lake** at about Km 727 (Mile 454) there are often stone sheep on the road, there is a mineral lick nearby. If you follow the short trail to the lick your chance of spotting animals is even better.

In Kluane National Park at Km 1,029 (Mile 1,708) at the south end of Kluane Lake Dall sheep are often visible on **Sheep Mountain**. There's a visitor center there with a viewing scope. The sheep are in the area in the spring and fall.

STONE SHEEP ARE OFTEN SEEN ALONG THE ALASKA HIGHWAY

# THE ROUTES, TOWNS AND CAMPGROUNDS

## DAWSON CREEK
### Population 12,000, Elevation 2,200 feet

Dawson Creek is the kick-off point for a drive up the Alaska Highway. Don't confuse this town with Dawson City, the gold rush town located on the Yukon River north of Whitehorse. Dawson Creek is well equipped to provide groceries and vehicle supplies. This might be a good place to have any vehicle modifications done in preparation for gravel farther north, see Vehicle Preparation in Chapter 2. Don't be deceived by the small population figure above, Dawson Creek really serves as the main town in the agricultural Peace River Block with a population of over 50,000 people.

The **Dawson Creek Visitor Information Centre** (900 Alaska Avenue, Dawson Creek, BC, V1G 476, Canada; 250 782-9595) with leaflets about sights and campgrounds north along the highway is located near the intersection of Highway 49 and Highway 2 near the center of town. They can also give you information about road conditions farther north. It is in a complex called the NAR (Northern Alberta Railway Station) Complex which also houses the **Dawson Creek Station Museum** which concen-

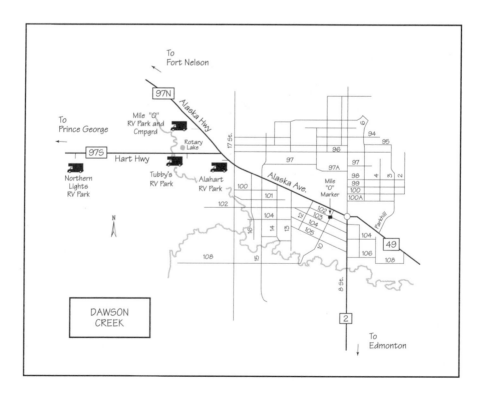

trates on the agricultural history of the area and the Alcan. In the same complex is the **Dawson Creek Art Gallery**. A short two-block stroll away is the all-important **Mile 0 Marker**. You'll probably want to take a photo before mounting your expedition north.

If you have a little more time in Dawson Creek you might want to visit the **Walter Wright Pioneer Village** and **Gardens North** at the **Mile 0 Rotary Park**, there are historical buildings from before the highway was constructed and 9 separate gardens. The park is located near the intersection of the Hart and Alaska Highways.

There are four campgrounds in Dawson Creek and many more north as far as Fort St. John. Dawson Creek's shopping malls are located off Highway 2, the road that leaves Dawson City to the south toward Grand Prairie and Edmonton.

## Dawson Creek Campgrounds

✦ MILE "O" RV PARK AND CAMPGROUND
    Address: 900 Alaska Avenue (P.O. Box 2383),
    Dawson Creek, B. C. V1G 4T9, Canada
    Telephone: (250) 782-2590, Fax (250) 782-1479
    Price: Medium

*GPS Location: N 55° 46' 10.1", W 120° 15' 37.3"*

We think this is the nicest campground in Dawson Creek. Its attractiveness at any given time depends greatly upon the quality of the management, the folks managing it for the last couple of years have been doing a good job.

This is a large grassy park-like campground with scattered shade trees. Camping spaces are widely separated and have picnic tables. Most of the 56 sites are back-ins but 9 are pull-throughs. There are also tent sites. Vehicle sites have either water and electricity or are dry, there is a dump station. The combination restroom, laundromat, and kitchen shelter building is well maintained and there are hot showers. A large picnic shelter is planned for 1998.

The campground is on the west side of the Alaska Highway just north of its junction with Highway 97 from Prince George.

✦ NORTHERN LIGHTS RV PARK
    Address: Box 2476, Dawson Creek, B. C.
    V1G 4T9, Canada
    Telephone: (250) 782-9433, Fax: (250) 782-9445,
    Internet: http://www.pris.bc.ca/rvpark
    Price: Medium

*GPS Location: N 55° 45' 59.4", W 120° 17' 30.1"*

If you are approaching Dawson Creek from the direction of Prince George this is the first RV park you'll see. It may not look too impressive from the road but this is a good facility with views over Dawson Creek to the east.

There are some 55 sites, a large proportion of them are pull-throughs. Some are full hookup sites with 20 and 30-amp service. Sites have picnic tables and grass strips separate them. There are some fire pits. Restrooms have free hot showers, there is a laundromat, and also a dump station and RV-wash area. The owners of this campground specialize in onsite mechanical work on Alaska-bound rigs including installation of gravel guards, mud flaps, and headlight protectors.

The campground is located on the south side of Highway 97S from Prince George about 2.4 km (1.5 miles) west of its intersection with the Alaska Highway, Highway 97N.

✦  TUBBY'S R.V. PARK
        Address: Comp 29-1725 Alaska Avenue,
        Dawson Creek, B.C. V1G 1P5, Canada
        Telephone and Fax: (250) 782-2584
        Price: Medium

*GPS Location: N 55° 45' 57.3", W 120° 15' 38.9"*

You'll find that Tubby's seems to have lots of customers even when the other parks in town are virtually empty. Many caravans stop here and Tubby's is very easy to spot from the highway. They have a car and RV wash and do RV oil changes.

The campground has at least 100 campsites although some of these are separated from the others and used for permanently located mobile homes. The camping area is a large gravel lot with a little grass, a grassy tent camping area lines the western edge. There are a variety of hookup options including full-hookups (20 and 30-amp). Pull-throughs are available. There are some fire pits, the campground has free hot showers and a laundromat, also a dump station.

Tubby's is one of the three campgrounds clustered around the junction of the Alaska Highway (Hwy. 97N) and the Hart Highway (97S). It is .3 miles west of the junction on the south side of the Hart Highway.

✦  ALAHART RV PARK
        Address: 1725 Alaska Avenue, Comp. 43,
        Dawson Creek, B.C. V1G 1P5, Canada
        Telephone: (250) 782-4702, Fax (250) 782-1179
        Price: Medium

*GPS Location: N 55° 45' 56.1", W 120° 15' 08.9"*

Alahart RV Park is the most centrally located of the Dawson Creek RV parks, the closest to the central business area. This campground is open all year long, they keep several spaces cleared of snow and have heated restrooms and showers in the motel for winter use.

The Alahart has some 50 large back-in spaces arranged around a circular drive on a gently sloping grassy lot. Grass separates the spaces and small trees have been planted. 40 sites have electric, sewer, and water hookups, the remaining ten have electricity and water. A restroom building with hot showers is in the center of the campground and there are dump and water fill stations and a laundromat.

From the intersection of Highway 97 from Prince George with the Alaska Highway head south toward central Dawson Creek. The campground is on the right almost immediately. You might miss it because it sits behind a small restaurant next to the motel.

## FROM DAWSON CREEK TO TAYLOR AND FORT ST. JOHN
### (47 miles)

When the US Army arrived in Dawson Creek to begin building the Alcan there was already a small road north to Fort St. John. Unfortunately there were several rivers along the road with no bridges so the first order of business was to hurry up and get supplies north to Fort St. John before the ice melted.

Today the road is excellent and the bridges are all in so the hour-long drive north is uneventful. You might want to take a short side trip at Km 35 (Mile 22) to visit the old curved wooden Kiskatinaw Bridge. This is the only original timber bridge remaining along the Alaska Highway. The access road is part of the original highway and is no longer on the main route.

## Campgrounds
## Dawson Creek to Taylor and Fort St. John

✦ FARMINGTON FAIRWAYS AND CAMPGROUND
    Address: P.O. Box 32, Farmington, B.C.
    V0C 1N0, Canada
    Telephone: (250) 843-7774
    Price: Medium

*GPS Location: N 55° 51' 34.7", W 120° 23' 48.4"*

Here's a one-of-a-kind stop along the Alaska Highway, a combination campground and golf course. The course is 9 holes, and there is also a driving range and a licensed clubhouse.

There are actually two campgrounds here. One is a 23-site RV campground with electrical and water hookups. Sites are large and located in an open area near the clubhouse. There is also a camping area with no hookups set in a wooded area nearby. This camping area has picnic tables and fire pits. Facilities include a portable-type building housing restrooms with free showers and a laundromat. There is also a dump station.

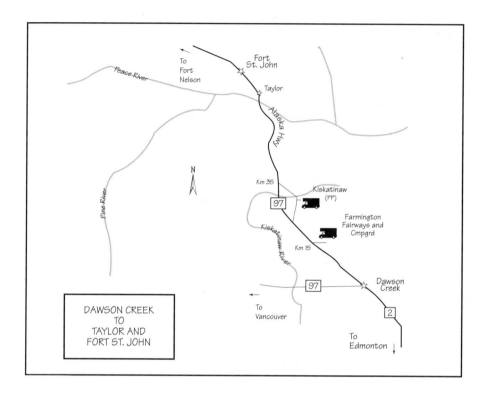

DAWSON CREEK
TO
TAYLOR AND
FORT ST. JOHN

The Farmington Fairways in located near Km 15 (Mile 10) of the Alaska Highway on the east side of the highway.

◆  KISKATINAW PROVINCIAL PARK CAMPGROUND
      Location: 5.3 Kilometer on Old Alaska Highway loop
      which leaves the Alaska Highway near Km 35 (Mile 22)
      Price: Low

*GPS Location: N 55° 57' 34.2", W 120° 33' 48.1"*

The Kiskatinaw River Bridge is a popular sight for visitors traveling the Alaska Highway. This is the only original wood bridge still in use and is interesting because it curves as it crosses high above the river. The campground is right next to the bridge.

This government campground offers 28 back-in sites on a rather narrow access loop. The sites are well-separated in poplar and spruce trees and some are right along the river. All have picnic tables and fire pits, there are outhouses and a water pump.

To reach the campground you must drive 5.3 km along a paved section of the old Alcan which leaves the new road near Km 35 (Mile 22). You'll reach and pass over the bridge just before the campground entrance. There is also access to the bridge and campground from Km 28 (Mile 17) at the other end of the loop of old road.

## TAYLOR AND FORT ST. JOHN

Population Taylor 1,050, Fort St. John 15,000, Elevation 2,300 feet

You'll drive through the town of Taylor about 13 miles south of Fort St. John and just north of the Peace River bridge at Km 55 (Mile 34). This is a nicely laid out town with several huge industrial complexes including a gas processing plant and a pulp mill.

Fort St. John was originally a fur trading post, but today gas and oil are the biggest industries. The largest oil and gas field in British Columbia is nearby.

The **Fort St. John-North Peace Museum** at Centennial Park covers the town's history as a fur trading center as well as the construction of the Alaska Highway. It is located near the easy to spot oil derrick to the north of the highway as it passes south of town. The **Visitor Info Center** (9923-96 Ave., Fort St. John, B.C. V1J 1K9, Canada; 250 785-6037) is also located here.

The drive to the **W.A.C. Bennett Dam** is a popular side trip from Fort St. John. Drive north on the Alaska Highway to Km 140 (Mile 87) and then on Highway 29 west through Hudson's Hope to the dam. The total distance one-way is 99 km (61 miles). This huge earth-filled dam provides 20% of British Columbia's electricity and forms Williston Lake, pilots who have flown the "trench" will be familiar with the long, skinny lake, British Columbia's largest. Tours of the power station are available. Another dam nearby, the **Peace Canyon Dam**, has self-guided tours. The town of **Hudson's Hope** is an old fur trading center and has a museum with exhibits related to the dinosaur fossils found in the area.

Fort St. John is just as good a place to stock up for your trip up the highway as Dawson Creek. The Totem Mall is on the right as you enter town from the south and there is a city dump station near Km 73 (Mile 46) on the right as you drive north.

### Taylor and Fort St. John Campgrounds

✦ PEACE ISLAND PARK CAMPGROUND
    Location: 24 Pringle Creek Rd., C/O Box 300,
    Taylor, B.C. V0C 2K0, Canada
    Price: Low

*GPS Location: N 56° 07' 52.5", W 120° 40' 55.3"*

The crossing of the Peace River has always been problematic. Rafts were used to move road-building equipment after an ice bridge went out during the spring thaw of 1942. Several timber bridges were built and washed out before a suspension bridge was finished in 1943, but this collapsed in 1957. The current bridge looks pretty solid, but the river isn't completely tamed. Although now dammed upstream, in 1997 we found the Peace Island Park closed because of an emergency water release from the dam.

The campground sits on an island in the middle of the river and is reached by a cause-

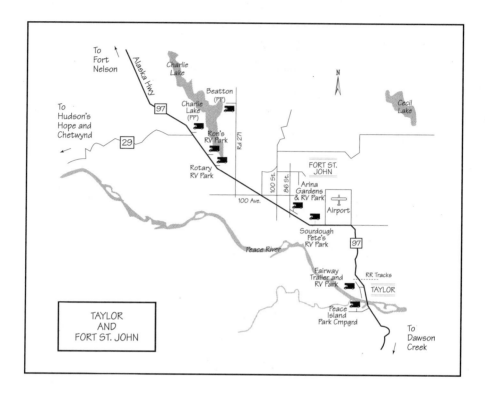

way from the south. The park has large playing fields and picnic areas but also camp-sites. There are 26 formal campsites plus an overflow area and tent sites. The camping sites have picnic tables and fire pits and there are outhouses and free firewood.

To reach the campground drive west along the river on Pringle Creek Road from the south end of the Peace River bridge near Km 55 (Mile 34) of the Alaska Highway. The campground entrance is at .4 miles, turn in and follow the driveway through the trees and across the causeway to the park.

✦  FAIRWAY TRAILER AND RV PARK
      Address: 10034 100th Street, C/O Box 429,
      Taylor, B.C. V0C 2K0, Canada
      Telephone: (250) 789-3792
      Price: Medium

*GPS Location: N 56° 09' 30.5", W 120° 41' 13.1"*

The little town of Taylor on the north bank of the Peace River is neat and attractive. Unfortunately the town has a natural gas processing plant and there is often a faint smell of rotten eggs. The Fairway is one of the nicest urban campgrounds along the highway.

There are 19 back-in spaces with parking on gravel surrounded by nicely clipped grass. Big rigs can usually arrange to drive directly into their spaces without backing. All sites are full hookup with 30-amp electricity. The restrooms are beautiful with individual tiled rooms and hot showers. There is also a laundry area.

Coming from the south zero your odometer at the north end of the Peace River Bridge. At 1.8 km (1.1 miles) turn left onto a parallel access road just before an Esso station and follow the access road north for another .3 km (.2 miles) to the campground. From the north turn right onto the parallel access road just after crossing the railroad tracks and you will come to the campground in about .2 km (.1 mile).

✦ SOURDOUGH PETE'S RV PARK
Address: Box 6911, Fort St. John, B.C. V1J 4J3, Canada
Telephone: (250) 785-7664 or (800) 227-8388, Fax (250) 785-7663
Price: Medium

*GPS Location: N 56° 13' 26.2", W 120° 48' 18.3"*

Sourdough Pete's is one of the newest and nicest campgrounds on the Alaska Highway. Next door and with related ownership is Troy's Amusement Park with mini-golf, a driving range, go karts, and more.

The campground is relatively new so the trees that have been planted in the grassy areas between sites haven't had much time to grow. The 64 sites are all pull-throughs with lots of room for big rigs. All have picnic tables and about half have full hookups with 30-amp electricity. There are also some tent spaces. The restrooms have hot showers (small fee) and there is a laundromat. At the back of the park is a gazebo with a campfire area. There is also a dump station.

The campground is located at Km 70 (Mile 44) of the Alaska Highway about 2 miles south of Ft. St. John. Watch for the big blue derrick with the park sign on top.

✦ ARINA GARDENS AND RV PARK
Address: 8428 Alaska Road, Ft. St. John, B.C. V1J 5L6, Canada
Telephone: (250) 785-4218
Price: Medium

*GPS Location: N 56° 13' 37.5", W 120° 49' 06.9"*

The Arina Gardens is now the closest campground to Ft. St. John, it is located near the southeast entrance to town. The campground is operated in conjunction with a commercial greenhouse, not a bad place to spend the night.

The campground has about 25 sites arranged on gravel with some grass and flowers behind the office and convenience store out front. There are full and partial hookup sites (15 and 30 amp) as well as tent sites. The restrooms have free showers and a laundromat. Sites have picnic tables and fire pits.

The campground is located on an access road that parallels the north side of the Alaska Highway. Turn onto the access road on 86th at about Km 72 (Mile 45) of the Alaska Highway just north of the big sign for a Chevrolet dealer. Immediately turn right and drive past the Coachman Inn, the campground office is the building next to the Chevrolet dealer.

✦ BEATTON PROVINCIAL PARK CAMPGROUND
     Location: East side of Charlie Lake
     Price: Low

*GPS Location: N 56° 19' 59.0", W 120° 56' 59.3"*

Beatton is not right next to the highway, you must drive around the south side of Charlie Lake to reach this campground which is located on the east shore of the lake. In addition to swimming, boating and fishing in the lake this park has miles of cross country ski trails that double as good hiking trails in the summer.

The campground has 37 paved back-in sites off paved access roads. Like other B.C. Provincial parks this one offers picnic tables and fire pits at each site, outhouses, and a water pump. Camping sites are set in trees and some are along the lake. There is also a nearby boat-launching ramp.

The paved road to the park leaves the Alaska Highway near Km 80 (Mile 50). Head north on Beatton Nontney Rd. 271 for 7.7 km (4.8 miles), then follow the pavement as it makes a left 90 degree turn and drive another mile to the park entrance on the left.

✦ ROTARY R.V. PARK
     Address: Box 6306, Ft. St. John, B.C.
     V1J 4H9, Canada
     Telephone: (250) 785-1700
     Price: Medium

*GPS Location: N 56° 16' 37.3", W 120° 57' 16.4"*

With a tall chain-link fence surrounding it this has got to be the most secure campground on the Alaska Highway. It has spacious grassy areas between sites and good facilities and is a popular campground. There is a nearby boat ramp for fishermen interested in the walleye that Charlie Lake is known for and limited groceries are available in the vicinity.

The Rotary R.V. Park has 40 serviced sites. Some are pull-throughs and there is lots of room to maneuver. Each has a picnic table and fire pit. Restrooms are spic-and-span and have hot showers (small fee). There is also a laundromat and a dump station.

To reach the campground just turn east off the highway near Km 81(Mile 51). You can see the campground from the highway,

✦ RON'S RV PARK
   Address: Box 55, Charlie Lake, B.C.
   V0C 1H0, Canada
   Telephone: (250) 787-1569
   Price: Medium

*GPS Location: N 56° 17' 04.4", W 120° 58' 03.8"*

Camping at Ron's feels a lot like pitching the tent in the back yard of your house when you were a kid, you'll feel right at home. The campground is near but not on the shore of Charlie Lake. There are 37 sites. Most are back-in RV spaces with full hookups but there are 6 nice tent sites and a few pull-throughs and also some sites with only electricity. Small trees provide decent separation. Sites have picnic tables and fire pits. The restrooms have hot showers (small fee) and there is a laundry area.

The campground is located east of the Alaska Highway near Km 83 (Mile 51.5).

✦ CHARLIE LAKE PROVINCIAL PARK CAMPGROUND
   Location: West shore of Charlie Lake near
   Km 86 (Mile 54) of the Alaska Highway
   Price: Low

*GPS Location: N 56° 18' 22.8", W 121° 00' 06.8"*

This large Provincial campground is convenient to the highway and very nice, it has paved access roads and large back-in sites. There are 61 of them, set in a grove of trees. Each has a picnic table and fire pit, there are outhouses and a picnic/kitchen shelter and children's playground. A 2-kilometer (1.2-mile) trail leads to the lake and there is even a dump station.

## FROM FORT ST. JOHN TO FORT NELSON
### (236 miles)

The section of the Alaska Highway between Fort St. John and Fort Nelson is in excellent condition. The road skirts the eastern edge of the Rocky Mountains as if waiting for the chance to leave the plains and climb toward the west. When the troops arrived to build the Alaska Highway in 1942 there was only a winter road between Fort St. John and Fort Nelson and it was not deemed suitable for an upgrade to an all weather road. Instead the road was moved westward into the foothills of the Rockies where the terrain was better drained and the road easier to build.

During the mid-summer berry season keep an eye on the brush line along the highway. We've spotted many bears, both blacks and browns, along this section of highway feeding on the berries.

Just 9 kilometers (6 miles) north of Fort St. John near Km 81 (Mile 51) is Charlie Lake. There are two provincial park campgrounds here and two private ones. The lake

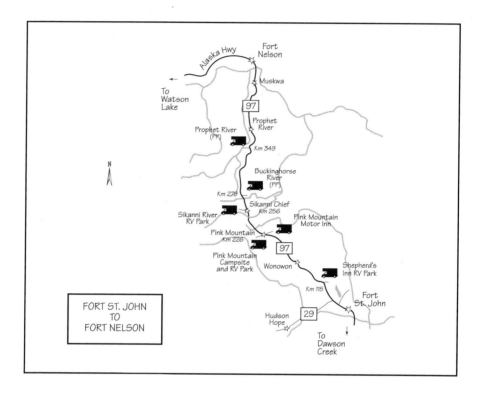

FORT ST. JOHN
TO
FORT NELSON

is famous for its walleye fishing. We've included these Charlie Lake campgrounds under the Fort St. John heading above since they are so close.

North of Charlie Lake you'll find miles of empty highway with the occasional tiny settlement. These include Wonowon at Km 163 (Mile 101, get it?), Pink Mountain at Km 226 (Mile 140), Sikanni Chief at Km 256 (Mile 159) and Prophet River at Km 365 (227). Most of these settlements have little more than a roadhouse and perhaps a campground.

## Campgrounds
## Fort St. John to Fort Nelson

✦ SHEPHERD'S INN RV PARK
    Address: P.O. Box 6425, Fort St. John, B.C.
    V1J 4H8, Canada
    Telephone: (250) 827-3676, Fax (250) 827-3559
    Price: Low

*GPS Location: N 56° 31' 27.2", W 121° 14' 00.4"*

The Shepherd's Inn is a restaurant, motel, and gas station with five pull-through full-service sites located in a large grassy field. One of the hotel rooms has been set aside as restrooms and showers for the campers. The facility is located at Km 115 (Mile 72) of the Alaska Highway.

✦ PINK MOUNTAIN MOTOR INN
  Address: Km 225 (Mile 143) Alaska Highway,
  Pink Mountain, B.C. V0C 2B0, Canada
  Telephone: (250) 772-3234, Fax (250) 774-1071
  Price: Medium

*GPS Location: N 57° 02' 28.3", W 122° 30' 31.6"*

The Pink Mountain Motor Inn is a motel, restaurant, gas station, laundromat, and campground. The campground has 26 back-in sites with electric hookups set in spruce trees. Water is available and there's a dump station. Sites have picnic tables and there is a restroom building with coin-op showers.

✦ PINK MOUNTAIN CAMPSITE AND R.V. PARK
  Address: Box 73, Pink Mountain, B.C.
  V0C 2B0, Canada
  Telephone: (250) 774-1033
  Price: Medium

*GPS Location: N 57° 02' 22.9", W 122° 30' 32.2"*

Behind a log building housing a post office, grocery and liquor store, and gift shop with gas out front you'll find a variety of campsites set in spruce trees. Some have full hookups and some are pull-throughs, there are also some very good tent sites. This campground also has a dump station and laundromat.

Look for the campground on the west side of the Alaska Highway near Km 225 (Mile 143) across from the Pink Mountain Motor Inn.

✦ SIKANNI RIVER RV PARK
  Address: Box 4, Pink Mountain, B.C.
  V0C 2B0, Canada
  Telephone and Fax: (250) 774-1028
  Price: Medium

*GPS Location: N 57° 14' 17.3", W 122° 41' 42.7"*

This is our favorite place to stay in the neighborhood of Pink Mountain. If you're coming from the south watch carefully as you approach Mile 159 and the Sikanni River because you won't see the campground until you're almost past as you highball down the hill and cross the river.

This campground has about 40 sites along the edges of a large gravel area near the river. Some have full hookups. There's lots of maneuvering room and sites have picnic tables and fire rings. There are hot showers, flush toilets, and a laundromat, as well as a dump station. Power here is produced by a generator but it is hardly noticeable and the setting is very scenic.

Sikanni River RV Park is located on the north shore of the Sikanni River near Km 256 (Mile 159, Historic Mile 162) of the Alaska Highway.

✦  Buckinghorse River Provincial Park Campground
      Location: Near Km 279 (Mile 173) of the
      Alaska Highway
      Price: Low

*GPS Location: N 57° 23' 04.3", W 122° 50' 45.6"*

The Buckinghorse River campground has 33 back-in spaces next to the Buckinghorse River. They are not separated, this is really more of a parking lot than a campground. The camp sites are some distance from the highway and are along a creek that has some grayling so this is a good place to overnight. A nice feature is the Buckinghorse River Lodge across the highway which has a cafe, showers, and phone (also free dry camping). Sites have picnic tables and fire pits and there are outhouses and a hand operated water pump.

✦  Prophet River Provincial Park Campground
      Location: Near Km 349 (Mile 217) of the
      Alaska Highway
      Price: Low

*GPS Location: N 57° 58' 11.7", W 122° 46' 33.5"*

This is another Provincial campground that is good for an overnight stop. The Prophet river is nearby and you can follow a trail down to take a look or maybe wet a line. There are reported to be a lot more sites here than we could find. We counted 25, the rest must be tent sites. Seven of the vehicle sites are pull-throughs with plenty of room for big rigs, the rest are back-ins. There are the usual picnic tables, fire pits, outhouses, free fire wood, and hand water pump.

## Fort Nelson
### Population 4,500, Elevation 1,400 feet

Little Fort Nelson has become something of an economic center in recent years. Before the construction of the Alaska Highway the population of this fur town was fewer than 500 people. Today the town is a rail head and has wood processing plants (including a chopstick factory), a natural gas processing plant, and serves as trade center for the McConachie Creek agricultural subdivision.

Fort Nelson visitors usually take in the **Fort Nelson Heritage Museum** which has displays about local history, wildlife, and the construction of the Alaska Highway.

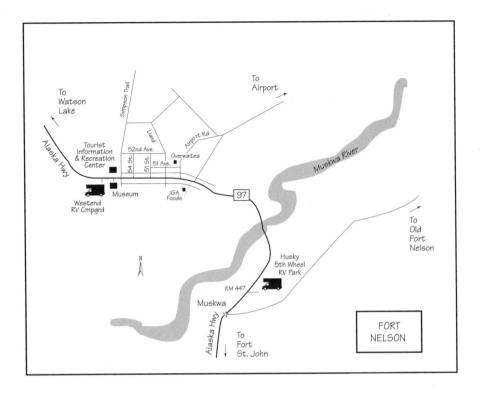

Across the street from the museum is the **Travel Info Center** (Bag Service 399, Fort Nelson, B.C. V0C 1R0, Canada; 250 774-6400 or 250 774-2541). An interesting offering in Fort Nelson is the **Fort Nelson Welcomes Visitors Program** where local residents give presentations explaining their lifestyle. It's held at the Phoenix Theater, ask about it at the visitor's center.

There are two small supermarkets in town for groceries and also two campgrounds.

### Fort Nelson Campgrounds

◆ HUSKY 5TH WHEEL RV PARK
      Address: RR#1, Alaska Hwy., Ft. Nelson, B.C.
      V0C 1R0, Canada
      Telephone: (250) 774-7270, Fax: (250) 774-7800
      Price: Medium

*GPS Location: N 58° 44' 35.8", W 122° 40' 41.2"*

One of two good RV parks in Ft. Nelson, the Husky 5th Wheel is the most southerly of the two, you'll see it as you approach town on the Alaska Highway from the south.

This is a large Husky gas station with a restaurant, a grocery store, and an RV park in the rear. They have over 70 large fully-serviced sites with 30-amp electricity in a large field behind the station. Many of them are long pull-throughs, separated by grassy strips with small trees and with a picnic table at each site. There's lots of room to maneuver, caravans with big rigs often stay here. The restrooms are clean and warm, they're located in the main building along with the restaurant and store. Showers are free. There's also a dump station.

Watch for this campground near Km 447 (Mile 278) of the Alaska Highway, about 5 miles south of Ft. Nelson.

✦ WESTEND R.V. CAMPGROUND
    Address: Box 398, Ft. Nelson, B.C.
    V0C 1R0, Canada
    Telephone: (250) 774-2340, Fax: (250) 774-3091
    Price: Medium

*GPS Location: N 58° 48' 16.9", W 122° 43' 15.8"*

Located in the western outskirts of Ft. Nelson this campground is right next door to the museum and across the street from the town's recreation center.

The Westend has an almost bewildering array of sites. There are long pull-throughs, star-burst back-ins, and treed partial hookup sites, some 140 in all. Most have picnic tables and fire pits with free firewood provided. Recreational facilities include the cable TV that is available, a mini-golf course and a playground. Showers are available for a small fee and there are also a laundromat, a vehicle washing area, and a dump station.

As you enter Ft. Nelson on the Alaska Highway from the west watch for the Westend on the right.

## FROM FORT NELSON TO WATSON LAKE
### (330 miles)

The miles from Fort Nelson to Watson Lake are some of the most scenic along the Alaska Highway. The road climbs through the Rocky Mountains and reaches the highest point of the highway near **Summit Lake** at Km 578 (Mile 374)—4,250 feet. The road is paved but narrow in some places and drivers shouldn't expect to make the same kind of speeds that were possible in the Dawson Creek to Fort Nelson section.

When army crews started cutting the Alaska Highway west from Fort Nelson toward Watson Lake the route through the mountains had not been surveyed. In fact, the route had not even been scouted on foot. There was some concern that there might not even be a suitable route through the mountains. Some quick work including getting help from local trappers was necessary. One of the toughest challenges on this part of the highway was building the section of road along Muncho Lake near Km 725 (Mile 453).

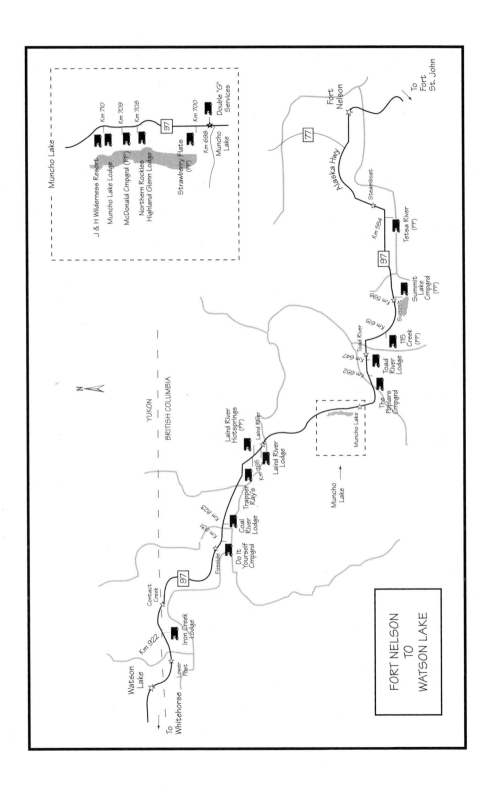

Muncho Lake

J & H Wilderness Resort
Muncho Lake Lodge
McDonald Cmpgrd (PP)
Northern Rockies
Highland Glenn Lodge
Strawberry Flats (PP)

Km 710
Km 709
Km 708
Km 700
97
Km 698
Muncho Lake
Double "G" Services

Fort Nelson
To Fort St. John
77
Alaska Hwy
Steamboat
Km 554
Tetsa River (PP)
97
Km 596
Summit Lake Cmpgrd (PP)
Summit
Km 615
Toad River
115 Creek (PP)
Km 647
Toad River Lodge
Km 652
The Poplars Cmpgrd
Muncho Lake

N

YUKON
BRITISH COLUMBIA

Laird River Hotsprings (PP)
Laird River
Laird River Lodge
Km 765
Trapper Ray's
Coal River Lodge
Km 823
Km 831
Fireside
Do It Yourself Cmpgrd

Contact Creek
97
Km 922
Iron Creek Lodge
Watson Lake
Lower Post
To Whitehorse

FORT NELSON TO WATSON LAKE

There are three Provincial Parks between Fort Nelson and the Yukon border. The first of these (heading north) is **Stone Mountain Provincial Park** near Km 597 (Mile 373). You cross the highest pass along the whole highway here right next to a cute little campground along Summit Lake. There are several hiking trails in the vicinity and you stand a good chance of seeing stone sheep or caribou here.

**Muncho Lake Provincial Park** is near Km 698 (Mile 437) of the Highway. The road runs along the shore of this long, deep lake for about 11 kilometers (7 miles). There are two provincial campgrounds and several commercial campgrounds. The lake has huge lake trout and boat tours are available. Watch for stone sheep along the highway just north of the lake, they are attracted by mineral licks in the area and are often on the road. There's a short trail to the mineral licks at Km 727 (Mile 454) to view the mineral seeps and perhaps see sheep or caribou.

**Liard River Hotsprings Provincial Park** is near Km 765 (Mile 478). There is a provincial campground and two commercial campgrounds nearby. The two hot pools at the springs have temperatures to 110° F. Almost everyone stops here for a dip. There is a half-mile boardwalk to the pools.

After Liard Hotsprings the road gets better and you can cruise into Watson Lake at a good clip. A point of interest is **Contact Creek** at Km 909 (Mile 570, Historical Mile 590) where crews working west from Fort Nelson and east from Whitehorse hooked up when building the Alaska Highway.

The highway crosses into the Yukon Territory at Km 910 (Mile 568). It crosses and re-crosses the border 7 times before reaching Watson Lake.

## Campgrounds
## Fort Nelson to Watson Lake

✦ TETSA RIVER CAMPGROUND (PROVINCIAL)
    Location: At the end of a 2-km (1.2 mile) road
    leaving the Alaska Hwy. near Km 554 (Mile 346)
    Price: Low

*GPS Location: N 58° 38' 37.8", W 123° 56' 35.6"*

This is a quiet provincial campground located far enough from the highway for peace and quiet but close enough for convenience. Grayling fishing in the river here is good.

There are 25 large back-in sites, many overlooking the river. This is a wooded campground with separated sites having the normal picnic table and fire pit. There are also outhouses and free firewood.

The road into the campground leaves the highway near Km 554 (Mile 346). A construction camp is situated along the road, just drive on by and back to the campground, a distance of about 2 km (1.2 miles).

✦ SUMMIT LAKE PROVINCIAL CAMPGROUND
    Location: Near Km 598 (Mile 374) of the Alaska Hwy.
    Price: Low

*GPS Location: N 58° 39' 08.0", W 124° 39' 06.4"*

This campground is located in high alpine country in Stone Mountain Provincial Park. Its site is at the east end of Summit Lake very near the highway. Several excellent hiking trails leave the road from the vicinity of the campground. We've also seen caribou at the campground during September.

There are 28 sites that are separated but since there are no trees here they are not really very private. Road noise is a problem and the weather can be harsh since the altitude is high and this is a pass. Sites have picnic tables and fire pits and the campground has outhouses. There's also a boat launch but fishing in the lake and on MacDonald Creek running by the campground is poor due to the cold water.

✦ 115 CREEK PROVINCIAL CAMPGROUND
    Location: Near Km 615 (Mile 384) of
    the Alaska Highway
    Price: Low

*GPS Location: N 58° 43' 03.5", W 124° 54' 45.9"*

This campground is nothing more than a wayside along the highway. There are 8 back-in side-by-side spaces. They have picnic tables and there are outhouses and a hand water pump nearby. You can fish in 115 Creek. Caribou and moose are often seen in the vicinity.

✦ TOAD RIVER LODGE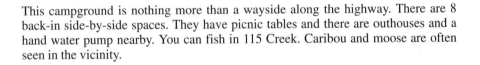
    Address: Mile 422, Alaska Highway, B.C.
    V0C 2X0, Canada
    Telephone: (250) 232-5401, Fax: (250) 232-5215
    Price: Low

*GPS Location: N 58° 50' 47.3", W 125° 14' 05.0"*

The Toad River Lodge offers a motel, gas, and a small restaurant with 6 back-in RV sites behind the buildings. The sites overlook a large marshy area, bird watching is pretty good. Sites have electricity provided by a generator which, unfortunately, is very near and quite loud. Restrooms have flush toilets and showers are available. There is also a dump and water fill station. The lodge is located near Km 647 (Mile 405, Historic Mile 422) of the Alaska Highway.

◆  THE POPLARS CAMPGROUND
     Address: Box 30, Toad River, B.C.
     V0C 2X0, Canada
     Telephone: (250) 232-5465
     Price: Medium

*GPS Location: N 58° 51' 08.2", W 125° 18' 33.4"*

The Poplars is a pleasant RV campground located in magnificent mountain country. There are 35 sites, some are full-hookup and there are pull-throughs. Sites have picnic tables and fire rings. Restrooms have hot showers, there are dump and water fill stations, and also a small grocery store.

The Poplars is located near Km 652 (Mile 407, Historical Mile 426) of the Alaska Highway.

◆  DOUBLE "G" SERVICE AND MOTEL
     Address: Box 36, Muncho Lake, B.C.
     V0C 1Z0, Canada
     Telephone: (250) 776-3411
     Price: Low

*GPS Location: N 58° 55' 50.7", W 125° 46' 02.1"*

Double "G" Service is located near Muncho Lake and has gas, a restaurant, post office, licensed mechanic, a gift shop, a few cabins, and 15 nice camping sites set in spruces behind the buildings. These are dry sites but there is a dump and water fill station. Sites have fire pits and picnic tables. Restrooms have flush toilets and showers. Boat tours of the lake are available here.

The campground is located near Km 698 (Mile 436) of the Alaska Highway.

◆  STRAWBERRY FLATS CAMPGROUND
     IN MUNCHO LAKE PROVINCIAL PARK
     Location: In Muncho Lake Provincial Park
     near Km 700 (Mile 438) of the Alaska Highway
     Price: Low

*GPS Location: N 58° 56' 53.3", W 125° 46' 12.9"*

This is a nice provincial campground on the shore of Muncho Lake. The 15 sites are separated and many are on the lake shore. All have picnic tables and fire pits. There are outhouses, free firewood, and a dock. Given a choice between this provincial campground and the one just down the road we'd stay here because it is quieter.

✦  NORTHERN ROCKIES HIGHLAND GLEN LODGE
     Address: Box 8, Muncho Lake, B.C.
     V0C 1Z0, Canada
     Telephone: (250) 776-3481 or (800) 663-5269
     Fax: (250) 776-3482
     Price: Medium

*GPS Location: N 59° 00' 31.5", W 125° 46' 17.0"*

You can't miss this beautiful log lodge on the shores of Muncho Lake even if you aren't looking out for it. In addition to the hotel they sell gas, have a restaurant and bakery, and also operate an active bush-flying operation off the lake out front.

There are also some 20 RV camping sites here. Four are real beauties, large back-in sites along the lake shore with electric and water hookups. The remaining sites are farther back but still near the lake and also have hookups. The lodge also offers flush toilets and showers, a laundromat, and a dump station.

The lodge is located at Km 708 (Mile 442) of the Alaska Highway.

✦  MCDONALD CAMPGROUND -
     MUNCHO LAKE PROVINCIAL PARK
     Location: Near Km 709 (Mile 443) of the Alaska Highway
     Price: Low

*GPS Location: N 59° 01' 05.6", W 125° 46' 23.2"*

This lakeside campground has 15 back-in separated spaces located along the lake. They have picnic tables and fire pits. The campground also has outhouses, free firewood, and a hand operated water pump.

✦  MUNCHO LAKE LODGE
     Address: Box 10, Muncho Lake, B.C.
     V0C 1Z0, Canada
     Telephone: (250) 776-3456, Fax: (250) 776-3457
     Price: Low

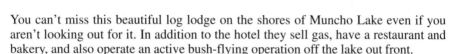

*GPS Location: N 59° 01' 42.6", W 125° 46' 31.2"*

The camping sites at this lodge occupy a large clearing that slopes down to the lake. There are some 40 large pull-throughs, most with water hookups, and about 18 of them have electrical hookups. There are also some tent sites in trees down near the lake with firepits. Flush toilets and hot showers are available, as is a dump station. The lodge also sells gas and has a restaurant and hotel.

The Muncho Lake Lodge is located right next to the J&H Wilderness Resort on the shore of Muncho Lake near Km 710 (Mile 444) of the Alaska Highway.

◆ J&H WILDERNESS RESORT
　　Address: P.O. Box 38, Muncho Lake, B.C.
　　V0C 1Z0, Canada
　　Telephone: (250) 776-3453, Fax: (250) 776-3454
　　Price: Medium

*GPS Location: N 59° 01' 48.4", W 125° 46' 34.5"*

The J&H has about 60 sites of various kinds arranged on a terraced lot sloping down to Muncho Lake. Some are large pull-throughs and there are a variety of hookup options including full, partial and dry sites. Sites have picnic tables and fire pits. Restrooms have flush toilets and hot showers and the campground also offers gas, a cafe, a small grocery store and a dump station.

The resort is located near Km 710 (Mile 444) of the Alaska Highway.

◆ LIARD RIVER LODGE
　　Address: P.O. Box 9, Muncho Lake, B.C.
　　V0C 1Z0, Canada
　　Telephone: (250) 776-7341, Fax: (250) 776-7340
　　Price: Low

*GPS Location: N 59° 24' 57.1", W 126° 05' 42.4"*

The Liard River Lodge is located just down the highway from Liard Hot Springs. Since the springs are an institution along the highway the Provincial campground is often full. When this happens the Liard River Lodge can be a popular place, and it is less expensive than the Provincial campground.

Camping facilities are limited. There is a large gravel lot near the lodge and also a grassy area for tenters. Outhouses are convenient to the camping area and flush toilets and showers are available in the lodge building. There is a dump station and the lodge has a nice cafe and dining room and sells gas.

The lodge is located near Km 765 (Mile 478) of the Alaska Highway overlooking the Lower Liard River suspension bridge. The hot springs are .6 mile down the road.

◆ LIARD RIVER HOTSPRINGS PROVINCIAL PARK
　　Location: Near Km 765 (Mile 478)
　　of the Alaska Highway
　　Price: Low

*GPS Location: N 59° 25' 37.1", W 126° 06' 02.1"*

Almost everyone traveling the highway stops at Laird Hotsprings for a soak, even if only for a short time. The outdoor pools are just the right temperature and a great place to meet other travelers.

The Provincial campground is located right next to the springs. There are 50 well-separated back-in sites, each has a picnic table and fire pit. There are outhouses, a hand water pump, and free firewood. While there are no showers you can always take a dip in the springs which have lots of water flow and no sulfur smell.

✦ TRAPPER RAY'S
    Address: Mile 497, Alaska Highway, Liard River,
    B.C. V1G 4J8, Canada
    Telephone and Fax: (250) 776-7349
    Price: Medium

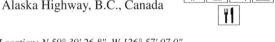

*GPS Location: N 59° 25' 31.1", W 126° 06' 23.0"*

If you are looking for a campground with hookups in the Liard Hotsprings area Trapper Rays is your only choice, and it's not a bad one.

There are about 35 RV sites located in a clearing a short distance behind the gas pumps and garage. They have electric hookups and many sites are pull-throughs. Grass separates the sites. Some picnic tables are available and many sites have fire pits. There is also a tent camping area in trees nearby. Showers are available for a small fee and there is a dump and water fill station. In addition there is a cafe, a small grocery store, gas sales, and guest rooms.

Trapper Rays is located near Km 765 (Mile 479) of the Alaska Highway, about .1 mile from the hot springs parking lot.

✦ COAL RIVER LODGE
    Address: Mile 533, Alaska Highway, B.C., Canada
    Price: Low

*GPS Location: N 59° 39' 26.8", W 126° 57' 07.0"*

This roadhouse-style campground has gasoline, a cafe, lodging and a campground. There are 12 sites with electricity and water in a gravel lot next to the other facilities. These are side-by-side pull-throughs with a rail between the sites. Restrooms have flush toilets and hot showers and there is a laundromat. The Coal River Lodge is at Km 823 (Mile 514, Historical Mile 533) of the Alaska Highway.

✦ DO IT YOURSELF CAMPGROUND
    Location: Near Km 831 (Mile 520) of the Alaska Highway
    Price: Free

*GPS Location: N 59° 37' 27.9", W 127° 05' 11.4"*

This small primitive campground has about 8 sites, one or two are large enough for large rigs. There are no utilities but sites have picnic tables and fire pits. One small site is very scenic and overlooks the Mountain Portage Rapids of the Liard River. There are outhouses but no other amenities.

◆  IRON CREEK LODGE
    Address: Mile 596 Alaska Hwy., Iron Creek,
    Y.T. Y0B 1L0, Canada
    Telephone: (867) 536-2266
    Price: Medium

*GPS Location: N 60° 00' 10.4", W 127° 55' 20.3"*

This roadhouse-style facility offers a lake stocked with fish and has plans for expanding its camping offerings. Keep an eye on it.

Currently (1997) there are about 7 side-by-side sites with electricity and water hookups on gravel next to the highway. Other dry sites are down the hill behind the lodge near the lake. These have picnic tables and fire pits. There's also a large gravel area farther from the road that may become a campground with utilities soon. The lodge has restrooms with flush toilets and coin-op showers and there is a dump station. Other lodge facilities include gas sales, a motel, a small store, and a cafe.

The lodge is located near Km 922 (Mile 576, Historic Milepost 596) of the Alaska Highway.

## WATSON LAKE
### Population 1,750, Elevation 2,250 feet

Watson Lake serves as the trade center for the southeastern Yukon. The little town is located near the junction of the Cassiar Highway and the Alaska Highway. It also is at the junction of the gravel-surfaced Campbell Highway running northwest to meet the Klondike Loop at Carmacks. For travelers on the Alaska Highway Watson is often an overnight stop between Fort Nelson and Whitehorse. Either of these towns is a one-day drive away although driving from Fort Nelson to Watson Lake in one day makes for a long day of driving, especially if you stop at Liard Hotsprings.

Probably the most famous sight in Watson Lake is the **signpost forest**. Started by a highway worker during the construction of the Alaska Highway the original signpost has grown to a true forest with over 10,000 signs. You can put one up yourself if you wish. Right next to the signpost forest is the **Watson Lake Travel Info Center** (867 536-7469) and **Alaska Highway Interpretive Center**. The latter is full of information about the building of the highway. Watson Lake also has a new attraction, the **Northern Lights Centre**. This is a planetarium featuring northern lights shows. If you feel like stretching your legs after a long day on the road you might want to follow the nature trail around **Wye Lake**. It's a good trail with boardwalks to let you get closer to the birds. Another way to stretch them might be a round of **golf** at the 9-hole Greenway's Greens (867 536-2477) course in Upper Liard, 6 miles north of Watson Lake on the Alaska Highway at Km 1,033 (Mile 620).

Watson Lake has two decent campgrounds in or near town. To the west is a government campground and a commercial one is at the junction with the Cassiar Highway. These last two are included in the next section. There are also small supermarkets and

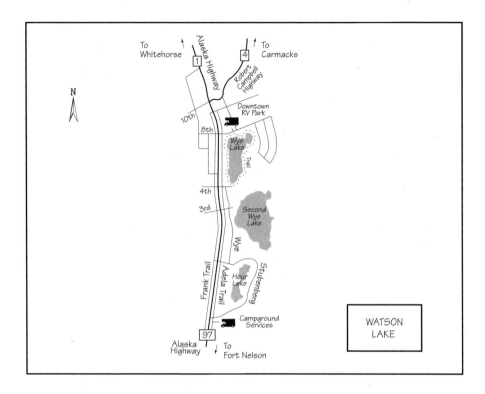

vehicle repair facilities. For major repairs, however, we recommend waiting for Whitehorse if at all possible.

## Watson Lake Campgrounds

◆ CAMPGROUND SERVICES,
  GATEWAY TO THE YUKON RV PARK
     Address: Box 268, Watson Lake, Y.T.
     Y0A 1C0, Canada
     Telephone: (867) 536-7448, Fax: (867) 536-7971
     Price: Medium

*GPS Location: N 60° 03' 02.0", W 128° 39' 15.7"*

This is the largest of the Watson Lake RV parks and our favorite. It is the first RV park you'll come to in Watson Lake if you are approaching on the Alaska Highway from the south. You'll have to drive if you want to visit central Watson Lake, probably the only important disadvantage to this campground. If you want to walk in the distance is nearly 2 miles.

There are about 140 camping sites in this large campground. Many are pull-throughs with electricity, sewer, and water. Many others sites, both pull-throughs and back-ins, offer electricity and water or are dry. Cable TV is available at some sites. The campground has many trees and a layout that is a little hard to figure out, it is pleasantly unorganized. When you check in you'll be led to your site so this isn't a problem. There are quite a few amenities: flush toilets and coin-op showers, laundromat, vehicle wash, a decent sized grocery store, a children's playground, hiking trails, a meeting pavilion, and gas sales.

If you're approaching Watson Lake from the south on the Alaska Highway watch for the campground on the right near Km 1,018 (Mile 610).

✦ DOWNTOWN R.V. PARK
    Address: Box 609, Watson Lake,
    Y.T. Y0A 1C0, Canada
    Telephone: (867) 536-2646 or (867) 536-2224
    Price: Medium

*GPS Location: N 60° 03' 51.7", W 128° 42' 23.5"*

For convenient access to central Watson Lake there's no beating the Downtown RV Park. The lack of ambiance here—the park is basically a big gravel lot—is mitigated by Wye Lake which is located just across the road and is encircled by a walking and nature trail. You can easily walk from the campground to buy groceries or visit Watson Lake's biggest attractions: the signpost forest and visitor's center.

The Downtown has about 70 full-hookup sites (20-amp). Most are back-ins but about 20 are pull-throughs. There are clean restrooms with flush toilets and hot showers and a very popular large area with hoses to wash down your rig with no fee. There is also a laundromat.

The campground is well-signed in the middle of Watson Lake. It sits about a block north of the highway.

## FROM WATSON LAKE TO WHITEHORSE
### (282 miles)

The Alaska Highway between Watson Lake and Whitehorse is an excellent paved two-lane road with long flat straight stretches, particularly near Whitehorse.

The road actually crosses the continental divide as it gently climbs up through the Rancheria Valley and then descends along the Swift River. It then follows the shores of two large lakes through the upper Yukon basin: Teslin Lake and Marsh Lake.

At Km 1,043 (Mile 626), about 21 kilometers (13 miles) west of Watson Lake is the junction with Highway 37, the **Cassiar Highway**. The Cassiar is an alternate route for many people traveling to Alaska and is covered in Chapter 5 in this book.

At Km 1,163 (Mile 699) the highway crosses the **Continental Divide**. The waters to the east drain into the Mackenzie, those to the west into the Yukon.

The small town of **Teslin** at Km 1,294 (Mile 776) is the only community of any size along the highway between Watson Lake and Whitehorse. Teslin has a large RV park, restaurants, and service stations. There's also a store in the village of Teslin just off the highway. Teslin has a population of about 500 and has one of the largest Native populations in the Yukon. The town has an interesting museum, the George Johnston Museum, which is well worth a stop.

There are several more campgrounds, both government and commercial, along the shore of **Teslin Lake**. This huge lake has excellent fishing for lake trout and near inlets and the outlet you will find grayling and pike.

At Km 1,392 (Mile 837) is **Jake's Corner**. From here Yukon Highway 8 (the Tagish Road) leads 55 kilometers (34 miles) west to a junction with the Skagway-Whitehorse road (Klondike Highway 2) at Carcross. We cover this road in Chapter 12 - Skagway and Haines. Just 2 kilometers (1 mile) down the Tagish Road is another junction, this one with Yukon Highway 7 to Atlin. A trip to **Atlin** is a good two-day side trip into a region of large lakes and scenic mountains. The road runs along Little Atlin Lake and Atlin Lake to the gold-mining town of Atlin, British Columbia, a distance of 90 kilometers (56 miles). Atlin has an RV park and there are several government campgrounds en route. There's also a large provincial park but there are no campgrounds, trails, or access roads in this park.

## Campgrounds
## Watson Lake to Whitehorse

✦ WATSON LAKE TERRITORIAL CAMPGROUND
    Location: Near Km 1,025 (Mile 615) of
    the Alaska Highway
    Price: Low

*GPS Location: N 60° 05' 28.9", W 128° 48' 58.4"*

If you are heading north this is probably the first Yukon government campground you will have a chance to visit, and it's a good one.

There are about 55 sites off two circular drives. Some are large pull-throughs. All sites are well separated with lots of big trees and natural vegetation, they have picnic tables and fire pits. Free firewood is provided and there are outhouses. None of the campsites are actually next to the lake but there is a day-use area with a boat launch at the lake. Trails connect the lake with the campground.

To reach the campground you head north on a gravel road from near Km 1,025 (Mile 615) of the Alaska Highway. This is about 2.5 miles west of central Watson Lake. At 1.3 miles the road bends right and at 3.8 miles reaches the campground.

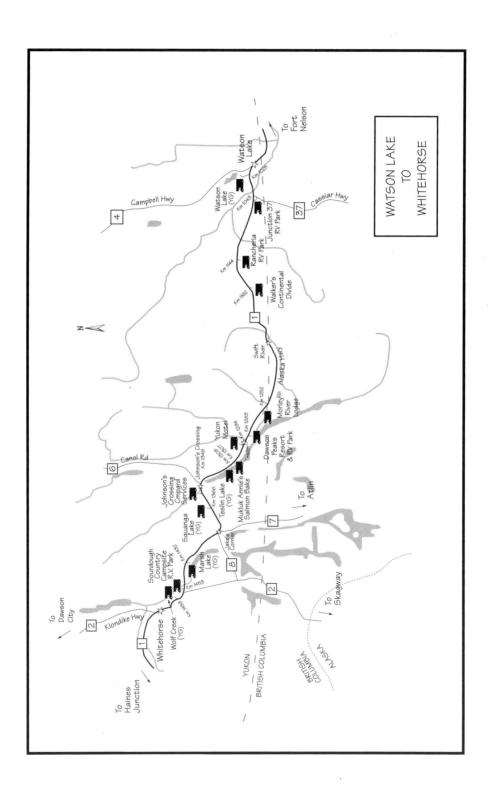

✦ JUNCTION 37 RV PARK
   Address: Mile 649, Watson Lake, Y.T., Canada
   Telephone: (867) 536-2794
   Price: Medium

*GPS Location: N 60° 01' 36.2", W 129° 03' 37.9"*

Travelers coming north on the Cassiar Highway meet those traveling the Alaska Highway at a junction about 21 kilometers (13 miles) west of Watson Lake. On the corner is a large establishment with a gas station, repair shop, cafe, motel, small grocery store, souvenir shop and an RV park.

There are about 70 camping sites located on gravel behind the other facilities. 26 sites have full hookups (20 and 30-amp), some are pull-throughs and there is lots of maneuvering room. There are quite a few trees separating sites and some have picnic tables and fire rings. Hot showers are available. There's also a dump station.

✦ RANCHERIA RV PARK
   Address: Historic Milepost 710 Alaska Highway,
   Y.T. Y0A 1A0, Canada
   Telephone: (867) 851-6456 or (867) 667-1016
   Price: Medium

*GPS Location: N 60° 05' 17.2", W 130° 36' 22.5"*

At first glance this appears to be one of the ubiquitous roadhouse-style operations with campgrounds that are little more than an afterthought. There are the usual gas pumps, cafe, cocktail lounge, and motel. However, in the trees to the west is an unusually nice little campground.

Rancheria has about 50 camping sites. All are back-in but if the campground is not full some back-to-back sites make good pull-throughs. 16 sites have electric hookups and there is a dump and water fill station. This campground is laid out like a government campground (it used to be one) with trees and natural vegetation separating sites and one of them overlooks the river. The restrooms have hot showers.

Rancheria is located near Km 1,144 (Mile 687, Historical Milepost 710) of the Alaska Highway.

✦ WALKER'S CONTINENTAL DIVIDE
   Address: Mile 721, Swift River, Y.T.
   Y0A 1A0, Canada
   Telephone: (867) 851-6451
   Price: Medium

*GPS Location: N 60° 04' 43.0", W 130° 54' 43.7"*

Walker's is a roadhouse-style campground. There are 6 back-in sites with electricity and water, a dump station, and hot showers. Walkers also offers gas and has a cafe and pub. They are located at Km 1,162 (Mile 698, Historical Milepost 721) of the Alaska Highway.

✦ Morley River Lodge
    Address: Mile 778 Alaska Highway, Y.T., Canada
    Telephone and Fax: (867) 390-2639
    Price: Low

*GPS Location: N 60° 00' 39.4", W 132° 09' 43.8"*

A roadhouse-style campground, Morley River Lodge has a few sites in a treed area that is near the river but also right along the highway. A few sites have power and there are picnic tables. There's also a dump station. Showers can be purchased and there is a motel, a restaurant, and gas station. The lodge is located at Km 1,252 (Mile 753, Historic Milepost 778) of the Alaska Highway.

✦ Dawson Peaks Resort & RV Park
    Address: Box 80, Teslin, Y.T. Y0A 1B0, Canada
    Telephone: (867) 390-2310 (Answering Service),
    Fax: (867) 390-2244
    Price: Medium

*GPS Location: N 60° 06' 33.9", W 132° 33' 11.8"*

Dawson Peaks Resort stands out as one of the better places to stay along this section of the Alaska Highway. They have a very good restaurant, a gift shop, and a pleasant RV park.

The campground has 24 sites, 14 of them with 15 or 30-amp power. Several are pull-throughs. The sites are separated and situated above the lake. A small road leads down to a boat ramp. There is a dump station and hot showers are available.

Watch for the Dawson Peaks near Km 1,283 (Mile 770) of the Alaska Highway.

✦ Yukon Motel
    Address: Box 187, Teslin, YT Y0A 1B0, Canada
    Telephone: (867) 390-2443, Fax: (867) 390-2003
    Price: Medium

*GPS Location: N 60° 10' 02.4", W 132° 42' 31.8"*

The Yukon Motel in Teslin is a large modern facility with a motel, a very popular restaurant, cocktail lounge, and gas station. It sits near the bridge on Nisutlin Bay.

Below the restaurant near the water is a large RV park. There are about 80 sites. Many are pull-throughs. A few have full hookups but most offer electricity and water, there are also a few dry sites. Satellite TV connections are available. Restrooms have flush toilets and hot showers and there is a laundromat and a dump station.

The campground is located near Km 1,294 (Mile 776, Historical Mile 804) of the Alaska Highway in the small town of Teslin.

✦ MUKLUK ANNIE'S SALMON BAKE
   Address: Box 101, Teslin, Y.T. Y0A 1B0, Canada
   Telephone: (867) 667-1200
   Price: Low

*GPS Location: N 60° 13' 22.4", W 132° 53' 47.6"*

Mukluk Annie's is one of the most popular campgrounds along the highway, almost a required stop. This is a restaurant that specializes in salmon. It has a large associated camping area which has free sites for those who eat in the restaurant. Since the restaurant prices are reasonable and the food good this is an excellent deal.

The campground has about 40 sites with electricity (15-amp)and water hookups. These sites are not free. There are an additional 100 or so dry vehicle and tent sites. The campground is set in trees overlooking Teslin Lake. A dump and water fill are included with the free sites, showers cost $3 but are free to those in the utility sites. If you participate in the special salmon bake you can also take a free boat ride on the lake and wash your RV for no charge.

Mukluk Annie's is located on the shore of Teslin Lake near Km 1,307 (Mile 784) of the Alaska Highway.

✦ TESLIN LAKE CAMPGROUND (YUKON GOVERNMENT)
   Location: Near Km 1,308 (Mile 785)
   of the Alaska Highway
   Price: Low

*GPS Location: N 60° 13' 57.3", W 132° 54' 37.8"*

This is a government campground set in trees overlooking Teslin Lake. There are 27 spaces, many are long parallel-types that are good for big rigs. Of course there are picnic tables, fire pits, outhouses, a picnic shelter, a water well and free firewood. There's also a playground. Fishing in the lake is good for lake trout and there is a nearby boat ramp.

✦ JOHNSON'S CROSSING CAMPGROUND SERVICES
   Address: Milepost 836 Alaska Highway,
   Johnson's Crossing, YT Y1A 9Z0, Canada
   Telephone: (867) 390-2607
   Price: Medium

*GPS Location: N 60° 29' 00.2", W 133° 18' 29.6"*

Although Johnson's Crossing is a roadhouse it is an attractive historic one with a good campground. The old roadhouse building houses a souvenir shop and small grocery store as well as a bakery. It sits on the shore of the Teslin River near Teslin Lake and offers good grayling fishing in the river.

The campground is set in trees with separated sites. There are 35 sites, many of them are pull-throughs. Full hookup (20 and 30 amp), partial hookup, dry, and tent sites are available. Fire rings and picnic tables are provided and there is also a dump station. A wash house has flush toilets and hot showers.

The roadhouse is located near Km 1,346 (Mile 809, Historical Milepost 836) of the Alaska Highway.

✦ SQUANGA LAKE CAMPGROUND (YUKON GOVERNMENT)
    Location: Near Km 1,366 (Mile 821) of the Alaska Highway
    Price: Low

*GPS Location: N 60° 26' 36.4", W 133° 35' 56.2"*

This small government campground has 13 spaces, one is a pull-through. None are on the lake. The campground has picnic tables, fire pits, free firewood, outhouses, a picnic shelter, and a boat launch. You can fish here for pike, grayling, and rainbows.

✦ MARSH LAKE CAMPGROUND (YUKON GOVERNMENT)
    Location: Near Km 1,432 (Mile 860)
    of the Alaska Highway
    Price: Low

*GPS Location: N 60° 33' 38.4", W 134° 26' 55.3"*

This large government campground has 41 separated sites off a loop road. Some are pull-throughs and 4 are tent sites. There are picnic tables, fire pits, outhouses, free firewood, a picnic shelter, and a playground.

✦ SOURDOUGH COUNTRY CAMPSITE R.V. PARK
    Address: Site 20, Comp. 346, Whitehorse,
    Y.T. Y1A 4Z6, Canada
    Telephone and Fax: (867) 668-2961
    Price: Medium

*GPS Location: N 60° 35' 51.8", W 134° 55' 07.8"*

The Sourdough is probably a little far from town to be convenient to Whitehorse, but that means there is often room when the others are full. There are 50 sites in a field with electric and water hookups. An additional 40 sites are dry and tent sites, many in trees. Restrooms with hot showers are very nice, there is also a laundromat. The campground has a dump station, a basic grocery store, and a dishwashing station for tent campers.

The entrance road for the Sourdough is located near Km 1,453 (Mile 874) of the Alaska Highway.

✦ WOLF CREEK CAMPGROUND (YUKON GOVERNMENT)
   Location: Near Km 1,459 (Mile 877)
   of the Alaska Highway
   Price: Low

*GPS Location: N 60° 36' 26.7", W 134° 56' 40.7"*

Wolf Creek Campground has 33 vehicle sites and additional tent sites arranged off a circular drive in a treed valley not far from Whitehorse. Several of the sites are pull-throughs. Wolf Creek runs right through the middle of the campground, There are picnic tables, fire pits, free firewood, a playground, a water pump, and outhouses.

## WHITEHORSE
### Population 23,000, Elevation 2,300 feet

Whitehorse is the capital of the Yukon Territory and by far the largest town with about 60% of the territory's population. This is the best place along the Alaska Highway for vehicle repairs, banking, grocery shopping, and acting like a tourist.

Whitehorse was founded during the Klondike gold rush. The section of river upriver from town, Miles Canyon and the White Horse Rapids, was so dangerous that a rail tram was built around it to portage the boats and goods of the prospectors floating down to Dawson City. This was also the head of navigation of the Yukon, a natural place for a town. Large steamboats could go no farther although other steamboats plied the waters of the lakes upstream. Very soon the railroad from Skagway tied Whitehorse to the sea and cemented Whitehorse's position as the supply center for the Yukon. For a long time, though, Dawson City remained the capital of the territory, only in 1953 was the government moved to Whitehorse.

The **Tourism Yukon Visitor Reception Centre** is located on 2nd Avenue (Box 2703, Whitehorse, Y.T. Y1A 2C6, Canada; 867 667-5340). The town is well supplied with interesting things to see and do. Those aimed specifically at the tourist trade include the **Frantic Follies** show, the **MV Schwatka** tour of Miles Canyon, the **Yukon Botanical Gardens**, and the **SS Klondike** restored riverboat. Tickets and transportation to most of these are available at RV parks. You might also find the town's museums to be interesting. The **MacBride Museum** is located downtown and has gold rush era exhibits. The **Yukon Transportation Museum** at the airport covers the full range of transportation in the Yukon. Finally, **Beringia**, also near the airport, is a brand new museum with displays covering the ice age era when this particular area was ice free and home to woolly mammoths.

An interesting hike is the one to Canyon City. Drive to Km 1,467 (Mile 882) of the Alaska Highway and follow the Miles Canyon Road .5 km (.3 Mile) to a Y and then turn right to a parking lot. A trail leads to a suspension bridge across **Miles Canyon**. Turn right on the far side of the river and in another 1.7 km (1.1 mile) you'll come the site of the gold rush town of **Canyon City**. Boats coming down river offloaded here and trams carried passengers and goods downstream past the rapids. Not much remains except the site and the former tram grades.

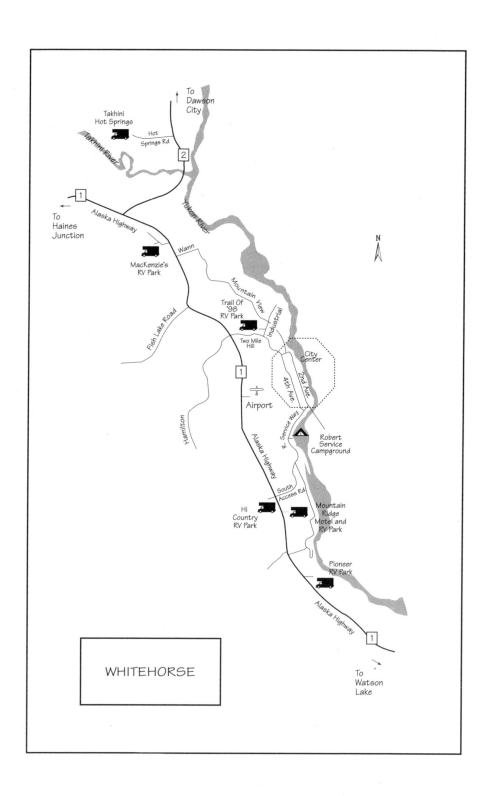

To
Dawson
City

Takhini
Hot Springs

Hot
Springs Rd

Takhini River

2

Yukon River

1

To
Haines
Junction

Alaska Highway

Wann

MacKenzie's
RV Park

Mountain View

Trail Of
'98
RV Park

Industrial

Fish Lake Road

Two Mile
Hill

City
Center

1

4th Ave.

2nd Ave.

Airport

R. Service Way

N

Hamilton

Alaska Highway

Robert
Service
Campground

South
Access Rd.

Hi
Country
RV Park

Mountain
Ridge
Motel and
RV Park

Pioneer
RV Park

Alaska Highway

1

To
Watson
Lake

WHITEHORSE

There is enough to see and do in Whitehorse to justify several days of visiting. Whitehorse is also something of a crossroads so you may find yourself here more than once. From Whitehorse the Klondike Highway leads south to Skagway and the Klondike Loop leads northward to Dawson City. The Alaska Highway and this book lead east toward Haines Junction and Alaska.

## Whitehorse Campgrounds

✦ PIONEER RV PARK
    Address: Site 8, Comp. 4, Whitehorse,
    Y.T. Y1A 5V9, Canada
    Telephone: (867) 668-5944, Fax: (867) 668-5947
    Price: Medium

*GPS Location: N 60° 38' 59.1", W 135° 01' 15.3"*

The Pioneer is a very large and popular RV park located some four miles from downtown Whitehorse. There are about 140 sites with something to please almost everyone. Sites include full and partial hookups, pull-throughs, back-ins in the trees, and dry or tent sites. Cable TV is available and there is a dump station. Other amenities include showers, laundromat, small grocery store, a recreation hall, gas sales, a gift shop, and a RV wash facility. You can get tickets here for most of the tours and attractions in Whitehorse and bus service into town is available.

The campground is located near Km 1,465 (Mile 881) of the Alaska Highway.

✦ MOUNTAIN RIDGE MOTEL AND RV PARK
    Address: P.O. Box 5211, Whitehorse,
    Y.T. Y1A 4Z1, Canada
    Telephone: (867) 667-4202
    Price: Medium

*GPS Location: N 60° 40' 32.0", W 135° 03' 09.0"*

The small Mountain Ridge Motel has 6 sites with full hookups in the parking lot. There are two restrooms with showers and a laundromat accessible to those camping in the sites. The Mountain Ridge Motel is located near Km 1,468 (Mile 883) of the Alaska Highway. This is 3 miles south of the South Access Road junction.

✦ HI-COUNTRY RV PARK
    Address: P.O. Box 6081, Whitehorse,
    Y.T. Y1A 5L7, Canada
    Telephone: (867) 667-7445, Fax: (867) 668-6342
    Price: Medium

*GPS Location: N 60° 41' 03.1", W 135° 03' 37.0"*

This is our favorite Whitehorse campground. It is close enough to town for conve-nience and has campsites with trees and decent facilities. It's also located right next door to a popular Whitehorse attraction, the Yukon Gardens.

The Hi-Country has about 130 sites. Some are in open areas without trees and others have some trees separating sites. Electricity and water hookups are available as are dry sites. Some sites are pull-throughs. There are some picnic tables and fire rings. They have good restroom facilities with hot showers, a laundromat, and a dump sta-tion. Bus transportation in to town is available.

The Hi Country is located just off the Alaska Highway with the access road near Km 1,470 (Mile 884).

✦ T<small>RAIL OF</small> 98 RV P<small>ARK</small>
Address: Box 4145, Whitehorse,
Y.T. Y1A 3S9, Canada
Telephone and Fax: (867) 668-3768 or
(800) 377-2142
Price: Medium

*GPS Location: N 60° 44' 05.9", W 135° 04' 47.6"*

This large campground is the closest to downtown Whitehorse although it is still a bit of a hike in to town, about a mile and a half with a good paved bike trail and sidewalk.

The Trail of 98 is a large gravel lot sitting on the side of a hill overlooking the indus-trial area of Whitehorse. There are about 150 sites with a variety of amenities and services: 15-amp and 30-amp electricity, water, sewer and cable TV in varying com-binations. Some sites are pull-throughs. The office, restrooms, showers and a restau-rant are located in a central building. You may be ready to wash your rig by the time you reach Whitehorse, this campground offers the free use of a washing area to their guests. They specialize in a pancake breakfast. City busses stop nearby and the shuttle bus to local attractions visits regularly.

To find the campground follow the northern access road off the Alaska Highway toward downtown Whitehorse. As you descend the hill you'll see the campground on your left, take the left immediately after it and then turn left again in a block at the campground entrance road.

✦ R<small>OBERT</small> S<small>ERVICE</small> C<small>AMPGROUND</small>
Address: Box 5418, Whitehorse,
Y.T. Y1A 5H4, Canada
Telephone: (867) 668-3721
Price: Low

*GPS Location: N 60° 42' 07.3", W 135° 02' 55.9"*

Whitehorse has a tent-only campground located within easy walking distance of down-town. The Robert Service Campground has 48 tent sites set in the woods. Sites have picnic tables and fire pits. There are flush toilets and hot showers, a small grocery store and bakery, free firewood, and a picnic shelter.

To reach the campground from downtown walk or drive south. You'll end up on what is called the South Access Road and soon see the campground sign on the left.

✦ MacKenzie's RV Park
   Address: 18 Azura Road, Whitehorse,
   Y.T. Y1A 6E1, Canada
   Telephone: (867) 633-2337, Fax: (867) 667-6797
   Price: Medium

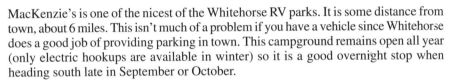

*GPS Location: N 60° 46′ 44.1″, W 135° 09′ 46.6″*

MacKenzie's is one of the nicest of the Whitehorse RV parks. It is some distance from town, about 6 miles. This isn't much of a problem if you have a vehicle since Whitehorse does a good job of providing parking in town. This campground remains open all year (only electric hookups are available in winter) so it is a good overnight stop when heading south late in September or October.

MacKenzie's has about 120 sites in three different locations. Near the main services buildings and the entrance is a large open gravel area with full hookup sites, many are pull-throughs. Behind these is a treed area with mostly dry back-in sites. On a treed plateau above this area are more full-hookup back-in sites with their own services building. All sites have picnic tables. There are flush toilets, free showers (for 2 guests per night), dump stations, coin-op laundromat, cable TV, groceries, video rentals, and coin-op pressure vehicle wash.

The campground is located west of Whitehorse just off the Alaska Highway. Turn onto Azure Road at Km 1,484 (Mile 892), you'll see the campground to your left. It is well signed. This location is about 3 miles toward Whitehorse from the intersection of the Alaska Highway and Highway 2 to Dawson City.

✦ Takhini Hot Springs
   Address: RR 2, Site 19, Comp 4, Whitehorse,
   Y.T. Y1A 5X2, Canada
   Telephone: (867) 633-2706
   Price: Low

*GPS Location: N 60° 52′ 43.2″, W 135° 21′ 36.0″*

For something different near Whitehorse you might try the city's favorite swimming hole: Takhini Hot Springs. They have a shallow but nice swimming pool that is kept comfortably hot, but not steaming, about 100° F.

The hot springs has a 90-site campground. There are 15 sites with low amp power, the remainder are dry. Most sites are set in a grove of pine and aspen and have decent separation with fire pits and picnic tables. There are flush toilets and showers at the pool as well as a laundromat, and a snack bar. There's also a dump station and a water fill point. Horse trail rides are offered. Bathing facilities are limited to the pool and showers in the dressing room which have an additional fee, but the hot water feels great and there's no smelly sulfur in it.

To find the campground follow the paved access highway from Km 198 (Mile 123) of the North Klondike Highway for 9.2 kilometers (5.7 miles).

## FROM WHITEHORSE TO TOK
### (396 miles)

The Alaska Highway from Whitehorse to Tok is paved, but much of it is narrow. This is where you will meet the nemesis of road maintenance in the north, the frost heave. Frost heaves are the result of building roads across permafrost, and they are virtually impossible for road builders to conquer. These unpredictable dips and mounds mean that you must often hold your speed down, especially if you are driving a large rig or trailer. The road gets better each year but it pays to stay alert.

Because this is a slower section of highway you might consider covering it in two days rather than one. We like to overnight at one of the campgrounds near beautiful Kluane Lake.

Almost immediately after leaving Whitehorse you will come to the junction with Highway 2 north to Dawson City. This road, known as the Klondike Loop, is covered in Chapter 11 of this book.

Continuing east the next important settlement is **Haines Junction** at Km 1,635 (Mile 985). Watch yourself in Haines Junction, if you aren't alert you'll end up on the road to Haines rather than the Alaska Highway to Tok. The 245-kilometer (152-mile) long Haines Highway is covered in Chapter 12 of this book. Haines serves as the jump-off point for expeditions into Kluane National Park. This small town of about 800 has the **Kluane National Park Visitors Center** (P.O. Box 5339K, Haines Junction, Yukon YOB 1L0; 867 634-2293), as well as stores, restaurants, gas stations, and RV parks.

From Haines Junction the highway gradually climbs over 3,280 foot **Bear Creek Summit** and then descends to skirt the west side of emerald green **Kluane Lake**. Near the southwest shore of the lake at Km 1,707 (Mile 1,029) is Kluane Park's **Sheep Mountain** visitor center where you can often see Dall sheep in the spring and fall.

Kluane Lake is the largest lake in the Yukon and there are two communities—Burwash Landing and Destruction Bay—and several campgrounds along its length. The lake's unusual color is caused by glacial silt suspended in the water and reflecting the sky.

After Kluane Lake the road deteriorates somewhat because of swampy ground and permafrost. Construction has been underway here for several years and you may run into sections of gravel. On the other hand, there are also some sections of brand-new beautiful highway.

At Km 1,935 (Mile 1,169) is the little town of Beaver Creek. This is the site of the Canadian border station and also of several hotels and a good RV park.

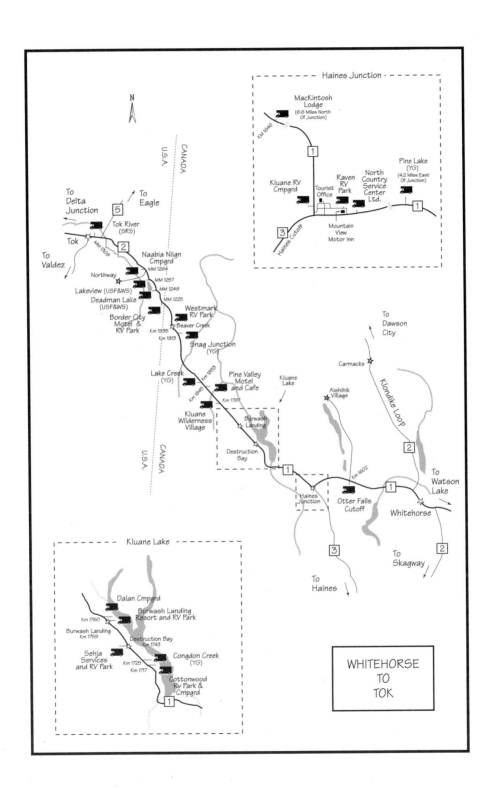

You reach the **Alaska border** at Km 1,966 (Mile 1,222). At the top of the hill is the U.S. border station and customs. There is usually little or no delay.

With recent improvements to the Alaska Highway on the Canadian side you may not notice much difference in the road on the Alaska side. Not many years ago crossing the border brought pure bliss, smooth pavement after more than 1,200 miles of gravel. From the border you can reach the first Alaska town of any size, Tok, in a little over an hour and a half, the distance is 92 miles.

### Campgrounds
### Whitehorse to Tok

✦ OTTER FALLS CUTOFF
   Address: Box 5450, Haines Jct.,
   Y.T. Y0B 1L0, Canada
   Telephone and Fax: (867) 634-2812
   Price: Medium

*GPS Location: N 60° 51' 12.0", W 137° 02' 11.4"*

The Otter Falls Cutoff is a combination gas station, grocery store and RV park along a section of the highway that doesn't have many other establishments of any kind, including campgrounds.

There are about 50 sites with electricity and water hookups in an open gravel and grass lot next to the store. If the campground isn't full many of the sites can be used as pull-throughs, this is probably the normal situation. Additional dry sites are located under trees nearby and on the opposite side of the store and gas pumps. Some sites have fire pits and picnic tables. Showers are available and there is a playground. There is also a dump station.

The Otter Falls Cutoff is at the junction with Aishihik Road at Km 1,602 (Mile 965) of the Alaska Highway. This is 126 Km (78 miles) north of Whitehorse and 32 kilometers (20 miles) south of the Haines Junction.

✦ PINE LAKE CAMPGROUND (YUKON GOVERNMENT)
   Location: Km 1,628 (Mile 981)
   of the Alaska Highway
   Price: Low

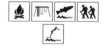

*GPS Location: N 60° 47' 53.9", W 137° 29' 24.5"*

This government campground is located just outside Haines Junction, gateway to the Kluane National Park. There are 33 sites here, 5 are pull-throughs, and there is plenty of room for big rigs. All sites have picnic tables and fire pits and are well-separated with spruce trees and other natural vegetation. There are outhouses, a covered kitchen and picnic area, drinking water, a boat launch, and swimming in Pine Lake for the hardy.

✦ NORTH COUNTRY SERVICE CENTER LTD.
    Address: P.O. Box 5502, Haines Junction,
    Y.T. Y0B 1L0, Canada
    Telephone: (867) 634-2505
    Price: Low

*GPS Location: N 60° 45' 39.9", W 137° 31' 03.8"*

About the first thing you see when you approach Haines Junction from the Whitehorse direction is a Petro-Canada gas station on the west side of the road. This is North Country Service Center. They have 23 new RV spaces with electricity (20 and 30-amp) and water hookups in an open area next to the station. Many are pull-throughs. Plans are in the works for sewer hookups but there is no definite timetable. On the opposite side are several dry parking sites. The price of an overnight stay includes a water fill-up and a holding tank dump. There are no showers but flush toilets are available when the station is open.

✦ RAVEN RV PARK
    Location: Behind the Mountain View Motor Inn
    Price: Medium

*GPS Location: N 60° 45' 25.4", W 137° 30' 55.5"*

This tiny RV park with 6 pull-through full-hookup spaces is easy to miss. As you approach from the Whitehorse direction watch for the Mountain View Motor Inn and Chevron station. Turn on the road just north of the inn and you'll see the Raven RV Park just ahead. It has flush toilets and hot showers in a small building near the sites. Instructions for checking in are posted if no one is around. The campground is not associated with the Motor Inn.

✦ KLUANE RV CAMPGROUND
    Address: Box 5496, Haines Junction,
    Y.T. Y0B 1L0, Canada
    Telephone: (867) 634-2709, Fax: (867) 634-2735
    Price: Medium

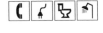

*GPS Location: N 60° 45' 06.0", W 137° 31' 15.0"*

This is the largest full-service RV park in Haines Junction. There are about 90 spaces, most are pull-throughs and there is lots of room for maneuvering since the campground is a large open gravel field. Full hookup, partial hookup, and dry sites are available, as are tent sites. There are some picnic tables but not at most sites. The Kluane has restrooms and showers (individual rooms) in the main building as well as a small store and laundromat. There is also a dump station, a vehicle wash, and a gas station. A good 3-mile hiking trail leads from the campground.

The campground is located at Km 1,636 (Mile 985) of the Alaska Highway, about 1.1 km (.7 mile) west of the junction.

◆   MACKINTOSH LODGE
         Address: Historic Mile 1022, Alaska Hwy,
         Y.T. Y1A 3V4, Canada
         Telephone: (867) 634-2301, Fax: (867) 634-2302
         Price: Medium

*GPS Location: N 60° 47' 42.3", W 137° 40' 24.6"*

The Mackintosh is a lodge-type highway stop offering rooms, gas, and a restaurant as well as the RV park. There are about 14 pull-through spaces on a gravel area behind the motel building. Each has electricity and water hookup. Quite a few additional rigs can park with no utilities. There are also tent sites in a nearby area of trees. Showers are available in the motel building as are flush toilets. There is also a dump station. The Alsek Pass Trail starts across the road, this would be a good place to camp if you want to hike it.

The Mackintosh is at Km 1,646 (Mile 992, Historical Milepost 1,022) of the Alaska Highway, about 7 miles north of the Haines Junction.

◆   COTTONWOOD RV PARK AND CAMPGROUND
         Address: Km 1,717 Alaska Highway,
         Destruction Bay, Y.T., Canada
         Telephone: Mobile Operator
         Destruction Bay Channel 2M 3972,
         Reservations: (867) 634-2739, Fax (867) 634-2429
         Price: Medium

*GPS Location: N 61° 05' 13.3", W 138° 32' 01.0"*

The Cottonwood is one of our favorite stops along the Alaska Highway. It is a beautiful campground in a beautiful location.

The campground must have at least 70 camping sites of various types scattered along the shore of Kluane Lake. The small trees and shrubs that occur naturally in the area separate the sites, much like in a government campground. About 30 sites have electricity and 20 of these also have water hookups. The electric-only sites are on the waterfront while many of the water and electric sites are pull-throughs. Sites have fire pits and picnic tables. The restroom building has flush toilets and free hot showers. Power here is produced by a generator but the noise is almost impossible to hear from the camping sites and the generator operates 24 hours. There's a small grocery and gift store, Gopher Golf (mini golf), a rental hot tub, a laundromat, and dump and water fill stations.

The campground is located at Km 1,717 (Mile 1,035) of the Alaska Highway, about 16 miles south of Destruction Bay and on the shore of Kluane Lake.

✦ CONGDON CREEK CAMPGROUND
   (YUKON GOVERNMENT)
        Location: Near Km 1,725 (Mile 1,040)
        of the Alaska Highway
        Price: Low

*GPS Location: N 61° 09' 08.0", W 138° 32' 51.9"*

Congdon Creek is a large government campground adjoining Kluane Lake. There are some 80 spaces here, about 25 are pull-throughs. They are well separated and set in spruce and alder, many are along the lake shore. All have fire pits and picnic tables. The campground also offers outhouses, free firewood, kitchen shelters, hand water pump, playground and a boat launch.

✦ SEHJA SERVICES AND RV PARK
        Address: Historical Mile 1,083, Destruction Bay,
        Y.T. Y0B 1V0, Canada
        Telephone: (867) 841-4807, Fax: (867) 841-4807
        Price: Medium

*GPS Location: N 61° 15' 22.1", W 138° 48' 39.3"*

The camping slots at this facility occupy a large gravel lot beside and behind the gas station, restaurant, and gift shop. There are 40 sites with water and electric hookups. Many of these are pull-throughs. There is also lots of space for dry camping. Restrooms are inside the restaurant building and are individual rooms with toilet and free shower. There is also a laundromat and a dump station.

Sehja Services is near Km 1,743 (Mile 1,052, Historical Mile 1,083) of the Alaska Highway.

✦ BURWASH LANDING RESORT AND RV PARK
        Address: Historical Mile 1,093, Burwash Landing
        Telephone: (867) 841-4441, Fax: (867) 841-4040
        Price: Medium

*GPS Location: N 61° 21' 27.7", W 138° 59' 50.6"*

This resort has about 10 back-in (or pull-in) sites with electricity and water hookups situated along the water next to a restaurant/bar/lodge. The site is an open gravel area and visitors to the lodge park in pretty much the same lot. The surrounding area is available for dry camping and parking. There was one picnic table available when we visited. Showers are available in the lodge.

To reach the camping area turn in at the sign near a gas station near Km 1,759 (Mile 1,061, Historical 1,093) of the Alaska Highway. Drive down to the lake, a distance of about .3 miles.

✦ DALAN CAMPGROUND
    Address: Box 20, Burwash Landing, Y.T.
    Y0B 1V0, Canada
    Price: Low

*GPS Location: N 61° 21' 56.2", W 138° 59' 57.8"*

Although now run by the Kluane First Nation this campground appears to have been a Yukon Government campground at one time. There are 25 separated sites, one is a pull-through. Several sites are near the lake shore. There are picnic tables, fire pits, free firewood, a water pump, outhouses, and even a dump station. The .6 mile access road leaves the Alaska Highway near Kilometer 1,760 (Mile 1062, Historic Mile 1093).

✦ KLUANE WILDERNESS VILLAGE
    Address: Mile 1118 Alaska Highway, Y.T.
    Y1A 3V4, Canada
    Telephone: (867) 841-4141
    Price: Medium

*GPS Location: N 61° 34' 53.8", W 139° 22' 38.3"*

This large roadhouse-style operation offers lots of pull-through sites. There are about 50 of these side-by-side sites, mostly with full hookups including satellite TV. There are also some sites with only electricity and water and many dry sites. Showers are free to campers and quite nice. There is also a laundromat, small grocery store, restaurant, saloon, motel and gas station. The Kluane Wilderness Village is located near Km 1,797 (Mile 1,085, Historic Mile 1,118) of the Alaska Highway.

✦ PINE VALLEY MOTEL AND CAFE
    Address: Mile 1,147 Alaska Highway, Y.T., Canada
    Telephone and Fax: (867) 862-7407
    Price: Medium

*GPS Location: N 61° 48' 21.6", W 140° 02' 51.7"*

This roadhouse-style campground has decent campsites with trees separating the sites and a small creek alongside. There are about 40 sites, 11 with electricity and water hookups. There are pull-throughs, picnic tables, and hot showers. Maneuvering room for really big rigs is limited. There's also a dump station, a cafe, and gas. You can fish in Edith Creek. The Pine Valley is near Km 1,845 (Mile 1,114, Historic Mile 1,147) of the Alaska Highway.

✦ LAKE CREEK CAMPGROUND (YUKON GOVERNMENT)
    Location: Near Km 1,853 (Mile 1,119) of the Alaska Highway
    Price: Low

*GPS Location: N 61° 51' 25.6", W 140° 08' 56.7"*

This small 27-site government campground has large separated sites, many are pull-throughs and several border the creek. There are picnic tables, fire pits, free firewood, outhouses, a kitchen shelter, and a hand water pump.

✦ SNAG JUNCTION CAMPGROUND (YUKON GOVERNMENT)
    Location: Near Km 1,913 (Mile 1,155) of
    the Alaska Highway
    Price: Low

       *GPS Location: N 62° 14' 19.2", W 140° 41' 15.2"*

Snag Junction is a small government campground with 15 separated back-in sites. Some are near a small lake and all have picnic tables and fire pits. There are outhouses, free firewood, and a kitchen shelter.

✦ WESTMARK RV PARK
    Address: Mile 1,202 Alaska Highway,
    Beaver Creek, YT, Y0B 1A0 Canada
    Telephone: (867) 862-7501 or
    (800) 544-0970
    Internet: www.westmarkhotels.com
    Price: Medium

    *GPS Location: N 62° 22' 56.9", W 140° 52' 27.5"*

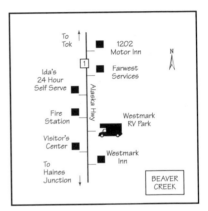

This big new campground stands out along this section of the Alaska Highway. It is associated with the very nice Westmark Inn next door, an overnight stop for cruise ship passengers traveling by bus between Haines and Fairbanks. They even offer entertainment, the hotel puts on a musical in its dinner theater.

There are 67 sites here with electric (30 and 50-amp) and water hookups. Over half of them are large pull-throughs. Each site has a small tree but it will be a long time before they offer much shade. Sites also have picnic tables and barbecues. There are hot showers and flush toilets in the washrooms, there's also a laundromat, a mini-mart, gas sales, and two dump stations.

Watch for the campground just north of the Westmark Inn in Beaver Creek.

✦ BORDER CITY MOTEL & RV PARK
    Address: Mile 1,225 Alaska Highway, Alaska
    Telephone: (907) 774-2211
    Price: Medium

       *GPS Location: N 62° 39' 51.2", W 141° 03' 28.1"*

Border City is the first stop north of the Alaska border. If you've been pushing all day to reach Alaska this isn't a bad place to stop at the end of the day and celebrate. Behind the huge gas station, motel, and gift shop are 26 large RV sites in a large grass field. Many of the sites are pull-throughs, five have full hookups (30 and 50 amp) and most of the rest offer electricity and water. There are also dry and tent sites. There are flush toilets and hot showers, a laundromat, and a dump station. The lodge is located at Mile 1,225 of the Alaska Highway, 3.5 miles north of the U.S. Customs station.

✦   DEADMAN LAKE CAMPGROUND (USF&W)
     Location: Near Mile 1,249 of the Alaska Highway
     Price: Free

*GPS Location: N 62° 53' 21.9", W 141° 32' 33.0"*

This is a small campground and very easy to miss. The roads and spaces are small and narrow, it isn't suitable for big rigs. There are 18 separated sites set in black spruce along Deadman Lake. Sites have picnic tables and fire pits and there are outhouses. There's a boat ramp and the lake is good for pike, there's also a nature trail. This is prime mosquito country. Leave the highway at about Mile 1,249 and follow the gravel and dirt road for 1.1 miles to the campground.

TYPICAL BLACK SPRUCE FOREST SEEN ALONG THE ALASKA HIGHWAY

✦ LAKEVIEW CAMPGROUND (USF&W)
    Location: Near Mile 1,257 of the Alaska Highway
    Price: Free

*GPS Location: N 62° 57' 50.0", W 141° 38' 01.4"*

Another very small public campground on a lake. This one has some 11 sites and little maneuvering room. There are picnic tables, fire pits, and outhouses. None of these sites is directly on Yarger Lake. The entrance road here is about .3 miles long.

✦ NAABIA NIIGN CAMPGROUND
    Address: P.O. Box 476, Northway, AK 99764
    Telephone and Fax: (907) 778-2297
    Price: Medium

*GPS Location: N 63° 00' 35.5", W 141° 48' 06.5"*

Naabia Niign Campground has 20 sites set in trees behind and below a gas station, laundromat, mini-mart, and gift shop. Sixteen sites have full hookups (20 and 30-amp). Sites have picnic tables and fire pits. Flush toilets and showers are located up in the laundromat. There is also a dump station.

The campground is located at Mile 1,264 of the Alaska Highway.

✦ TOK RIVER STATE RECREATION SITE
    Location: Near Mile 1,309 of the Alaska Highway
    Price: Low

*GPS Location: N 63° 19' 33.1", W 142° 49' 48.3"*

This campground now has about 43 sites but many of them are nothing more than side-by-side slots in a parking lot. The others are separated by trees but have shared double parking pads. There are picnic tables and fire pits, as well as outhouses and a boat ramp. This campground has a host and firewood is on sale.

## TOK
### Population 1,400, Elevation 1,650 feet

You would be perfectly justified to wonder why Tok exists. There is little here other than RV parks, service stations, restaurants, and stores. In fact the town does little more than serve as a transportation center. Tok's residents will welcome you to Alaska when you arrive and bid you farewell when you leave.

The **Tok Visitor Center** and **Alaska Public Lands Information Center** (P.O. Box 359, Tok, AK 99780; 907 883-5667) are located together in a large log building in the northwest quadrant of the intersection of the Alaska Highway and the Tok Cutoff. This is an important stop, you can pick up a ton of information about the whole state.

You can also try to make Alaska State Ferry Reservations, although you should have done that long before you left home.

The public lands information center is one of four in the state, the others are in Fairbanks, Anchorage, and Ketchikan. There is so much federal and state land in Alaska that the governing organizations - eight different ones including the National Parks Service, the Bureau of Land Management, the U.S. Fish and Wildlife Service, and the State of Alaska - have set these information centers up in an attempt to make it easy for people to find all the information they need in one place. The information centers are a good place to start, but often it is necessary actually go to the governing organization for all the information you need. This center caters more to highway travelers than the others and may not be the best place to look for information about off-highway camping possibilities. See Chapter 14 - Camping Away From the Road System for more information.

In Tok you must make an important decision. Will you continue up the Alaska Highway to Fairbanks or will you turn south toward Valdez and Anchorage? An amazingly large number of people head for Fairbanks and never see the southern part of the state. Don't be one of them. See it all. You've come a long way.

## Tok Campgrounds

✦ TOK GATEWAY SALMON BAKE
    Address: P.O. Box 577, Tok, AK 99780
    Telephone: (907) 883-5555
    Price: Low

*GPS Location: N 63° 20' 03.0", W 142° 57' 17.1"*

The Gateway Salmon Bake has 28 no-hookup spaces set in spruce trees behind the restaurant. Some are pull-throughs. Coming from Canada this is the first campground you will come to in Tok and you should check it out. Camping is free if you have dinner at the restaurant, and it's one of the best places to eat in town. There are no showers but the restrooms have flush toilets and hot water in the sinks. There's also a dump station and water fill point.

The Gateway is on the north side of the Alaska Highway near Mile 1,313. It is 1 mile east of the intersection of the Tok Cutoff and the Alaska Highway.

✦ BULL SHOOTER RV PARK
    Address: P.O. Box 553, Tok, AK 99780
    Telephone: (907) 883-5625
    Price: Medium

*GPS Location: N 63° 20' 03.4", W 142° 57' 43.5"*

The Bull Shooter is a nicely groomed and conveniently located campground tucked behind a sporting goods store. There are about 30 sites, most are pull-throughs with

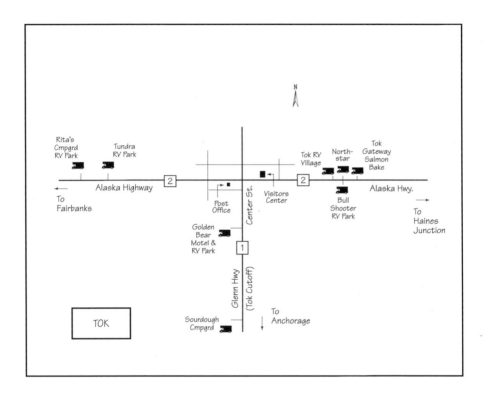

grass separating them. There are full service sites with 30-amp power, sites with just water and electricity, and dry sites. Maneuvering room for big rigs is more than adequate. The washrooms have flush toilets and free showers and there is a dump station. There's also a good restaurant across the highway.

Watch for the Bull Shooter on the south side of the Alaska Highway .9 miles east of the intersection with the Tok Cutoff.

✦  NORTHSTAR
        Address: P.O. Box 504, Tok, AK 99780
        Telephone: (907) 883-4501
        Price: Medium

*GPS Location: N 63° 20′ 03.0″, W 142° 57′ 31.0″*

The Northstar is a combination gas station, restaurant, laundromat and RV park. There are 7 pull-through sites with 30-amp electricity and water hookups behind the large main building. Showers are included in the nightly rate. There is also a dump station.

The Northstar is located at mile 1,313 of the Alaska Highway about .9 miles east of the intersection with the Tok Cutoff.

✦ TOK RV VILLAGE
   Address: P.O. Box 739, Tok, AK 99780
   Telephone: (907) 883-5877 or (800) 478-5878
   Fax: (907) 883-5878
   Price: Medium

*GPS Location: N 63° 20' 04.3", W 142° 57' 57.9"*

The Tok RV Village claims to be Alaska's finest RV park. There are many other parks in the state that could justifiably argue this point, but this is a nice campground.

The large campground advertises 95 sites. There are all types of sites including pull-throughs. 50-amp power is available at some sites. This campground, like most in Tok, is set in a spruce grove. The campground offers free showers to overnighters, a laundromat, and a gift shop which also has a few RV supplies. There is a dump and water-fill station.

The campground is located at mile 1,313 of the Alaska Highway, about .8 miles east of the intersection with the Tok Cutoff.

✦ THE GOLDEN BEAR MOTEL AND RV PARK
   Address: P.O. Box 500, Tok, AK 99780
   Telephone: (907) 883-2561 or (888) 252-2123
   Fax: (907) 883-5950
   Internet: http://www.tokalaska.com/901
   Price: Medium

*GPS Location: N 63° 19' 51.9", W 142° 59' 24.3"*

The Golden Bear has about 60 sites. Most are pull-throughs, full-hookup, water and electric, and dry sites are offered. There are also tent sites The campground sits in a grove of spruce trees and sites have picnic tables. There are a surprisingly large number of showers for a campground of this size, they are included in the price of your site. This campground also offers a laundromat, dump station, and a restaurant.

The campground is located just south of the intersection of the Tok Cutoff and the Alaska Highway on the west side of the highway.

✦ SOURDOUGH CAMPGROUND
   Address: Box 47, Tok, Alaska 99780
   Telephone: (907) 883-5543, (800) 789-5543
   Price: Medium

*GPS Location: N 63° 18' 42.5", W 143° 00' 06.7"*

The Sourdough is a little farther from town than the other Tok campgrounds and is on the road to Anchorage so many Fairbanks-bound travelers never even see it until they return home after a visit to Southcentral. As a result this campground seems to get a little less traffic than the others in town and is usually a quieter place to stay,

This is an older medium-sized campground with about 75 camping sites in a fairly dense patch of spruce. Parking pads are gravel and have picnic tables. Both 15 and 30-amp plugs are offered, and sites are available with various combinations of electrical, water, and sewer hookups as well as without any services at all. Some pull-throughs are available, also a tent-camping area. There is a restaurant serving a sourdough breakfast, a gift shop, a laundromat, and a coin operated vehicle wash. Hot showers are free. There is a dump station.

To reach the campground take the Tok Cutoff toward Anchorage from central Tok, the campground is about a mile and a half from the intersection on the right.

✦ TUNDRA RV PARK
    Address: P.O. Box 760, Tok, AK 99780
    Telephone: (907) 883-7875, Fax (907) 883-7876
    Internet: http://www.tokalaska.com/tundra
    Price: Medium

*GPS Location: N 63° 20' 19.5", W 143° 01' 05.5"*

The Tundra is another good RV park that probably suffers a little for business because it is on the wrong side of Tok.

This is a large park. There are some 80 sites here, pull-throughs, full-hookups, partial hookups, and dry. 20, 30, and 50-amp electricity is available. All are in a nice setting with many trees, they also have picnic tables and fire pits with wood. Showers are free and there is a laundromat, a vehicle wash, a dump station, and even a cocktail lounge and meeting room.

The campground is located at Mile 1,315 of the Alaska Highway, about .8 miles west of the junction with the Tok Cutoff.

✦ RITA'S CAMPGROUND RV PARK
    Address: P.O. Box 599, Tok, AK 99780
    Telephone: (907) 883-4342
    Price: Medium

*GPS Location: N 63° 20' 29.0", W 143° 02' 42.1"*

One of the smallest parks in Tok is also one of the best. Rita's is the last park as you leave town toward Fairbanks, but really not far out, so you might want to drive over to take a look before settling into one of the large places in town.

Rita's has 18 spaces, 6 are huge pull-throughs with electricity and two more will soon be added. Other spaces are back-ins and have picnic tables and fire pits with free firewood provided. There's a good tent-camping area. Big spruce trees shelter the sites. The campground provides free hot showers, a dump and water fill station and a gift shop.

The campground is at mile 1,316 of the Alaska Highway, about 1.5 miles west of the Tok Cutoff intersection.

## From Tok to Delta Junction
### (108 miles)

From Tok the Alaska Highway follows the wide Tanana Valley northwest to Delta Junction. The road is excellent, the entire trip takes less than two hours. At Delta Junction the Alaska Highway ends. The Richardson Highway runs north 98 miles to Fairbanks and south 266 miles to Valdez.

## Campgrounds
## Tok to Delta Junction

✦ Moon Lake State Recreation Site
    Location: Mile 1,332 of the Alaska Highway,
    18 miles west of Tok
    Price: Low

*GPS Location: N 63° 22' 31.3", W 143° 32' 36.7"*

This campground is located alongside Moon Lake, a pretty little swimming lake just off the highway. There are 14 back-in sites near the water with picnic tables, fire pits, and outhouses. There's also a hand water pump and boat launch. The short access road leads north from the Alaska Highway at Mile 1,332.

✦ Gerstle River Wayside
    Location: Along the Alaska Highway at mile 1,393,
    about 29 miles east of Delta Junction
    Price: Free

*GPS Location: N 63° 49' 12.7", W 144° 55' 42.3"*

This wayside has a large circular drive that is back off the highway. In the center are picnic tables and fire pits. Outhouses are provided.

Watch for the entrance road just west of the Grestle River at mile 1,393 of the Alaska Highway.

## Delta Junction
### Population 750, Elevation 1,200 feet

Delta Junction started as a construction camp on the old Richardson Highway before

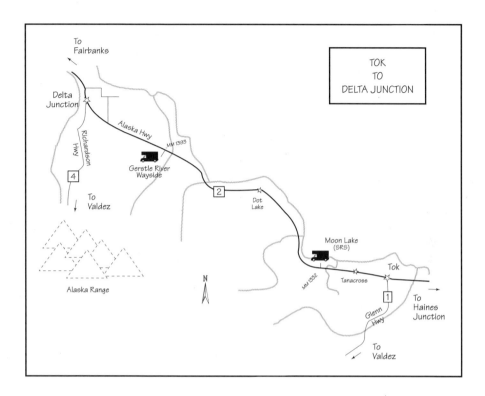

the Alaska Highway was built. The surrounding country has become an important agricultural area.

Delta is known for the **bison** that were transported into the area in the 1920's. There are now over 400 of them and they roam pretty much where they want to. You may be fortunate enough to see some, a popular place to try is the overlook at Mile 241 of the Richardson Highway about 25 miles south of town. Watch for them along the road too, a collision with a bison will do your rig no good.

**Rika's Roadhouse**, 9 miles north toward Fairbanks, was constructed at a ferry crossing of the Tanana River. This was one of the original Richardson Highway roadhouses and is today a state park. A walk around the grounds is rewarding, there's a restaurant and a gift shop. You can even camp in the parking area.

Delta Junction has a several campgrounds in the vicinity and makes a good overnight stop. Some are actually on the Richardson Highway but are included here because they are close enough to Delta to be considered when spending the night here.

## Delta Junction Campgrounds

✦ BERGSTAD'S TRAVEL AND TRAILER COURT
   Address: Mile 1421 Alaska Highway,
   Delta Junction, Alaska 99737
   Telephone: (907) 895-4856
   Price: Medium

*GPS Location: N 64° 01' 53.4", W 145° 41' 52.3"*

Bergstad's has a line of full-hookup sites in a large grassy field next to the highway.
There are either 50 pull-through sites or 100 back-ins, it depends upon the number of
folks staying in the campground. There is also lots of room for rigs not needing hookups and for tenters in a wooded area. There are restrooms with hot showers and a
laundromat as well as a dump station.

Bergstad's is the first of the Delta RV parks you reach if you are approaching on the
Alaska Highway from the east. It is on the north side of the road at Mile 1,421, 1 mile
from the intersection of the Alaska Highway and the Richardson Highway.

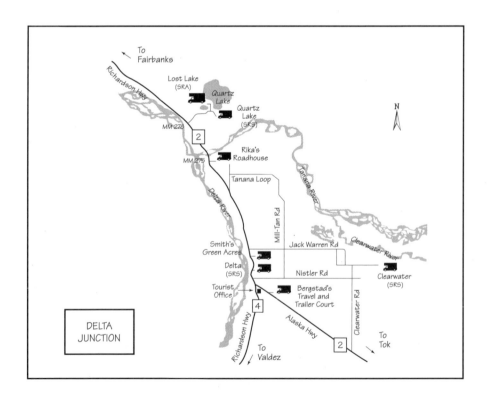

✦ SMITH'S GREEN ACRES
   Address: P.O. Box 1129, Delta Junction, AK 99737
   Telephone: (907) 895-4369 or (800) 895-4369
   Fax (907) 895-4110
   Price: Medium

*GPS Location: N 64° 03' 47.8", W 145° 44' 33.0"*

This is an excellent campground, one of our regular stops. If you are headed north on the Alaska Highway and still have some driving left in you when you reach Tok you might consider pushing on another easy 100 miles or so to Delta.

Smith's Green Acres has about 80 sites of all types: pull-throughs, full utilities (30-amp electric), electric and water, dry, and even tent sites. They cover a large field with a few trees and some grass. There are also a few permanents near the rear of the campground. The services building houses restrooms with free hot showers and a laundromat. There is also a dump station and water fill station.

Watch for this campground on the east side of the road about 1.5 miles north of the junction of the Richardson and the Alaska Highway. The Richardson mileage is 268.

✦ DELTA STATE RECREATION SITE
   Location: In Delta, about 1.1 miles north
   of the junction of the Alaska Highway and Richardson Highways
   Price: Low

*GPS Location: N 64° 03' 17.3", W 145° 44' 18.8"*

This is a pleasant and convenient state campground. It is located right next to the Delta airport, a real plus for us aviation lovers. If you happen to be flying the Alaska Highway this is a convenient camping spot.

There are 24 spaces, four are pull-throughs . The campground is set in a grove of trees but there is still plenty of light. There are picnic tables and fire pits. A water tap is provided and there are outhouses.

The campground is located along the east side of the Richardson Highway in Delta about 1.1 miles north of the intersection of the Alaska Highway and Richardson Highways.

✦ CLEARWATER STATE RECREATION SITE
   Location: East of Delta Junction about 10
   miles on back roads.
   Price: Low

*GPS Location: N 64° 03' 14.3", W 145° 25' 51.0"*

This campground is located on what is known locally as the Delta Clearwater (to distinguish it from another nearby river with the same name). It is a very clear river offering good grayling fishing. The campground is a popular access point for river boaters, there is a boat ramp.

There are 18 sites, most but not all are back-ins. They have picnic tables and fire pits and decent separation and surrounding vegetation with trees. There are outhouses and a hand-operated water pump.

There are two ways to access this campground. The first is the paved Clearwater Road from the Alaska Highway at mile 1,415, about 7 miles east of the Alaska Highway-Richardson junction in Delta. Follow signs about 8.5 miles to the campground. The second is the Jack Warren Road, also paved, which leaves the Richardson at Mile 268, about 2 miles north of the Alaska Highway-Richardson junction in Delta. Follow signs about 11 miles to the campground on this road.

✦ RIKA'S ROADHOUSE (BIG DELTA STATE HISTORICAL PARK)
      Location: Mile 275 Richardson Highway
      Price: Low

*GPS Location: N 64° 09' 16.1", W 145° 50' 33.4"*

You should stop and take a look at Rika's Roadhouse even if you don't want to camp here. This restored roadhouse was one of the originals along the old Valdez to Fairbanks trail. A ferry crossed the very dangerous Tanana River at this point. There is a self-guided tour, a museum, a restaurant, and also a gift shop. The Trans-Alaska oil pipeline crosses the Tanana just down the road.

The camping area is really just the parking lot for the park. There are nearby outhouses. There is also a dump and water fill station nearby.

The roadhouse is located near Mile 275 of the Richardson near the bridge over the Tanana. A short road leads back to the roadhouse from the highway.

✦ QUARTZ LAKE CAMPGROUND
      (QUARTZ LAKE STATE RECREATION AREA)
      Location: Mile 278 of the Richardson Highway,
      about 11 miles north of Delta
      Price: Low

*GPS Location: N 64° 11' 53.4", W 145° 49' 37.9"*

This is a nice little campground on a popular area lake. Quartz lake gets warm enough for swimming and is also a popular float plane lake. You may see a few visiting planes tied up down on the shore.

There are two camping areas here. The large lakeshore parking lot can be used for camping. It has a few picnic tables, fire pits, and outhouses. On the hillside above this lot is a more normal state campground with 16 back in spaces separated by trees and natural vegetation. Some are long enough for medium -sized rigs. These sites have picnic tables, fire pits, and there are outhouses.

The campground is located about 2.7 miles from the Richardson Highway on a gravel road. The access road leaves the highway at about Mile 278.

✦  LOST LAKE CAMPGROUND
    (QUARTZ LAKE RECREATION AREA)
        Location: Mile 278 of the Richardson Highway,
        about 11 miles north of Delta
        Price: Low

*GPS Location: N 64° 11' 43.5", W 145° 50' 28.7"*

Near the Quartz Lake Campground is another much smaller one, the Lost Lake Campground. Trails lead between the two.

This campground has 11 medium to short sites. They are normal state campground back-in type sites with picnic tables and fire pits. Separation is good. There are outhouses and a hand-operated water pump. One site is right along the lake.

You come to this campground before reaching the Quartz Lake Campground. Follow the access road from mile 278 of the Richardson Highway. The Lost Lake Campground is at mile 2.3 of the gravel road.

## ALASKA HIGHWAY DUMP STATIONS

Dump stations (called sani dumps in Canada) are sometimes hard to find in the north. Even when you do find one you will probably have to pay to use it because handling sewage in an area with few sewer systems can be expensive. Plan ahead by dumping when you can, preferably when in a larger town that has a sewer system. Many of the campgrounds listed in this book have dump stations, you can usually pay to use them even if you aren't staying at the campground.

Here are some additional sites, this information is taken from government publications and has not been confirmed:

In **Ft. St. John** there is a city dump station near Km 73 (Mile 46) on the right as you drive north.

In **Watson Lake** try Sign Post Services Chevron station, Watson Lake Esso Service, Kal Tire Ltd./Gulf Station or Wye Lake Park.

In **Whitehorse** try Yukon Tire Centre, Trails North Esso, 2nd Avenue Chevron, or Shell Service.

In **Haines Junction** try the Haines Junction Self-Serve Chevron.

In **Destruction Bay** try the sewage lagoon at the south side of town.

In **Tok** try Young's Chevron at Mile 1314.1 of the Alaska Highway.

In **Delta Junction** try Interior Texaco at 1600 Richardson Highway.

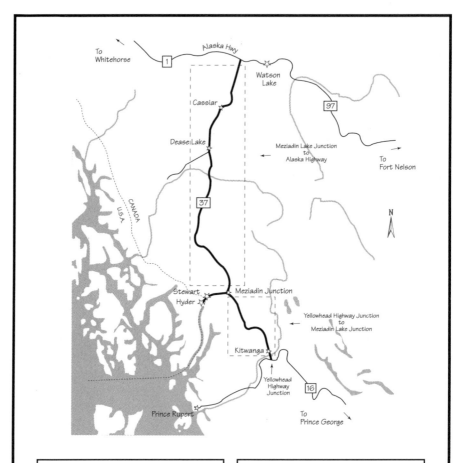

To Whitehorse

Alaska Hwy

1

Watson Lake

97

Cassiar

DeaseLake

Meziadin Lake Junction
to
Alaska Highway

To Fort Nelson

CANADA
U.S.A.

37

N

Stewart
Hyder

Meziadin Junction

Yellowhead Highway Junction
to
Meziadin Lake Junction

Kitwanga

Yellowhead
Highway
Junction

16

Prince Rupert

To Prince George

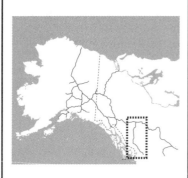

# THE CASSIAR HIGHWAY

# CHAPTER

. . . . . . . . . 5

# THE CASSIAR HIGHWAY

## INTRODUCTION

The Cassiar follows a proposed route for the Alcan highway that wasn't chosen back during World War II. When the decision was made to build a highway to Alaska there was fear that the Cassiar route was too close to the coast and therefore might be in danger from the Japanese. Because the Cassiar Highway wasn't completed until 1972 it is the newest route to Alaska and therefore something of an adventure. Portions of the road remain unpaved and fuel and supply stops can be far apart. On the other hand, wildlife is sometimes more plentiful and the scenery is great!

### Highlights

Just 62 scenic kilometers (38 miles) west of the Cassiar Highway are the coastal towns of **Stewart, British Columbia** and **Hyder, Alaska**. There's a drive-up glacier en route (the **Bear Glacier**) and when you reach the coast you'll find two entirely different kinds of towns: orderly Canadian Stewart and the tiny Alaskan bush town of Hyder. Even better, just outside Hyder when the fish are running is one of the better places to see bears in all of Alaska. The road to Stewart and Hyder is excellent, don't miss this side trip.

### The Road

The Cassiar Highway runs 720 kilometers (446 miles) north through the wilderness from the small town of Kitwanga on the Yellowhead Highway (Hwy. 16) to join the Alaska Highway near Watson Lake in the Yukon Territory. It is a good alternate route to the Alaska Highway, from Prince George the distance to the

Alaska border is 124 miles shorter via the Cassiar than via the Alaska Highway from Dawson Creek. If you drive the Cassiar to Alaska you will still drive much of the Alaska Highway, the two roads join near Watson Lake.

The Cassiar is now paved most of the way but there are several unpaved stretches north of the cutoff to Stewart and Hyder, they total about 131 kilometers (80 miles). The condition of these gravel stretches varies, when we last traveled them in 1997 it was poor with vehicle speeds limited to about 25 MPH at times. They were soon behind us, however, and the uncrowded and scenic nature of the route more than compensates for the few hours of gravel. Many truckers now use the Cassiar rather than the longer and therefore slower Alaska Highway so it is clear that the Cassiar is a viable alternate to the southern portion of the Alaska highway.

The Cassiar remains less traveled than the Alaska Highway and has fewer service stops. You should be well prepared when traveling and plan ahead, don't run out of gas or forget to bring a spare tire.

Distance and location markings along the Cassiar are in kilometers. Posts are placed every 5 kilometers. The kilometer posts are not necessarily accurate, they have not always been corrected for mileage changes due to road straightening. Campground locations in this book are based upon the kilometer posts. They start at the junction with the Yellowhead Highway in the south and increase heading north.

### Fishing

The Cassiar Highway passes over or along many rivers, lakes and streams. Many of them offer excellent fishing. Take the time to stop and give a few a try. Several of the campgrounds listed in this section are on lakes with fishing possibilites. See the individual campground listings for more information. As always, don't hesitate to ask the locals for fishing tips.

### Wildlife Viewing

One of the best reasons to visit Hyder is to see the bears. When the salmon are running in August there are a lot of them around, both blacks and grizzlies. The best place to see them is at **Fish Creek**, a 5 Km (3 Miles) drive on a good gravel road on the far side of Hyder.

The northern section of the Cassiar also offers wildlife-viewing possibilities. We've often seen stone sheep near the road near Km 615 (Mile 376), and if you are traveling in the early spring you may see woodland caribou along the section of road between Dease Lake and the Alaska Highway.

# THE ROUTES, TOWNS, AND CAMPGROUNDS

### FROM YELLOWHEAD HIGHWAY JUNCTION TO THE MEZIADIN LAKE JUNCTION
### (97 miles)

The Cassiar Highway leaves the Yellowhead highway some 501 kilometers (307 miles) west of Prince George and 243 kilometers (149 miles) east of Prince Rupert. It immediately crosses the Skeena River Bridge and passes by the small town of Kitwanga.

Kitwanga is the home of the **Kitwanga Fort National Historic Site** and has an RV park and a very small village campground.

From Kitwanga the road runs north through gently rolling scenic country with a few lakes to big Meziadin Lake and its provincial campground at Km 155 (Mile 96). The cutoff to Stewart and Hyder is at Km 156 (Mile 97).

### Campgrounds
### Yellowhead Highway Junction to the Meziadin Lake Junction

✦ CASSIAR RV PARK
   Address: P.O. Box 301, Kitwanga, B.C.
   V0J 2A0, Canada
   Telephone and Fax: (250) 849-5799
   Price: Medium

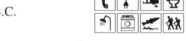

*GPS Location: N 55° 06' 49.0", W 128° 01' 57.5"*

This RV park is the first of a thin line of campgrounds along the Cassiar as you are heading north. It has probably the nicest facilities of them all and is especially popular with folks arriving from the north. Arriving here feels like arriving back in civilization.

The campground has at least 25 full-hookup spaces and additional sites with partial or no hookups. Many are large pull-throughs. There is well-clipped grass separating the sites. There are also some tent sites. Restroom, shower, and laundry facilities are first-rate. There's a dump station and a pressure vehicle wash.

From the Cassiar highway at Km 4 (Mile 2.5) drive .6 kilometer (.4 miles) west on Barcalow Rd. The campground is on the left.

✦ KITWANGA CENTENNIAL PARK
   Location: Across from the Tempo gas station
   on Kitwanga Valley Rd.
   Price: Donation

*GPS Location: N 55° 06' 44.2", W 128° 01' 25.7"*

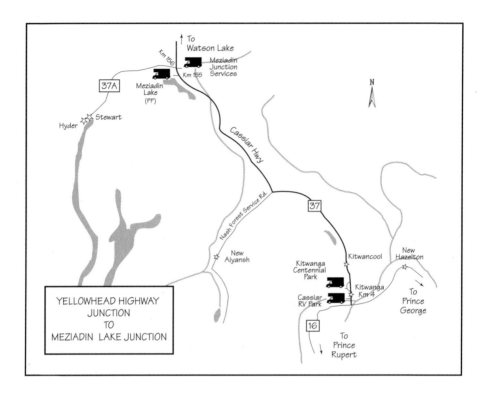

This is a simple village-run campground in Kitwanga. There are 12 small back-in sites in a grove of trees with no utilities. Outhouses are provided, they are in poor condition.

Easiest access is from Km 4.2 (Mile 2.6) of the Cassiar. Follow Kitwanga Valley Road for .6 kilometer (.4 mile) to the Tempo service station, the campground is across the street. Campground maintenance contributions are accepted at the service station.

✦ MEZIADIN LAKE PROVINCIAL PARK
(B.C. GOVERNMENT)
·    Location: Km 155 (Mile 95) of the Cassiar Highway
Price: Low

*GPS Location: N 56° 05' 16.7", W 129° 18' 19.3"*

Meziadin Lake campground is located on the shores of huge Meziadin Lake near the junction where the Stewart/Hyder road meets the Cassiar. This is also very near the point where you will have a chance to experience your first gravel if you are traveling north. The lake has good Dolly Varden and rainbow trout fishing and the campground has a boat ramp. Bears are common at this campground so don't leave food outside your rig and dispose of garbage properly.

There are now 62 spaces at Meziadin Lake with many along the lake. The remaining sites are above and behind the lakefront ones, most of these have views. Facilities include the boat ramp, picnic tables, outhouses and a well for drinking water.

The campground is located west of Highway 37 near Km 155 (Mile 95).

✦ MEZIADIN JUNCTION SERVICES
    Address: Box 100, Stewart, BC V0T 1W0, Canada
    Telephone: (250) 636-9240
    Price: Medium

*GPS Location: N 56° 06' 02.7", W 129° 18' 21.8"*

This roadhouse-style operation offers gas, repairs, a restaurant, a laundromat and RV spaces. The RV sites are basic but functional. There are at least 30 back-in sites with electricity, water and sewer hookups. Showers are available at a bunkhouse. There is a dump station.

The campground is located at Km 156 (Mile 96) of the Cassiar. It is at the junction with the 65-kilometer (40-mile) road to Stewart and Hyder on the coast.

## STEWART AND HYDER
Population Stewart 1,000, Hyder 100, Elevation sea level

The 65 kilometer (40-mile) road that descends from the Cassiar Highway down to Stewart and Hyder on the coast is one of the most scenic in British Columbia. The entire distance is paved and grades are no problem for even the largest rigs. At about Kilometer 24 (Mile 15) is an overlook with excellent views of the **Bear Glacier** just across the valley. Near the coast the highway threads its way through Stewart, laid out in an organized grid pattern, and then follows the shore of the **Portland Canal**, a huge fjord, to the border and little Hyder. There is no U.S. border post going into Hyder but there is a new Canadian post when you return to Stewart.

Much larger Stewart with its paved streets is the best place for purchasing supplies and has a gas station and decent-sized grocery store. There is also a town dump station. Funky Hyder is more interesting with gravel streets, several bars and souvenir stores and an excellent bear-viewing area in August during the chum (dog) and pink salmon run on **Fish Creek** about 3 miles (5 km) outside town.

Hyder is an Alaska State Ferry stop. In 1997 British Columbian fishermen blockaded an Alaska State Ferry in Prince Rupert which is the southern end of most Alaska ferry runs. Alaskan politicians talked about abandoning Prince Rupert for Hyder. Both provide excellent access to the road system. The problem is that Hyder is well off the inside passage ferry routes and a longer ferry run than Prince Rupert. The narrow Portland Canal providing water access to Hyder is about 90 miles long.

## Stewart and Hyder Campgrounds

✦ Lions Rainey Creek Municipal Campground
   Address: P.O. Box 306, Stewart, B.C.
   VOT 1WO, Canada
   Telephone: (250) 636-2537 Fax: (250) 636-2668
   Price: Medium

*GPS Location: N 55° 56' 17.1", W 129° 59' 59.5"*

This is the most popular campground in Stewart/Hyder. It was originally started by the local Lion's Club and now is run by the chamber of commerce. The many campers traveling down to this campground each summer are a big boost to the local economy. The office people are excellent sources of information about the area.

The campground has just over 100 sites. More than half of them have electricity, some 15-amp and some 30-amp. One water fill station services the campground, there is a dump station but when we visited it was not in use. Campers were using a station provided by the city several blocks away. Restrooms are in a cement block building and are well-maintained and clean. Stewart's downtown area is within walking distance.

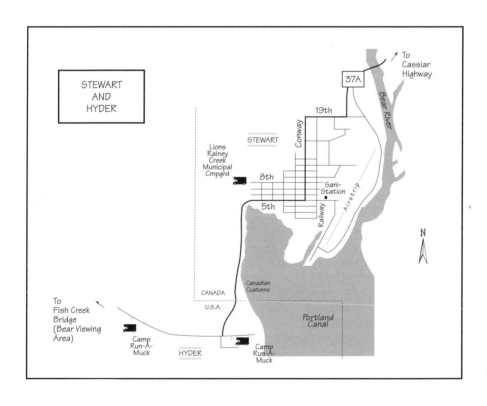

ENTERING HYDER

As you enter downtown Stewart watch for 8th. Turn right and follow this street to where it ends against the mountain. That's where the campground entrance is located.

✦ CAMP RUN-A-MUCK
    Address: 1001 Premier Avenue, Hyder, AK 99923
    Telephone: (250) 636-2486 or (888) 393-1199
    Fax: (250) 636-9003
    Price: Medium
        *GPS Location: N 55° 55' 09.5", W 130° 01' 58.0"*

It is now possible to find a decent campsite in Hyder. The new Camp Run-A-Muck, really two campgrounds, has both tent sites and pull-through RV sites with full hook-ups.

After crossing the border into Hyder you will come to a T in the road. Just half a block or so to the left is the Sealaska Inn. You can check into either campground in the bar. Just to the left of the hotel is the tent-camping area. It has it's own newish laundromat and shower building.

If you had turned right at the T and driven about a half mile you would have come to the RV camping area. It adjoins the road out to Fish Creek (the local bear-watching area). There are 38 sites, 36 with 30-amp service and two with 50-amp. Most sites are pull-throughs, all have electric and water service, some have sewer. There is a dump station and this campground also has a new laundromat and shower building. The entire camping area is a bare gravel pad next to the road but there is little traffic and lots of maneuvering room.

## FROM THE MEZIADIN LAKE JUNCTION TO THE ALASKA HIGHWAY
### (350 miles)

Almost immediately after leaving the Meziadin Junction the nicely paved highway turns to gravel. This road can be fine and allow speeds of 40 MPH and up, or it can have potholes and washboards that mean speeds down to 25 MPH if you want to keep the cabinets on the walls. Fortunately the gravel sections only total about 80 miles and end near Iskut, about 150 miles to the north.

There are really only a few small population centers along this section. One is little Iskut (population about 300) at Km 406 (Mile 249) and the other Dease Lake at Km 488 (Mile 299). Iskut sits between the **Spatsizi Wilderness Provincial Park** to the east of the highway and **Mount Edziza Provincial Park** to the west, both are becoming popular wilderness destinations and along the highway are a string of lakes that are popular for fishing and canoeing.

The community of Dease Lake marks the junction with a cutoff to Telegraph Creek on the Stikine River. The original route into the Cassiar area was along this road from Telegraph Creek, the Stikine is a navigable river and was traveled by large sternwheelers almost to Telegraph Creek from the mouth near Wrangell, Alaska. Now the 70 mile-long gravel road is used to go the other way, it is suitable for small rigs only and is a bit of an expedition. Check in Dease Lake about road conditions. Telegraph Creek has a population of about 300.

## Campgrounds
## Meziadin Lake Junction to the Alaska Highway

✦ WILLOW RIDGE RESORT
    Address: P.O. Box 99, Iskut, B.C. V0J 1K0, Canada
    Telephone: (250) 234-3705
    Price: Medium

*GPS Location: N 57° 26' 21.8", W 130° 13' 17.5"*

This little campground sites on a ridge well above the highway. There are about 20 sites, 6 are pull-throughs with electrical, sewer, and water hookups. The others are a mix of pull-throughs and back-in sites with no utility hookups. There are also tent camping areas. Sites are set in trees and are decently separated. Showers are available and there is a laundromat and small store.

Watch for the entrance road to the resort leading to the east from Km 353 (Mile 216) of the Cassiar Highway. The decent road leads a short distance to the top of the ridge and the resort.

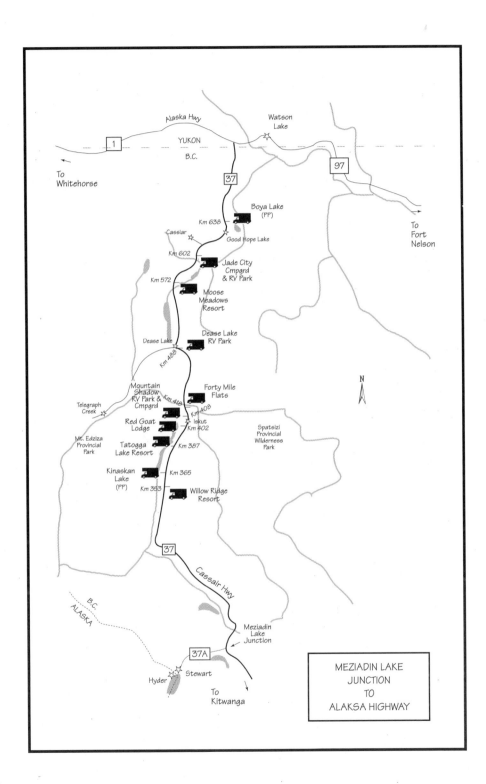

Alaska Hwy

Watson Lake

1  YUKON

B.C.

To Whitehorse

37

To Fort Nelson

97

Boya Lake (PP)

Km 638

Cassiar

Good Hope Lake

Km 602

Jade City Cmpgrd & RV Park

Km 572

Moose Meadows Resort

Dease Lake

Dease Lake RV Park

Km 488

Mountain Shadow RV Park & Cmpgrd

Km 416

Forty Mile Flats

Telegraph Creek

Km 408

Red Goat Lodge

Iskut
Km 402

Spatsizi Provincial Wilderness Park

Mt. Edziza Provincial Park

Tatogga Lake Resort

Km 387

Kinaskan Lake (PP)

Km 365

Km 353

Willow Ridge Resort

N

37

Cassair Hwy

B.C.
ALASKA

Meziadin Lake Junction

37A

Hyder    Stewart

To Kitwanga

MEZIADIN LAKE
JUNCTION
TO
ALAKSA HIGHWAY

✦ Kinaskan Lake Provincial Park
   (B.C. Government)
      Location: Km 365 (Mile 225) Cassiar Highway
      Price: Low

*GPS Location: N 57° 31' 46.9", W 130° 10' 59.5"*

Kinaskan Lake is a beautiful lakeside campground with much more separation and privacy than is found at the next lakeside park to the south - Meziadin Lake. Rainbow trout fishing in the large lake is an attraction here (during late summer) as is the Mowdade Trail to volcanic Mt. Edziza Park to the west. Some visitors even swim in the lake. The last time we visited the campground was full, there was a large caravan from the states occupying most of the sites.

The campground has 50 spaces, many of them quite large, and also many along the lake. All have the customary picnic table and fire pit. The campground has outhouses, a water pump, free firewood, and a boat launching ramp.

✦ Tatogga Lake Resort
      Address: Box 59, Iskut, B.C. V0J 1K0, Canada
      Telephone: (250) 234-3526
      Price: Medium

*GPS Location: N 57° 42' 44.0", W 129° 59' 36.8"*

This establishment seems less like a resort than a traditional roadhouse. The log restaurant building is tastefully decorated with moose antlers. They also sell gas. Hiking, fishing, and canoeing excursions are available, including fly-in trips. Behind the buildings located along the highway is a large field with campsites that slopes down toward (but not all the way to) Tatogga Lake.

The campground itself has about 40 sites, most of them offer 15-amp electricity and water hookups. Hot showers are available and there is a laundromat and a dump station.

The resort is located on the west side of the Cassiar Highway near Km 387 (Mile 237).

✦ Red Goat Lodge
      Address: Box 101, Iskut, B.C. V0J 1K0, Canada
      Telephone: (250) 234-3261 or (888) RED-GOAT
      Price: Medium

*GPS Location: N 57° 48' 55.2", W 129° 57' 39.3"*

The Red Goat Lodge is a bed and breakfast and hostel with a campground next to the lake out front. The campground was being improved when we visited in 1997, electricity was being installed. Canoes are available for rent, guided canoe tours can be arranged, and fishing on Eddontenajon Lake out front is decent in July and August.

The campground at the lodge has about 18 sites, several are along the lake. Electricity was being installed when we visited. Access for larger rigs is tight here, leave your big rig on the highway and walk down to take a look if you are thinking of stopping. Showers and a laundromat are available.

Watch for the sign and driveway on the west side of the Cassiar Highway near Km 402 (Mile 246) about 3 kilometers (2 miles) south of Iskut.

✦  MOUNTAIN SHADOW RV PARK AND CAMPGROUND
    Address: Box 3, Iskut, B.C. V0J 1K0, Canada
    Telephone: Summer (250) 234-3333,
    Winter (415) 897-4445
    Price: Medium

*GPS Location: N 57° 51' 34.3", W 130° 00' 28.7"*

When we're looking for a campground in this section of the Cassiar we head for the Mountain Shadow RV Park. It's a meticulously laid out and maintained facility with both large pull-through sites and secluded back-ins. Views to the west are spectacular and a short path takes you to a small lake which offers rainbow trout fishing and bird watching.

The campground has two different camping areas. For large rigs there are 10 pull-throughs with lots of room and water and electricity hook-ups. Smaller rigs and tent campers will appreciated the 10 back-in spaces in trees, three with electrical hook-ups. Showers are available, there are flush toilets, and there is a dump station.

A wide and well-maintained entrance road leads down a gentle slope to the campground from near Km 408 (Mile 250) of the Cassiar Highway. Watch for the sign on the west side of the highway.

✦  FORTY MILE FLATS
    Address: Iskut, B.C. V0J 1K0, Canada
    Price: Medium

*GPS Location: N57° 56' 07.9", W130° 02' 35.0"*

This is a roadhouse-style facility with a restaurant, gas station, garage, and campground in the trees to the rear. There are about 11 sites, some pull-throughs, on soft gravel. Most have electrical hookups and there is a dump station. Picnic tables are provided and hot showers are available.

The facility is located on the East side of the Cassiar Highway near Km 418 (Mile 256).

✦  DEASE LAKE R.V. PARK
    Address: P.O. Box 129, Dease Lake, B.C.
    V0C 1L0, Canada
    Telephone: (250) 771-4666, Fax (250) 771-4667
    Price: Medium

*GPS Location: N 58° 25' 56.8", W 129° 59' 09.5"*

STONE SHEEP LEAD THE PILOT CAR

Large RV owners will appreciate this campground. Although it is little more than a large gravel lot filled with RV sites there is lots of room, full hookups, and the surface is solid and well drained.

There are about 25 sites, all have electricity and water and half also have sewer hookups. The new tiled bathrooms have flush toilets and showers and a new RV pressure wash is being installed.

The campground is located on the East side of the Cassiar Highway near the Telegraph Creek Road junction and Dease Lake at Km 488 (Mile 299).

✦  MOOSE MEADOWS RESORT
      Address: P.O. Box 299, Dease Lake, B.C.
      V0C 1L0, Canada
      Price: Low

*GPS Location: N 59° 04' 10.6", W 129° 43' 09.2"*

Moose Meadows is a rustic resort with friendly management in a beautiful location on the shore of Cotton Lake. Canoes are available for exploring and fishing. If you feel like going on a longer expedition shuttle service is available for Dease River floats of up to 180 miles.

The facilities at Moose Meadows are more appropriate to tent campers and self-contained rigs than to RVers looking for hookup sites. There are several very nice parking spots on the shore of the lake and others nearby. There is no dump station and no electricity available. The campground has only outhouses but does have showers.

Moose Meadows is located just off the highway near Km 572 (Mile 323) of the Cassiar Highway. This is about 50 miles north of the Dease Lake junction.

✦  JADE CITY CAMPGROUND AND RV PARK
      Address: P.O. Box A8, Jade City, Cassiar, B.C.
      V0C 1E0, Canada
      Price: Low

     *GPS Location: N 59° 14' 50.7", W 129° 38' 52.4"*

Jade City is a popular stop although there's little here except a gas station and a jade and jewelry store. The store offers a good selection of jade carvings and jewelry and a nice little campground next door. It will remind you of a government campground, the amenities are similar. It has about 30 back-in spaces in a grove of trees. There are no hookups but there are outhouses. No showers are available.

Jade City is on the east side of the Cassiar Highway near Km 602 (Mile 369).

✦  BOYA LAKE PROVINCIAL PARK (B.C. GOVERNMENT)
      Location: Km 638 (Mile 394) of
      the Cassiar Highway
      Price: Low

     *GPS Location: N 59° 21' 52.2", W 129° 08' 44.6"*

The farthest north provincial park campground along the Cassiar is on the shores of crystal clear Boya Lake. On a clear day this lake is a beautiful bright blue, great for photos. Unfortunately the fishing is very poor in the lake. The nearby Dease River does have grayling.

The campground has about 44 sites. Some are along the lake, a few are pull-throughs, and some are tent sites. All sites have picnic tables and fire pits, there are outhouses, free firewood, and a boat ramp. There's a hiking trail along the lake shore and to the river.

The 2.4-kilometer (1.5-mile) entrance road heads east from near Km 638 (Mile 391) of the Cassiar Highway. This is about 93 kilometers (57 miles) south of the junction of the Cassiar and the Alcan.

## CASSIAR HIGHWAY DUMP STATIONS

Most of the dump stations (called sani dumps in Canada) are in private campgrounds. We've noted those campgrounds offering dump stations by a symbol, expect to pay a fee if you aren't staying at the campground, and sometimes if you are.

There is one important exception. The town of **Stewart** has a free city-operated dump station with excellent access. See the Stewart map in this book for the location.

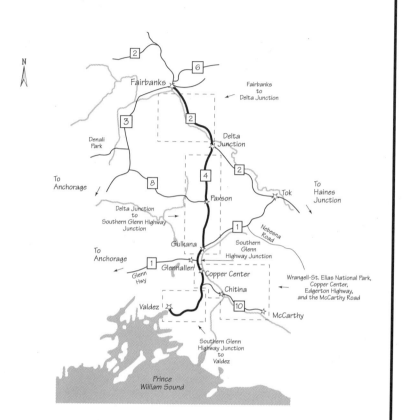

N

2

6

Fairbanks

Fairbanks
to
Delta Junction

3

2

Denali
Park

Delta
Junction

8

4

2

To
Anchorage

Paxson

Tok

To
Haines
Junction

Delta Junction
to
Southern Glenn Highway
Junction

1

Nebesna
Road

Gulkana

Southern
Glenn
Highway Junction

To
Anchorage

1

Glennallen

Copper Center

Wrangell-St. Elias National Park,
Copper Center,
Edgerton Highway,
and the McCarthy Road

Glenn
Hwy

Chitina

Valdez

10

McCarthy

Southern Glenn
Highway Junction
to
Valdez

Prince
William Sound

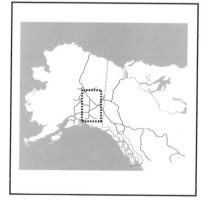

# THE RICHARDSON HIGHWAY

# CHAPTER

. . . . . . . . . . 6

# THE RICHARDSON HIGHWAY

## INTRODUCTION

The Richardson is Alaska's oldest major highway. It runs from tidewater at Valdez to Fairbanks in the interior. The Richardson is also one of the state's most scenic highways with natural scenery including distant mountain peaks, wide interior valleys, overhanging glaciers, and mountain passes.

In this guide we'll cover the Richardson from north to south. You are likely to travel only segments of the Richardson. If you've driven the Alaska Highway from the south you'll probably join it at Delta Junction near Mile 266 and drive north to Fairbanks. Alternately, you may drive the Richardson for only a few miles between the two segments of the Glenn Highway on your way to Anchorage. If you decide to visit Valdez you'll drive quite a bit of the Richardson, including some of its most scenic sections.

In this book we'll cover the Richardson from north to south. This may seem strange at first. After all, the highway mileposts go from south to north. We think most people will first drive most of this road from north to south so that's the way we laid things out.

### Highlights

The cities at each end of the Richardson, **Fairbanks** and **Valdez**, are two of the most popular destinations in the state. They're very different, of course, but most people want to see them both.

The **Trans-Alaska Oil Pipeline** has been a top Alaska news story for many years.

You'll have lots of chances to see it while driving the Richardson since the pipeline parallels the highway for most of its length. There will be times when you can't see the pipeline from the highway but it is usually not far away. There are viewing areas and displays at Mile 215, Mile 88, and Mile 65. You'll probably also spot Pump Station 9 at Mile 258, Pump Station 10 at Mile 219, and Pump Station 12 at Mile 65. It is sometimes possible to tour Pump Station 9, call ahead for reservations at (907) 869-3270.

The Richardson began as a gold rush trail to Eagle, Alaska even before Fairbanks was founded. Very soon, however, most people traveling along it were following a new left fork toward Fairbanks. In 1910 the road was upgraded to allow the use of automobiles. Roadhouses were built along the road at approximately 10 mile intervals (one day's travel before automobiles) by private individuals. Most roadhouses disappeared but a few remain. **Rika's Roadhouse** at Mile 275 just north of Delta Junction is now a state park and makes an interesting stop. Another that is still standing and operating is the **Copper Center Lodge**, in Copper Center just off the main highway near Mile 101.

The Richardson will give you several opportunities to take a good look at glaciers. The best of the bunch is the **Worthington Glacier** at Mile 30 just north of Thompson Pass. You can walk right up to it or take a hike along a lateral moraine to overlook it.

As Denali National Park gets more and more crowded the National Park Service would like us to visit Alaska's other national park with road access. This is the **Wrangell-St. Elias National Park**. Unfortunately, opportunities for access to Wrangell-St. Elias National Park are limited. There are two driving routes, the Nabesna Road (from Mile 60 of the Tok Cutoff - See Chapter 7 - The Glenn Highway) and the Edgerton Highway and McCarthy Road (from Mile 83 of the Richardson) but both are rough and not really suitable for larger RV's. We cover the Edgerton Highway and McCarthy Road in more detail later in the chapter.

 **The Road**

The Richardson Highway was once the major route into the interior of the state. Until the Alaska Railroad from Seward to Fairbanks was finished in 1923 the choice was between the Richardson Highway and river boat down the Yukon. Much later, in 1971, the Parks Highway opened. Today most Anchorage to Fairbanks traffic follows the Parks so the Richardson is not really heavily traveled.

All of the Richardson is paved. Most is pretty good road but not up to the same standards as the much newer Parks Highway. There are some sections of road that have permafrost problems. Most of the wear and tear of the pipeline construction years along this route has been repaired.

The Richardson Highway, from Fairbanks to Valdez, is 368 miles long. Mile markers along the highway count up from just outside Valdez to Fairbanks. We'll travel in the opposite direction in this chapter, from Fairbanks to Valdez.

## Fishing

In Alaska timing is an important part of catching fish, particularly salmon. You can't catch fish if they aren't there. Salmon arrive in runs and may be entirely absent the rest of the time. For timing purposes there are two regions traversed by the Richardson Highway: the Tanana Valley and Prince William Sound/Copper Valley. In general the Tanana fish arrive later because they have farther to travel. In the Tanana Valley July is the king month, in the Copper Valley they show up in the middle of June while in salt water it's early June. Copper Valley reds are present from late June to the end of August, Copper valley silvers are present from the middle of August until the middle of September. In Valdez expect pinks in July and August with a July peak and silvers just a little later with an August peak.

Many of the good fishing locations near Fairbanks are actually north of town. See Chapter 10 - North of Fairbanks for information about them.

From Fairbanks to Paxson most of the fishing along the Richardson Highway is lake fishing. A small boat is a big help. Try the **Chena Lakes** (Mile 347) for rainbows and silvers, **Harding Lake** (Mile 321) for lake trout and northern pike, **Lost Lake** (off a side road at Mile 306) for rainbows, **Birch Lake** (Mile 306) for rainbows, **Quartz Lake** (Mile 278) for rainbows, **Fielding Lake** (Mile 200) for lake trout and grayling, and **Summit Lake** (Mile 195) for grayling and lake trout.

At Paxson (Mile 185) the Denali Highway heads west toward Denali Park and the Parks Highway. Along the Denali try fishing **Ten Mile Lake** (Mile 10) for lake trout and grayling, **Denali-Clearwater Creek** (Mile 18) for grayling, the **Tangle Lakes** (at about Mile 21) for grayling and lake trout, **Clearwater Creek** (Mile 56) for grayling, and **Brushkana Creek** (Mile 104) for grayling.

Back on the Richardson Highway and heading south from Paxson try **Paxson Lake** (Mile 175) for grayling and lake trout; **Dick Lake** (Mile 173) for grayling; **Meiers Lake** (Mile 170) for grayling; **Gillespie Lake** (Mile 168) for grayling; **Sourdough Creek** (Mile 147) for grayling in the creek and also access to the Gulkana River; **trails to the Gulkana River** (Mile 141, 136, and 129) for kings, reds, rainbows, and grayling; **Bear Creek** (Mile 127) for grayling; the **Gulkana River mouth** (Mile 123 with a 1.5 mile trail to mouth) for kings, reds, grayling, and rainbows; the **Klutina River** at Copper Center for kings, reds, grayling and Dollies; the **Squirrel Creek gravel pit** (Mile 80) for grayling and rainbows; the **Little Tonsina River** (Mile 65) for Dollies; **Worthington Lake** (Mile 28) for rainbows; **Blueberry Lake** (Mile 24) for rainbows and grayling; and **Robe River** (Mile 5) for Dollies and reds using flies.

At Mile 83 the Edgerton Highway leads east to Chitina, the Copper River, the McCarthy Road, and eventually, McCarthy. The Copper River near Chitina is the scene of one of Alaska's most interesting fisheries, the salmon dip-net fishery. It is open only to Alaska residents and special permits are required. Big nets with handles over 20 feet long are used to catch fish in water that is just too silt-laden to be fished using other methods. It's fun to just watch. Other fishing possibilities along the road are **Liberty Falls**

(Mile 25) for grayling, **Second Lake** (Mile 36) for rainbows and grayling, **First Lake** (Mile 37) for rainbows and grayling, **Chitina Lake** (Mile 39) for grayling, the **Copper River** (Mile 1 McCarthy Road) for red salmon and king salmon, **Strelna Creek** (Mile 15, McCarthy Road) for Dollies, **Lou's Lake** (Mile 26, McCarthy Road) for silvers and grayling, and **Long Lake** (Mile 45, McCarthy Road) for grayling, lake trout, silvers, and Dollies.

**Valdez** is the top sport fishing destination on Prince William Sound. This is a great place to join a charter operator for a day of salmon fishing. Valdez also has some of the best and easiest beach fishing for pinks and silvers in Alaska at **Allison Point** near the **Solomon Gulch Hatchery** on Dayville Road. There are three different fishing derbies with prizes in Valdez. Dates vary slightly from year to year but the Halibut Derby runs all summer, the Pink Salmon Derby is in July, and the Silver Salmon Derby is in August. Check out the rules before you go fishing, you must follow them to win.

A large proportion of the campgrounds along the Richardson are in locations that offer fishing possibilities. This is a little surprising since most people don't think of this area of Alaska as being a top fishing destination.

### Boating, Rafting, Canoeing, and Kayaking

When Fairbanks residents head out for a day of swimming, water skiing, and fun on the water they generally end up at **Harding Lake** (Mile 321, Richardson Highway) or **Birch Lake** (Mile 306, Richardson Highway). The **Chena Lakes Recreation Area** (Mile 347, Richardson Highway) is dedicated to non-powered boats and aquatic sports. North of Fairbanks there are several possibilities for river float and canoe trips, see Chapter 10 - North of Fairbanks, for information.

Between Delta Junction and the Gakona Junction there are two popular floatable rivers—the north-flowing **Delta River** and the south-flowing **Gulkana River**. Both are designated Wild and Scenic Rivers and are administered by the BLM (Glennallen District Office, P.O. Box 147, Glennallen, AK 99588; 907 822-3217). A Delta River trip starts by crossing the Tangle Lakes from a put in at the Tangle Lakes Campground at Mile 21 of the Denali Highway. From the lakes the float is mainly Class II with a portage around a falls. The first takeout is at Mile 212 of the Richardson Highway. This trip is suitable for canoes, kayaks, and rafts. The **Gulkana River** has several different forks and possible routes, but the most popular float is from Paxson Lake (Mile 175, Richardson Highway) to takeouts at Sourdough Campground (Mile 148, Richardson Highway), Poplar Grove (Mile 137, Richardson Highway with 1-mile trail) or the Richardson Highway Bridge (Mile 127, Richardson Highway). You can also put in at Sourdough to avoid the worst stretches of whitewater. Water is mostly Class II and a portage is required around Canyon Rapids. The Gulkana is a well-known fishing stream offering excellent red and king fishing during their respective runs. Rafts, kayaks, and canoes (only for good canoers) are suitable. Both of these rivers have long stretches that are remote from road access and can be dangerous. If you plan to float them prepare yourself with adequate research and make sure you have the proper experience and equipment.

Several large lakes along this stretch of road are also popular with boaters. They are **Fielding Lake** (Mile 200), **Summit Lake** (Mile 195), and **Paxson Lake** (Mile 175).

Visitors to the Wrangell-St. Elias National Park will find that commercial operators offer whitewater rafting on rivers in the park including the **Chitina River**, the **Kennicott River**, and the **Nizina River**. Some of these rivers can be pretty challenging and entrance and exit points are often not obvious or easy to reach. Commercially guided tours are the best way to float these rivers.

Valdez sits on the shore of the Valdez Arm which leads out into **Prince William Sound**. These waters are some of the best in the world for ocean kayaking. Possible routes are unlimited and range from a day trip on the Arm to something much longer, say a 150-mile crossing to Whittier. Several state marine parks with tent campsites are within a day's paddle of Valdez. Use of a charter vessel to drop you far out in the sound can save many days of paddling if you want to explore some of the more remote reaches of the sound.

### Hiking and Mountain Biking

Most good hikes in the Fairbanks area are north of town. See Chapter 10 - North of Fairbanks for information about them. One exception is Creamers Field, formally known as **Creamer's Field Migratory Waterfowl Refuge**. The refuge is located on the northern outskirts of Fairbanks along College Road. There is a 2-mile guided nature trail with observation platforms. The best months for observing waterfowl are April, May, and August.

The entire **Denali Highway** has become a popular mountain bike route. 114 miles of gravel are hard going on a touring bike, but mountain bikes have no problems and traffic is minimal. There are also some high-country hiking routes from the highway. This is a popular hunting area and there are many off-road vehicle trails, many are not very good for hiking because the wheeled vehicles tend to tear up the tundra leaving a muddy mess. Some of the best hikes are away from the trails. The **Landmark Lake** hike from Mile 25 follows an old dirt road 2.4 miles to Landmark Gap Lake, you can catch grayling in the lake and hike the surrounding hills. The route in is suitable for hiking or mountain bikes. From Mile 37 just west of **Maclaren Summit** (4,086 ft.) you can hike north on an old vehicle trail through a region of small lakes and big views. Go as far as you want across the open tundra, the first part of the trail is fine for mountain bikes. Mountain bikers will also like the 12-mile **Maclaren River Road** heading north for 12 miles from Mile 43 to the Maclaren Glacier.

There are several decent trails in the Wrangell-St. Elias National Park accessible from the Edgerton Highway and the McCarthy Road. Two trails lead from the Nugget

Creek Road near Mile 13.5 of the McCarthy Road. **Dixie Pass** is an 11-mile strenuous back-packing trip that takes at least three days. Much of the route is not on well-defined trail, you must have good maps and route instructions before attempting it. The **Nugget Creek Trail** is easier to follow since it follows an old mining road. The 15-mile trail is also suitable for mountain bikes and leads to an old mining works and an unmaintained park cabin overlooking the Kuskulana Glacier.

At the end of the McCarthy Road there's a parking lot where you can camp in your RV or tent, from there you must either walk or hitch a ride to McCarthy (1 mile) and Kennicott (5 miles). A mountain bike comes in very handy here for transportation since you must cross a foot bridge to reach the towns from the parking lot. From Kennicott there are at least three trails for strenuous day hikes or easy overnighters: **Bonanza Mine Trail**, **Jumbo Mine Trail**, and **Root Glacier Trail**. Portions of these trails can be done on mountain bikes.

Mountain bikers might want to try the **Bernard Creek Trail** at Mile 79 of the Richardson. The BLM recommends this 15-mile road east to Kimball Pass and it looks good on the map. There's another similar road called the **Klutina Lake Trail** from about Mile 101 of the Copper Center Bypass section of the Richardson that goes east for 25 miles up the Klutina River to Klutina Lake.

At Mile 29 of the Richardson Highway is the **Worthington Glacier State Recreation Site**. There's an opportunity for a hike here, you can climb the lateral moraine and follow its summit above the glacier for views even better than those from the overlook.

In Valdez the most popular hike is probably the **Solomon Gulch Trail**. The trail starts across from the Solomon Gulch Fish Hatchery on Dayville Road. The 1.3-mile trail climbs steeply to the Solomon Creek power plant dam and offers great views of the town of Valdez across Port Valdez.

### Wildlife Viewing

Bird lovers will love the **Creamer's Field Migratory Waterfowl Refuge**. It is located just north of Fairbanks, there are nature trails and a visitor's center with displays and volunteers to answer questions and lead hikes. Spring and fall are the best times to visit because the area is full of migrating waterfowl. The visitor center telephone number is (907) 459-7213.

Almost **anywhere along the Richardson** you are likely to suddenly spot a moose, maybe when you least expect them. Keep your eyes peeled. Isolated caribou are also often spotted on portions of road passing through the Alaska Range. Also watch along streams for signs of beaver.

Bison were introduced into the Delta Junction area in 1928. They did well, today there are over 400 of them and there is an annual hunt to keep the numbers in check. The huge animals can be a problem, they love the barley that is grown by the farmers around Delta Junction and no fence seems to keep them out of the fields. The **Delta Junction State Bison Range** has been set aside for them but they tend to go where they want. In early summer you can often see them on the flats near the Delta River from viewpoints between Mile 265 and Mile 241. A pair of binoculars will help you spot them.

The **Denali Highway** is an excellent place to spot animals, perhaps because the country is so open and the traffic so sparse. The Nelchina Caribou herd is present during the fall. Caribou and grizzly bears tend to stick to the wide open areas, watch for moose and black bears where there are trees. It pays to stop occasionally and examine the open country with a pair of binoculars.

**Wrangell-St. Elias National Park** is accessible from the Richardson Highway by following the Edgerton Highway east to McCarthy. There's lots of game in this largest of U.S. national parks including Dall sheep, mountain goats, brown and black bear, moose, caribou, and even bison. Viewing the animals, however, isn't quite as easy as in Denali Park. There's no long road through the park with vistas in all directions as there is at Denali. Watch for animals along the McCarthy access road, you're likely to see a moose or two. To really see animals in this park, however, you need to get out and hike away from the roads or take a sightseeing flight.

In Valdez make sure to stop at the **Crooked Creek salmon spawning area** which is just outside town along the highway. From Valdez you can access the waterways of **Prince William Sound** on charter boats, cruise boats, ferries, or even with a kayak. The sound is home to Steller sea lions, seals, sea otters, orcas, gray and humpback whales, eagles, and a virtually unlimited number of marine birds, shore birds, raptors, and ducks.

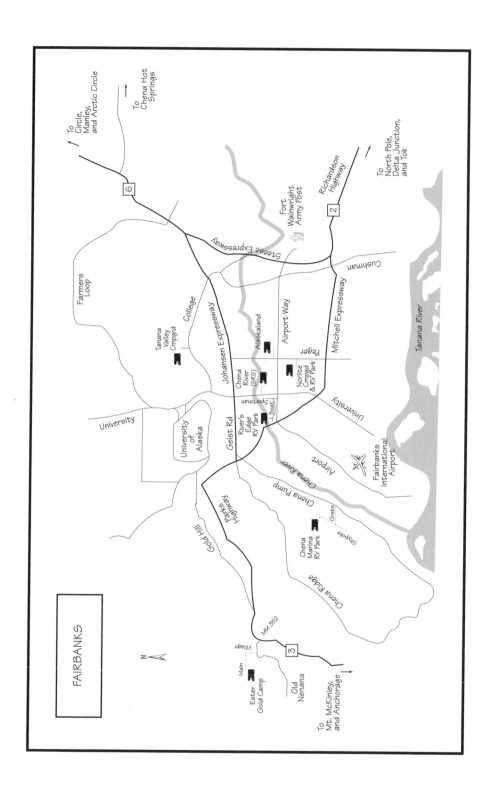

# THE ROUTES, TOWNS, AND CAMPGROUNDS

## FAIRBANKS
### Population 33,000, Elevation 440 feet

Fairbanks may be only Alaska's second largest town but there is no doubt that the interior city is a more popular destination among Alaska Highway RVers than much larger Anchorage. This may be because Fairbanks appreciates its RVing visitors. There are lots of things to do in the area and many good RV parks. Fairbanks serves as a gateway to both the Denali Park area (121 miles south on the Parks Highway) and the roads extending to the north, one as far as Prudhoe Bay (see Chapter 10 of this book). Fairbanks may also be more popular than Anchorage because its summer weather is much nicer. There's a lot less rain in the interior and evenings never really get dark because of the midnight sun.

Fairbanks is by far the older of the two largest Alaska cities. The town was founded in 1901 and soon became a supply center for nearby gold fields, gold continues to be mined in the area. Today Fairbanks is still a supply center, but now the area served includes most of interior Alaska and the North Slope.

You'll have no problem finding out about the available attractions in Fairbanks and the whole northern part of the state. The **Fairbanks Visitors Information Center** sits on the banks of the Chena River downtown near the corner of First and Cushman (550 First Avenue; 907 456-5774 or 800 327-5774). The **Alaska Public Lands Information Center** is nearby (250 Cushman Street, Fairbanks, AK 99701; 907 456-0527). All of the major commercial RV parks in town can set you up with commercial tour operators or give you suggestions for exploring on your own.

**Alaskaland**, the town's historical theme park, makes a good afternoon's destination that can easily stretch into the evening. On the grounds you'll find several museums, the stern wheel riverboat Nenana, historical displays, souvenir shops, a salmon bake restaurant and a even a musical comedy show.

After seeing the riverboat at Alaskaland you'll probably want to take a ride on one. The most popular attraction in Fairbanks has got to be the **Riverboat Discovery**. This sternwheeler makes twice daily trips down the Chena to the Tanana and is usually packed with visitors enjoying an extremely well-done trip including a stop at Old Chena Indian Village.

On the campus of the University of Alaska you'll find one of the most interesting museums in the state. The **Otto William Geist Museum** has displays about gold mining, natural history, the Alaska Highway, mastodons and dinosaurs, the northern lights, and lots more. You don't want to miss it! Nearby you'll find the University's **Georgeson Botanical Gardens**, these experimental gardens are a great place to see big vegetables and beautiful flowers.

A big part of the history of Fairbanks and Alaska is gold mining. Near Fairbanks are two areas that have been extensively mined using huge floating dredges that left rows and rows of gravel "tailing piles". Both have exhibits that are well worth visiting. North of town out the Steese Highway is the Goldstream area around the little town of Fox. There you'll find both **Dredge No. 8** and the **El Dorado Gold Mine**. Both are commercial operations with hefty entrance fees and both are well worth the money. West of Fairbanks along the Parks Highway is another region of tailing piles along Ester Creek. Here you'll find the **Ester Gold Camp**, another commercial operation best known for its Malamute Saloon but also offering a restaurant and RV parking.

Fairbanks has 3 golf courses: Chena Bend (907 353-6223) has 18 holes, Fairbanks Golf and Country Club (907 479-6555) and the North Star Golf Club (907 457-4653) both have 9 holes. All are open to the public.

## Fairbanks Campgrounds

✦ CHENA MARINA RV PARK
   Address: 1145 Shypoke Dr., Fairbanks, AK 99709
   Telephone: (907) 479-4653
   Price: High

*GPS Location: N 64° 49' 02.5", W 147° 54' 49.7"*

For aviation enthusiasts this is the best Fairbanks campground. The Chena Marina Campground is on the shore of the Chena Marina float-plane pond. Most good-weather days see a lot of takeoffs and landings.

The campground has about 45 sites, many are large pull-throughs. The majority of the sites have 30-amp electricity, water, and satellite-TV hookups although there are also a few full hook-up slots with sewer. The sites are very large with lots of grass separating them, there are picnic tables. Restrooms are individual rooms with toilet, sink and shower. There is a laundromat and comfortable indoor and outdoor lounge areas provide a place for trip planning and to watch TV. The campground has a dump station and water fill station. There is also a vehicle wash station. Campground staff is more than willing to help you arrange local tours and excursions. Fishing for Northern Pike in the float-plane pond is allowed. Reservations are recommended.

To get to the campground follow the Chena Pump Road for 2.8 miles from its intersection with the Parks Highway near the University. Turn right on Grebe Drive, then right again on Shypoke Dr. The campground will soon appear on your left.

✦ CHENA RIVER STATE RECREATION SITE
   Location: On the banks of the Chena River
   off University Ave.
   Price: Medium

*GPS Location: N 64° 50' 25.9", W 147° 48' 34.4"*

This is a state campground right in the middle of Fairbanks, it has a convenient location and is very popular. Two large supermarkets are within easy walking distance.

There are 58 long back-in sites well separated with trees and natural vegetation. There are also 5 tent sites. All have picnic tables and fire pits. There are flush toilets but not showers. The campground also has a boat launch and a dump station. There is a 5 day camping limit.

You will find the site on the east side of University Avenue just south of the bridge over the Chena River.

✦ RIVERS EDGE RV PARK & CAMPGROUND
    Address: 4140 Boat St., Fairbanks, AK 99709
    Telephone: (907) 474-0286 or (800) 770-3343
    Price: High

*GPS Location: N 64° 50' 21.8", W 147° 50' 00.9"*

One of the nicest and most popular campgrounds in Fairbanks is the Rivers Edge. It sits on the banks of the Chena River, has lots of grass and trees and a very helpful staff.

The campground has about 160 sites. There are a variety of types, full and partial hookups, pull-throughs with lots of room for big rigs, dry sites for vehicles and also tent sites. All have picnic tables. The restrooms offer flush toilets and free hot showers, there is a coin-op laundromat and a gift shop. There is also a vehicle wash station and dump and water-fill stations. Reservations are recommended.

The campground is located just off what most people now consider the major arterial in Fairbanks, Airport Way. Take Sportsman's Way across from the Fred Meyer store, immediately turn left on Boat Street, and then watch for the campground on the right.

✦ ALASKALAND
    Location: Just off Airport Way at Peger Road
    Price: Low

*GPS Location: N 64° 50' 14.6", W 147° 46' 35.60"*

The Alaskaland city-run theme park offers dry camping in its huge parking lot. Lots of people take them up on it. There are no hookups but there is a water-fill station. There is also a city dump station very nearby where Moore Rd. (just east of Alaskaland) meets 2nd Ave. Either chemical toilets are provided or you are allowed to use the restrooms inside the park which are open all night. Signs in the parking lot will tell you where to go to check in.

Alaskaland is centrally located just off Airport Way near the Peger Road intersection.

✦ NORLITE CAMPGROUND & RV PARK
  Address: 1660 Peger Road, Fairbanks, AK 99709
  Telephone: (907) 474-0206 or (800) 478-0206
  Fax: (907) 474-0992
  Internet: http://www.alaskaone.com/norlite
  Price: High

*GPS Location: N 64° 50' 02.0", W 147° 46' 49.2"*

The Norlite is the largest campground in Fairbanks, there are about 250 spaces here. This campground seems to be a little older than the others but the facilities are fine. There are a variety of site types: pull-throughs, back-in, full-hookup, partial hook-up, dry, and tent sites. They have picnic tables and many are set in trees. Restrooms have hot showers and there is a laundromat. There are also dump stations, a vehicle washing station, and a small gift shop with some groceries, tour ticket sales and tourist information,

To get to the campground follow Peger Road south from its intersection with Airport Way near Alaskaland. The campground is on the right about .2 mile south of the intersection.

✦ TANANA VALLEY CAMPGROUND
  Address: 1800 College Rd., Fairbanks, AK 99709
  Telephone: (907) 456-7956
  Price: Medium

*GPS Location: N 64° 51' 51.5", W 147° 45' 30.7"*

The Tanana Valley Fair is a popular area attraction during the first or second week of August. Don't try to stay in this campground that week, the place is probably a madhouse. At other times, however, the campground makes a convenient and pleasant base.

There are about 33 camping sites. They are set in a grove of trees and have pretty good separation. Provision has been made to provide electricity to 18 of the sites. The provision is very long electrical cords leading to a couple of outlet boxes, but it works. There are also some tent sites reserved for hikers and bikers. The campground has flush toilets, free hot showers, a dump station, and a coin-op laundry. There is a conscientious host at this campground and firewood for sale. There is convenient bus service along College Road to downtown and the college. The Creamer's Field Bird Sanctuary is also close by.

The campground is located at the Tanana Valley Fairgrounds on College Road. From the Parks Highway take the Geist Road exit and head east to University Ave., a distance of 1.5 miles. Turn left and drive north for .4 miles to College Road, turn right on College Rd. and drive .3 miles. You will see the campground on your left.

✦ ESTER GOLD CAMP
   Address: P.O. Box 109B, Ester, Alaska 99725
   Telephone: (907) 479-2500 or (800) 676-6925
   Price: Low

*GPS Location: N 64° 50' 44.9", W 148° 01' 18.2"*

The Ester Gold Camp (officially listed on the National Register of Historic Places as Ester Camp Historic District) is the restored town of Ester City. This gold camp had its heyday in the early 1900's, it has been restored and offers gold rush-style entertainment in the Malamute Saloon, a restaurant, a hotel, a gift shop, and most importantly, a small RV park.

There are 16 back-in sites on a gravel lot and three tent sites nearby, none of the sites has hookups. Restrooms and free showers are located in the bunkhouse. There are picnic tables but no fire pits. There is a dump station and potable water is available.

Ester Gold Camp is located just off the Parks Highway at Mile 352, about 6 miles from Fairbanks. Follow the signs west for a half mile to the camp.

## North Pole and Badger Road Campgrounds

✦ RIVERVIEW RV PARK
   Address: P.O. Box 72618, Fairbanks, AK 99705
   Telephone: (907) 488-6281 or (888) 488-6392
   Price: High

*GPS Location: N 64° 49' 57.1", W 147° 30' 55.9"*

The Riverview is a large campground with a quiet location along the Chena River several miles outside Fairbanks.

The campground has about 120 spaces, many are large pull-throughs. Full utility hookups are offered including cable-TV and spaces are separated by grass and some trees. Picnic tables are provided. Individual shower rooms provide privacy. The campground sits behind a gas station and convenience store with the same ownership and also has a restaurant, the Riverside Seafood Cookout, next to the river.

The Riverview is located on Badger Road. The best access route is from the Richardson Highway near Mile 357. Follow Badger Road for 2.7 miles, you'll see the campground on the left.

✦ ROAD'S END RV PARK
   Address: 1463 Wescott Lane, North Pole, AK 99705
   Telephone: (907) 488-0295
   Price: Medium

*GPS Location: N 64° 48' 06.7", W 147° 33' 03.8"*

This is a fairly small RV park located right on the Richardson between North Pole and Fairbanks. The Road's End accepts permanents, but it also has some good spaces for travelers.

The campground has about 40 full-hookup spaces out of a total of about 65 sites. Interior roads are gravel and parking is on grass. There are some pull-throughs. Showers are included in the daily rate. There is a laundromat and also a dump station.

Watch for the Road's End on the north side of the Richardson at about Mile 356. This is about 6 miles from Fairbanks.

✦ SANTALAND RV PARK & CAMPGROUND
    Address: 125 St. Nicholas Drive (P.O. Box 55317),
    North Pole, AK 99705
    Telephone: (907) 488-9123 or (888) 488-9123
    Price: Medium

*GPS Location: N 64° 45' 17.1", W 147° 20' 39.6"*

Everyone knows that Santa lives at the North Pole, this campground is right next to the Santa Clause House. The RV park is decorated to match with red and green picnic tables and a big Santa Clause statue out front. There are even live reindeer to fascinate the younger campers in your family.

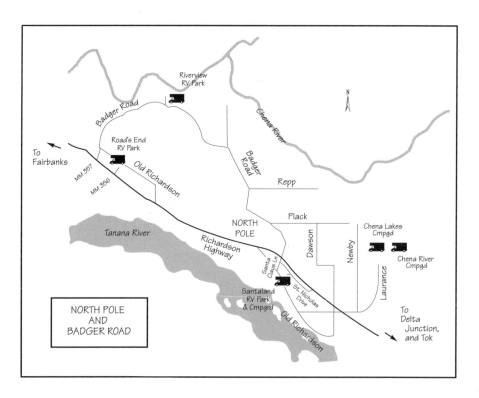

SANTA AT NORTH POLE

The campground is one of the largest and most popular in the Fairbanks area with about 85 RV spaces and also a tent-camping area. There are full and partial hookup sites, also pull-throughs with plenty of room for the largest rigs. Sites have picnic tables and are separated by grass. The large building at the front of the park houses the office, a gift shop, the laundromat, and individual bathrooms with sink, shower, and toilet. Any of the many local excursions and tours can be booked here and the very popular Santa Clause House (with it's gift shop) is right next door.

The campground is located in North Pole, a Fairbanks suburb. Take the Santa Clause Lane exit from the Richardson Highway near Mile 349, then head south. Just before the Pizza Hut turn left on St. Nicholas Drive, the campground is on the right just after Santa Clause House some .6 mile from the freeway exit. If you were coming from out of town you probably saw the huge Santa as you passed on the freeway before taking the exit.

✦ CHENA LAKES RECREATION AREA
   Location: 19 miles from Fairbanks off the
   Richardson Highway
   Price: Low

*GPS Location: N 64° 45' 16.0", W 147° 13' 07.4"*

One of the big disasters in modern Alaskan history was the almost complete flooding of Fairbanks by the Chena River in 1967. To prevent this from happening again a major flood control project was undertaken. Huge dikes were built to divert flood water, and some of the gravel came from what is now the Chena River Lakes Recreation Area. Built by the Corps of Engineers and managed by the North Star Borough this is one of the best camping areas in the Fairbanks region and certainly one of the best deals.

There are actually two campgrounds in the Recreation area. One is the Lake Park with 45 sites and the other is the River Park with 35 sites. There are also additional tent sites. Both camping areas offer large back-in and pull-through wilderness-type sites with good separation by trees and natural vegetation. Sites have picnic tables and fire pits. There are outhouses and hand-operated water pumps. The recreation area also has a dump and water-fill station as well as boat ramps, covered picnic areas and swimming beaches.

Follow Laurance Road from its intersection with the Richardson Highway at Mile 347 for 2.6 miles to the recreation area entrance gate.

## FROM FAIRBANKS TO DELTA JUNCTION
### (98 miles)

Between Fairbanks and Delta Junction the Richardson follows the north bank of the Tanana River. Much of the time the river is not visible from the highway. The Tanana is a very dangerous, muddy, fast moving river that carries tons of mud and silt. Where it does adjoin the road it is often a problem because it threatens to wash out the highway as it unpredictably tries to change course.

For the first miles or so the Richardson is a new four-lane divided highway. You'll cruise past Fairbanks's southern suburb, North Pole, at Mile 349, about 14 miles from Fairbanks. Most people stop in North Pole to visit Santa Claus House where you can pick up a toy or Christmas ornament and arrange to have Santa send a letter to someone back home. Twenty-five miles from Fairbanks you'll see the long runway at Eielson Air Force Base on your left, watch for a long line of KC-135 tankers and the occasional flight of A-10 Thunderbolts.

At Eielson the road narrows down to two lanes and stays that way all the way to Valdez. For most of the distance to Delta Junction you'll have low bluffs on your left and the river on your right. At Mile 275 the road crosses the Tanana. The Trans-Alaska oil pipeline crosses at this same spot, you can't miss it.

Just south of the river crossing, at Mile 275 is the entrance road to the Big Delta State

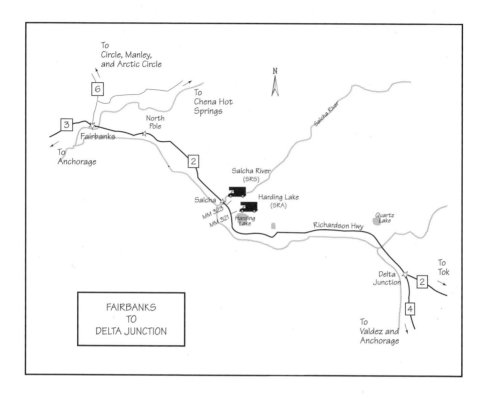

Historical Site and Rika's Roadhouse. This is one of the few remaining roadhouses along the Richardson and a good place to stop and stretch your legs. Delta Junction is just 9 miles farther south.

See Chapter 4 - The Alaska Highway for information about Delta Junction and its campgrounds.

## Campgrounds
## Fairbanks to Delta Junction

◆ SALCHA RIVER STATE RECREATION SITE
   Location: 41 miles south of Fairbanks on
   the Richardson Highway
   Price: Low

*GPS Location: N 64° 28' 05.0", W 146° 55' 31.0"*

Designed primarily to be a boat-launching area for the clear-running Salcha River, this recreation site also allows camping. There is a huge parking lot that the state says represents 90 camping sites and also 3 designated campsites along its borders. It is also possible to camp along the river upstream but don't get stuck in the soft gravel. The recreation site has the customary picnic tables, fire pits, outhouses and hand-operated water pump. This campground also has a host. The boat ramp is well-used, particularly on weekends.

The access road for this area is at Mile 323 of the Richardson Highway.

✦ HARDING LAKE STATE RECREATION AREA
    Location: 44 miles from Fairbanks off
    the Richardson Highway
    Price: Low

*GPS Location: N 64° 26' 15.9", W 146° 52' 51.4"*

Harding Lake is one of the few large lakes near Fairbanks, it is surrounded by cabins owned by local residents. The Harding Lake State Recreation Area gives the rest of us access to the lake. The recreation area offers swimming, picnicking, sports fields and hiking trails as well as camping. Week-ends can be crowded because Fairbanks is so close.

This campground has about 90 back-in sites and additional tent sites. These are wilderness sites with surrounding natural vegetation and trees, however, they are not as well separated as the sites in most State of Alaska campgrounds. They sit back from the lake and have no views. Sites have picnic tables, fire pits and dish-water drains. The campground has outhouses. There is a dump station, a water-fill station, and a boat ramp.

The paved access road to the campground leaves the Richardson Highway at Mile 321. It will lead you about .6 mile to the campground.

## FROM DELTA JUNCTION TO THE SOUTHERN GLENN HIGHWAY JUNCTION
### (151 miles)

Driving south from Delta Junction you'll pass through **Fort Greeley**, probably without even noticing. Fort Greeley is the army's Arctic training and testing center. Winter training exercises held in this area teach troops from around the country how to survive operations in sub-zero temperatures. Plans are underway for closing the base, Delta Junctions population is trying to think of something else to use it for.

At Mile 244 there is a pull-off and overlook that in good weather offers views of three Alaska Range peaks to the southwest. These are **Mount Deborah** (12,339 ft.), **Mount Hess** (11,940 ft.), and **Mount Hayes** (13,832 ft.). This viewpoint is also a popular place to glass for the **Delta bison herd**.

The Richardson soon begins climbing through the Alaska Range to **Isabel Pass**. This 3,284 foot crossing is very gradual, you'll hardly know when you reach the top at Summit Lake at Mile 198. Before reaching the summit watch for pipeline Pump Station Number 10 at Mile 219. Also watch for the **Gulkana Glacier** at Mile 197.

From Summit Lake the road gradually descends to the Paxson Junction with the Denali Highway at Mile 185. The Denali Highway is discussed in a following section in this chapter.

Another important junction, this time the North Junction with the Glenn Highway (also called the Tok Cut-off), is at Mile 128. For 13 miles the Glenn and the Richardson are the same highway, then at Mile 115 is the South Junction where the Glenn heads west through Glennallen to Anchorage.

## Campgrounds
## Delta Junction to the Southern Glenn Highway Junction

✦  DONNELLY CREEK STATE RECREATION SITE
    Location: Near Mile 238 of the Richardson Highway
    Price: Low

*GPS Location: N 63° 40' 26.5", W 145° 53' 02.6"*

Donnelly Creek campground is one of the older ones in the state and doesn't get a lot

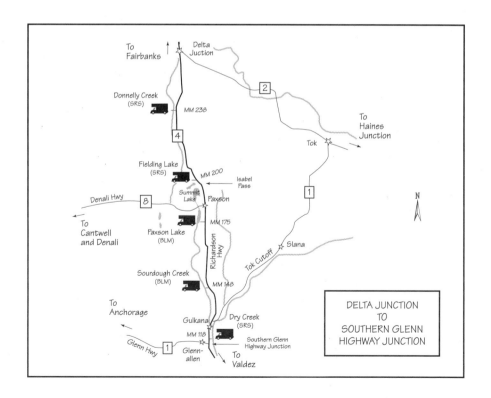

of visitors except during hunting season. Still, this small campground makes a good place to spend the night along a section of road that doesn't have many places to stay.

There are 12 back-in sites arranged around a loop road. Spaces are well separated in willows and white spruce. All have fire pits and picnic tables. The campground has outhouses and a hand operated water pump.

Watch for the campground near Mile 238 of the Richardson Highway on the west side of the road.

✦ FIELDING LAKE STATE RECREATION SITE
　　　Location: Near Mile 200 of the Richardson Highway
　　　Price: Free

*GPS Location: N 63° 11' 33.5", W 145° 39' 06.0"*

Fielding Lake campground sits near the shore of a lake offering good lake trout and grayling fishing. There are a few private cabins in and near the campground vicinity. This lake is situated above the tree line so the surroundings are a little barren and unprotected from the weather.

There are 17 back-in side-by-side parking lot type sites along a stream that runs into the lake. Any size rig will find maneuvering room. Fire pits, picnic tables, and out-houses are available. There is also a boat ramp.

To reach the campground follow the gravel road which leaves the Richardson High-way near Mile 200 for 1.6 miles. The condition of this entrance road varies but even large rigs should always be able to negotiate it.

✦ PAXSON LAKE BLM CAMPGROUND
　　　Location: Near Mile 175 of the Richardson Highway
　　　Price: Low

*GPS Location: N 62° 52' 59.3", W 145° 31' 28.2"*

This large campground is popular with RVers because it offers nice large spaces, some are even pull-throughs. There is also a dump station. Paxson Lake is quite large and offers lake trout, grayling, and even red salmon fishing. Many people float the Gulkana River from here to the Sourdough Campground mentioned below.

The campground has 39 vehicle spaces, 9 of these are pull-throughs. There is also a tent-camping area. Spaces are well separated with many spruce trees. They have fire pits and picnic tables but are not located along the lake shore. This campground has outhouses, a hand-operated water pump, and a dump station. There is also a boat ramp.

From Mile 175 of the Richardson Highway follow a wide gravel access road west for 1.6 miles to the campground.

✦ SOURDOUGH CREEK BLM CAMPGROUND
   Location: Near Mile 148 of the Richardson Highway
   Price: Low

*GPS Location: N 62° 31' 38.6", W 145° 30' 58.3"*

This large campground is located along the Gulkana River and is a take-out point for people floating from Paxson Lake and a put-in point for people planning to float the lower river. A large area is set aside for parking rigs belonging to floaters. Fishing in the Gulkana and Sourdough Creek for grayling, rainbows and king salmon is quite good.

The campground itself has 43 sites. Some are pull-throughs. The sites are separated by natural vegetation including black spruce and have picnic tables and fire pits. There are outhouses, a nature trail, a boat launch area, and a covered picnic area.

✦ DRY CREEK STATE RECREATION SITE
   Location: Mile 118 of the Richardson Hwy.
   Price: Low

*GPS Location: N 62° 09' 10.3", W 145° 28' 15.3"*

Dry Creek campground is conveniently located just north of the junction of the Glenn and Richardson Highways at Glennallen. Be ready, at certain times of the year the mosquitoes can be terrible at this campground. During one visit they were so bad that we couldn't go outside without a head net, even to walk to the toilets.

There are about 60 well-separated vehicle sites at this campground. Most are back-ins but one area has a number of pull-throughs. There are also some walk-in tent sites. All sites have picnic tables and fire pits. There are outhouses and a hand-operated water pump.

The campground is located just east of the highway across from the Gulkana Airport, it is near Mile 118 of the Richardson Highway. This is three miles north of the junction with the Glenn Highway at Glennallen.

## Denali Highway Side Trip

The Denali Highway runs from Paxson at Mile 185 on the Richardson Highway to the Parks Highway at Mile 210. This is a distance of 135 miles, only the eastern-most 21 miles are paved. Before the Parks Highway was finished the Denali Highway served as an access route to Denali National Park, today the road is little used and traversed mostly by outdoors-oriented travelers. In the fall it is a popular hunting area but all summer the road is used almost exclusively by wildlife watchers, fishermen, hikers, canoers, and scenery lovers. It really doesn't serve as a preferred route to anywhere else.

There are three formal BLM campgrounds along the highway but there are many more place where an RVer can just pull over and spend the night. The route covered is

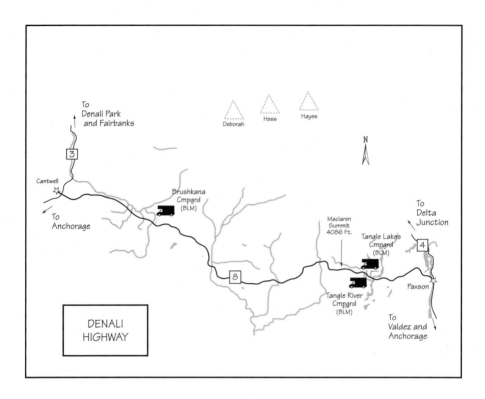

mostly high plateau dotted with lakes, fishing in many of them is good and it's not hard to see wildlife if you take the time to search with your binoculars. Maclaren Summit at Mile 35 is the second highest highway pass in the state (4,086 ft.), second only to Atigun Pass on the Dalton Highway.

✦  TANGLE LAKES CAMPGROUND (BLM)
     Location: Mile 21 Denali Highway
     Price: Free

*GPS Location: N 63° 02' 59.4", W 146° 00' 25.9"*

The Tangle Lakes Campground is located in high country with little in the way of trees. In good weather the vistas are wonderful. The campground is often used as a starting point for floats of the Delta River which is a designated National Wild and Scenic River.

The campground has about 28 sites. They are separated by small bushes and are really not well defined, they're spread over a large area. Some are pull-throughs or parallel parking spots suitable for big rigs. Some sites are also right along the lake. Each has a fire pit and picnic table. The campground has a hand pump for water, outhouses, and a boat ramp.

The campground is located on the north side of the Denali Highway near the end of the pavement at Mile 21.

✦  TANGLE RIVER CAMPGROUND (BLM)
   Location: Mile 22 Denali Highway
   Price: Free

*GPS Location: N 63° 02' 43.4", W 146° 01' 32.7"*

This is a very small campground on the opposite side of the road from the much larger Tangle Lakes Campground. About seven camping sites are scattered below the road along the Tangle River. There are tables, fire pits and outhouses. There's also a boat launch. This is a put-in point for a long canoe route through the Tangle Lakes with a portage to the Middle Fork of the Gulkana River. The BLM now calls it the Delta National Wild & Scenic River Wayside which may indicate that they don't consider it a campground at all.

✦  BRUSHKANA CAMPGROUND (BLM)
   Location: Mile 105 Denali Highway
   Price: Free

The Brushkana Campground has about 18 back-in camping sites as well as an over-flow area suitable for RVs. Sites have picnic tables and fire pits, there are outhouses. Fish for grayling in Brushkana Creek.

## WRANGELL-ST. ELIAS NATIONAL PARK, COPPER CENTER, EDGERTON HIGHWAY AND THE McCARTHY ROAD

Not far south of the Glenn Highway junction is an old town, **Copper Center**, which was founded in 1896 as a government agricultural experimental station. The main road now bypasses Copper Center, if you want to drive through town take a left at the junction at Mile 106 for the Old Richardson Highway. Just under a mile down this road, on the right, is the **Wrangell-St. Elias National Park Visitor's Center** (PO Box 439, Copper Center, AK 99573; 907 823-2205. The visitor center is not in the park, it's in Copper Center so that it is more accessible to the public, and because you need to stop and get information before heading for the park. The ranger here can fill you in on the park which has very limited road access. The two access roads into the park are the Nabesna Road off the Tok Cut-off (see Chapter 7 - The Glenn Highway) and the Edgerton Highway at Mile 83 of the Richardson (see below).

Copper Center is more than just home to the park visitor center. Near Mile 100 (off the Old Richardson loop) are the two entrances to an inner loop road which runs through old Copper Center. Off this road is the old **Copper Center Lodge**, one of the original roadhouses along the Richardson and still in operation. Copper Center now has a population of about 500 and has several interesting stops including the lodge, the **George Ashby Memorial Museum**, the log **Chapel on the Hill**, and a couple of king and red salmon fishing oriented camping areas along the Klutina River which runs into the Copper River here.

The Copper Center loop rejoins the Richardson Highway at Mile 100 and heads south to another junction, this one with the **Edgerton Highway** at Mile 83. The Edgerton provides access to McCarthy and the Wrangell-St. Elias National Park. Think of the road as having two sections. The first is the Edgerton Highway. It is a 35-mile long paved highway running through Kenny Lake and Chitina and then crossing the Copper River on a good modern bridge. At Chitina the paving ends and at the Copper River the McCarthy Road begins. The **McCarthy Road** is an unpaved 58-mile long rough road following an old railway roadbed. Occasionally spikes from the old railroad have been known to work loose and puncture tires. The road is not suitable for large RVs. A van service runs from Glennallen to McCarthy and is an excellent way to get to McCarthy if you don't want to drive, check at the park visitor's center in Copper Center for information. There are several small commercial campgrounds along the McCarthy Road near Mile 9, Mile 15, and near the end of the road.

At the end of the McCarthy road is a parking lot that can be used for camping. There is a fee. From the parking lot there is now a walking bridge across the Kennicott River to McCarthy and Kennicott. Transportation is sometimes available on the far side of the river. The distance to McCarthy is about a mile, Kennicott is about 5 miles distant.

McCarthy, with a population of about 25, is the service center for this area. You'll find lodging, a restaurant or two, and guide services in McCarthy. Services are limited so check at the park visitor's center in Copper Center to determine what is available before heading in to McCarthy.

Kennicott is the reason for the development in this area. From 1910 to 1930 this was the location of a huge copper mine. Ore was transported to tidewater at Cordova along the railroad that formed the base for the road you probably traveled to get here. Red-painted buildings remain (they're off limits) and there is a lodge. Hiking trails lead up the adjoining Kennicott Glacier and up the mountainside above the structures.

### Campgrounds
### Wrangell-St. Elias National Park, Copper Center, Edgerton Highway and the McCarthy Road

✦  TAZLINA RIVER RV PARK
     Address: P.O. Box 277, Glennallen, AK 99588
     Telephone: (907) 822-3546
     Price: Medium

*GPS Location: N 62° 03' 01.8", W 145° 26' 03.0"*

This small RV park is co-located with a mobile home park. It is a little incongruous considering its location in the middle of the Alaska wilderness, but this campground is one of the best places to overnight in the area.

There's a small unattended sign-in booth across the road from about 12 RV sites,

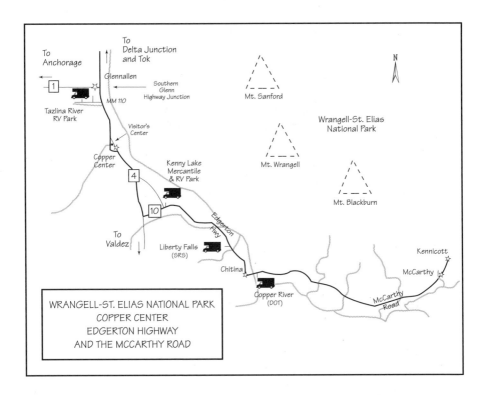

mostly back-ins but with a couple of pull-throughs. They have electricity (20-amp plugs) and water hookups. The campground has hot showers (included in the nightly fee), a laundromat, and a dump station. Tenters aren't allowed even though there's a nice grassy area in the middle of the park with a covered barbecue area. There are small tables and seats, maybe from some long-gone McDonalds, at every space.

The entrance to the subdivision and the RV park is at Mile 110.5 of the Richardson Highway, about 14.5 miles south of the intersection of the Glenn and the Richardson Highways in Glennallen. The entrance road goes west from the highway, take the second right for the campground. The huge empty lot to the south was one of the pipe storage yards when the oil pipeline was being built.

✦ KENNY LAKE MERCANTILE & RV PARK
    Address: HC 60, Box 230, Mile 7.5 Edgerton Hwy.,
    Copper Center, Alaska 99573
    Telephone: (907) 822-3313
    Price: Medium

*GPS Location: N 61° 44' 11.5", W 144° 57' 07.1"*

Kenny Lake Mercantile is located on the Edgerton Highway between Chitina and the

Richardson Highway. It is a well-run fairly new roadhouse-style facility with restaurant, laundromat, hotel, groceries and campground. This is a good place to base your rig when catching the shuttle into McCarthy.

There are 19 camping spaces. 10 are back-in sites with electrical hookups in the cleared yard near the store and laundromat/shower building. Nine others are pull-through camping sites with no utility hookups set in trees in a secluded area nearby. The restrooms and showers are private rooms in the laundromat. Both a dump station and water fill station are provided.

This campground is on the north side of the Edgerton Highway some 7.5 miles from its junction with the Richardson Highway.

✦   LIBERTY FALLS STATE RECREATION SITE
     Location: Mile 24 of the Edgerton Hwy.
     Price: Low

*GPS Location: N 61° 37' 19.1", W 144° 32' 50.0"*

This very small campground is probably most suitable for tent campers. It sits in a small canyon next to the highway with a creek running through. Little Liberty Falls forms the centerpiece of the campground.

There are about five tent camping sites, some with platforms located on a sloping hillside. For vehicles there are 2 back-in sites in trees and another 5 or so parking slots that could be used for camping. Large rigs will find the roads narrow with little maneuvering room and parking slots too short. There are picnic tables, fire pits, outhouses and a water pump.

Watch for the campground on the south side of the Edgerton Highway near Mile 24.

✦   DEPARTMENT OF TRANSPORTATION COPPER
     RIVER CAMPGROUND
       Location: East end of Copper River Bridge
       on the Edgerton Hwy.
       Price: Free

*GPS Location: N 61° 31' 46.5", W 144° 24' 14.3"*

This small camping area on the banks of the Copper River is extremely popular when the salmon are running, any other time you're likely to be on your own.

There are about 12 sites with picnic tables and fire pits located in a grove of cottonwoods. This little-developed campground has few amenities but does offer outhouses.

To find the campground follow the Edgerton Highway to Chitina, through town, and across the Copper River Bridge. The camping area is on the south side of the highway just after the bridge near what would be Mile 35 of the Edgerton except that this part of the highway is called the McCarthy Road.

## FROM THE SOUTHERN GLENN HIGHWAY JUNCTION TO VALDEZ
### (115 miles)

As the road leads south from the junction it passes the two entrances to the Copper Center loop at Mile 106 and Mile 101. It then passes the Edgerton Highway junction at Mile 83. This area is covered in the immediately preceding section titled Wrangell-St. Elias National Park, Copper Center, Edgerton Highway and the McCarthy Road. The highway then gradually climbs along river valleys into the Chugach Mountains towards Thompson Pass.

At Mile 29 a short side road leads to a parking lot and overlook for the **Worthington Glacier** which is very close to the overlook.

The road crosses **Thompson Pass** at Mile 26. Thompson is only 2,678 feet high but seems higher. The huge snowfall here means that the vegetation is truly alpine. After the pass the road descends steeply and then passes through scenic **Keystone Canyon** to end, according to the mileposts, four miles short of Valdez. This is because Valdez was moved to a new site after the 1964 Good Friday earthquake. Continue straight ahead to the new town site.

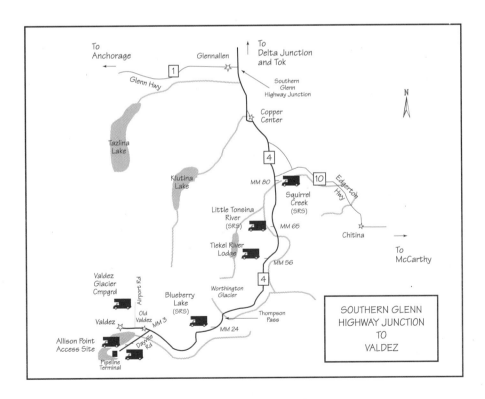

## Campgrounds
## Southern Glenn Highway Junction to Valdez

✦ Squirrel Creek State Recreation Site
   Location: Near Mile 80 of the Richardson Hwy.
   Price: Low

*GPS Location: N 61° 39' 59.3", W 145° 10' 38.1"*

A small campground with nice sites and offering some fishing for grayling where Squirrel Creek empties into the Tonsina River. There are also fish in the gravel pit next to the campground.

There are about 25 sites of various types, some are around a gravel lot and others are individual separated sites. Take a look on foot before driving into any blind entrances if you have a large rig, you might have to back out. The area has cottonwood trees and some sites are along Squirrel Creek. They all have fire pits and picnic tables, there are outhouses and a hand-operated water pump.

The campground is situated just east of the Richardson Highway near Mile 80.

✦ Little Tonsina River State Recreation Site
   Location: Near Mile 65 of the Richardson Hwy.
   Price: Low

*GPS Location: N 61° 28' 52.5", W 145° 09' 22.0"*

This is a very small campground but it does offer some Dolly Varden fishing, there are Kings but fishing for them isn't allowed. Pump Station Number 12 of the Trans-Alaska pipeline is very near, at times you'll probably hear the turbine faintly roaring in the distance.

There are 8 sites, one is pull-through. Watch to make sure you don't get yourself into a position where you have to back your large rig out of a dead-end. There are picnic tables, fire pits, outhouses and a hand-operated water pump.

The campground is located on the west side of the Richardson near the 65 Mile point.

✦ Tiekel River Lodge
   Address: Mile 56, SR Box 110, Valdez, AK 99686
   Telephone: (907) 822-3259
   Price: Medium

*GPS Location: N 61° 23' 01.5", W 145° 14' 15.1"*

This roadhouse-style facility is located on the banks of the Tiekel River. They offer a restaurant, motel, gas, and a gift shop.

WORTHINGTON GLACIER

The campground area has 13 neglected sites near the river. Five have water and electric hookups but the better sites are along the river and have none. They are suitable for smaller rigs only. The lodge offers hot showers for a fee.

The lodge is on the west side of the Richardson Highway near the 56 Mile point.

✦ BLUEBERRY LAKE STATE RECREATION SITE
   Location: Near Mile 24 of the Richardson Highway
   Price: Low

*GPS Location: N 61° 07' 12.3", W 145° 42' 05.5"*

This is a small campground, fairly close to Valdez, with a spectacular location. It sits below the summit of Thompson pass, surrounded by mountains and meadows. Little Blueberry Lake adjoins the campground. Bears are frequently seen nearby.

There are 8 numbered vehicle sites, four picnic shelters, and a few tent-camping sites. Stunted alders are the primary local vegetation. Fire pits, picnic tables, outhouses, and a water pump are available.

Watch for the .8 mile access road near Mile 24 of the Richardson Highway.

✦ ALLISON POINT ACCESS SITE (CITY OF VALDEZ)
   Location: Near the Alyeska Terminal
   across from Valdez
   Price: Low

This campground's reason for being is salmon fishing. Either pink or silver salmon can be caught from the shore during their respective runs. There is a salmon hatchery nearby which explains the fish.

65 back-in parking lot spaces line the road for about a half mile. Some, on the ocean side of the road, are pretty nice sites with excellent views across the fiord to Valdez. There is no separation between adjoining parking slots. Some fire pits and picnic tables are available. Outhouses are provided and drinking water is hauled to the campground.

The camping area is located along the access road to the oil-tank farm across the bay from Valdez. To get there follow Dayville Road from Mile 3 of the Richardson Highway. The campground lines the road from Mile 3.6 to Mile 4 of the Dayville Road.

✦ VALDEZ GLACIER CAMPGROUND (CITY OF VALDEZ)
   Location: 2.3 miles on Valdez Airport Rd.
   Price: Low

*GPS Location: N 61° 08' 19.4", W 146° 12' 16.6"*

This very large government campground is run by the city of Valdez. It offers the services you would expect in a government campground, the price is reasonable and Valdez is only a short drive away.

There are 101 camping spaces arranged off paved access roads. About 13 sites are pull-throughs, the rest are back-ins. Each space has a picnic table and fire pit, toilets are outhouse-type and there is a water pump. Tent camping sites are available. Most of the vegetation is cottonwood or alder and spaces are well separated.

The campground is located past the airport on the paved Airport Road that leaves the Richardson Highway at Mile 3.4. You'll pass the airport at .8 miles and find the campground at 2.3 miles. Just beyond is the Valdez Glacier parking area.

## VALDEZ
### Population 4,100, Elevation sea level

Since the Exxon Valdez oil spill in 1989 this little town has become very well known. Most people even know how to pronounce it now (Val-DEEZ). Before the pipeline the town may have been best known for its tremendous winter snowfall which sometimes exceeds 40 feet.

The oil spill wasn't the first disaster to strike Valdez. In 1964 the town was virtually destroyed during the Good Friday Earthquake. The present town is brand new, not much is left of old Valdez which was four miles to the east.

The top summer attraction in Valdez seems to be the fish. Three fishing derbies run throughout the summer: the Halibut Derby for most of the summer, the Pink Salmon Derby at the end of June and most of July, and the Silver Salmon Derby in August. You can easily charter a boat, use your own, or fish from the beach. Fishermen practically fill Valdez's many campgrounds during the summer.

The **Valdez Visitor Center** is at 200 Chenega St. (Box 1603, Valdez 99686; 907 835-2984) at the center of town near the Municipal Building and Library. You'll see that the new version of Valdez built after the earthquake doesn't have a traditional downtown area, things are pretty spread out for such a small town.

Valdez is a port for the **Alaska Marine Highway**. From here you can catch a ferry to Cordova, Whittier, or Seward. A very popular trip is to ride the ferry to Whittier past the Columbia Glacier, then put your vehicle on a train for the short shuttle to the Seward Highway just south of Anchorage.

For a better view of the **Columbia Glacier** you'll want to take a cruise boat. The ferry doesn't really get close enough for a great view.

The **Valdez oil terminal** is located across the Port Valdez from the town. You can easily see the huge oil storage tanks and usually a loading tanker from the Valdez waterfront. Tours are available to get a closer view of the operations there, check with the office at one of the local RV parks.

COLUMBIA GLACIER

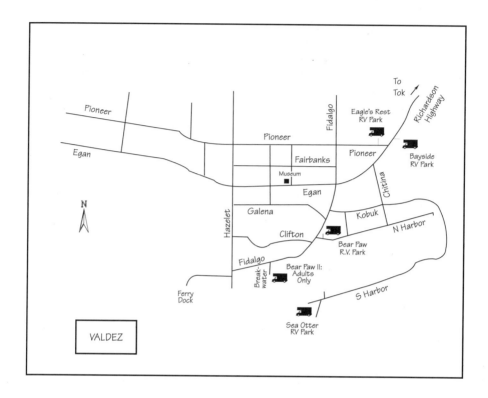

Valdez also has a **museum** (217 Eagan Drive). It has displays on the history of the area and on the oil pipeline.

Valdez is a small town but very busy during the summer. Tourism, fishing, and pipeline activities are all happening at the same time. There are lots of camping slots in Valdez and also, for such a small town, an adequate service infrastructure including a medium-sized supermarket.

## Valdez Campgrounds

✦ SEA OTTER R.V. PARK
   Address: P.O. Box 947, Valdez, AK 99686
   Telephone: (907) 835-2787, (800) 831-2787
   Price: Medium

*GPS Location: N 61° 07' 25.0", W 146° 21' 06.7"*

Our favorite of the Valdez campgrounds is the Sea Otter R.V. Park. It is located next to the ocean on the peninsula that forms the ocean side of the small boat harbor.

The Sea Otter has 200 or more sites set on a large flat gravel area (there is some landscaping) next to the water. 55 of the sites are waterfront. Most sites have electricity and water hookups and are wide back-ins but a few are available with full hookups and there are also pull-throughs. Restrooms are private rooms with showers, there is a laundromat, and the campground has a dump station. Reservations are recommended.

As you arrive in Valdez on the Richardson you'll pass the Eagles Rest and Bayside RV Parks. Watch for Chitina Ave. Turn left here and follow the road until you see a sign to the left for the Sea Otter and Kobuk. Turn left and follow the road as it curves around the small boat harbor. The campground is on the left at .8 miles near the road end.

✦  BEAR PAW R.V. PARK
    Address: 101 North Harbor Dr. (P.O. Box 93),
    Valdez, AK 99686
    Telephone: (907) 835-2530
    Internet: http://alaska.net/~bpawcamp/
    Price: High

*GPS Location: N 61° 07' 39.2", W 146° 21' 01.9"*

The Bear Paw is conveniently located just across the road from the small boat harbor. If you are in Valdez to take advantage of the available fishing charters this is a good base.

The campground is a large fenced gravel lot, but not quite as huge as a couple of the other campgrounds in Valdez. There are a variety of site types, some are pull-throughs. Full hookup, electric only, and dry sites are available. The campground has restrooms with hot showers in private rooms and is convenient to a laundromat, restaurants, charter boat operators and central Valdez. The same owners also operate an adult park and a tent camping area nearby. The tent camping area is in a small grove of alders behind the adult park and has tent platforms and picnic tables. Reservations are recommended.

The easiest way to find the campground is to follow the Richardson into town until you see Fidalgo. Turn left on Fidalgo and drive .1 miles to the corner with N. Harbor Dr. The Bear Paw is on the corner on the left.

✦  BEAR PAW II: ADULTS ONLY
    Address: P.O. Box 93, Valdez, AK 99686
    Telephone: (907) 835-2530
    Price: High

*GPS Location: N 61° 07' 30.8", W 146° 21' 19.0"*

The Bear Paw Adult Camper Park is nicely located right on the water at the entrance to the Valdez small boat harbor. While not quite as convenient as the other Bear Paw campground scenic location easily compensates.

There are about 25 back-in spaces in this park. They have 30-amp electricity, sewer, water and cable TV (to be installed in 98) hookups. There are picnic tables and a dump station.

To find this campground follow the Richardson into town until you see Fidalgo. Turn left here and drive .3 miles until you see a small street (Breakwater) going left. Turn here and you'll soon come to a dead end at the water with the campground to your left.

◆ Bayside RV Park
     Address: P.O. Box 466, Valdez, AK 99686
     Telephone: (907) 835-4425 or (888) 835-4425
     Price: High

*GPS Location: N 61° 07' 49.4", W 146° 20' 37.4"*

The Bayside is the newest RV park in Valdez. It is so new that when we visited in the fall of 1997 there was not yet a restroom and shower building or laundromat. The portable building to house these had been ordered, however, and they are expected to be operational in 1998. This is not a waterfront campground but it is within walking distance of the boat harbor.

The campground has almost 100 vehicle spaces. 75 are full-service sites and 35 are pull-throughs. The campground is a large gravel lot. It has a dump station.

You can't miss the Bayside. As you arrive in Valdez on the Richardson Highway you'll see the campground on your left as you enter town.

◆ Eagle's Rest RV Park
     Address: 630 E. Pioneer (P.O. Box 610),
     Valdez, AK 99686
     Telephone: (907) 835-2373 or (800) 553-7275
     Fax: (907) 835-5267
     Internet: http://www.alaskaoutdoors.com/eagle/
     Price: High

*GPS Location: N 61° 07' 51.7", W 146° 20' 39.5"*

Valdez's largest RV park is also probably its best promoted. You'll undoubtedly run into pamphlets and cards singing its praises long before you reach Valdez. It is also likely to be the first place you see when you reach town. All of this means that the Eagle's Rest may be the most successful park in town, but not necessarily the place for everyone.

The Eagle's Rest has over 250 vehicle spaces and also a grassy area for tents. The vehicle area is a large gravel lot with little landscaping. Full hookup (30 and 50-amp power), partial, and dry sites are available. The central office building has restrooms with hot showers, a laundromat, and a fish cleaning area. This is the farthest campground from the waterfront, but still within easy walking distance.

As you enter Valdez on the Richardson Highway watch for the Eagle's Rest on the right.

## RICHARDSON HIGHWAY DUMP STATIONS

Travelers in Alaska should try to use dump stations in larger cities, on the Richardson that means Fairbanks and Valdez. Many of the campgrounds in this chapter have dump stations or sewer hookups. There is generally a fee, particularly if you are not staying at the campground, which is only fair. The section of road between Delta Junction and Glennallen has few places to dump, note that the Paxson Lake BLM Campground near Mile 175 has a dump station.

In **Fairbanks** there is a municipal dump station near Alaskaland at the intersection of Moore Road and 2nd Avenue. Gas stations with dump stations available to customers include MAPCO Express Store 5022 at 2300 Cushman Street, Alaska Chevron Service at 333 Illinois Street, Southgate Texaco at 1603 South Cushman Street, 7-Eleven #101 (Tesoro) at 3569 South Cushman, Mike's University Chevron at 3245 College Road, and Sourdough Fuel at 1555 Van Horn Road.

In **North Pole** there is a dump station at North Pole Plaza Gas at 301 North Santa Claus Lane.

See Chapter 4 - The Alaska Highway for Delta Junction dump stations.

See Chapter 7 - The Glenn Highway for Glennallen dump stations.

In **Valdez** most campgrounds have dump stations but also try the Tesoro Station at the corner of Meals and Egan.

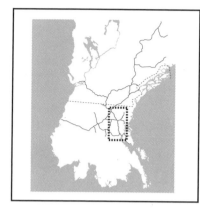

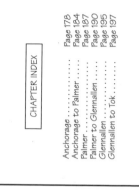

To Haines
Junction

Tok

To
Fairbanks

Glennallen
to
Tok

Slana

Tok Cutoff

Gakona

Wrangell-St. Elias
National Park

Glennallen

Gulkana

To Delta
Junction

To
Valdez

To
Denali

Palmer
to
Glennallen

Matanuska Glacier

N

To
Fairbanks

Sutton

Palmer

Wasilla

Anchorage
to
Palmer

To
Keani,
Soldotna,
and Seward

Prince
William Sound

Anchorage

THE GLENN HIGHWAY

# CHAPTER 7

# THE GLENN HIGHWAY

## INTRODUCTION

The Glenn Highway runs northeast 189 miles from Anchorage on the shores of Cook Inlet to meet with the Richardson Highway near Glennallen. It then follows the Richardson north just 14 miles. Leaving the Richardson again at Gakona Junction the Glenn becomes the Tok Cutoff and crosses the northern Copper River country, threads through Mentasta Pass, and meets the Alaska Highway at Tok, a distance of 125 miles. The entire Glenn Highway from Anchorage to Tok is 328 miles long.

If you are starting your trip in Anchorage, the Glenn to the Gakona Junction is the first part of one of two possible routes to Fairbanks. If you have driven up the Alaska Highway, the Glenn is your quickest route from Tok to Anchorage and the Kenai Peninsula.

### Highlights

The Glenn highway starts in **Anchorage**, the state's largest town and commercial center. Visitors from outside the state shouldn't skip a visit to Anchorage, your trip to Alaska isn't complete until you've seen this city that is so different from the rest of the state.

The **Matanuska Valley** is Alaska's most successful agricultural area. In recent years it has also become something of an Anchorage suburb. This large area north of Knik Arm is usually known as the Mat-Su Valley because it combines the valleys of two rivers, the Matanuska River in the east and the Susitna River in the west. The Glenn Highway travels through the Matanuska Valley while the Parks Highway (see Chapter 9 - The Parks Highway) cuts off to head up the Susitna Valley.

As the Glenn climbs out of the Matanuska Valley you'll have a chance to see some very scenic country. A highlight is the **Matanuska Glacier** descending out of the Chugach Mountains to the south and visible from scenic viewpoints near the highway.

Once you reach the Glennallen area and turn north you'll have some great views of the mountains of the **Wrangell-St. Elias National Park** to the southeast. You'll find more about this park in Chapter 6 - The Richardson Highway.

### The Road

The Glenn Highway was only a rough trail until World War II. Then it was improved to connect the military bases in Anchorage with the Alcan. Until the Parks Highway was completed in 1971 the Glenn was Anchorage's only connecting road to the rest of the state and the "Lower 48".

From Anchorage to Tok is a distance of 328 miles, a long drive but possible in a long day. The entire highway is paved but it is all two-lane road except for a short segment near Anchorage. Many sections, particularly on the Tok Cutoff, have permafrost problems and larger rigs are forced to drive slowly to stay in one piece.

Mileposts on the Glenn Highway run from south to north, but there are three segments of them. From Anchorage to the junction with the Richardson Highway near Glennallen they run from 1 to 189. Then there is a short section of the Richardson Highway with mileposts indicating the distance from Valdez. Back on the Tok Cutoff mileposts start at the south end at 1 and run up to 125 at Tok.

### Fishing

**Ship Creek**, almost in downtown Anchorage, is the second most popular fishing site in the state with only the Russian River receiving more angler/days of fishing pressure. The best campground for fishing here is Ship Creek Landing RV Park which is within walking distance.

Many lakes in the Matanuska Valley are stocked with rainbow trout. See Chapter 9 - Parks Highway for more information about other fishing lakes in the Matanuska Valley, but also consider spending the night at "The Homestead" RV Park which is just across the Glenn Highway from the **Kepler-Bradley Lakes State Recreation Area**. You'll find stocked rainbow trout in the lakes.

**Lake Louise** is an large lake reached by gravel road from the Glenn Highway at Mile 160 and offers campers with their own boats the opportunity to catch large lake trout and grayling. The state's Lake Louise Recreation Area with the Lake Louise and Army Point Campgrounds is right on the lake.

As you drive up the Glenn Highway you may want to wet a line in one or another of the many small streams and lakes along the road. Here are a few to try: **Moose Creek** (Mile 55), **Granite Creek** (Mile 62), **Kings River** (Mile 66), **Chickaloon River** (Mile

78), **Long Lake** (Mile 85), **Mendeltna Creek** (Mile 153), **Gergie Lake** and **Arizona Lake** (Mile 155), **Mae West Lake** (by 1-mile trail from Mile 169), **Tolsona Lake** (Mile 170), **Tolsona Creek** (Mile 173), **Moose Creek** (Mile 186), the **Gulkana River** (access trail at 123 of the Richardson), **Tulsona Creek** (Mile 15 to 18 Tok Cutoff), **Sinona Creek** (Mile 35 Tok Cutoff), **Ahtell Creek** (Mile 61 Tok Cutoff), **Carlson Creek and Lake** (Mile 68 Tok Cutoff, trail 2.5 miles up creek to lake), **Mable Creek** (Mile 76 Tok Cutoff), and **Mentasta Lake** (Mile 81.5 on the old Slana-Tok bypass). In the low country expect Dollies and rainbows, in higher country you are more likely to find grayling.

### Boating, Rafting, Canoeing, and Kayaking

Anchorage is a waterfront city but don't expect to see many small boats on the Inlet out front. Cook Inlet is notoriously dangerous with a tidal range of near 30 feet, extremely cold muddy water, and frequent strong winds from nearby passes. Much farther south, off the Kenai Peninsula and in Kachemak Bay many people do use small boats on the Inlet but even there extreme caution is advised.

The glacial **Eagle River** near Anchorage is a convenient and popular canoe, kayak and rafting river just outside Anchorage. Commercial rafting companies run the river. Access is from near the Eagle River Visitor Center and there are several take-out points. The first portion of the float is Class I, but Class II and Class III rapids near Eagle River require caution. Check with Chugach State Park personnel for more information. The Eagle River Campground sits on the river and is used as a takeout point by rafters, but note that it is just below the Class III Campground Rapids. After the campground the river passes under the Glenn Highway, do not continue past this point because the river becomes very dangerous.

The **Knik River** near Palmer is a braided river running from Knik Glacier for about 26 miles to Knik Arm. This is a Class I - II glacial river with access to the upper river off the Knik River Road. The operators of the Mt. View RV Park run jet boat tours up the river. There are also commercial rafting tours of the Knik River.

Commercial raft tour companies run raft excursions on the glacial **Matanuska River** from Chickaloon which is near Mile 76 of the highway.

**Lake Louise** is a very large lake in the Copper Valley region west of Glennallen. It connects to Susitna Lake and Tyone Lake. Fishing and water sports are both popular on the lake, you can stay at the Lake Louise Recreation Area campgrounds on the lake shore.

### Hiking and Mountain Biking

**Anchorage** has one of the best systems of bike paths in the country, there are 121 miles of paved trails. Don't miss the chance to explore them on foot or on a bike. The best is the **Tony Knowles Coastal Trail** which runs along the shore of Cook Inlet from Westchester Lagoon past the airport and connects with miles of cross-country ski trails in Kincaid Park. This trail has been designated a National Recreation Trail. Other trails connect at Westchester Lagoon and lead downtown or east to the universities and Russian Jack Park. In fact, bike trails lead out along the Glenn Highway past Eagle River.

**Chugach State Park** just outside Anchorage has some of the best hiking and mountain bike trails in the state. The mountainous terrain means mostly dry trails and great views over Anchorage and Cook Inlet. There are access points to the trails in Anchorage's Upper Hillside area as well as from Eklutna Lake and the Eagle River Visitor Center. An excellent place to camp while taking advantage of the park is the Eklutna Lake Campground. See Chapter 14 - Camping Away From The Road System for more information about Chugach State Park.

### Wildlife Viewing

The city of **Anchorage** offers an amazing variety of wildlife viewing opportunities. Hikers on the bike trails, particularly the Tony Knowles Coastal Trail, will see a variety of birds. Chances of meeting a moose are pretty high, there are thought to be about 1,000 of them living in Anchorage, as well as about 50 black bears and another 10 or so browns. Bird lovers will also want to visit Potter Marsh, see Chapter 8 - The Kenai Peninsula for more information. During the summer it is often possible to see white beluga whales chasing salmon and hooligan from the Resolution Park viewing platform overlooking Cook Inlet at the corner of 3rd and L Street.

To get warmed up (especially if you have kids along) visit the **Alaska Zoo** (907 346-3242) for guaranteed sightings of Alaska wildlife. Head out the Seward Highway and take the O'Malley off ramp. Turn toward the mountains and watch for the entrance on the left side of the road.

Chugach State Park's **Eagle River Visitor Center** has wildlife displays, videos about local wildlife, and you can often see Dall sheep on the mountainsides. There's also a nature trail. Along more remote trails in **Chugach State Park** you may see both brown and black bears, moose, goats, bald eagles, and sharp-shinned hawks. You reach the visitor center by exiting the Glenn Highway at Mile 13 and then following the paved Eagle River Road for just over 12 miles. For more about Chugach State Park see Chapter 14 - Camping Away From the Road System.

Just a little farther from Anchorage the **Eklutna Lake Valley** and surrounding hillsides, also inside Chugach State Park, is a good place to see Dall sheep, moose, and perhaps even mountain goats if you are willing to hike the trails leading into the mountains from the campground.

The **Palmer Hay Flats** are a good place to watch ducks and moose. Take the Rabbit Slough access road at Mile 35 of the Glenn Highway.

BIRD WATCHING AT POTTER FLATS

In the Matanuska Valley there is another quite unusual animal viewing stop. The **Musk Ox Farm** (Mile 50.1 Glenn Highway; 907 745-4151) has a herd of 35 domestic musk oxen. They're being raised for their fur (called qiviut and harvested by combing the animals) and as a tourist attraction. There is a visitor's center and opportunities for photographing the oxen. Other possible opportunities for seeing a musk ox near the road network are on the Dalton or Dempster Highways, a much longer drive.

As you travel up the Glenn Highway stop to search for Dall sheep on the mountainside at **Sheep Mountain**. It's on the north side of the road from about Mile 106 to Mile 113. You may also recognize that this extremely scenic stretch of road is used as a location for many cover photos on publications about driving or RVing in Alaska.

As you cross the high open country between Mile 115 and Glennallen keep you eyes peeled for caribou, this is part of the range of the **Nelchina herd**.

# THE ROUTES, TOWNS, AND CAMPGROUNDS

## ANCHORAGE
### Population 260,000, Elevation near sea level

Anchorage is by far the largest town in Alaska, almost half of the state's population lives here. Many visitors to the state avoid Anchorage because they see no reason to spend time in a place that is much like any medium-sized western city in the Lower 48.

The fact is that Anchorage has its own charm. It sits on a point of land bounded on two sides by water and on the third by the Chugach Mountains. The city/borough (they're one entity) covers 1,955 square miles, about the same area as the state of Delaware. This largest city in Alaska is really not far from the surrounding wilderness, the huge Chugach State Park overlooks the city from the east and offers hiking trails, wildlife, and mountains to 8,000 feet.

Anchorage's central downtown area along 4th Avenue seems to have been almost totally dedicated to summer tourism. On the corner of 4th and F Street is the **Log Cabin Visitor's Information Center** (524 W. 4th Ave., Anchorage, AK 99501; 907 274-3531). This little sod-roofed cabin looks like a prospector's shack decked out with flower baskets, you can find information at the center about almost anything to do with Anchorage. A walking tour route starts at the information center, you can get a map inside. Across the street and on the next block is the **Alaska Public Lands Information Center** (605 West Fourth Avenue, Suite 105, Anchorage, AK 99501; 907 271-2737) one of four similar centers with exhibits and information about public land and parks (both national and state owned) all around the state. The others are in Tok, Fairbanks, and Ketchikan. Near these two Anchorage information centers you will find many small shops and a mall complete with a Nordstrom's and a Penny's.

An important downtown site is the **Anchorage Museum of History and Art** (121 West 7th Ave.; 907 343-4326). It has excellent historical and art exhibits. Another good museum is the **Heritage Library Museum** located in the National Bank of Alaska building at the corner of Northern Lights and C Street (907 248-5325). It has displays of Alaska paintings and native artifacts.

The Anchorage International Airport is a busy place, but even busier (in terms of landings and takeoffs) and more interesting during the summer is the nearby **Lake Hood Seaplane Base**. With over 800 takeoffs or landings in a peak summer day it is the busiest water airfield in the world and a great place to find a bush pilot to fly you out into the real Alaska. It can be fun to find a quiet place to park along the lakeshore and watch the constant coming and going of small aircraft, particularly on Friday evening or Sunday afternoon on a good-weather summer weekend.

Anchorage is known for its **bicycle and walking paths**. They run through many wooded areas of town as well as along the shore of Cook Inlet from downtown to well past the airport. Get out and stretch your legs, walkers often see a moose or two along the trail.

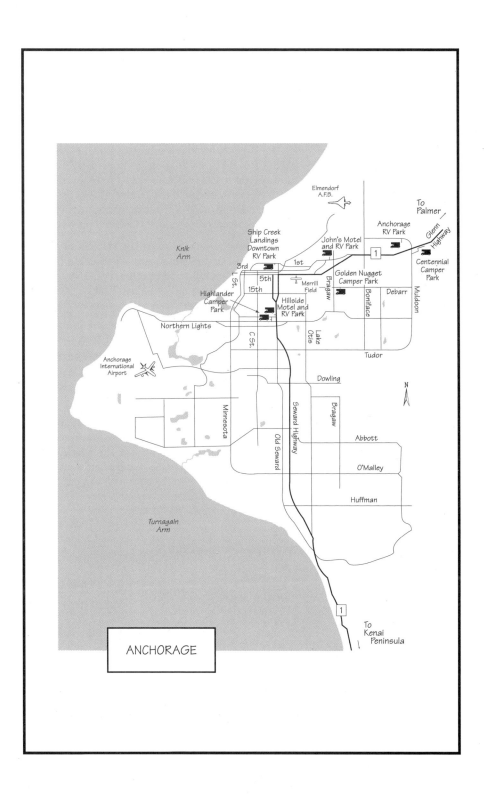

ANCHORAGE

Anchorage's weather, due to the city's location along the ocean and near several mountain passes, tends to be much cooler and cloudier than the weather in the interior around Fairbanks. 70° F is a heat wave in this part of the state. The dry summer month is June. July and August get quite a bit of rain.

Even though Anchorage is the largest town in the state you will find driving to be very easy. Locals complain, but the morning and evening rush hours are really quite short and roads are plentiful and wide. The large stores in the suburban area outside downtown Anchorage have huge parking lots and lots of room to maneuver. The large grocery chains are Carr's and Safeway, you'll also find Wal-Mart, Fred Meyer, Costco, and Barnes & Noble. The city has a bus system called the People Mover (Ride Line information number is 907 343-6543) and most city RV parks are on the routes. The downtown Transit Center is at 6th and G Street. Bus service is limited on weekends.

Those interested in catching a salmon have an opportunity to do so right in Anchorage. **Ship Creek** has good runs of king and silver salmon and is within a mile of the central downtown area. The king run is in June, the silver run is in late August and early September. Even-numbered years (like 1998 or 2000) also bring a run of pink salmon. This is shoulder-to-shoulder combat fishing at it's best (or worse) but can be amazingly productive. At least drive down and take a look.

Anchorage has four golf courses. The Anchorage Golf Course (3651 O'Malley Road; 907 522-3363 has 18 holes. Russian Jack Springs Park (907 333-8338) is a 9-hole course with astroturf greens. Two military courses are open to civilian: Eagle Glen Golf Course (907 552-2773) is an 18-hole Air Force course and Moose Run Golf Course (907 428-0056) is an 18-hole Army course.

If you are planning to fly to Alaska and rent an RV Anchorage is your best choice for a base. See Chapter 2 for a listing of RV rental companies. Almost all direct flights into Alaska (except those into Southeast) stop first in Anchorage. From here you can hit the road and head south for the scenery and fishing of the Kenai Peninsula or North to Denali Park or the Copper River Valley. RVers who have driven a rig up the highway will find that Anchorage has the most complete and reasonably-priced collection of service facilities available anywhere in Alaska or the Yukon.

### Anchorage Campgrounds

✦ ANCHORAGE RV PARK
    Address: 7300 Oilwell Road, Anchorage, AK 99504
    Telephone: (907) 338-7275 or (800) 400-7275
    Price: High

*GPS Location: N 61° 13' 50.9", W 149° 44' 29.8"*

This newest RV park in Anchorage is also the nicest. Located near the Glenn Highway entrance to the city the large campground has quiet, well-spaced sites, and brand-new facilities. Last time we were there they were also offering free coffee and donuts in the morning.

There are almost 200 spaces, all with full hook-ups including 20, 30, and 50-amp service. Some of the sites are pull-throughs, all are gravel surfaced and surrounded by native ground cover. You'll probably notice that a lot more land was used to build this campground than most comparable commercial operations. Restrooms are spacious and clean and the hot showers are free. The campground also offers a coin-operated laundry, a small store, and a dump station. The nearby Muldoon area of Anchorage offers good shopping for necessities, the downtown area is a 10-minute drive from the campground and city bus service (Routes 3 and 4) is available. A bike trail starts near the campground and runs out the Glenn Highway past Eagle River.

From the Glenn Highway northeast of central Anchorage take the Muldoon Road exit. Head north, the road soon curves to the left and you will see the campground on the left.

✦ HIGHLANDER CAMPER PARK
   Address: 2706 Fairbanks St. #11, Anchorage,
   AK 99503
   Telephone: (907) 276-2632
   Price: Medium

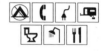

*GPS Location: N 61° 11' 46.6", W 149° 52' 22.9"*

It's hard to beat the Highlander for convenience, we find that this is our most frequently-visited Anchorage RV park, just right for short visits to the big city.

The Highlander is nothing if not simple. There are about 50 back-in spaces in a gravel lot on Fairbanks Street just off Northern Lights Blvd. The large Sears Mall and Carrs grocery store are just across Northern Lights. Most sites have full-hookups with 15 or 20-amp service. There is a decently maintained restroom building with free hot showers. We have found the location to be quiet although there is no fence or formal security. A manager lives on-site and the office is in the building to the south.

As you head west on Northern Lights from its intersection with the Seward Highway watch for Fairbanks Street. The campground will be on your left just after the turn.

✦ HILLSIDE MOTEL AND RV PARK
   Address: 2150 Gambell Street, Anchorage,
   AK 99503
   Telephone: (907) 258-6006 or (800) 478-6008
   Fax: (907) 279-8972
   Internet: http://www.servcom.com/hillside
   Price: High

*GPS Location: N 61° 12' 05.1", W 149° 52' 14.4"*

The Hillside has a convenient central location near Anchorage's Sullivan Arena and next to the Chester Creek bike trails. These trails will lead you down Chester Creek to Cook Inlet and then either downtown or along the Inlet past the airport. They're one of Anchorage's nicest features. This motel and campground have recently been spiffed up, making it a popular place to stay. The Hillside is one of the few Alaska campgrounds that are open year-round.

FLOAT PLANES ON LAKE HOOD

All of the 70 or so slots in this campground are back-in. Most have full-hookups although a few electric-only spaces are available. There is a central services building with bathrooms, showers and laundry for the RV park. The motel office can book excursions and tours. Rigs over 35 feet long will find this campground a tight fit. Reservations are recommended.

The campground is most easily reached by driving south on Gambell Street from just east of the downtown area. Gambell is the street that becomes the Seward Highway farther south. Gambell crosses 15th and descends into the Chester Creek Valley, you will see the Sullivan Arena on your right. As the road begins to ascend you will see the Hillside Motel and RV Park on your right. From the south you'll have to go north to 15th and return toward the south to enter the park.

✦ GOLDEN NUGGET CAMPER PARK
    Address: 4100 DeBarr Road, Anchorage, AK 99508
    Telephone: (907) 333-5311 or (800) 449-2012
    Price: High

*GPS Location: N 61° 12' 32.7", W 149° 47' 55.0"*

The Golden Nugget is a huge RV Park. Some folks think the campground's location across the street from the Costco store is its best feature, but it is also conveniently close to the 9-hole golf course (astro-turf greens) at Russian Jack Park and the city's bike-trail system. The campground also has good city bus service to downtown (Route 12).

The campground has 215 RV sites, most are full hook-ups. Some sites are pull-throughs, many have room for large rigs. There is also a tent area. The restrooms are well-maintained and clean with free showers and there is also a laundry, a playground, and a picnic area.

The campground is located near the corner of Bragaw and DeBarr. One possible access route would be to take the Muldoon Road exit from the Glenn Highway. Travel south on Muldoon Road to DeBarr, then west on DeBarr. You will cross the Boniface Parkway and then climb and descend a small hill, just after descending the hill you will see a Costco store on your right, the campground is on your left. Turn left on Hoyt Street and then right into the campground.

✦ CENTENNIAL CAMPER PARK
   (MUNICIPALITY OF ANCHORAGE)
      Address: Box 196650, Anchorage, AK 99519
      Telephone: (907) 333-9711
      Price: Medium

*GPS Location: N 61° 13' 38.1", W 149° 43' 21.1"*

Centennial Park is a Municipality of Anchorage campground. Government campgrounds tend to offer more space and Centennial Park is no exception. While most sites are not overly large they are well-separated and there are lots of trees. This is also the least expensive formal campground in town (excluding some store parking lots).

The campground offers about 90 spaces for vehicle campers and also large grassy areas for tenters. There are no hook-ups. Several sites are very large, the rest are medium-sized back-ins, some will accommodate larger rigs. Restrooms are very basic but do offer hot coin-operated showers. There is also a dump station. Campfires are allowed in this campground. City bus service is available. The bike trail to Eagle River is just across the Glenn Highway from this campground.

To reach Centennial Park head south on Muldoon Road from the Glenn Highway interchange. Almost immediately turn left onto Boundary Ave. From there it is easy to follow signs for about a half-mile to the campground.

✦ JOHN'S MOTEL AND RV PARK
      Address: 3543 Mountain View Drive, Anchorage,
      AK 99508
      Telephone: (907) 277-4332 or (800) 478-4332
      Fax: (907) 272-0739
      Price: High

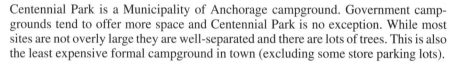

*GPS Location: N 61° 13' 23.8", W 149° 48' 47.1"*

This older RV park and motel in Anchorage's Mountain View district is easy to find and conveniently located. This is an adult-only campground. Good city bus service

(Route 45) is available.

The campground has about 50 back-in sites, most with full hookups including 30-amp service. Parking is on concrete wheel pads with gravel or grass surrounding them. There are restrooms with free showers, a laundromat, a gift shop, and a dump station. Groceries and RV supplies are available nearby as are restaurants. The staff in the motel office will help you arrange tours or excursions. City bus stops are conveniently close to the campground. John's is open year-round.

To reach the campground turn north from the Glenn Highway on Bragaw. Drive .2 miles to the first stop light (Mountain View Drive) and turn left. The campground will be on your right in another .1 mile.

✦  SHIP CREEK LANDINGS DOWNTOWN RV PARK
    Address: 150 North Ingra Street (P.O. Box 200947),
    Anchorage, AK 99520-0947
    Telephone: (907) 277-0877, Fax: (907) 277-3808
    Price: High

*GPS Location: N 61° 13' 20.6", W 149° 52' 06.4"*

Ship Creek Landing is the closest RV park to downtown. Visitors interested in the central tourist area will love the fact that they can walk there in about ten minutes.

This campground is relatively new. There are about 150 campsites, almost all are large back-in spaces but there are a few pull-throughs. An area is provided for tent camping. The campground itself is a large gravel area below a bluff which blocks much of the southern sun. There is lots of room for big rigs and most spaces have full utility hookups. There are no picnic tables or fire pits. Electricity is 20 and 30-amp. The restrooms are in reasonably good condition with hot showers and there is a laundromat.

If you are arriving on the Glenn Highway from the north zero your odometer as you pass the Muldoon Road interchange at the entrance to town. Continue for 4.5 miles to Ingra Street (the sixth stoplight the last time we were in town). Turn right on Ingra and go three blocks to the stop sign at the bottom of the hill. Turn left on First and you will see the campground entrance on your left.

## FROM ANCHORAGE TO PALMER
### (42 miles)

From Anchorage a four-lane divided highway runs north through a region of rolling hills between the Chugach Mountains and Knik Arm. The small Anchorage suburb of **Eagle River** is at Mile 13, it has a population of about 18,000. Eagle River has grocery shopping and restaurants. The paved Eagle River Road runs back into the Chugach Mountains for 13 miles to the **Chugach State Park Nature Center**. Trails lead from the center into the park.

At about Mile 26 the road becomes two-lane, near this point watch for local residents sitting on old couches on a small bluff west of the highway watching the traffic go by. At Mile 31 the highway crosses the Knik River and enters the Matanuska Valley. At a junction at Mile 35 the Parks Highway cuts off to the west. Follow this road to Denali Park and for the shortest route to Fairbanks. See Chapter 9 - The Parks Highway for information about the route.

A few miles after the Parks Highway junction the road reaches Palmer at Mile 42.

## Campgrounds
## Anchorage to Palmer

✦ EAGLE RIVER CAMPGROUND (CHUGACH STATE PARK)
    Location: Near Mile 12 Glenn Highway
    Price: Medium

*GPS Location: N 61° 18' 22.9", W 149° 34' 18.8"*

This large state campground is said to be one of the most popular in Alaska. This is understandable considering its location near the largest city in the state. Still, it doesn't seem to be hard to find a site if you arrive reasonably early in the day and avoid week

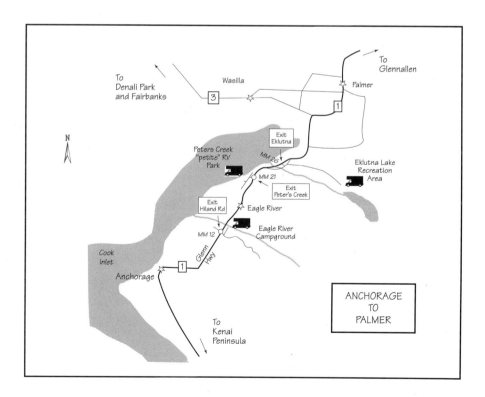

ends. The campground is set along the Eagle River near the Glenn Highway.

This large campground has 57 spaces. There are a few tent sites, the rest are back-in vehicle slots. Many are roomy enough for large rigs. All interior roads and parking pads are paved and sites have picnic tables and fire pits. The camping sites are well-separated and there are lots of trees and natural area. This campground also has a large overflow area for RVs when the regular sites are filled. Most toilets are outhouses. There are also flush toilets available at one building but no showers. There is a dump station and water is available at the station for rig fill-ups. The campground has a 4-day limit.

Take the Hiland Road Exit from the Glenn Highway near the 12 mile marker. The campground access road entrance is right at this interchange. The road runs north along the east side of the highway for about 1.4 miles to the campground.

✦  EKLUTNA LAKE RECREATION AREA
   (CHUGACH STATE PARK)
      Location: Mile 9 Eklutna Lake Road
      Price: Low

*GPS Location: N 61° 24' 40.3", W 149°08' 58.9"*

This very nice state campground near Anchorage has only one major drawback, 7 miles of rough gravel road. Some folks see this as one of its best features. The campground sits next to Eklutna Lake, source of drinking water and hydroelectric power for Anchorage. There are several good hiking and biking trails from the campground leading into the surrounding Chugach State Park.

Eklutna Lake has about 50 sites, most are back-in vehicle sites set in a birch grove. There are also some tent sites near the lake. The interior roads and parking pads are gravel, there are picnic tables and fire pits. The campground has outhouses and water faucets. There is also an overflow camping area and a walk-in boat launching area (for canoes and kayaks). The campground has a 15-day limit.

Access to the campground is via the Eklutna Road which leaves the old Glenn Highway just east of the Eklutna exit from the 26 mile point of the new Glenn Highway in Eagle River. The first two miles of the road are paved, the remaining seven miles are rough dirt and gravel but easily passable in any rig most of the time.

✦  PETERS CREEK "PETITE" RV PARK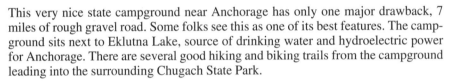
      Address: 20940 Old Glenn Highway, Chugiak,
      AK 99567
      Telephone: (907) 688-2487
      Price: Medium

*GPS Location: N 61° 24' 34.8", W 149°26' 48.3"*

This small campground is conveniently located near the Glenn Highway with easy frequent bus connections into Anchorage. There are about 20 spaces with full hook-ups and another eight or nine with none. The campground is suitable only for self-contained rigs, there are no restrooms or showers.

To reach the campground take the south Peters Creek exit from the Glenn Highway near the 21 mile point. The campground is on the west side of the freeway, Almost immediately as you head west the road T's, turn left at the T and drive about a tenth of a mile, the campground will be on your right.

## PALMER
### Population 40,000, Elevation 250 feet

Palmer was founded in 1916 as a stop on the newly constructed Alaska Railroad and served as the supply center and rail head for the surrounding area. In 1934 the Matanuska Valley around Palmer was the destination for 202 families from depressed areas in the lower 48, the U.S. government moved them to the Matanuska Valley to take advantage of the area's obvious agricultural potential. Today's Palmer is surrounded by both farms and residential areas that stretch westward through the valley to Wasilla on the Parks Highway.

The **Mat-Su Visitor's Center** (HC01, Box 6166J21, Palmer, Alaska 99645; 907 746-5000) is actually located just off the Parks Highway at about Mile 35. This is very near the junction of the Glenn and Parks Highways. Palmer also has its own visitor's center, the **Palmer Visitors Center** (Palmer Chamber of Commerce, P.O. Box 45, Palmer, Alaska 99645; 907 745-2880) in town near the railroad tracks at South Valley Way and East Fireweed. It has a gift shop and a small museum describing the valley's agricultural history. Across the street is the **Palmer Farmers and Crafts Market** where you can buy local vegetables. You'll also find them at several roadside stands along major roads in the valley. If you are in the area during the week before Labor Day (the last week in August) be sure to visit the **Alaska State Fair** and take a look at some of the really big prize-winning vegetables that result from the long summer daylight hours.

Golfers will be glad to hear that Palmer has a course. The 18-hole **Palmer Golf Course** (907 745-4653) is located behind the State Fairgrounds on Inner Springer Road which leaves the Glenn Highway at about Mile 40 and is open from 6 AM to 11 PM.

A very interesting side trip from the Palmer area is **Hatcher Pass**. There's more about Hatcher Pass and the Independence Mine in Chapter 9 - The Parks Highway, but one of the best access routes is Fishhook Road which heads east from the Glenn Highway at Mile 49.5 near Palmer.

## Palmer Campgrounds

◆ MOUNTAIN VIEW RV PARK
    Address: P.O. Box 2521, Palmer, AK 99645
    Telephone: (907) 745-5747 or (800) 264-4582
    Fax: (907) 745-1700
    Price: Medium

*GPS Location: N 61° 35' 39.1", W 149° 01' 28.3"*

This large and friendly park in the quiet countryside east of Palmer offers an unusual attraction, airboat tours up the nearby Knik River to the foot of the Knik Glacier.

The campground has about 120 spaces, most are large pull-throughs with 30-amp electricity, water, and sewer. The entire campground is a large open field, perhaps not as attractive as a treed area but a popular feature here since it means fewer mosquitoes and lots of sunshine. There's also lots of room for big rigs. A designated tent camping area is provided. Another popular feature at this campground is the many individual bathrooms, each with toilet, sink and shower. There is also a coin-operated laundromat and a community fire pit with wood supplied by the campground.

To drive to the campground follow Arctic Street east from its junction with the Glenn Highway just outside Palmer near Mile 42. This takes you along the route of the Old Glenn Highway, it used to swing much closer to the mountains than the current routing across the hay flats to Anchorage. Follow the highway east for 2.8 miles, then turn left onto Smith Road, drive .6 miles, and turn right. You'll see the campground on your left in .3 mile.

◆ MATANUSKA RIVER PARK
    (MATANUSKA-SUSITNA BOROUGH)
    Location: 1 Mile East of Palmer on Old Glenn
    Highway
    Price: Low

*GPS Location: N 61° 36' 22.7", W 149° 05' 12.4"*

This is a nice campground operated by the local government, called a borough instead of a county in Alaska. The 101 acre park is more than a campground, there are hiking trails along the Matanuska River, playing fields, and a picnic area.

There are two camping areas. One is an open grassy area with back-in slots for about 34 rigs. The other has about 45 back-in slots along winding roads through a forested area with picnic tables and fire-pits, a traditional government-type Alaska campground. Less traditional are the flush toilets and coin-operated hot showers at this campground. There are no hook-ups but water is available and there is a dump station.

Follow Arctic (Old Glenn Highway) east from its intersection with the Glenn Highway near Palmer, the campground entrance is on the left at .9 miles.

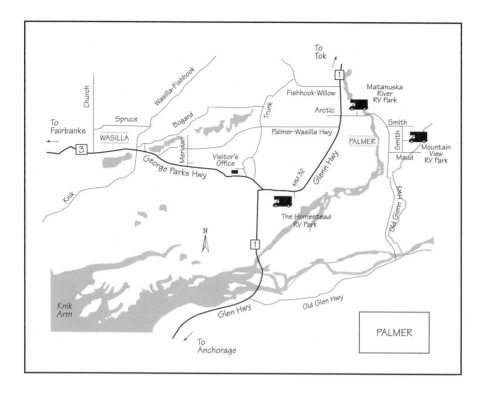

✦ THE HOMESTEAD RV PARK
   Address: P.O. Box 354, Palmer, AK 99645
   Telephone: (907) 745-6005 or (800) 478-3570
   Price: Medium

*GPS Location: N 61° 33' 06.5", W 149° 13' 54.2"*

This popular campground has an extremely convenient location, a sunny setting, and some of the nicest restrooms in Alaska. They even feature soothing music.

The campground has 64 sites sitting on a birch-covered bluff overlooking the Knik Valley and mountains to the east. Most sites are large pull-throughs, they have 30-amp electric and water hook-ups. There is also a tent-camping area and a public campfire ring. Restrooms are in a modern but sod-roofed log building and offer hot showers (and music), there is also a coin-operated laundry and a dump station. Fishing is possible in the lakes across the highway. Some evenings entertainment is available in the form of square dances or musical narratives in the on-site amphitheater. The people in the office can help you with local tours and excursions.

The campground is easy to find since it is right next to the Glenn Highway near Mile 32. This is about .9 miles north of the intersection of the Parks and Glenn Highways.

## FROM PALMER TO GLENNALLEN
### (147 miles)

After Palmer the highway begins to wind its way through a mountain pass and climb toward the Copper River Valley. At Mile 101 is the Matanuska Glacier State Recreation Site which has a viewing area overlooking the **Matanuska Glacier**. For a closer look at the glacier you can drive in to the private Glacier Park, which allows RV and tent camping. For many miles along the highway there are spectacular views to the south of the Chugach Range. The mountains to the north are the Talkeetna Mountains.

After climbing out of the Matanuska Valley the road runs through **Tahneta Pass** and across 3,322-foot **Eureka Summit**, then through a high plateau region with hundreds of little lakes and scattered black spruce trees. Many of the lakes have good fishing but they're difficult to access. There is a gravel road that runs north for 17 miles from Mile 160 to **Lake Louise** which has excellent fishing and two state campgrounds.

Once you pass the Lake Louise junction you'll start to see the Wrangell Mountains ahead. From left to right the peaks are **Mount Sanford** (16,237 feet), **Mount Drum** (12,010 feet), and **Mount Wrangell** (14,163 feet). All of them are in the Wrangell-St. Elias National park. See Chapter 6 - The Richardson Highway for more about this park. The road reaches Glennallen at Mile 187.

## Campgrounds
## Palmer to Glennallen

✦ RIVER'S EDGE RECREATION PARK
   Address: P.O. Box 364, Sutton, AK 99674
   Telephone: (907) 746-2267
   Price: Medium

*GPS Location: N 61° 42' 42.7", W 148° 50' 58.5"*

This private campground seems a lot like a well-run state campground, except that there are some electrical hookups and restrooms with flush toilets and hot showers. Unfortunately, the location next to Granite Creek doesn't mean that you can camp right on the water, there is a large gravel dike separating the campground from the creek. Overall, though, this is a very pleasant little campground.

There are about 20 sites, most are scattered back-ins but there are several pull-throughs offering electrical hookups Many sites have picnic tables and fire pits and there is a dump and water fill station. The new and modern restroom building is accessible to handicapped campers and there is an extra fee for showers. You can fish in Granite Creek and there is a bicycle path along the highway to the little town of Sutton.

The campground is located on the Glenn Highway near Mile 62, some 20 miles from Palmer.

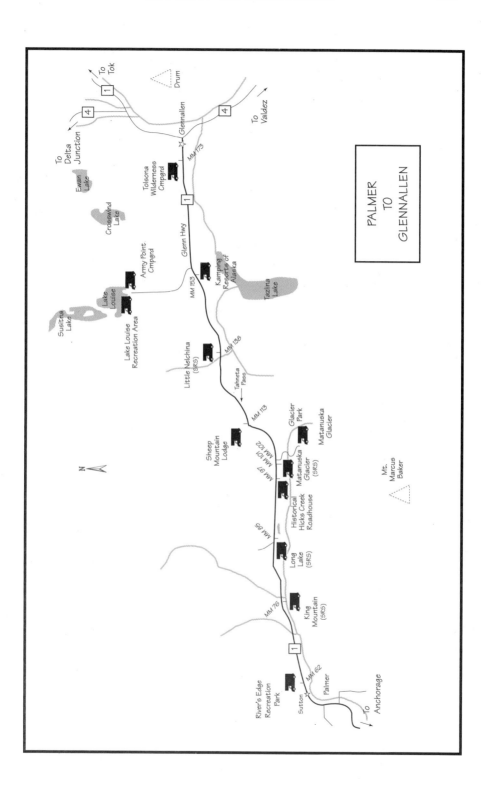

PALMER
TO
GLENNALLEN

✦ KING MOUNTAIN STATE RECREATION SITE
  Location: Mile 76 Glenn Highway
  Price: Low

*GPS Location: N 61° 46' 32.5", W 148° 29' 40.6"*

The best of the state campgrounds for smaller rigs along this section of the Glenn Highway is undoubtedly King Mountain. There are some 24 smallish back-in sites in a wooded setting next to the milky Matanuska River. Sites have picnic tables and fire pits and there are outhouses and a water pump. This campground also has a boat launch and a kitchen/picnic shelter. There is a 15-day stay limit at this campground.

✦ LONG LAKE STATE RECREATION SITE
  Location: Mile 85
  Price: Free

*GPS Location: N 61° 48' 08.9", W 148° 14' 19.4"*

At first glance Long Lake campground seems an idyllic location, especially if your are descending from the high country toward Glennallen. There's the sheltered little lake surrounded by trees, fishermen in small boats dot the surface. A closer look, however, reveals that the 9 camping sites are really just parking slots in a small gravel lot next to the busy highway. Nonetheless, this is a popular campground. There are picnic tables, fire pits, and outhouses and the price is right. There's a small boat ramp and you can catch grayling in the lake. The camping limit here is 15 days.

✦ HISTORICAL HICKS CREEK ROADHOUSE
  Address: HC 3 Box 8410, Palmer, AK 99645
  Telephone: (907) 745-8213
  Price: Medium

*GPS Location: N 61° 47' 34.1", W 147° 56' 03.8"*

Back behind this little roadhouse-style operation is a pleasant little camping area. To date most of the improvement efforts of the current energetic owners have been toward the restaurant and restrooms and laundromat, but they promise that the campground's time will come. Now (1997) there are about 15 campsites set in cottonwood trees. Four of them are pull-throughs and a couple of these offer electrical hookups (really long extension cords). Some sites have picnic tables and some have fire pits. The laundromat building also houses some decent coin-op showers. The lodge is located on the south side of the Glenn Highway near Mile 97.

✦ MATANUSKA GLACIER STATE RECREATION SITE
  Location: Mile 101 of the Glenn Highway
  Price: Low

*GPS Location: N 61° 48' 06.4", W 147° 48' 54.3"*

This recreation site gets lots of visitors because it offers a viewpoint with good views of the Matanuska Glacier. Many tour busses and passing motorists make the stop.

There are also about 12 vehicle camping sites and also a tent camping area. The sites are well separated and have picnic tables and fire pits. The campground has outhouses and a water pump.

Watch for the recreation site on the south side of the Glenn Highway near Mile 101.

✦  GLACIER PARK
      Address: HC03 Box 8449, Palmer, AK 99645
      Telephone: (907) 745-2534
      Price: Medium

*GPS Location: N 61° 47' 34.1", W 147° 47' 46.5"*

Glacier Park is a unique private operation. They've built an impressive road that descends from the highway to the flat bench near the Matanuska Glacier. You leave the highway near Mile 102 and descend to a gatehouse area at about .8 miles. Here you'll find a small restaurant and gift shop. To pass on to the glacier overlook you must pay a fee of $6.50 per person. The overlook is at 3.1 miles and is popular for picnics. From the parking area it is usually possible to walk to the rapidly retreating glacier.

Camping facilities at Glacier Park are limited. At the overlook it is possible to dry camp in the parking area if you have a self-contained rig. There are picnic tables and a hard-to-find outhouse but this is an exposed location with often blustery weather. Near the gatehouse complex there is a 10-space tent camping area suitable for tents or small rigs with picnic tables, fire rings, and an outhouse.

✦  SHEEP MOUNTAIN LODGE
      Address: HC 03 Box 8490, Palmer, AK 99645
      Telephone: (907) 745-5121, Fax: (907) 745-5120
      Internet: http://www.alaska.net/~sheepmt/
      Price: Medium

*GPS Location: N 61° 48' 42.8", W 147° 29' 50.8"*

The real reason for stopping here is the restaurant, it is excellent. There are also nice rental cabins. Camping is limited to parking in the lot in front of the lodge near the highway. Electrical hookups are available. Tents are not accommodated. You can pay a little extra for a hot shower in the immaculate restrooms or to soak in the hot tub.

The lodge is located on the north side of the highway near Mile 113 of the Glenn Highway.

✦  LITTLE NELCHINA STATE RECREATION SITE
      Location: Mile 138 of the Glenn Highway
      Price: Free

*GPS Location: N 61° 59' 22.5", W 146° 56' 43.8"*

This little state recreation site is tucked into a small canyon near the highway. Access is via a short stretch of the old highway that was abandoned during road-straightening construction.

There are 11 sites in this typical state campground. Several of them are along the creek in spruce and cottonwoods. Most are fairly small and are back-ins or tent sites. There are outhouses and a raft launching area. The price charged for camping here reflects the lack of drinking water, but this isn't a bad place to stop for the night if you have a smaller rig. You can hike upriver to some fossil beds. There is a 15-day camping limit.

◆ KAMPING RESORTS OF ALASKA (K.R.O.A.)
    Address: HC 1 Box 2560, Glennallen, AK 99588
    Telephone: (907) 822-3346
    Price: Medium

*GPS Location: N 62° 02' 54.4", W 146° 32' 16.1"*

K.R.O.A. is a full service campground seemingly situated in the middle of nowhere. There are at least 100 camping spaces in a large gravel lot behind the restaurant, cabins, and gas station out front. Trees break up the large expanse of the campground. Many sites are pull-throughs and both full hookup and partial hookup sites are available. Some sites are along the Little Mendeltna, a small stream running along the side of the campground. There are picnic tables and some sites have circles of rocks forming fire rings. The laundromat/shower building has flush toilets and hot showers. There is also a dump station.

The campground is located on the south side of the Glenn Highway near Mile 153. This is about 30 miles from Glennallen and near the half-way point if you are driving between either Tok or Valdez and Anchorage.

◆ LAKE LOUISE RECREATION AREA
    LAKE LOUISE AND ARMY POINT CAMPGROUNDS
        Location: Mile 17 Lake Louise Road,
        Leaves Glenn Highway at Mile 160
        Price: Low

*GPS Location: N 62° 16' 54.0", W 146° 32' 33.9"*

Lake Louise is a huge lake that is very popular year-round, which is surprising considering its remote location. In the summer fishing, especially for lake trout, is popular. In late summer the water is warm enough for swimming (you've got to be tough) and water sports. During the fall this is a popular hunting area and in the winter this can be great snow mobiling and ice fishing country.

There are two modern state campgrounds located right next to each other on the southwest shore of the lake with about 60 camping spaces. They really make up one large campground. Most of the sites here are back-ins in large gravel parking areas but a few are separated sites. The trees in the area are very small dwarf species or shrubs so don't expect a lot of privacy even if you get one of the separated spaces. There are picnic tables and fire pits. Other offerings are outhouses, water pumps, a boat launching area, and a nice little beach with a walking trail between the two campgrounds.

To reach the campgrounds you must follow the often rough gravel Lake Louise Road from near Mile 160 of the Glenn Highway. The campgrounds are at Mile 17.

◆ Tolsona Wilderness Campground
   Address: P.O. Box 23, Glennallen, AK 99588
   Telephone: (907) 822-3865
   Price: Medium

*GPS Location: N 62° 06' 49.4", W 145° 58' 32.1"*

Probably the best spot to stop for the evening or a week along the whole Glenn Highway is the Tolsona Wilderness Campground. This is a commercial campground with the advantages and ambiance of a government campground. If you are looking for an interesting hike ask how to reach the nearby Tolsona mud volcanoes.

Tolsona is a large campground, there are some 70 sites. Most are back-ins but there are also a few pull-throughs. About 30 of the sites have electricity and water hookups. The remainder are dry. Many sites are on the banks of Tolsona Creek which runs right through the campground, and which has grayling. Sites are well separated and the campground is wooded with white spruce. Each site has a picnic table and fire pit. There are restrooms with flush toilets and coin-op showers, a laundromat, a dump station and water fill site, and even playing fields.

The .8 mile long gravel access road leaves the Glenn Highway near Mile 173. This is about 13 miles west of Glennallen.

## Glennallen
### Population 1,000, Elevation 1,450 feet

Glennallen occupies a strategic position just west of the south junction of the Richardson and Glenn highways. It serves as the supply center for the huge but sparsely populated Copper River Valley and has lots of government offices including the Bureau of Land Management, State Troopers, and Fish and Game. You'll find that the services are strung along the highway and include RV parks, grocery stores, restaurants, and gas stations. The **Copper River Valley Information Center** (Box 469, Glennallen, Alaska 99588; 907 822-555) is a sod-roofed log cabin located right at the junction of the Glenn and Richardson Highways.

## Glennallen Campgrounds

✦ MOOSE HORN RV PARK
   Address: Mile 187.7 Glenn Hwy., Glennallen, AK 99588
   Price: Medium

*GPS Location: N 62° 06' 26.6", W 145° 31' 23.6"*

If you happen to reach Glennallen late in the day and need a place to stop for the evening with full hookups you might try this small campground. There are 10 back-in spaces with 30 amp electric, sewer and water in an open gravel field. The campground is located south of the Glenn Highway in Glennallen some 1.5 miles west of the junction with the Richardson Highway.

✦ BISHOP'S RV PARK AND CAR WASH
   Address: P.O. Box 367, Glennallen, AK 99588
   Telephone: (907) 822-3310
   Price: Medium

*GPS Location: N 62° 06' 27.3", W 145° 30' 56.8"*

Self-contained campers who like to keep things simple will like this place. Bishop's

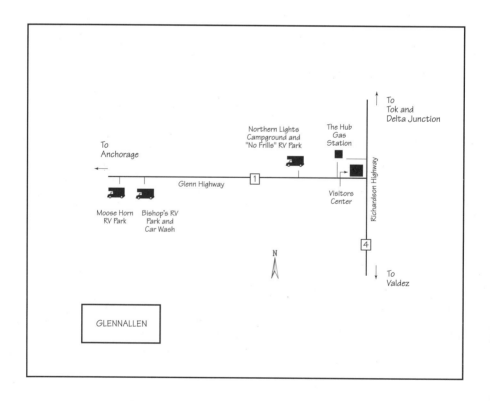

has 13 sites including 7 pull-throughs and 6 back-ins. There are 30-amp electric and water hookups and also a dump station. All are set on a gravel lot behind a small office building and next to the large car wash building owned by the same folks. Watch for Bishops on the south side of the highway in Glennallen about 1.3 miles west of the Glenn's junction with the Richardson Highway.

✦ NORTHERN NIGHTS CAMPGROUND AND RV PARK
    Address: Mile 188.7 Glenn Hwy.,
    Glennallen, AK 99588
    Telephone: (907) 822-3199
    Price: Medium

*GPS Location: N 62° 06' 27.0", W 145° 29' 10.5"*

The name of this campground is deceiving because this campground has more in the way of frills than either of the other two campgrounds in Glennallen.

There are 23 sites set in a mixed white and black spruce grove. The gravel sites are well separated for a commercial campground and many are pull-throughs. There are 30-amp electrical and water hookups and a dump station. When we visited there were chemical toilets serving as restroom facilities. Five nice tent sites with parking pads and tent platforms are located in the rear of the campground.

The campground is located on the north side of the Glenn Highway in Glennallen about .3 miles west of the intersection of the Glenn and Richardson Highways.

## FROM GLENNALLEN TO TOK
### (139 miles)

From Glennallen the Glenn and Richardson are the same road for 14 miles northward to the Gakona junction. From there a section of road runs northeast to Tok, it is commonly called the Tok Cutoff.

For many miles the Tok Cutoff runs along high ground overlooking the Copper River. At higher points there are great views toward the southeast and the Wrangell-St. Elias National Park and Mt. Drum (12,010 feet) and Mt. Sanford (16,237 feet). Much of this road is on permafrost and the frost heaves are terrible.

At Mile 60 there is a junction with the **Nabesna Road**. This gravel road runs 45 miles into the Wrangell-St. Elias National Park and Preserve to the former gold-mining town of Nabesna. There's a ranger station for the park about a quarter-mile in. They can fill you in on road conditions and camping possibilities. There are no formal government campgrounds but there are lots of places to park your rig and dry camp. The road is paved for just 4 miles, it is decent gravel to Mile 28, then it deteriorates further with some sometimes dicey stream fords. There are no park facilities along the road but the scenery is spectacular. There are several good fishing lakes and also some hiking possibilities. The park service seems to be trying to interest visitors in this part of the park, you will probably be able to get some good information from the ranger at the station.

After passing the Nabesna Road the highway runs through **Mentasta Pass** and crosses the 2,234-foot summit to pass through the Alaska Range from the Copper River drainage into the Tanana and Yukon drainage. The road reaches Tok junction at Mile 125 where it joins the Alaska Highway some 93 miles from the Alaska border. See Chapter 4 - The Alaska Highway for information about Tok.

## Campgrounds
## Glennallen to Tok

✦ GAKONA, ALASKA R.V. PARK
   Address: P.O. Box 299, Gakona, AK 99586
   Telephone and Fax: (907) 822-3550
   Price: Medium

*GPS Location: N 62° 18' 27.6", W 145° 13' 52.9"*

This campground has about 50 sites sitting on a large open gravel area next to the Copper River. Some spaces are pull-throughs and some back-ins, all have lots of room for maneuvering. Full service (20, 30 and 50-amp), water and electric, electric only, and dry sites are available. An older restroom building has flush toilets and hot showers and there is a laundromat and dump station. Other attractions include a playground, some picnic tables, and some fire pits.

The entrance road to the campground is on the Tok Cutoff some 4 miles northeast of the junction of the Richardson and the Tok Cutoff (Gakona Junction).

✦ CHISTOCHINA RV PARK
   Address: SR 224 Mile 34.4 Tok Cut-Off,
   Chistochina, AK 99586
   Telephone: (907) 822-3914
   Price: Medium

*GPS Location: N 62° 35' 09.2", W 144° 39' 04.8"*

The Chistochina RV Park has about 15 sites, many are pull-throughs. Sites have 20-amp electric, sewer, and water hookups. The gravel sites are separated by grass strips and there are some trees scattered around the camping area. There are also tent sites. Restrooms have flush toilets and hot showers and firewood is available.

The campground is located near the highway at Mile 34.4 of the Tok Cut-Off.

✦ GRIZZLY LAKE RANCH
   Address: P.O. Box 340, Gakona, AK 99586
   Telephone: (907) 822-5214 or (907) 822-3239
   Price: Medium

*GPS Location: N 62° 42' 45.5", W 144° 11' 52.3"*

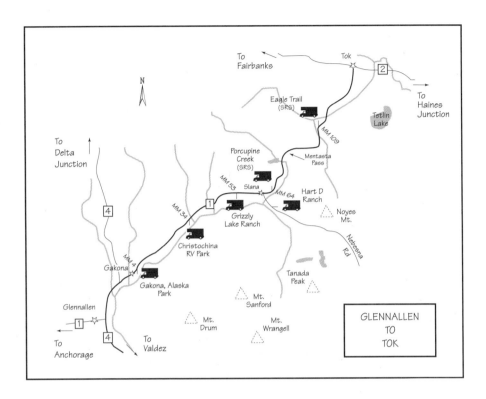

This small bed and breakfast occupies a scenic site near the Tok-Cutoff on a small lake with great views toward the east. They plan to have parking with no hookups for RVs and tent sites beginning in 1998. They'll also offer showers, a water fill station, and perhaps a dump station. If you are interested in stopping here and have a large rig you should probably walk the short distance down from the highway to check maneuvering room. Watch for the sign and entrance road on the east side of the highway near Mile 53 of the Tok Cutoff.

✦   HART D RANCH
       Address: Slana, AK 99586
       Telephone and Fax: (907) 822-3973
       Price: Medium

*GPS Location: N 62° 42' 20.9", W 143° 58' 07.0"*

This campground was under construction when we visited in the fall of 1997. The sites had been laid out and utilities were mostly in. 1998 should see it open.

The campground has about 30 sites, most are pull-throughs with electricity and water hookups. They are nicely arranged and separated by vegetation and trees, Maneuvering room appears tight but it is hard to tell at this time. A generator is used to provide power. You'll probably quickly become accustomed to the slow putt-putt, many rural Alaskans do. There will be a dump station and restrooms will be available with hot showers.

To reach the campground follow the Nabesna Road east from near Mile 60 of the Tok Cutoff. At .7 miles turn left into the post office parking lot and continue on through to the campground.

✦ PORCUPINE CREEK STATE RECREATION SITE
    Location: Near Mile 64 of the Tok Cutoff
    Price: Low

*GPS Location: N 62° 43' 39.9", W 143° 52' 16.2"*

This very small state campground has 12 back-in sites arranged around an open cleared driveway area. Each site as a picnic table and fire pit. There are outhouses and a water pump.

✦ EAGLE TRAIL STATE RECREATION SITE
    Location: Near Maaile 109 of the Tok Cutoff
    Price: Low

Eagle Trail is a large and pleasant state campground. It celebrates the Eagle Trail, built from Valdez to Eagle (and including a telegraph line) to improve communications with the gold fields. A short trail from the campground follows portions of the Eagle Trail.

The campground has about 40 sites including 5 for tenters. They are arranged in 5 wheel-like groups with back-in sites for RVs. There is good separation between sites and they are set in wooded area. All have picnic tables and fire pits. There are pit toilets and a water pump.

## GLENN HIGHWAY DUMP STATIONS

Many of the campgrounds in this chapter have either dump stations or sewer hookups. In most cases use of the dump stations is either restricted to people staying at the campground or requires payment of a fee. Try to plan to empty your holding tanks in one of the larger cities where proper sewer treatment is guaranteed and isn't a financial burden to the campground owner.

In **Anchorage** many gas stations have dump stations available to customers. Here are some of them: Mapco Express Store #5010, 1500 East 5th Ave.; Earl's Chevron, International Airport Road and Arctic; Ed's Chevron Service, 832 East 6th Ave.; Fountain

Chevron, Spenard and Minnesota; Indian Hills Chevron, 6470 Debarr Road; Triple A Service Station, 1304 Airport Heights; MAPCO Express Store #5008, 717 E. Northern Lights; and Garrett's Tesoro #1, 2811 Seward Highway.

In **Eagle** River try Frontier Texaco, 11301 Old Glenn Highway.

In **Palmer** go to Palmer Chevron, 439 West Evergreen or Glacier View Tesoro, Glacier View Drive and Glenn Highway.

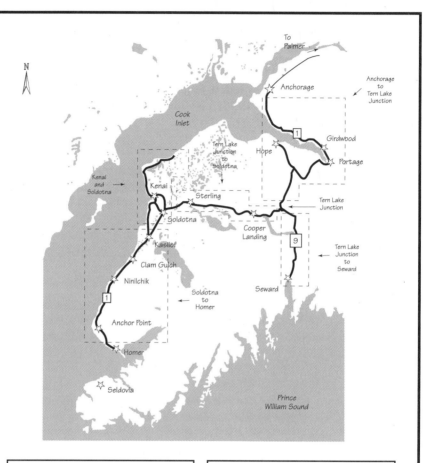

N

To
Palmer

Anchorage

Anchorage
to
Tern Lake
Junction

Cook
Inlet

Girdwood

1

Portage

Tern Lake
Junction
to
Soldotna

Hope

Kenai
and
Soldotna

Kenai

Sterling

Tern Lake
Junction

Soldotna

Cooper
Landing

Tern Lake
Junction
to
Seward

9

Kasilof

Clam Gulch

Ninilchik

Soldotna
to
Homer

Seward

1

Anchor Point

Homer

Seldovia

Prince
William Sound

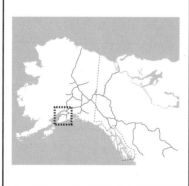

# THE KENAI PENINSULA

# CHAPTER

. . . . . . . . . 8

# THE KENAI PENINSULA

## INTRODUCTION

The one region in Alaska with the most to offer campers has got to be the Kenai Peninsula. This huge wilderness playground, almost an island, has something for everyone.

We're often amazed when talking to RVers returning down the highway after a summer in Alaska to find that they did not even visit the Kenai. We hear many reasons: didn't want to drive through Anchorage, didn't want to drive so far, it's too crowded, the weather isn't very good. We think that the real reason is that they didn't know what they were missing.

The Kenai is the most popular place in the state for campers from Anchorage. The state's largest city is home to the state's largest group of campers, and on weekends during the summer they head south every Friday night and usually return on Sunday evening. That means that there are many camping sites on the Kenai. If you plan ahead you can easily arrange to enjoy the Kenai during the week when it isn't very crowded, on weekends you can be comfortably ensconced in a beautiful campsite and watch the weekenders arrive with a cocktail in your hand.

### Highlights

Three major population centers are located on the Kenai Peninsula, these are **Seward**, **Kenai-Soldotna**, and **Homer**. Each of them has many campgrounds and is covered in more detail below.

The **Seward Highway** is a designated National Forest Scenic Byway. Attractions along the way like **Turnagain Arm**, the **Alyeska Ski Area**, **Portage Glacier**,

**Turnagain Pass**, **Kenai Lake**, and the **Exit Glacier** are excellent reasons to make this drive.

Much of the Peninsula is federal or state land. While there you'll visit **Chugach National Forest**, **Kenai Fjords National Park**, the **Kenai National Wildlife Refuge**, and the **Kachemak Bay State Park**. If you like the outdoors you'll love the Kenai Peninsula. It's one of the best places in Alaska to find beautiful scenery, fishing, hiking, canoeing, kayaking, and just about anything you want to do in the outdoors.

### The Road

Two highways combine to give access to the Kenai Peninsula. From Anchorage the only route to the south is the **Seward Highway**. The Seward Highway is very scenic and has been designated a National Forest Scenic Byway. This two-lane paved road hugs the cliffs along Turnagain Arm until reaching Girdwood, then circles around the end of Turnagain to climb into the mountains onto the Kenai Peninsula proper. Ninety-two miles from Anchorage the peninsula's second highway, the Sterling Highway, branches off to the west. The Seward Highway continues south, eventually ending at Seward on the south coast. By law headlights are required to be on at all times along this road.

The **Sterling Highway** leads west from its junction with the Seward highway. After some 11 miles it leaves the mountains and crosses the flatlands until reaching Soldotna near the west coast of the Kenai. The highway then follows the coast south to Homer, ending at the point of the Homer Spit.

From Anchorage to Seward along the Seward Highway is a distance of 127 miles. Mileposts along the Seward Highway start in Seward and run north to Anchorage. Several important side roads lead off from the Seward Highway including the Alyeska Access Road (Mile 90), the Portage Glacier Road (Mile 79 ), and the Hope Highway (Mile 57). From Mile 90 at Girdwood to Mile 7 about 6 miles from Seward there is no gas available on the Seward Highway so be prepared. If you find yourself running low you can turn west on the Sterling Highway at Mile 37 and drive 8 miles to buy gas at the Sunrise Inn.

The Sterling Highway from Tern Lake Junction to Homer is 143 miles long. Mileposts along this highway are confusing because they start in Seward which is not even on the highway. Tern Lake Junction, the highway's starting point, is at Mile 37. Mileposts count up from there. Important side roads off the Sterling Highway include the Skilak Lake Loop (Mile 58 and Mile 75) and the Kenai Spur Road (Mile 94).

The Highway designation system used on these two roads is also confusing because the names and numbers do not designate the same stretches of roads. Highway 1 includes the Seward Highway from Anchorage to Tern Lake Junction and then the Sterling Highway to Homer. The Seward Highway from Tern Lake Junction to Seward is known as Highway 9.

### Fishing

Probably the most popular attraction on the Kenai is the fishing. You have lots of choices: king salmon on the world famous Kenai River and other streams, halibut out of Homer, silver salmon in Seward, red salmon at the Russian River, trout from dozens of lakes and streams. The truth is that there are excellent fishing opportunities on the Kenai during the entire summer. The fish are almost everywhere so we'll only mention the highlights.

The possibilities for catching salmon start almost as soon as you start down the Seward Highway from Anchorage. **Indian Creek** (Mile 103) and **Bird Creek** (Mile 101) have heavy runs of pink salmon in July and August. Remember, Cook Inlet pinks only run in large numbers during even numbered-years like 1998 and 2000. The **Twentymile River** (Mile 81) and the **Placer River** (Mile 78) has an interesting dip net fishery for hooligan in May. It's as much fun to watch as it is to fish.

**Seward** is best-known for its silver salmon. You can catch them from the beach or from boats during August. The Seward Silver Salmon derby is held during the second week of August. Seward also offers fishing for kings, pinks, halibut, and sea-run Dollies.

Heading down the Sterling Highway from the intersection at Tern Lake the fishing action is dominated by the **Kenai River** all the way to Soldotna/Kenai. There are fish, especially trout and Dollies, in other places, notable Quartz Creek and the lakes of the Kenai Mountains and the Kenai Moose Range, but most people are after big salmon in the Kenai.

The first stop is the **Russian River**. This tributary of the Kenai is fished in two places, the Russian itself and the Kenai where the Russian flows in. The area of the Kenai just below the mouth of the Russian receives extremely heavy fishing pressure. During late June and again in late July fishermen are elbow to elbow flipping flies to red salmon on both side of the river. They wouldn't be there if their chances of catching fish weren't extremely good. Access to the far side of the Kenai away from the road is by ferry from Mile 55 of the Sterling Highway. Silver fishing in the Russian is good in August, so is Dolly and catch-and-release rainbow fishing. Fishing regulations for the Russian can be complicated and different from those for the surrounding area so check them out.

The **Upper Kenai**, from the outlet of Kenai Lake to Skilak Lake, is a beautiful emerald-colored stream 17 miles in length. The Sterling Highway runs along it between Mile 48 and Mile 57, then the river turns away from the road and enters a canyon. You can fish from the bank or from a raft or drift boat to reach otherwise inaccessible waters. Fish for reds in late June and late July into August. Silvers appear in August and September and again in October and November. The area is closed to king fishing. This is also a good place to fish for rainbows and Dollies, especially in the fall. Again, the regulations should be checked carefully when fishing this water.

The **Lower Kenai** is the king fishery. It runs 50 miles from the Skilak Lake outlet to salt water near Kenai. The Sterling Highway does not run along this river very much, but there is access all along its length using side roads. A lot of the fishing is from boats, this is big water. There are two runs of kings, one in June and the other starting in mid July. There are also two runs each of reds and silver salmon, and there are also Dollies and rainbows. For best results on the lower Kenai hire a guide, they have the knowledge and the boats. No fisherman should visit Alaska and not spend at least a day on a guided Kenai king fishing expedition.

From Soldotna the Sterling highway heads south, and along the way it passes over a string of extremely productive rivers flowing west into Cook Inlet. These include the **Kasilof River and Crooked Creek** (Mile 109), the **Ninilchik River** (Mile 135), **Deep Creek** (Mile 137), and the **Anchor River** (Mile 157). All have large state campgrounds near the river and offer fishing for kings, and silvers.

There is also a substantial salt water fishery in **Cook Inlet from Ninilchik to Anchor Point**. Along the shore fishermen find kings, pinks, silvers, and even halibut. Charter operators from **Deep Creek** in larger boats offer excellent halibut fishing, they fish some of the same waters as charter boats out of Homer.

**Homer** is at the end of the road. Most fishermen come to Homer for the halibut. They fish from charter boats and often limit out with two halibut in the ten to thirty pound range. Occasionally a halibut as large as 400 pounds (that's right!) is caught. Homer also has its "fishing hole" near the end of the spit which is designed just to give tourists a better-than-fighting chance to catch a king or silver. This is a terminal fishery with no place to spawn. Hatchery king and silver fingerlings are released here and come back as adults just to be caught.

Have you ever gone claming? Digging for razor clams along Cook Inlet beaches is like claming·nowhere else. During the lowest tides (you can't reach them any other time) it is easy to get your limit, and the limit in 1997 was 60 clams per day. You can easily equip yourself for claming in Soldotna or Kenai, you only need a fishing license, a clam shovel, boots and a bucket. Head for either Clam Gulch or Ninilchik. Once you're on the beach just watch someone who's finding clams, it's easy if you use the right technique. You'll also need a few tips on cleaning those clams. Check around your campground, during the clam tides you'll probably have no trouble finding an expert. A word to the wise, limit your enthusiasm when you're digging, cleaning clams can take longer than digging them.

### Boating, Rafting, Canoeing, and Kayaking

The Kenai has an excellent canoe trail system. The Kenai National Wildlife Refuge's **Swanson River Canoe Route** is a week-long trail passing through lakes and along the Swanson River. Another trail in the moose range, the **Swan Lake Route**, is similar. See Chapter 14 - Camping Away From the Road System.

A popular rafting trip is a float of the **Upper Kenai**. The section from the Kenai Lake outlet to Jean Creek is primarily a fishing trip but there are sections of Class III water. From Jean Creek to Skilak Lake is Class III water in the Kenai Canyon. Neither section is a place for inexperienced rafters. Your best bet is to float with a commercial operator. They can be found in Anchorage and Cooper Landing. Canoers also like to float the **Lower Kenai** between Skilak Lake and Jim's landing, the take-out there allows them to avoid rapids below the landing.

Ocean kayakers will find three exceptional areas accessible on the Kenai Peninsula. The first is world-famous **Prince William Sound**. While not really on the Kenai Peninsula we'll mention it here since access is possible by rail shuttle from Portage near Mile 80 of the Seward Highway. Resurrection Bay near Seward has excellent kayaking waters, since the **Kenai Fjords** are a long paddle away try catching a lift with a excursion or charter boat operator. Finally, **Kachemak Bay** has miles of relatively protected shoreline across from Homer. All of these areas are further described in Chapter 14 - Camping Away From the Road System.

### Hiking and Mountain Biking

The Kenai Peninsula has the best selection of good hiking trails in all of Alaska. Probably the best known is the **Resurrection Pass Trail** that runs from Hope to Cooper Landing and then on to Seward. Hiking the whole thing would take over a week. This is a popular mountain bike trail but be careful. Grizzly bears are often on the trail and it is possible to get very close on a bike before you or the bear is aware of each other, that's a recipe for trouble. Other trails lead to lakes, ridges, and glaciers. Several hiking guidebooks describe hikes in this area, check our Chapter 2 - Details, Details, Details for our suggestions. Here are a few of our favorite hikes.

The **Primrose Trail** from Primrose Campground on Kenai Lake and the **Lost Lake Trail** from Lost Lake Subdivision near Mile 5 of the Seward Highway both go to the same place, a big alpine lake called Lost Lake. The one-way distance from either is 7 miles, you can also make a traverse out of this hike. This trail is open to bikes.

**Johnson Pass** is usually hiked as a traverse. This is a historic trail that was originally part of a pack route from Seward to Sunrise and Hope. It is also part of the historic Iditarod Trail. This 23-mile trail is a popular mountain bike route. Trailheads are near Mile 32 and Mile 64 of the Seward Highway.

Across Kachemak Bay from Homer is **Kachemak Bay State Park**. It has lots of hiking trails, see Chapter 14 - Camping Away From the Road System for more information.

### Wildlife Viewing

Almost as soon as you leave Anchorage heading south you'll come to one of the most-visited bird watching sites in the state—**Potter Marsh**. Near Mile 117 of the Seward Highway is a quarter-mile boardwalk leading into the marsh.

Best viewing is in April and May but all summer long you might spot a variety of ducks, Canada geese, bald eagles, grebes, loons, yellowlegs, and Arctic terns. There's also a salmon spawning area.

Just a little farther south, near Beluga Point (Mile 110) or Windy Corner (Mile 106) along **Turnagain Arm** Dall sheep often come all the way down to the road to pose for pictures. Also keep an eye open for bald eagles along the shoreline and beluga whales offshore when the hooligan or salmon are running, particularly near Bird Creek.

**Kenai Fjords National Park**, accessible in excursion boats from Seward, is one of the best places in the state to see seabirds and marine mammals. On a typical day trip you might spot whales (humpback, minke, or gray), orcas, Steller sea lions, harbor seals, sea otters, and Dall porpoises. Some trips visit the Chiswell Islands to see colonies of puffins, murres, and kittiwakes. You might even sight mountain goats or bears from the boat. This is also a good place to get away from the crowds, see Chapter 14 - Camping Away from the Road System.

The **Kenai Mountains** may seem almost civilized since they are laced with hiking trails, but stay alert. Hikers shouldn't be surprised to see grizzly bears in the high country, not to mention even more common black bears. Valleys often have moose and beaver. A desire to see some wildlife is an excellent reason to get out and do some hiking.

Near the north shore of Kenai Lake at Mile 46 of the Sterling Highway there's a parking area just for viewing sheep and goats with binoculars and spotting scopes. Directly north of the site is **Near Mountain** where Dall sheep are often visible. Across Kenai Lake is **Cecil Rhode Mountain** which sometimes has mountain goats. Also watch for bears a little farther down the mountains.

At the mouth of the Kenai River near the town of Kenai are the **Kenai River Flats**. In April the flats are covered with snow geese migrating to Siberia. There's also a small herd of caribou that uses the flats as a calving area in May. Later in the year birders can see a variety of water birds and ducks as well as several bald eagles. Best viewing is from the Kenai River Access Road. Another attraction here is the beluga whales and harbor seals attracted by hooligan and salmon runs, they may be best seen from the Kenai bluff.

The **Kenai National Wildlife Refuge** used to be known as the Kenai National Moose Range. That should give you some idea of what you should be watching for. It's a huge (2,000,000 acres) flatland covering across almost all of the western Kenai Peninsula. You've got to keep your eyes open, the moose in most areas are hunted in the fall so they may be wary. Still, there are so many of them that you're sure to spot some. Heading into the refuge stop at the visitor contact station at Mile 58 of the Sterling Highway for a map and information. The Kenai National Wildlife Refuge Headquarters (USF&W) is near Soldotna on Ski Hill Road (P.O. Box 2139, Soldotna, AK 99699; 907 262-7021). They also administer the Swanson River and Swan Lake Canoe Trails.

**Kachemak Bay** near Homer also has an excellent place to watch seabirds. **Gull Island** is a short excursion boat or kayak ride away, it is home to some 12,000 seabirds, much like the Chiswell Islands. Kayakers and other visitors to the south side of the bay often see sea otters, harbor seals, and Dall porpoises.

# THE ROUTES, TOWNS, AND CAMPGROUND

## FROM ANCHORAGE TO TERN LAKE JUNCTION
(90 miles)

The real start of the Seward Highway begins near central Anchorage at the corner of Gambell Street and 5th and 6th Avenues (the Glenn Highway). Gambell (the Seward Highway) heads south, stopping at many stoplights, and then turns into a four-lane expressway until meeting Turnagain Arm near **Potter Flats** at Mile 117. This is where you leave Anchorage's suburbs and abruptly find yourself in what would be considered wilderness in most places.

The highway now runs between cliffs and the rocky edge of muddy **Turnagain Arm**. In recent years this has become a popular if somewhat dangerous wind-surfing area. Stay off the mud flats, they can be like quicksand and the tides come in very rapidly. You're also likely to see climbers on the rocks along the road. Another frequent sight is Dall sheep on the rocks just above the road or even on the road itself.

At Mile 90, 25 miles from Potter Flats is the cutoff to **Girdwood** and the Alyeska Ski Resort. Girdwood is a popular weekend get-away for Anchorage residents and explains the excellent road from Anchorage to this point. Summer visitors will find some hiking possibilities and can ride a tram up onto the ski slope for a great view.

At Mile 80 of the Seward Highway you will see a large parking area next to the highway. This is the loading point for passengers and vehicles on their way to **Whittier**, only a few miles away on Prince William Sound. There is no road to Whittier, only rail access through a long tunnel. From Whittier there is Alaska State Ferry access to Valdez.

At Mile 79 the Seward Highway reaches the Portage Glacier Road. **Portage Glacier**, at the end of this 5.5-mile paved access road, is one of Alaska's most-visited tourist sites. The **Begich, Boggs Visitor Center** (907 783-2326) has a viewing area, displays, a film, and naturalists. You can also take a boat ride to get a closer view of the glacier which has retreated to the point that good views are not available from the visitor's center. Along the access road you can see small hanging glaciers above the road and also stop and watch spawning salmon at a viewpoint at Williwaw Creek near Mile 4. There are two good USFS campgrounds along this road.

After passing Portage the Seward Highway begins climbing into the mountains at Mile 75. This long hill has always been a problem area for trucks and RVers because they are forced to slow by the long climb. New passing lanes are making the road much safer. Before long the highway approaches the tree line at not much over 1,000 feet, you can glass for bears on the slopes on both sides.

At a junction at Mile 57 the Hope Highway descends north for 18 miles along Sixmile Creek to Turnagain Arm and the old gold-mining town of **Hope**. The virtual ghost town sits at the mouth of Resurrection Creek. There's good pink salmon fishing dur-

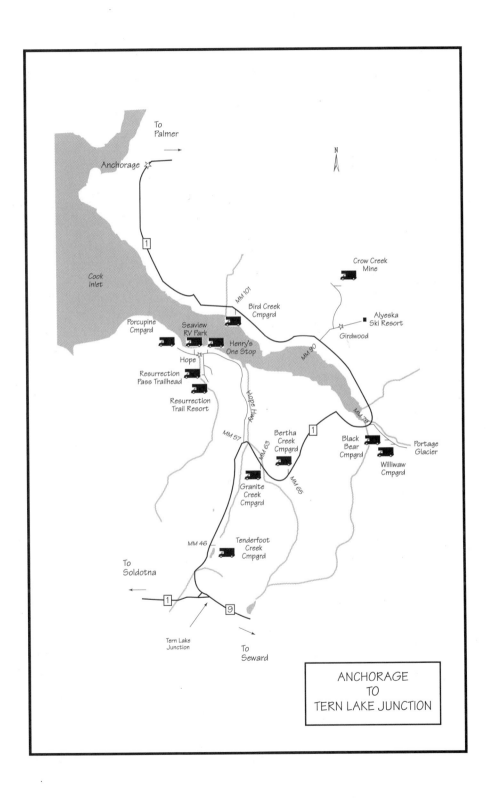

To Palmer

Anchorage

N

Crow Creek Mine

Cook Inlet

1

MM 101

Bird Creek Cmpgrd

Alyeska Ski Resort

Girdwood

Porcupine Cmpgrd

Seaview RV Park

Henry's One Stop

MM 90

Hope

Resurrection Pass Trailhead

Resurrection Trail Resort

Hope Hwy

Bertha Creek Cmpgrd

MM 79

1

Black Bear Cmpgrd

Portage Glacier

MM 57

MM 63

Williwaw Cmpgrd

Granite Creek Cmpgrd

MM 65

MM 46

Tenderfoot Creek Cmpgrd

To Soldotna

1

9

Tern Lake Junction

To Seward

ANCHORAGE
TO
TERN LAKE JUNCTION

ing August and upstream you'll find gold panning possibilities and the trailhead for the Resurrection Pass Trail.

After passing the Hope Highway junction the road continues through mountains past Upper and Lower Summit Lakes and Jerome Lake to the Tern Lake Junction with the Sterling Highway.

## Campgrounds
## Anchorage to Tern Lake Junction

✦ BIRD CREEK CAMPGROUND (CHUGACH STATE PARK)
    Location: Mile 101 Seward Highway
    Price: Low

*GPS Location: N 60° 58' 18.5", W 149° 27' 38.2"*

Bird Creek is the closest government wilderness campground to Anchorage. It is also conveniently located near Bird Creek, a popular and relatively good fishing spot for pink salmon in late July and August. Coastal views of the cliffs and tide flats along Turnagain Arm are spectacular. Bald eagles and Dall sheep are often seen nearby.

The small campground has 15 vehicle sites south of the highway. Many are long enough for larger rigs. There are also tent sites. The campground has well water, outhouses, a telephone, and picnic tables. There is also a host. Interior roads are gravel, so are camping pads. There is a paved lot across the road providing 16 overflow camping spaces. It sits well above the highway and provides excellent views south across Turnagain Arm to the Kenai Peninsula.

To find Bird Creek Campground just drive south from Anchorage on the Seward Highway. The campground is on the right about 16 miles after the highway meets Turnagain Arm just outside Anchorage. The campground is near Mile 101.

✦ CROW CREEK MINE
    Address: P.O. Box 113, Girdwood, AK 99587
    Telephone: (907) 278-8060 (Off-site)
    Price: Low

*GPS Location: N 61° 00' 00.4", W 149° 04' 58.2"*

If you are looking for an interesting campsite not far from Anchorage and are willing to do without hookups you will enjoy the Crow Creek Mine. Crow Creek was a working placer mine, it is now a National Historic Site, and offers displays and buildings from early days and the chance to pan for gold. Gold mining here was no joke, Crow Creek was the most productive placer stream in southcentral Alaska with over 40,000 ounces produced since 1896.

The mine has a small camping area next to the gravel parking lot with fire rings and picnic tables. RVs can park overnight in the parking lot. There are no hook-ups but

COMBAT FISHING ALONG BIRD CREEK

chemical toilets are available and drinking water can be purchased at the gift shop.

The Crow Creek Mine is located near Girdwood, home of Alyeska, Alaska's largest ski area. Girdwood is about 42 miles southeast of Anchorage off the Seward Highway. Take the Girdwood cutoff near Mile 90 and drive into the valley for 1.9 miles to the Crow Creek Road which goes left. Follow this gravel road for 3.1 miles, turn right at the mine entrance road, and you will reach the parking lot in another .4 miles.

✦  BLACK BEAR CAMPGROUND (USFS)
    Location: Mile 3.7 of Portage Glacier Road
    Price: Low

*GPS Location: N 60° 47' 20.9", W 148° 53' 22.2"*

Black Bear Campground is a small U.S. Forest Service campground located conveniently near Portage Glacier. It is small and has not been upgraded with paving and large sites like the nearby Williwaw Campground so there are often sites available here when Williwaw is full.

Black Bear is a wooded campground with 12 sites, two are pull-throughs. The entrance sign says that there is room for rigs 20 feet long or less but rigs to 30 feet often use the campground. There is a water pump, picnic tables, fire pits, and outhouses.

To find Black Bear take the Portage Glacier Road near Mile 79 of the Seward Highway (48 miles from Anchorage). Drive toward the glacier for 3.7 miles, the campground is on the right.

✦ WILLIWAW CAMPGROUND (USFS)
    Location: Mile 4.1 of Portage Glacier Road
    Reservation Number: (800) 280-CAMP
    Price: Low

*GPS Location: N 60° 47' 13.5", W 148° 52' 22.0"*

This government campground near Portage Glacier has been upgraded with wide paved roads and large paved sites. It sits below overhanging Middle Glacier and is right next to the Williwaw Creek salmon viewing area.

There are 60 sites in the campground. Many are pull-throughs and most are large enough for large rigs. Sites have picnic tables and fire pits. There is a hand-operated water pump and outhouses. The campground has a host and amphitheater for campfire programs and reservations are taken at 1-800-280-CAMP. There's also a nature trail.

You can find Williwaw on the Portage Glacier Road which leaves the Seward Highway at Mile 79 (48 miles from Anchorage). The campground is 4.1 miles from the junction.

✦ BERTHA CREEK CAMPGROUND (USFS)
    Location: Near Mile 65 of the Seward Highway
    Price: Low

*GPS Location: N 60° 44' 55.9", W 149° 15' 06.8"*

This is a small government campground in high country near the highway. There are 12 sites, some will take larger rigs. Roads in the campground are gravel and so are the sites. Picnic tables and fire pits are provided. There is a hand-pump water well and outhouses.

Bertha Creek Campground is located on the west side of the road near Mile 65 of the Seward Highway about 62 miles from Anchorage.

✦ GRANITE CREEK CAMPGROUND (USFS)
   Location: Near Mile 63 of the Seward Highway
   Price: Low

*GPS Location: N 60° 43' 36.3", W 149° 17' 59.4"*

Granite Creek Campground is a 19-site campground located in a spruce forest next to a rushing glacial stream. The roads in the campground are gravel and so are the sites. Many are located next to the creek. All are back-in sites, they have picnic tables and fire pits. The campground has a hand-operated water pump and outhouses. This campground has a host and firewood is available.

The access road to the campground leaves the Seward Highway near Mile 63 (64 miles from Anchorage). Drive south on the access road for .8 miles to reach the campground.

✦ HENRY'S ONE STOP
   Address: Box 50, Hope, AK 99605
   Telephone: (907) 782-3222
   Price: Medium

*GPS Location: N 60° 55' 09.0", W 149° 37' 14.5"*

Henry's is located about a mile from the historic Hope town site and is an important gathering place for Hope area residents since it has one of the few public telephones and grocery stores.

There are 12 camping sites located next to the store. All have 15-amp electrical outlets and water, all but one have sewer hook-ups also. A few are pull-throughs. There is also a dump station. Henry's has a small grocery store with movie rentals, offers showers, and has a public telephone. Reservations are recommended.

The campground is located near Mile 16 of the Hope Highway on the north side of the road. Just past Henry's the Resurrection Creek Road goes left providing access to the Resurrection Trail.

✦ SEAVIEW BAR, CAFE, MOTEL AND RV PARK
   Address: Box 27, Hope, AK 99605
   Telephone: (907) 782-3364 or (907) 782-3581
   Price: Medium

*GPS Location: N 60° 55' 12.6", W 149° 38' 40.6"*

For a convenient place to stay when you visit the old gold-mining town of Hope you'll probably want to stay at the Seaview. It is located right in town, you can take a walking tour right from your campsite.

The Seaview has 26 sites, 16 have power and water is available. The campground is located on the shore of Turnagain Arm next to the mouth of Resurrection Creek. In addition to a bar (beer and wine only) and a cafe the Seaview offers hot showers, a gift shop, a gold-panning table, and historic films. The campground is located right next to the mouth of Resurrection Creek so fishing for pink salmon is extremely handy.

To reach Hope and the Seaview follow the Hope Highway for 17 miles from its intersection near Mile 57 of the Seward Highway. The campground is well-signed from the edge of town.

✦  PORCUPINE CAMPGROUND (USFS)
      Location: Mile 18 of the Hope Highway, the end of the road
      Price: Low

*GPS Location: N 60° 55' 43.6", W 149° 39' 31.2"*

The Porcupine Campground makes a great destination for a weekend trip from Anchorage. There are hiking trails along Turnagain Arm and to other nearby locations and Hope and the Resurrection Creek mining area are nearby.

This state campground has 24 sites, most are back-in but there are a couple of pull-throughs. This is one of the state's upgraded campgrounds, interior roads are paved as are parking pads. Each site has a picnic table and fire ring and they are well-separated with natural vegetation and trees. The campground has outhouses and a hand-pump for water.

You reach the campground by following the Hope Highway all the way to the end, a distance of eighteen miles from the junction with the Seward Highway near Mile 57.

✦  RESURRECTION PASS TRAILHEAD
      Location: Near the end of Resurrection Creek Road
      Price: Free

*GPS Location: N 60° 52' 00.7", W 149° 37' 52.3"*

This is an almost undeveloped campsite that is very popular with gold panners searching for gold in the creek. From May 15 to July 15 you can be sure that this campground will be full of prospectors. The rest of the year it is almost empty.

There is room for about 10 parties to camp under cottonwood trees next to Resurrection Creek. There are no real designated sites but repeated use has resulted in established sites, most have fire rings but no tables. There are outhouses.

A hundred yards or so down the creek is the parking area for the very popular Resurrection Trail. There are also outhouses here and many people overnight in this parking area, particularly if they are getting ready to head out on the trail of if they are waiting for a party of hikers.

The Resurrection Creek Road leaves the Hope Highway at Mile 16. This is 1.8 miles from where the Hope Highway ends at the Porcupine Campground. Drive south on the Resurrection Creek Road following signs for the Resurrection Trail. The only Y is at .7 miles where the Palmer Creek Road goes left, you want to go right. The Resurrection Pass Trailhead Campground is 4.3 miles from the Hope Highway junction.

✦  RESURRECTION TRAIL RESORT
      Address: P.O. Box 1245, Sterling, AK 99672
      Telephone: (888) HAT-HAUN
      Price: Low

*GPS Location: N 60° 51' 45.7", W 149° 37' 52.4"*

This location has a lot of local history, some might call it notoriety. For years it was the home and mining works of Red Hat Haun who gave gold panning lessons to many visitors. Later it was the site of a modern-day gold camp which gained international attention when the occupants sent out a well-publicized call for mail-order brides. Today that camp is gone, it burned down a few years ago. The current operator is a descendant of Red Hat Haun, and he is developing the property to be a combination recreational gold-panning operation and natural history center. The resort's location at the north end of the Resurrection Trail makes it an excellent base for hiking and trail biking. Gold panning and fishing are also popular and often productive.

There are plans for 12 dry vehicle camping sites at the resort. Presently there are few sites, but lots of room to park. Chemical toilets are provided. You can pan for gold for a fee or rent a mountain bike. Cabins are under construction.

To reach the resort follow the directions given above for the Resurrection Pass Trailhead Campground. Continue past the campground for another .3 miles to the resort.

✦  TENDERFOOT CREEK CAMPGROUND (USFS)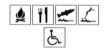
      Location: Near Mile 46 of the Seward Highway
      Price: Low

*GPS Location: N 60° 38' 34.1", W 149° 29' 52.5"*

This is a very nice campground on the shore of Summit Lake. It sits across the valley from the highway so there is little road noise, a nice feature. Nearby Summit Lake Lodge has a restaurant.

There are 27 separated sites, 6 are pull-throughs. Each site has a picnic table and fire ring and there are outhouses and a boat ramp. Some sites are right next to the beach.

The .5 mile gravel entrance road leaves the Seward Highway near Mile 46, just north of the Summit Lake Lodge.

## FROM TERN LAKE JUNCTION TO SEWARD
### (35 miles)

From Tern Lake the two-lane paved Seward Highway continues toward Seward. At Mile 29 it passes through a small town called **Moose Pass** and then passes the south end of Kenai Lake at Mile 17. Several good USFS campgrounds are located along this stretch of road. Very soon the outskirts of Seward begin to appear.

## Campgrounds
## Tern Lake Junction to Seward

✦  MOOSE PASS ALASKA RV PARK
    Location: Near Mile 29 of the Seward Highway
    Telephone: (907) 288-3184
    Price: Medium

*GPS Location: N 60° 29' 07.3", W 149° 22' 13.6"*

This small commercial RV park has about 30 sites on gravel with small trees separating sites. Many sites have 30-amp electrical hookups. The campground is for self-contained rigs only, there are no showers and the only restrooms are outhouses. A restaurant is nearby. The campground entrance is on the east side of the highway in Moose Pass, near Mile 29 of the Seward Highway.

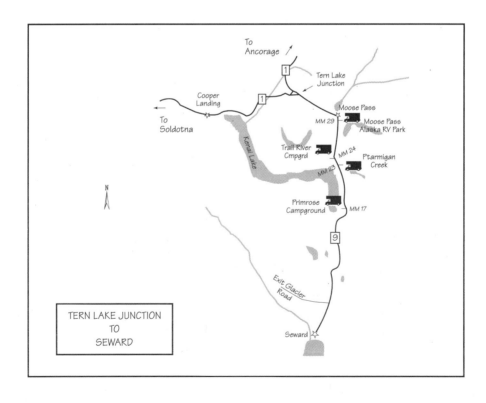

✦ TRAIL RIVER CAMPGROUND (USFS)
   Location: Near Mile 24 of the Seward Highway
   Reservation Phone: (800) 280-CAMP
   Price: Low

*GPS Location: N 60° 24' 32.7", W 149° 22' 58.1"*

The Trail River Campground is located along the Lower Trail River and Kenai Lake. Fishing is good for Dolly Varden and rainbows. You can make reservations for this campground, call (800) 280-CAMP.

There are about 65 separated campsites arranged off four different loops. Many of these are good-sized sites, there are even some pull-throughs. A few sites are along the lake. Each site has a picnic table and fire pit, there are outhouses and hand-operated water pumps. This campground also has some large group campsites available, to reserve call (907) 563-2524.

The 1.2 mile entrance road leaves the Seward Highway near Mile 24.

✦ PTARMIGAN CREEK (USFS)
   Location: Near Mile 23 of the Seward Highway
   Reservation Phone: (800) 280-CAMP
   Price: Low

*GPS Location: N 60° 24' 19.9", W 149° 21' 49.9"*

This is another USFS campground that takes reservations. A 3.5 mile long hiking trail to Ptarmigan Lake starts at the campground. Sites here are large, there are several pull-throughs. The campground has only 16 sites. They are separated and have picnic tables and fire pits. Toilets are outhouse-type. The campground entrance is on the east side of the Seward Highway near Mile 23.

✦ PRIMROSE CAMPGROUND (USFS)
   Location: Near Mile 17 of the Seward Highway
   Price: Low

*GPS Location: N 60° 20' 28.2", W 149° 22' 09.1"*

Primrose is a very small campground located near the southern shore of Kenai Lake. Unfortunately none of the sites are on the lake. A hiking trail leading to Lost Lake starts from the campground.

There are 10 sites here, they are separated back-ins and are pretty small. Each has its picnic table and fire pit, there are outhouses and a boat launch.

A one-mile access road leaves the Seward Highway near Mile 17 and runs past some private homes to the campground.

## Seward
### Population 4,000, Elevation near sea level

Seward was founded in 1903 as an ice-free port which could be the southern end of an Alaska railroad. Private attempts to build one didn't go well until the U.S. government took over in 1915. Construction of a line through newly settled Anchorage to Fairbanks was finished in 1923.

In 1980 the ice fields and coastline to the west of Seward were designated as the **Kenai Fjords National Park**. Gradually the park has attracted more and more visitors. The usual access is on excursion boats making day trips from Seward. Visitors see whales, sea otters, mountain goats, puffins, and other marine birds and animals. The only road access to the park is the Exit Glacier Road which leaves the Seward Highway at Mile 4. The 9-mile road leads to a parking lot, small tent campground, and trails to the glacier. Trails also lead to a view of the Harding Ice Field. The **Kenai Fjords National Park Headquarters** (P.O. Box 1727, Seward, Alaska 99664; 907 224-3175) is located near the boat harbor on Fourth Avenue. They have slide shows and can answer questions and supply information about the park. An elaborate **SeaLife**

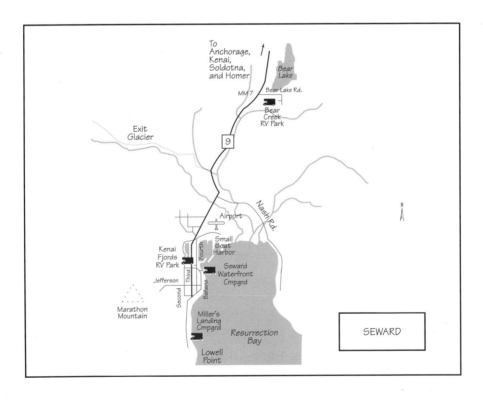

**Center** on the waterfront will open in 1998 with exhibits on the marine life in the area

Seward has 2 Visitor Information Centers. One is at Mile 2 of the Seward Highway as you enter town. The other is in a railroad car at 3rd and Jefferson downtown. For information contact: P.O. Box 749, Seward, Alaska 99664; 907 224-8051.

Seward is also well known for its fishing. A very popular and productive **silver salmon derby** is held in the middle of August. Charter operators are easy to find or you can use your own boat for fishing for salmon, rockfish, and halibut.

There are a couple of good hiking trails in the Seward area. The **Mt. Marathon Trail** is the scene of a race on the 4th of July. It goes to the top of 3,022 foot Mt. Marathon and back. For something flatter try the Caine's Head Trails leading south along the coast to **Caine's Head State Recreation Area.**

## Seward Campgrounds

✦ BEAR CREEK RV PARK
   Address: HCR 64, Box 386, Seward, AK 99664
   Telephone: (907) 224-5725, Fax (907) 224-2283
   Price: High

*GPS Location: N 60° 11' 01.4", W 149° 22' 19.3"*

For full-hookup camping in the neighborhood of Seward this is probably your best choice. Unfortunately the campground is located several miles from the town. There's a state-operated fish weir nearby that can be quite interesting when the salmon are running.

This commercial campground has about 75 sites that are mostly side-by-side back-ins without trees although trees do separate some parking areas. A few spaces are pull-throughs. Full-hookup, partial-hookup, and dry sites are available. There are some picnic tables. The campground has flush toilets, hot showers, a small grocery, a recreation room, propane sales, a dump station, and a high pressure vehicle wash. They can help you make arrangements for the various tours and boat excursions from Seward.

The campground is located at Mile .3 of the Bear Lake Road. This road leaves the Seward Highway at Mile 6.6.

✦ CITY OF SEWARD WATERFRONT CAMPGROUND
   Location: On waterfront south of small boat harbor
   Price: Medium

*GPS Location: N 60° 06' 48.9", W 149° 26' 22.2"*

Most of the thousands of RVers who visit Seward during the year dry camp in the huge gravel lots along the waterfront. There are no utility hookups. Flush toilets are available at several locations including near the small boat harbor and in a pavilion adjacent to the parking areas. There is also a grassy area for tent campers. Coin-op showers are available in the building that houses the harbormaster and also at nearby laundromats. Large signs will inform you of payment procedures. There's also a dump station near the small boat harbor.

◆  KENAI FJORDS RV PARK
      Address: P.O. Box 2772, Seward, AK  99664
      Telephone: (907) 224-8779
      Internet: http://www.ptialaska.net/~rvcampak
      Price: Medium

*GPS Location: N 60° 06′ 48.9″, W 149° 26′ 22.2″*

This gravel lot appears at first to be part of the huge city dry camping area. If you look closer you will see that there are 38 back-in slots arranged around the border of a gravel lot. All have electric hookups and many have water. There are no restroom or shower facilities. When we visited the manager occupied the large RV just to the right of the entrance. Reservations are recommended.

The campground is located just south of the small boat harbor and across the street off Fourth Avenue.

◆  MILLER'S LANDING CAMPGROUND
      Address: Box 81, Seward, AK 99664
      Telephone and Fax: (907) 224-5739
      Price: High

*GPS Location: N 60° 04′ 20.5″, W 149° 26′ 10.0″*

For something different in the Seward area try Miller's Landing. This beachfront campground looks at first like it is constructed of driftwood collected by a beach-comber, but they have electric hookups, hot showers, and offer lots of recreational options. You can rent kayaks or small outboard skiffs, ride a water taxi to a remote cove, hike to nearby Cain's Head State Park or Tonsina Creek, or just beach comb and fish right out front. Best of all, when the fish are running the location is far from the madness of central Seward.

The campground has over 50 sites. Some are lined up along the water, most are in trees back from the beach. Some have electric hookups, 20, 30, or 50-amp. Water is available but there is no dump station. Flush toilets and hot showers are provided. There is a small store for groceries and fishing tackle and you can get lots of advice about things to do and see in the area.

To reach Millers drive right through Seward and find the small gravel road that con-tinues to follow the shoreline below the cliffs to the south. This is Lowell Point Road. The campground is 2.2 miles from the end of the pavement. Big rigs should have no problem if they take it easy.

## FROM TERN LAKE JUNCTION TO SOLDOTNA AND KENAI
### (58 miles)

From its junction with the Seward Highway at Mile 37 the Sterling Highway starts west through scenic mountainous country. At Mile 45 it reaches the north edge of Kenai Lake and follows the lake shore to the Lake's outlet, the Kenai River.

The **Kenai River** is world famous for its king salmon. The current record for a Kenai king is 97 pounds. The river flows 17 miles from Kenai Lake to Skilak Lake. This part of the river is known as the upper Kenai. The lower Kenai flows from Skilak Lake 50 miles to Cook Inlet at Kenai. The river is a playground, it offers fishing for king, red, silver and pink salmon as well as opportunities for both white and flat-water boating.

The Sterling Highway follows the upper Kenai through the **Cooper Landing** area to a junction with the gravel Skilak Lake Road at Mile 58. This section of the Sterling Highway is lined with campgrounds and has probably the most heavily-fished location in the entire state, the Kenai River just below the **Russian River** mouth at Mile 55 of the highway. Even if you don't fish you'll enjoy watching the action during the red salmon runs.

The highway now enters the **Kenai National Wildlife Refuge**. The Skilak Loop Road is a 19-mile gravel road that leaves the Sterling Highway at Mile 58 and rejoins it at Mile 75. This road gives access to campgrounds and boat ramps on Skilak Lake at two points and also to a very nice campground on Hidden Lake.

After the Sterling Highway passes the junction with the Skilak Lake Road it crosses the flat Kenai National Wildlife Refuge and reaches little Sterling at Mile 81. Sterling has a few stores and services, it is located where the Moose River enters the Kenai, another popular fishing spot. Near Sterling, at Mile 83, the 29-mile Swanson River Road leads north to the Swanson River and Swan Lake Canoe Routes. See Chapter 14 for more about these routes.

After Sterling the highway begins to pass through the outskirts of Soldotna which it reaches at Mile 94.

## Campgrounds
## Tern Lake Junction to Soldotna and Kenai

✦ SUNRISE INN RV PARK
   Address: P.O. Box 701, Cooper Landing, AK 99572
   Telephone: (907) 595-1222
   Price: Medium

*GPS Location: N 60° 29' 12.9", W 149° 43' 53.0"*

This roadhouse-style facility has the traditional gas pumps, restaurant, lounge, gift

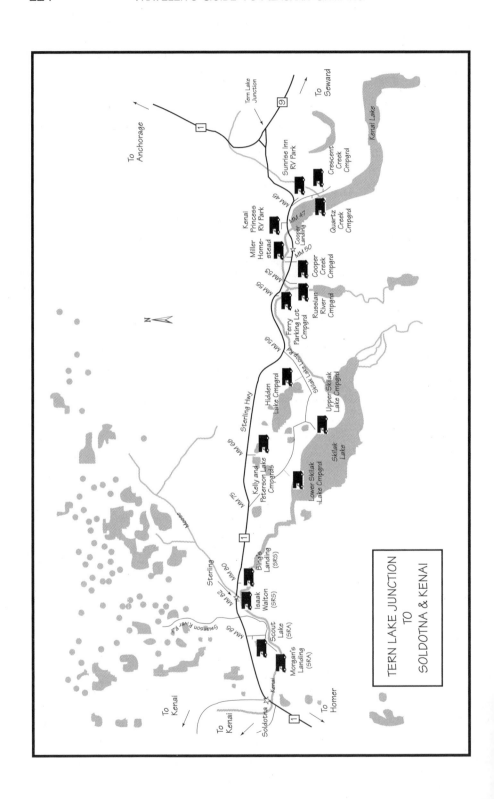

shop, and motel rooms. It also has a nicely wooded camping area out back. This is a small campground with separated spaces with picnic tables. Most have electrical hook-ups. Flush toilets and showers are provided and there is a laundromat and dump station. They'll even book a fishing, raft, or Kenai Fjords tour boat trip for you. The Sunrise Lodge is located near Mile 45 of the Sterling Highway, about 7 miles from the junction with the Seward Highway.

✦ QUARTZ CREEK CAMPGROUND (USFS)
    Location: .3 Mile on Quartz Creek Road
    Price: Low

*GPS Location: N 60° 28' 54.4", W 149° 43' 54.2"*

Quartz is one of the prettiest government campgrounds in Alaska, particularly if you manage to snag one of the few lakefront sites. Altogether there are 26 vehicle sites off two loops and also a tent area. Sites are separated and both the parking pads and access roads are paved. There are a few pull-throughs but most sites are back-ins, all sites have picnic tables and fire pits. An unusual feature here is flush toilets, there are no showers. There is also a boat ramp. Exercise caution boating on Kenai Lake, the wind comes up quickly.

Turn south on the Quartz Creek Road near Mile 45 of the Sterling Highway. This is right next to the Sunrise Inn. Drive .3 miles on the good gravel road to the first entrance road. An entrance to the second loop road is another 3 tenths farther along.

✦ CRESCENT CREEK CAMPGROUND
    Location: Mile 3 of the Quartz Creek Road
    Price: Low

*GPS Location: N 60° 29' 49.7", W 149° 41' 03.9"*

This small government campground is a good base if you plan to hike the good six-mile-long trail up to Crescent Lake or if you want to fish Quartz Creek. There are nine separated sites set in trees. Each site has a picnic table and fire pit. There are outhouses and a hand operated water pump. Plans are in the works for upgrade work here, we describe the campground as it was in 1997. To reach the campground drive 2.9 miles down the gravel Quartz Creek Road, the campground entrance is on the left.

✦ KENAI PRINCESS RV PARK
    Address: P.O. Box 676, Cooper Landing, AK 99572
    Telephone: (907) 595-1425
    Price: Medium

*GPS Location: N 60° 29' 22.7", W 149° 51' 01.4"*

Princess Cruises (of Love Boat fame) has several hotels scattered around Alaska where cruise boat passengers stay during the land portion of their Alaska visit. One of these is hidden on a back road in Cooper Landing. This one is different from all the others, it has an RV park. If you stay here you can recover from a hard day of fishing by relaxing in one of three hot tubs or in the hotel lounge.

There are 35 large back-in RV spaces. They are separated by grassy areas and have full hookups with 30-amp power. There are restrooms with flush toilets and hot showers as well as a small convenience store and a dump station. People staying at the RV park are welcome to use the hotel's facilities including restaurant, bar, hot tubs, and exercise room. Reservations are recommended.

To reach the campground turn north at Mile 47.7 of the Sterling Highway just east of the Kenai River bridge at the outlet of Kenai Lake. Follow the gravel Bean Creek Road for 2 miles to the hotel and campground.

✦   THE MILLER HOMESTEAD ON THE KENAI RIVER
      Address: P.O. Box 693, Cooper Landing, AK 99572
      Telephone: (907) 595-1406 or (941) 765-4195
      Price: Medium

*GPS Location: N 60° 29' 10.5", W 149° 51' 40.8"*

If you are looking for a place with hookups that is convenient to the Upper Kenai and Russian River fishery you'll like the Miller Homestead. Some folks check in for a month at time.

There are 18 pull-through sites with electricity and water connections. There are additional dry sites. Flush toilets and hot showers are provided and there is a dump station. You can bank fish at the campground or arrange a guided float trip.

The campground is located between the river and the road near Mile 50 of the Sterling Highway.

✦   COOPER CREEK CAMPGROUND (USFS)
      Location: On both sides of the Sterling
      Highway near Mile 51
      Reservation Phone: (800) 280-CAMP
      Price: Low

This little Forest Service campground is one of the oldest in the neighborhood and still popular. It is also one of the few government campgrounds where you can reserve a site. There are 29 medium-sized back-in sites. Seven are near the Kenai River on the north side of the highway and the rest occupy a circular drive on the other side of the road along little Cooper Creek. Each site has a picnic table and fire pit, there are outhouses on both sides of the road.

◆ RUSSIAN RIVER CAMPGROUND (USFS)
   Location: Entrance at Mile 53 Sterling Highway
   Reservation Phone: (800) 280-CAMP
   Price: Medium

*GPS Location: N 60° 28' 53.4", W 149° 56' 36.0"*

The huge Russian River campground is one of the most popular in the state, particularly when the red salmon are running in the Russian River. During the salmon runs you are limited to a three-day stay here, reservations are available. The very popular Russian Lakes hiking trail starts from this campground.

Approximately 80 separated sites are arranged off a number of circular drives. All access roads and parking pads are paved and sites are large. They all have picnic tables and fire pits. There are outhouses and some flush toilets, also a dump station. There's also a large paved overflow parking area with room for another 30 rigs.

The entrance road for the campground leaves the Sterling Highway near Mile 53. Almost immediately you'll come to the manned entrance kiosk where your fee will be collected and a site assigned.

◆ SPORTSMAN'S LODGE RUSSIAN RIVER
   FERRY PARKING LOT (USF&W)
   Location: Near Mile 55 of the Sterling Highway
   Price: Low

*GPS Location: N 60° 29' 10.8", W 150° 00' 11.0"*

The most crowded and perhaps the most productive sports fishery in the state of Alaska is located on the Kenai River downstream from the outlet of the Russian River. There is a cable ferry located here so fishermen can work both sides of the Kenai. The parking lot at the ferry is a popular dry-camping area. Fishing goes on 24 hours a day so don't expect much peace and quiet. This is a show not to be missed.

There is probably room for about two hundred rigs to park in back-in side-by-side spaces. Campers are separated into those with generators and those without. There are outhouses and fish-cleaning tables but no other amenities. The camping fee is collected at a kiosk on the entrance road when the fish are running. There's also a two-day time limit here. There is an additional fee for the pedestrian ferry.

◆ KELLY AND PETERSON LAKE CAMPGROUNDS (USF&W)
   Location: Near Mile 68 of the Sterling Highway
   Price: Low

*GPS Location: N 60° 31' 18.7", W 150° 23' 24.9"*

Near Mile 68 of the Sterling Highway a small road leads a mile south to two little lakes: Kelly and Peterson. Both have room for a few campers in open gravel lots next to the lakes. There are a few picnic tables and fire pits as well as outhouses. Both lakes have rainbow trout. The Seven Lakes Trail starts at Kelly Lake and connects with Skilak Road at Engineer Lake, a distance of 4.5 miles.

✦   HIDDEN LAKE CAMPGROUND (USF&W)
        Location: 4 Miles from the Eastern junction of
        Skilak Lake Loop Road and the Sterling Highway
        Price: Low

*GPS Location: N 60° 29' 00.7", W 149° 52' 58.0"*

This large and nicely laid out government campground is well worth negotiating four miles of gravel to reach. It adjoins Hidden Lake which has decent fishing for lake trout and rainbows in the early summer. You'll need a boat, however. Hidden Lake is much smaller than nearby Skilak Lake and much safer.

There are 58 large well-separated sites arranged off paved loop roads. Sites have large picnic tables and fire pits. Three of them are pull-throughs. There are outhouses and a dump station. Down by the lake are a boat launch ramp and a few camping spaces as well as an amphitheater where campfire programs are sometimes offered. The campground also has a large overflow parking area.

The gravel Skilak Loop Road leaves the Sterling Highway at Mile 58 (eastern junction) and at Mile 75 (western junction). The campground entrance road is 4 miles from the eastern junction and 15 miles from the western junction.

✦   UPPER SKILAK LAKE CAMPGROUND (USF&W)
        Location: 9 Miles from the Eastern junction of
        Skilak Lake Loop Road and the Sterling Highway
        Price: Low

*GPS Location: N 60° 26' 27.3", W 150° 19' 16.9"*

The Upper Skilak Lake campground has a boat launch that is used as a take-out by boats and rafts that float the Upper Kenai River from Cooper Landing. Boating on Skilak Lake is considered very dangerous because winds come up suddenly. This is another first class government campground with paved access roads and parking pads as well as some lakefront campsites.

There are 15 separated vehicle sites and 10 walk-in tent sites at this campground. Sites have the normal picnic tables and fire pits. There are outhouses and a water pump as well as a covered picnic area and a boat ramp and large boat trailer parking area. There is no dump station at this campground but there is one located nearby in the middle of nowhere along the Skilak Loop Road 12 miles from the east junction and 8 miles from the west junction.

To reach the campground follow a gravel access road for 2 miles from a point on the Skilak Loop Road that is 9 miles from the east junction and 11 miles from the west junction.

✦ LOWER SKILAK LAKE CAMPGROUND (USF&W)
   Location: 6 Miles from the western junction of
   Skilak Lake Loop Road and the Sterling Highway
   Price: Low

*GPS Location: N 60° 28' 16.8", W 150° 28' 14.5"*

Lower Skilak Lake Campground has a boat ramp that provides easy access to the Middle Kenai River, the Kenai leaves Skilak Lake about 2 miles from the campground. Exercise extreme caution when boating on Skilak Lake, winds come up very suddenly and this is a big lake.

The small campground has 14 separated sites. Sites are small and not suitable for big rigs. They have picnic tables and fire pits, there are outhouses and a water pump.

A 1-mile gravel access road leaves the Skilak Lake Loop Road 6 miles from the western junction with the Sterling Highway and 14 miles from the eastern junction.

✦ BING'S LANDING STATE RECREATION SITE
   Location: Near Mile 80 of the Sterling Highway
   Price: Low

*GPS Location: N 60° 31' 01.3", W 150° 41' 55.2"*

Bing's Landing is primarily used by fishermen accessing the Middle Kenai River. There are about 30 back-in side-by-side slots in a gravel parking lot and also tent sites. Outhouses are available as well as a boat ramp, picnic area with tables and fire pits, and parking for boat trailers.

✦ IZAAK WALTON STATE RECREATION SITE
   Location: Near Mile 82 of the Sterling Highway, in Sterling
   Price: Low

*GPS Location: N 60° 32' 10.7", W 150° 45' 00.8"*

As the name suggests this is a campground primarily used by fishermen. It is located at the point where the Moose River enters the Kenai in Sterling and is a popular place to fish from the bank for salmon using flies.

The campground has some 25 sites. A large number are short separated sites off a paved circular access road. Others are back-in side-by-side parking lot spaces. Picnic tables are provided as well as outhouses. There is also a boat launch.

✦ SCOUT LAKE STATE RECREATION SITE
   Location: Mile 85 of the Sterling Highway
   Price: Low

*GPS Location: N 60° 32' 11.0", W 150° 49' 46.2"*

This small campground near the highway has 8 back-in side-by-side slots. They really service tent sites in the trees behind but can be used by vehicles for camping. There are picnic tables, fire pits, and outhouses. There's also a covered picnic shelter and a water pump.

✦ MORGAN'S LANDING STATE RECREATION AREA
   Location: Scout Loop Road from Mile 85 of
   the Sterling Highway
   Price: Low

This fairly large state campground is another popular access point for the middle Kenai River. The Alaska State Parks headquarters for the district is also located here.

There are 40 sites with tables and fire pits. Some are pull-throughs suitable for large rigs. Toilets are outhouse-type.

Best access to the campground is from Mile 85 of the Sterling Highway. Follow the Scout Lake Loop Road for 1.6 miles, then turn right on Lou Morgan Road. The campground will appear in another 2.5 miles.

## SOLDOTNA AND KENAI
### Population Soldotna 4,000, Kenai 7,000, Elevation near sea level

**Soldotna** has grown because of its convenient location near the junction of the Sterling Highway and Kenai Spur Road. The settlement began to grow in the 1940's. The location along the Kenai River didn't hurt either, today the town really hops when the salmon are running. Soldotna has full services including a huge Fred Meyer and a Safeway. Right next to the Kenai River Bridge at Mile 96 is the **Soldotna Visitor's Center** (Greater Soldotna Chamber of Commerce, 44790 Sterling Highway, Soldotna, Alaska 99669; 907 262-1337). This is an essential stop, they have the huge 97 pound, 4 ounce record Kenai king salmon on display.

**Kenai**, by far the older of these towns, is located well west of the Sterling Highway. To get there follow the Kenai Spur Road for 8 miles from near Mile 94 of the Sterling Highway. This intersection is in Soldotna across from the Fred Meyer store. Kenai was originally an Indian village and then in 1791 became the second permanent Russian settlement in Alaska. You will still find signs of the Russians in Kenai in the form of the Holy Assumption Russian Orthodox Church with its blue onion dome and also St. Nicholas Chapel. Kenai has supermarkets, restaurants and other services. The town seems well-clipped and organized compared to upstart Soldotna. Kenai has its own visitor center called the **Kenai Bicentennial Visitors and Cultural Center** (11471 Kenai Spur Highway, Kenai, AK 99611; 907 283-1991).

The Kenai-Soldotna area offers two golf courses. **Kenai Golf Course** (907 283-7500) has 18 holes and a driving range. It is located in Kenai next to Oiler Park on Lawton Drive. The **Birch Ridge Golf Course** (907 262-5270) is a nine-hole course and driv-

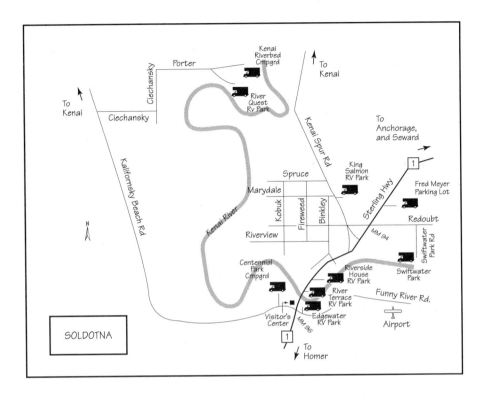

ing range located on the Sterling Highway east of Soldotna. Both courses have rental equipment.

Both Soldotna and Kenai are well supplied with campgrounds, they're the supply centers for the western Kenai Peninsula.

## Soldotna Campgrounds

✦ FRED MEYER PARKING LOT
    Location: In Soldotna at Mile 94 of the Sterling Highway
    Price: Free

*GPS Location: N 60° 29' 14.9", W 151° 03' 03.8"*

Fred Meyer is a huge and hugely popular grocery and discount store in Soldotna. To the chagrin of local RV park operators and the delight of frugal RVers it also is one of the more popular campgrounds in town since RVs are allowed to park overnight in the lot. There's no telling how long this situation will last as the commercial and political forces play out.

You can easily find the areas of the parking lot set out for RVers. There are two of them and they are marked with colored curbs and separators. There is even a dump station.

The store is impossible to miss, it is located on the east side of the highway near the point where the Sterling Highway enters Soldotna from the north.

✦ SWIFTWATER PARK (CITY OF SOLDOTNA)
    Location: Off Redoubt Road from Mile 94 of
    the Sterling Highway
    Price: Low

*GPS Location: N 60° 28' 59.2", W 151° 02' 28.9"*

The City of Soldotna maintains two large RV parks. This is the smaller of the two. There are about 40 spaces, many are pull-throughs or parallel-type spaces. Many are along the Kenai River. Picnic tables and fire pits are provided. There are outhouses, a boat launch, water fill hoses, and a dump station. A major drawback to this campground is that the access road continues through the campground to a subdivision and it is a thoroughfare.

To reach the campground leave the Sterling Highway in Soldotna near Mile 94, this is just south of the Fred Meyer store. Drive east on Redoubt for .5 mile, then turn right onto Swiftwater Park Road. You'll reach the park in another .3 miles.

✦ BEST WESTERN KING SALMON MOTEL AND RV PARK
    Address: 35546 A Kenai Spur Hwy.
    (P.O. Box 430), Soldotna, AK 99669
    Telephone: (907) 262-5857, Fax (907) 262-9441
    Price: High

*GPS Location: N 60° 29' 44.3", W 151° 04' 12.2"*

This motel has 39 sites located in a large open gravel lot. Most of the sites are pull-throughs suitable for big rigs, they have all hookups (20 and 30-amp). There are restrooms with flush toilets and hot showers, a laundromat, and the motel has a restaurant. To reach the motel just follow the Kenai Spur Road west from its junction with the Sterling Highway at Mile 94. You'll soon see the motel on your right.

✦ EDGEWATER RV PARK
    Address: 44770 Funny River Road
    (P.O. Box 976), Soldotna, AK 99669
    Telephone: (907) 262-7733 or (907) 262-9881
    Price: High

*GPS Location: N 60° 28' 32.6", W 151° 04' 58.1"*

One of the newer campgrounds in Soldotna, the Edgewater, is very popular, even when the fish aren't running. The attraction is probably good-sized sites and new facilities, that and good visibility from the highway. You can easily walk from this campground across the river into Soldotna and the Soldotna Visitor's Center with that record king salmon is about a block away across the Sterling Highway.

The campground has about 80 sites. Most have electricity (20, 30, and 50-amp), sewer, and water although there are some electricity-only and dry sites. There are many big pull-throughs, some grass separates sites, and there's lots of room for big rigs. Restrooms are individual rooms with toilet, sink and shower. There is also a coin-op laundry and fish cleaning table. A trail leads down to the south bank of the Kenai just upstream from the bridge, some bank fishing is possible. Reservations are recommended during the summer.

The campground is located very near the Soldotna bridge over the Kenai. From central Soldotna drive south across the bridge to the stop light. Turn left here onto Funny River Road and then almost immediately turn left into the campground.

✦ RIVER TERRACE RV PARK
     Address: P.O. Box 322, Soldotna, AK 99669
     Telephone: (907) 262-5593, Fax: (907) 262-9229
     Price: High

*GPS Location: N 60° 28' 39.3", W 151° 04' 45.1"*

The River Terrace is one of the older and better known campgrounds in Soldotna. You can't miss it as you drive across the bridge over the Kenai. It sits right on the river and is a popular base for fishermen during June, July, and August every year when the salmon are thick. The Soldotna Visitor's Center is just across the bridge and on the far side of the highway. You can easily walk to Soldotna's restaurants and stores from here.

The campground occupies a couple of terraces along the river bank. There are about 75 back-in or pull-into sites, many right along the river. Sites are either full-hookup or electric only (20, 30, and 50-amp). There is a dump station. Restrooms have flush toilets (there are also chemical toilets) and hot showers are available. Bank fishing is possible, there's even a fishing platform that is wheel chair accessible. Fishing is the mainstay of this campground, they can help you arrange charters and fish processing. Reservations are recommended during the summer.

The campground is located on the north bank of the river. As you drive south toward Homer it will be on your left just before you across the bridge in Soldotna.

✦ RIVERSIDE HOUSE RV PARK
     Address: 44611 Sterling Hwy., Soldotna, AK 99669
     Telephone: (907) 262-0500, Fax (907) 262-0406
     Price: Low

*GPS Location: N 60° 28' 44.8", W 151° 04' 33.2"*

The Riverside House is a motel with restaurant on the banks of the Kenai River. They also have a large RV parking area. There are 28 sites, all have electric hookups. There are two water taps, no dump station, and no dedicated restrooms although campers can use the toilets off the hotel lobby. While dedicated facilities at the campground may be limited you can find anything you need nearby including showers in a laundromat near at hand. The Riverside House has quite a bit of riverbank and fishing is possible.

✦ CENTENNIAL PARK CAMPGROUND
   (CITY OF SOLDOTNA)
      Location: Near the junction of the Sterling Hwy.
      and Kalifornsky Beach Road
      Price: Low

*GPS Location: N 60° 28' 39.8", W 151° 05' 12.7"*

This second campground operated by the City of Soldotna is huge. There are about 170 sites set in spruce trees along the Kenai River. Sites have picnic tables and fire pits. There are outhouses and dump stations. The person at the gatehouse kiosk can direct you to the nearby sports center for showers. There is a boat launch at the campground and large areas for parking boat trailers. The campground has lots of riverfront and bank fishing is possible.

To reach the campground turn onto the Kalifornsky Beach Road from the Sterling Highway at Mile 96. Turn right in just .1 mile into the campground entrance road.

✦ RIVER QUEST RV PARK
      Address: P.O. Box 3457, Soldotna, AK 99669
      Telephone: (907) 283-4991
      Price: High

*GPS Location: N 60° 30' 47.6", W 151° 06' 59.8"*

This is one of two huge campgrounds located along the Kenai River in a fairly isolated location (for everything except fishing). Many fanatical fishermen set up housekeeping here for the entire summer.

The River Quest has a variety of campsites, they report that they have 200 sites with power hookups and lots more dry-camping sites. Restrooms with flush toilets and showers are available, as are boat rentals, guide services, a convenience store, a restaurant, a coin-op laundry and a boat launch.

From the junction of the Sterling Highway and the Kalifornsky Beach Road at Mile 96 of the Sterling Highway drive to Mile 4.7 of the Kalifornsky Beach Road and turn right on the Ciechansky Loop Road. Follow the road to a T at .8 miles, turn left and then right on Porter Road. Finally at 2.4 miles take the right at the Y to reach the River Quest.

✦ KENAI RIVERBEND CAMPGROUND
   Address: P.O. Box 1270, Soldotna, AK 99669
   Telephone: (907) 283-9489, Fax 283-8449
   Price: High

*GPS Location: N 60° 30' 50.4", W 151° 06' 03.9"*

This large riverside campground is located right next to the River Quest RV Park. It also is totally dedicated to those interested in fishing the Kenai.

The Riverbend is a huge campground. There appear to be about 140 spaces with hook-ups, both full and partial, and at least another 150 without hookups. There are just a few pull-throughs. The campground has flush toilets, hot showers, a laundromat, a small grocery store, a tackle shop, boat rentals, and guide service.

From the junction of the Sterling Highway and the Kalifornsky Beach Road drive to Mile 4.7 of the Kalifornsky Beach Road and turn right on the Ciechansky Loop Road. Follow the road to a T at .8 miles, turn left and then right on Porter Road. Finally at 2.4 miles take the left at the Y to reach the Kenai Riverbed.

## Kenai Campgrounds

✦ OVERLAND RV PARK
   Address: P.O. Box 326, Kenai, AK 99611
   Telephone: (907) 283-4512 or (907) 283-4227,
   Fax (907) 283-4013
   Price: Medium

*GPS Location: N 60° 33' 14.8", W 151° 15' 43.0"*

Conveniently located right next to the information center in Kenai the Overland RV Park is a good base for those wanting to explore historic Kenai and bone up on the other offerings of the Kenai Peninsula. You can walk to shopping and restaurants.

The campground has some 50 full-hookup slots (30-amp) on neatly raked gravel. There are a few pull-throughs and lots of room for larger rigs. There are picnic tables at the sites. The campground has clean restrooms with flush toilets and coin-op showers. There's also a coin-op laundry and a dump station.

✦ BELUGA LOOKOUT RV PARK
   Address: 929 Mission Ave., Kenai, AK 99611
   Telephone: (907) 283-5999 or (800) 745-5999
   Price: High

*GPS Location: N 60° 33' 02.6", W 151° 15' 53.9"*

For a campground that takes full advantage of Kenai's view across Cook Inlet of the

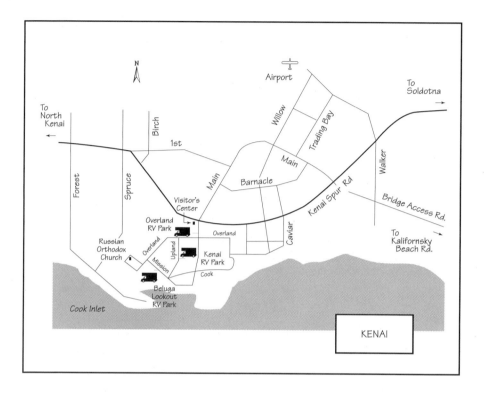

volcanoes of the Alaska Range you can do no better than the Beluga Lookout. High on a bluff overlooking the outlet of the Kenai River this is also a good place to watch for white beluga whales feeding off the mouth of the Kenai.

The campground has about 75 full-hookup spaces (20, 30, and 50-amp) occupying a large open lot at the top of a bluff overlooking Cook Inlet. Some 30 of the sites are large pull-throughs. Overnight telephone and cable-TV hook-ups are available. There are token-operated showers and flush toilets and a coin-op laundry. The restaurants, sights, and shopping of central Kenai are within walking distance.

To find the campground follow Main Street south from the visitor information center and turn right on Cook Drive. The campground is hard to miss on the lip of the bluff.

✦  KENAI RV PARK
      Address: 912 Highland Ave., Kenai, AK 99611
      Telephone: (907) 283-6699 or (907) 283-2851
      Price: Medium

*GPS Location: N 60° 33' 11.4", W 151° 15' 47.1"*

This small campground near the information center in Kenai is one of the homiest and friendliest around. The hosts at this site come back to the same campground year after year and love to introduce visitors to the joys of the Kenai Peninsula.

There are 18 full-service sites on a small grassy lot and some additional tent and dry-camping sites. Parking pads are gravel and are surrounded by grass, a few sites are pull-throughs. Restrooms have flush toilets and hot showers. There is a fish-cleaning station and even some loaner clam shovels and fish smoking equipment. The city of Kenai's attractions are within walking distance.

To reach the campground drive south of Main for one block next to the visitors center and turn right on Overland Street. You'll see the campground one block down Overland on the left but you must turn left on Upland Street to enter it.

KENAI'S RUSSIAN CHURCH

## North Kenai Campgrounds

✦ BISHOP CREEK STATE REC. SITE
    Location: Mile 36 of the Kenai
    Spur Road
    Price: Low

*GPS Location: N 60° 48' 17.4", W 151° 00' 55.3"*

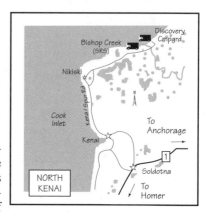

This little state campground has 15 side-by-side back-in slots near the highway but the real jewels are the ocean-side tent spaces located down a .3-mile trail from the parking area. There's a good beach and views of the mountains across Cook Inlet. There are a few picnic tables, fire pits, and outhouses both near the road and at the beach. The campground is located north of Kenai on the Kenai Spur Road that runs north inland from the coast.

✦ DISCOVERY CAMPGROUND -
    CAPTAIN COOK STATE RECREATION SITE
      Location: Near Mile 39 of the Kenai Spur Highway
      Price: Low

*GPS Location: N 60° 48' 17.4", W 151° 00' 55.3"*

Discovery Campground is a large and very nice government campground located a little off the beaten path. The fishing crowds found throughout the rest of the Kenai seldom venture out to the end of the Kenai Spur Highway. On the other hand, this makes a good place to stay if you are assigned pick-up duties for someone canoeing the Swanson River.

The campground has 53 back-in spaces off a circular access road. Sites have picnic tables and fire pits, there are outhouses. The campground sits near the bluff overlooking Cook Inlet and there are hiking paths.

From Kenai drive north 27 miles on the Kenai Spur Road past the refineries at Nikiski to the end of the road. Turn left and you'll soon see the campground.

## FROM SOLDOTNA TO HOMER

### (85 miles)

From Soldotna the Sterling Highway leads directly south toward Homer. At Mile 109 the road crosses the **Kasilof River** and from Mile 115 near Clam Gulch it never strays far from the bluffs overlooking Cook Inlet. The road can't really run along the water because high tides and storms eat away at the foot of the bluffs and they move to the

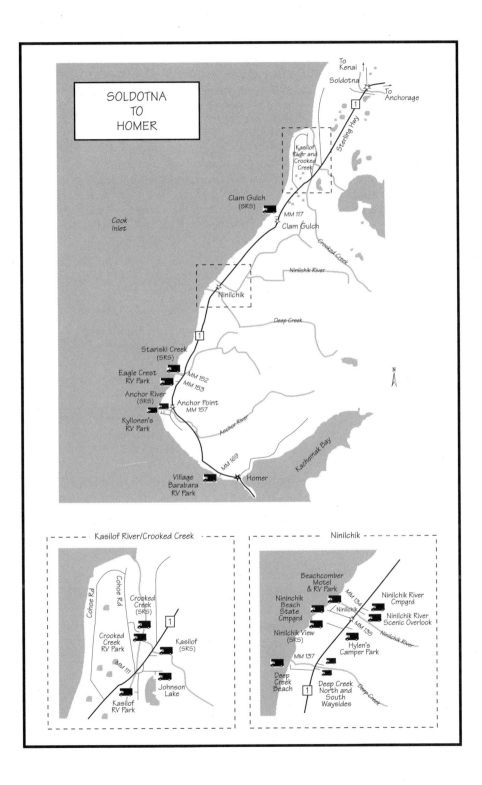

east a few feet each year. Nonetheless there are access roads to the beach at many places and often there are views across the inlet to the snowcapped volcanoes (from left to right): **Augustine** (4,025 ft.), last eruption 1986; **Illiamna** (10,016 ft.); **Redoubt** (10,197 ft.), last eruption 1989; and **Spur** (11,070 ft) last eruption 1992.

At Mile 117 an access road leads east to **Clam Gulch State Recreation Area**. This is the first of several beaches along Cook Inlet where razor clams can be found. Tides here can range 20 feet from low to high water so be careful if you take your rig onto the beach. If you get stuck you may lose it.

As the road continues south it crosses several rivers: the **Ninilchik River** at Mile 135, **Deep Creek** at Mile 137, and the **Anchor River** at Mile 157. Each of these rivers is a popular fishing stream with runs of king and silver salmon as well as Dolly Varden, rainbows, and steelhead. There are lots of campgrounds allowing easy access to the fishing.

Finally, at Mile 170 the highway crests the bluff overlooking **Kachemak Bay**. Pull off the highway at the overlook for one of the most scenic vistas in Alaska. Spread out before you are the Homer Spit, Kachemak Bay, and the snow-covered Kenai Mountains forming a magnificent backdrop.

## Campgrounds
## Soldotna to Homer

✦ KASILOF RIVER STATE RECREATION SITE
    Location: Mile 109 of the Sterling Highway
    Price: Low

*GPS Location: N 60° 18' 58.8", W 151° 15' 37.6"*

This is a very small campground near the highway and situated on a small knoll above the rushing Kasilof River. It makes a good place to base yourself for claming at Clam Gulch if you don't like the crowded parking lot-like campground there. The 10 sites at this campground are all small back-ins but are well separated. There is also a picnic area down by the river. Sites have picnic tables and fire pits and there are outhouses and a hand water pump.

✦ JOHNSON LAKE STATE CAMPGROUND
    Location: Near Mile 110 of the Sterling Highway
    Price: Low

*GPS Location: N 60° 17' 48.1", W 151° 15' 59.6"*

Johnson Lake is a larger government campground with a nice lake next to the campground and the Clam Gulch beaches not far away. You can catch small rainbows in the lake. It makes a good base for those planning to spend some time on the Kenai with visits to both the Homer and Kenai areas.

There are about 40 back-in sites off two loops. As you enter the campground the older and smaller sites are to the right, the newer and much larger sites are to the left. A few sites are along the lake, these go first. There's also a tent-camping area. Each campsite has a picnic table and fire pit and there are outhouses and water pumps.

You will find two entrance roads off the Sterling Highway marked with signs to this campground, one at Mile 110 and the other at Mile 111. Both are the same road, it forms a loop. In about the middle of the short loop is the Tustamena Lake Road, marked by a huge monument in the shape of a T. Turn here, you'll see the campground entrance on the right in a short distance.

◆ KASILOF RV PARK
   Address: P.O. Box 1333, Soldotna, AK 99669
   Telephone: (907) 262-0418, (800) 264-0418
   Internet: http://www.micronet.net/users/~kasilofrvpark
   Price: Medium

*GPS Location: N 60° 17' 26.6", W 151° 16' 15.7"*

Near the Johnson Lake State Rec. Area is an excellent little commercial RV park. This place has the same excellent location central to many western Kenai Peninsula attractions with the added advantages of hookups and showers. Johnson Lake is just across the road.

There are 39 sites on a wooded ridge between Crooked Creek and Johnson Lake. These are wooded and separated sites much like a government campground. 16 of them have electrical hookups. Restrooms are very clean and have hot showers. There is also a dump station and a laundry.

The best route to this campground is from Mile 111 of the Sterling Highway. Turn east on Johnson Lake Road and drive across Crooked Creek and past the fish hatchery. Take the first right past the hatchery and drive .5 mile to the campground on the right.

◆ CROOKED CREEK STATE RECREATION SITE
   Location: 1.8 Miles on Cohoe Loop Road
   Price: Low

*GPS Location: N 60° 19' 18.0", W 151° 17' 11.1"*

This has been a popular campground with fishermen because it is located near a good hole at the confluence of the Kasilof River and Crooked Creek. The Kasilof River is glacial and cloudy during the summer, fishing is best where clear-water streams empty into the river.

There are about 80 camping spaces at the campground. These are side-by-side back-in parking spaces in a gravel parking lot. Fishing is the attraction here, not peaceful enjoyment of an unspoiled setting. Outhouses are provided.

To reach the campground turn west on the Cohoe Loop Road from Mile 111 of the Sterling Highway. The campground access road is at 1.8 miles.

✦ CROOKED CREEK RV PARK
    Address: P.O. Box 601, Kasilof, AK 99610
    Telephone: (907) 262-1299
    Price: Medium

*GPS Location: N 60° 19' 18.0", W 151° 17' 11.1"*

This commercial campground is right next to the Crooked Creek State Recreation Area. The property borders Crooked Creek.

The campground has 43 full-hookup back-in sites and additional dry sites. These are separated sites with trees but laid out in a grid-like pattern. There are flush toilets, hot showers, laundry facilities, and a dump station.

To reach the campground follow the directions given for the Crooked Creek State Recreation Site but continue on past the state site entrance for just a short distance.

✦ CLAM GULCH STATE RECREATION AREA
    Location: Mile 117 Sterling Highway
    Price: Low

*GPS Location: N 60° 14' 21.6", W 151° 24' 07.9"*

The beaches along the west shore of the Kenai Peninsula along Cook Inlet provide some the best razor clam digging in the United States. Limits are huge - 60 clams per person per day in 1997. Clam digging can be really fun and easy if you know how, virtually impossible if you don't. You can find information in many places including at the information offices in Kenai and Soldotna. The Clam Gulch State Recreation Area is probably the best place to come for your introduction to this activity.

There are over 100 back-in side-by-side parking lot type camping spaces on the bluff above the beach. Picnic tables, fire pits, outhouses and sometimes potable water are provided. From the campground a steep sand road leads down to the beach. Four-wheel drive vehicles can be used on the beach, no permit is required. Keep in mind, however, that sea salt isn't very good for your rig. Most people just walk the beach, you can find clams directly in front of the campground. That can still be a healthy walk since Cook Inlet tides have a range of over 20 feet and the beach here is practically flat.

✦ NINILCHIK RIVER CAMPGROUND
    (NINILCHIK STATE RECREATION AREA)
    Location: Near Mile 134 of the Sterling Highway
    Price: Low

*GPS Location: N 60° 03' 10.1", W 151° 39' 08.0"*

LOTS OF CLAMS FROM CLAM GULCH

The Ninilchik Campground is one of four camping areas on the lower Ninilchik River. It is the largest and we think has the most pleasant setting, particularly when the fish are running and this area becomes a madhouse. There's a short trail from the campground down to the river.

There are about 40 back-in separated sites off two loop roads in a treed area near the highway north of the Ninilchik River. Spaces have picnic tables and fire pits. The campground has a host, outhouses and a hand water pump.

Watch for the campground on the east side of the highway near Mile 134 north of the Ninilchik River bridge.

✦ Ninilchik River Scenic Overlook
   (Ninilchik State Recreation Area)
      Location: Near Mile 134 of the Sterling Highway
      Price: Low

           *GPS Location: N 60° 03' 10.1", W 151° 39' 08.0"*

The Ninilchik River area needs lots of camping slots when the fish are running and this parking area provides about 25 of them. These are back-in side-by-side spaces in a parking lot. There are some picnic tables and fire pits and also outhouses. The overlook is just north of the Ninilchik River.

✦ NINILCHIK BEACH CAMPGROUND (NINILCHIK STATE REC. AREA)
  Location: At the beach on the Ninilchik Beach Road
  Price: Low

*GPS Location: N 60° 02' 56.9", W 151° 40' 21.3"*

Ninilchik is a popular fishing stream and also a good place to chase razor clams. This little campground has 35 back-in slots in an open parking lot next to the beach. There are picnic tables and fire pits as well as a pair of outhouses. Reach the campground by driving down the Ninilchik Beach Access Road from near Mile 135 of the Sterling Highway. The distance from the highway is .5 mile.

✦ BEACHCOMBER MOTEL & RV PARK
  Address: Box 367 Ninilchik, AK 99639
  Telephone: (907) 567-3417 or (907) 345-1720
  Price: Medium

*GPS Location: N 60° 03' 01.1", W 151° 40' 06.4"*

This little motel has an enviable location across a small access road from the Ninilchik Beach. Behind the hotel and its 15 back-in sites is the Ninilchik River where you can moor your small boat. Camping sites have full hookups with 30-amp power but there are no restroom or shower facilities for campers. A word of warning, this is a popular place and you are unlikely to find an empty space when the fish are running. Early reservations are recommended.

The Ninilchik Beach Access Road leaves the Sterling Highway near Mile 135. The road goes down the hill for .5 mile to the beach and turns right. The motel is on the right a short distance along the beach road.

✦ HYLEN'S CAMPER PARK
  Address: Box 39388, Ninilchik, AK 99639
  Telephone: (907) 567-3393
  Price: Medium

*GPS Location: N 60° 02' 41.3", W 151° 39' 56.5"*

If you like the Ninilchik area but don't want to stay in a government campground there is a good alternative. Hylen's Camper Park is a full-service campground and also offers guided fishing trips at Deep Creek and in Seward.

Hylen's has about 80 sites. Most of these are pull-throughs in a large open lot with either full (20 or 30-amp) or partial hookups. Satellite-TV hookups are available. There are also wooded tent and dry sites. The campground has good restroom facilities with hot showers, a laundromat, a dump station and a fish and clam cleaning area.

The campground is located near Mile 135.4 of the Sterling Highway.

✦ NINILCHIK VIEW CAMPGROUND (NINILCHIK STATE REC. AREA)
     Location: Near Mile 135.4 of the Sterling Highway
     Price: Low

*GPS Location: N 60° 02' 44.3", W 151° 40' 16.8"*

Ninilchik View is a nice wooded campground located at the top of the bluffs over the Ninilchik beaches. There are 13 separated sites with picnic tables and fire rings as well as outhouses. A trail leads down to the beach. There is also a dump station off the entrance road to the campground which serves this entire busy area. Watch for the sign marking the campground access road at Mile 135.4 of the Sterling Highway.

✦ DEEP CREEK NORTH AND SOUTH WAYSIDES
     (DEEP CREEK STATE RECREATION AREA)
     Location: Near Mile 137 of the Sterling Highway
     Price: Low

*GPS Location: N 60° 01' 50.2", W 151° 40' 50.6"*

Deep Creek, like the Ninilchik River just four miles north, is a popular fishing stream. On both sides of the creek where the Sterling Highway crosses there are open parking lot-style campgrounds. These have recently been paved and the long spaces marked off, a real improvement from years past. There are 25 back-in spaces in each lot, a total of 50. Picnic tables, fire pits, outhouses and information exhibits are provided.

✦ DEEP CREEK BEACH (DEEP CREEK STATE RECREATION AREA)
     Location: At the beach at the end of Deep Creek Access
     Road near Mile 137 of the Sterling Highway.
     Price: Low

*GPS Location: N 60° 02' 07.1", W 151° 42' 24.1"*

Deep creek is a very popular fishing stream but there is another attraction here. Sports fishing guides use the beach next to the creek mouth as a launching ramp for their halibut boats. These guides go after the same fish as those based in Homer, but the fishing grounds are much closer to Deep Creek.

The state campground at the mouth of Deep Creek is very well used. There are at least 300 back-in parking-lot style sites at this campground. It is so popular that there is a manned kiosk guarding the entrance. The campground has picnic tables, fire pits, outhouses and a boat-launching ramp into the protected river mouth.

To reach the campground drive down the Deep Creek Access Road from Mile 137 of the Sterling Highway. Turn right when you reach the beach, pass the commercial boat-launching area, and you'll find yourself at the entrance kiosk.

✦  STARISKI CREEK STATE RECREATION SITE
      Location: Near Mile 152 of the Sterling Highway
      Price: Low

*GPS Location: N 59° 50' 31.1", W 151° 48' 40.5"*

Stariski is a small state campground in a pleasant location at the top of the bluff above Cook Inlet. Since this isn't a good fishing base (at least not without a drive) it tends to have a different atmosphere than the combat fishing sites near Ninilchik and Deep Creek some 15 miles to the north.

There are 13 sites at Stariski. They are separated and located in spruce trees. Picnic tables and fire pits are at each site and there are outhouses.

✦  EAGLE CREST RV PARK
      Address: P.O. Box 249, Anchor Point, AK 99556
      Telephone: (907) 235-6851 or (888) 235-2905
      Internet: http://www.xyz.net/~eagle
      Price: High

Eagle Crest has 28 full-hookup sites on a bluff overlooking Cook Inlet just 3 miles north of Anchor Point. These are 30-amp hookups and there are also flush toilets, showers, and a laundry. Watch for the campground near Mile 153 of the Sterling Highway.

✦  ANCHOR RIVER STATE RECREATION AREA
      Location: Near Mouth of Anchor River
      Price: Low

*GPS Location: N 59° 46' 11.7", W 151° 50' 31.9"*

The Anchor River is another well-known Kenai Peninsula fishing destination. There are runs of king, silver and pink salmon but the river is probably most famous as a steelhead stream. Near the mouth of the river is an excellent state campground. Nearby are several good fishing holes with names like Slide Hole, Dudas Hole, Campground Hole and Picnic Hole.

Anchor River State Recreation Area has about 75 sites in five different areas called Silverking, Coho, Steelhead, Slide Hole and Halibut. Many are just side-by-side parking lot spaces but at the Slide Hole area there are about 25 nice back-in separated sites. Picnic tables and fire pits are at the sites and there are outhouses near all of the campsites. For tenters the best sites are at Halibut which is near the beach.

The access road to the campground, the Old Sterling Highway, goes west from today's Sterling Highway in the town of Anchor Point near Mile 157. Drive down the hill and across a bridge for .3 miles. Take the first right after the bridge onto Beach Road, you will immediately start seeing the campground entrance roads on your right. Slide Hole is the third one.

◆ Kyllonen's RV Park
    Address: P.O. Box 805, Anchor Point, AK 99556
    Telephone: (907) 235-7762, Fax (907) 235-6435
    Price: High

Right in the middle of the state campgrounds near the mouth of the Anchor River is a commercial one. Kyllonen's has 23 back-in or pull-in sites with either full or partial hookups. Sites are partially separated and there are flush toilets, hot showers, and a laundry. Fire pits and free firewood are available.

From Mile 157 of the Sterling Highway follow the old Sterling Highway west down the hill and across the bridge. Turn right onto Beach Access Road at .3 miles, you'll find Kyllonen's on your right at 1.2 miles.

◆ Village Barabara RV Park
    Address: P.O. Box 891, Homer, AK 99603
    Telephone: (907) 235-6404
    Price: High

*GPS Location: N 59° 39' 29.5", W 151° 38' 32.9"*

The Village Barabara must have the most spectacular view of any campground in Alaska. Rigs park at the lip of a bluff that must be 500 feet high overlooking the mouth of Kachemak Bay and the mountains on the far side of the bay.

There are 55 back-in sites here with lots of maneuvering room. All have electrical hookups and water and sewer hookups are also available. In 1997 the campground was only suitable for self-contained rigs since there were no toilets, hopefully this will change. Showers are available as is a laundromat. There is also a gift shop.

The campground is at the top of the long hill that descends into Homer near Mile 169 of the Sterling Highway.

## Homer
### Population 4,500, Elevation near sea level

Alaskans often think of Homer as something of an art colony. A combination of a beautiful setting, mild weather, and an isolated end-of-the-road location have combined to make Homer an attractive place to live. The largest part of the economy here, however, is tied to fishing. It's an interesting mix.

Homer spreads over a pretty large area. The central business district occupies a location overlooking Kachemak Bay. Here you'll find the schools, many stores, restaurants, and some RV parks. A 1.5-mile road runs from town, along Beluga Lake, past many roadside service establishments, to the base of the spit. 4.5 miles out on the spit is another center, this one with a small boat harbor, fish packing plants, and lots of tourist facilities. The windswept spit is the scene of lots of action during the summer with hundreds of RVs camped here and there, fishing charter boats heading out to catch halibut, ferries crossing to the far side of the bay, and hundreds of college-age cannery workers living in tents pitched on the beaches. The **Visitor Center** (Box 541, Homer, AK 99603; 907 235-7740) is located on the Homer Bypass at Main Street.

Homer is one of the best places in the state to take a trip out to catch a **halibut**. The limit is two fish, usually these are "chicken" halibut weighing less than 20 pounds, but halibut over 100 pounds are often caught. Its easy to set up a charter at one of the offices on the spit or at the reception desk of your RV park. There's a halibut derby from May 1 to Labor Day.

The **Pratt Museum** (3779 Bartlett St., 907 235-8635) has a wide range of exhibits including historical, natural science, and art.

Homer is home to the headquarters for the **Alaska Maritime National Wildlife Refuge** (509 Sterling Highway, Homer, AK 99603; 907 235-3691). This huge refuge includes rugged islands all along the Alaska coast all the way from the tip of the panhandle near Ketchikan to Barrow. The center has displays and programs including guided bird and beach walks. Naturalists from the facility also are on board the state ferry to Seldovia, Kodiak and down the Alaska Peninsula.

Kachemak Bay and the islands and fjords on the south side across from Homer are a huge attraction. The **Kachemak Bay State Park** covers 350,000 acres with islands, bays, glaciers, and lots of outdoor attractions, see Chapter 14 - Camping Away From the Road System for more information. **Gull Island** is home to huge numbers of

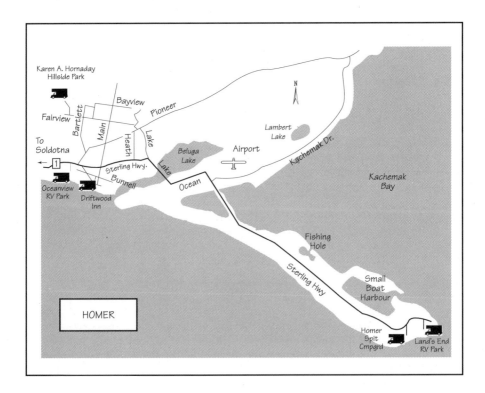

marine birds, a small ferry that runs over to Halibut Cover is an excellent way to see them. **Seldovia**, a small town of 300 people, makes a great place to visit if you want to get away from the crowds. The Alaska State Ferry stops there on the route between Homer and Kodiak but most people travel across the bay on smaller commercial passenger ferries or by airplane.

## Homer Campgrounds

✦ LAND'S END RV PARK
   Address: P.O. Box 273, Homer, AK 99603
   Telephone: (907) 235-2525
   Internet: http://akms.com/landsend
   Price: Medium

GPS Location: N 59° 36' 02.2", W 151° 24' 43.5"

If you want to be just as close to the end of the Homer Spit as possible and as close to the water as you can get this is the place. Planned to close at the end of 1997, reports now are that the campground will be open for the 1998 season.

The campground has 68 sites, 29 of them are right along the beach, views are great. Reserve early for these sites. Most sites have electric hookups (20, 30, and 50-amp) and both water and dump stations are easy to access. There are flush toilets and showers are available in private rooms.

To find the campground just drive to the end of the spit. The campground entrance is on the right just before you reach the oil tanks and Land's End Resort parking lot.

✦ HOMER SPIT CAMPGROUND
   Address: P.O. Box 1196, Homer, AK 99603
   Telephone: (907) 235-8206
   Price: Medium

GPS Location: N 59° 36' 02.7", W 151° 24' 56.9"

Much like the Land's End Campground the Homer Spit Campground occupies a waterfront site at the end of the Homer Spit. There are some 120 spaces at this campground, most with electrical hookups. Some are dry sites along the beach. Flush toilets and hot showers are available, there is a laundromat and a dump station.

The campground is located near the end of the Homer Spit. Watch for the sign. The Homer Spit Campground is located right next door to the Land's End Campground but just to the west. It is the first of the two that you will see.

✦ SPIT DRY CAMPING
   Location: Most of the Spit parking areas and
   beaches except where posted or on private property
   Price: Low

The City of Homer lets RVers and tent campers camp freely on much of the spit. Watch for signs designating parking and no parking areas. A fee is charged, the collection procedure varies from year to year, watch for signs. Restrooms and coin-op showers are located near the Harbormaster's Office near the Salty Dog at the end of the Spit. Large numbers of college-age fish-processing plant workers take advantage of this and set up tents along the beach.

✦  KAREN A. HORNADAY HILLSIDE PARK
      Location: Off Fairview Avenue
      Price: Low

*GPS Location: N 59° 39' 10.5", W 151° 33' 14.3"*

The City of Homer operates a campground that is located uphill from the central business area. The Karen A. Hornaday Hillside Park has about 33 separated sites set in alders. These are back-in sites and most are pretty small although there are a couple large enough for big rigs. Sites have picnic tables and fire pits. The restrooms in the campground are outhouses (very aromatic when we visited) but there are flush toilets at the ball park below the campground.

To reach this campground drive north on Bartlett from central Homer for .1 mile. Turn left on Fairview and then right in another .1 mile on Campground Road. The route is fairly well signed.

✦  DRIFTWOOD INN & RV PARK
      Address: 135 West Bunnell Ave., Homer, AK 99603
      Telephone: (907) 235-8019 or (800) 478-8019,
      Internet: http://www.alaskan.com/driftwood
      Price: High

*GPS Location: N 59° 38' 22.6", W 151° 32' 39.7"*

The Driftwood Inn is a hotel with a small RV park that is conveniently located near central Homer. It overlooks the beach which is a good place to walk and, like much of Homer, has a spectacular view of mountains and water. The campground has 22 back-in or drive-in spaces with electricity, water, and sewer hookups. There are also tent spaces on grass. The inn has restrooms with showers and a laundry. Easiest access is from the Homer Bypass. Turn south on Main Street and then west on Bunnell to the campground entrance.

✦  OCEANVIEW RV PARK
      Address: P.O. Box 891, Homer, AK 99603
      Telephone: (907) 235-3951, Fax (907) 235-2168
      Price: High

*GPS Location: N 59° 38' 29.7", W 151° 33' 11.2"*

The first campground you will see when you enter Homer (on the right) is the

Oceanview. This is a large and well organized campground, an excellent place to stay since it has convenient access to downtown, convenient access to a good walking beach, and excellent views of the water and mountains on the far side of Kachemak Bay.

The Oceanview has about 100 spaces. Most have full hookups including cable TV although a few have only electricity and water or are dry. Tent sites are available. There are a few large pull-throughs but most sites are large back-ins. The campground has flush toilets and hot showers as well as a gift shop and laundromat. They will help you arrange fishing charters or tours at the office.

## KENAI PENINSULA DUMP STATIONS

Because the Kenai Peninsula is such a popular RVing destination it has a better selection of dump stations than anywhere else in the state. Many of the campgrounds described in this chapter have their own dump stations, even some of the government campgrounds. Here are some other possibilities.

In **Girdwood** you can dump at a station near the gate of the municipal Girdwood Treatment Facility. It's on Ruane Drive which goes east a short distance up the Alyeska Access Road which intersects the Seward Highway at Mile 90.

**Seward** has a city dump station located on Fourth Avenue near the small boat harbor. Seward Tesoro at Mile 1.7 of the Seward Highway also has one.

On Skilak Road in the **Kenai National Wildlife Refuge** there is a dump station at Mile 11.5 about half way between Upper and Lower Skilak Campgrounds. It's hard to imagine anyone but users of one of the local campgrounds using it since the Skilak Road is gravel and often very rough.

In **Sterling** dump stations are at Sterling Tesoro at Mile 81.7 of the Sterling Highway and Big John's Texaco at Mile 91.3 of the Sterling Highway.

In **Soldotna** dump stations are located at Jack's Sourdough Tesoro Service at Mile 91.5 of the Sterling Highway, Soldotna "Y" Chevron at 44024 Sterling Highway, Soldotna Tesoro at 44152 Sterling Highway, Thompson's Corner at 44224 Sterling Highway, and the Fred Meyer at 43843 Sterling Highway.

In **Kenai** dump stations are at G&M Chevron at the junction of the Kenai Spur Highway and Willow and at Wildwood Chevron, 14096 Kenai Spur Highway.

Lots of people frequent the salmon streams near **Ninilchik**. There's a state-operated dump station near the Ninilchik View State Campground at Mile 135.4 to serve them.

Finally, in **Homer** the city has a dump station located next to the Homer Bypass near the junction with Lake Street where traffic heading for the spit turns to head across the Beluga Lake dam. Other dump stations are at Airport Texaco at 1495 Ocean Drive and Homer Tesoro at 1554 Homer Spit Road.

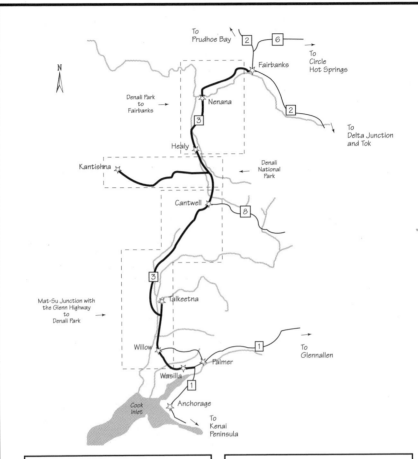

To
Prudhoe Bay

2   6

To
Circle
Hot Springs

Fairbanks

Denali Park
to
Fairbanks

Nenana

2

3

To
Delta Junction
and Tok

Healy

Denali
National
Park

Kantishna

Cantwell

8

3

Mat-Su Junction with
the Glenn Highway
to
Denali Park

Talkeetna

Willow

1

To
Glennallen

Palmer

Wasilla

1

Cook
Inlet

Anchorage

To
Kenai
Peninsula

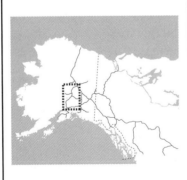

# THE PARKS HIGHWAY

# CHAPTER

......... 9

# THE PARKS HIGHWAY

## INTRODUCTION

The Parks Highway runs north from a junction on the Glenn Highway about 35 miles from Anchorage to the interior city of Fairbanks. This is the state's newest major road, until 1971 Fairbanks-bound travelers had to travel the Glenn north to Glennallen and then the Richardson through Delta Junction. The Alaska Railroad follows almost the same route, but the railroad is seldom within sight of the road.

We'll cover the Parks Highway from south to north. This is convenient for folks who are based in Anchorage or who rent rigs there, probably the larger part of the people who will be using this book.

### Highlights

Anchorage's northern suburb, **Wasilla**, is growing rapidly in the Mat-Su Valley. You'll find lots of recreation activities near what has become a week-end playground for many people. They include boating, hiking, fishing, and golf.

The **Hatcher Pass Road** runs for 49 miles from near Wasilla through the Talkeetna Mountains to meet the Parks Highway near Willow. You can stop and visit **Independence Mine State Historical Park** or hike above the timber line.

**Denali State Park**, not to be confused with Denali National Park, sits astride the Parks Highway south of the Alaska Range. There are at least one excellent state campground, high-country hiking trails, and wonderful views of the south face of Mount McKinley.

The most-visited attraction along the Parks Highway must be **Denali National Park**. At Mile 237 the park road leads westward into the park. The most popular activity at Denali is a bus ride into the park interior to see the wildlife. Vehicle access is limited but there are lots of camping sites in the park and nearby.

Fishermen will find lots of action on the Parks Highway. **Many good fishing streams** cross under the highway between Mile 57 and Mile 97. They include the Little Susitna, Willow Creek, Little Willow Creek, the Kashwitna River, Sheep Creek, and Montana Creek. The heavy fishing in these creeks is primarily for salmon.

The village of **Talkeetna** is located on a spur road from Mile 99 of the Parks Highway. Talkeetna is the base for Mt. McKinley climbing expeditions. It also is the base for riverboat salmon fishing expeditions, one of the most popular charter fishing options in the state.

 ### The Road

Building the Parks Highway was no easy project. Work started in 1959 and it wasn't until 1971 that it was completed. One of the toughest sections was across permafrost along a long section south of Nenana, you'll be able to identify this section by the heaves and dips in the road. Another challenge, a different kind, was the section through the Nenana Canyon north of Denali Park. The rest of the highway, however, is probably the nicest you'll find in all of Alaska and the Yukon. It was engineered from the beginning for modern traffic and has wide shoulders.

From Anchorage to Fairbanks along a short section of the Glenn Highway and then the entire length of the Parks Highway is 358 miles, you can easily drive it in one day. It is easy to maintain a constant speed of 60 MPH along virtually the entire distance. Mile markers on the Parks run from south to north. The highway begins at an intersection in the Matanuska Valley 35 miles from Anchorage. Mile markers start at 35 at this point.

 ### Fishing

The Matanuska Valley is full of small lakes, many of them stocked. Once established at a campground in the area you might want to check out **Finger Lake**, the **Kepler-Bradley Lakes State Recreation Area, Meirs Lake, Matanuska Lake, Seymour Lake, Nancy Lake**, or **South Rolly Lake** and the other lakes in the **Nancy Lake Recreation Area.** You'll notice that many of the campgrounds in the Mat-Su are near fishing lakes. Fishing in these lakes is best in the spring or fall. A boat is very helpful.

From Mile 57 at the Little Susitna River to Mile 97 at Montana Creek there are many small rivers flowing into Cook Inlet or the Susitna River that offer outstanding salmon fishing, much of it can be done from the bank without a boat. As in all salmon fishing timing is important. Kings (Chinook Salmon) peak in June, reds (Sockeye Salmon) peak in July, pinks (Pink Salmon) peak in the last half of July, and the first weeks of

August are best for silvers (Coho Salmon). Pinks only run in significant numbers in even years (1998, 2000, etc.). Salmon runs can't always be accurately predicted, sometimes the fish are early or late (or don't show up). Since the salmon ascend the rivers from the ocean they reach fishing holes downstream before those that are upstream. Information about the status of the salmon runs in this area is easy to obtain, just ask at sporting goods stores, information offices, campgrounds, or even check the newspapers. Fishing regulations may change during the run based upon the quantity of fish in the streams so make sure you stay abreast of the current rules.

Here are some of the streams and locations in the area: **Little Susitna River** (Mile 57) for kings, reds, silvers, pinks, rainbows, Dollies; **Willow Creek Recreation Area** (Mile 71) for kings, silvers, pinks, rainbows, Dollies, and grayling; **Willow Creek** (Mile 71) for kings, silvers, pinks, rainbows, Dollies and grayling; **Little Willow Creek** (Mile 75) for king salmon, pinks, silvers, grayling and rainbows; **Kashwitna Lake** (Mile 76) for stocked rainbows; **Grey's Creek** (Mile 81) for kings, silvers, pinks, grayling, and rainbows; **Kashwitna River** (Mile 83) for king salmon, silver salmon, grayling and rainbows; **Caswell Creek** (Mile 84) walk-in for kings, silvers, grayling and rainbows; **Sheep Creek mouth** (Mile 86) kings, silvers, pinks, grayling and rainbows; **Sheep Creek** (Mile 89) for kings, silvers, pinks, grayling and rainbows; **Montana Creek** (Mile 97) kings, silvers, pinks, grayling, and rainbows. Almost all of these fishing hot spots have campground along the creeks or nearby.

The **Susitna River** is a braided glacial river that is a very popular jet boat river. The Susitna can be dangerous to those who do not know it. You need the right equipment and local knowledge for this river. Charter boat operators offer guided fishing trips on the Susitna from several places including Susitna Landing (Mile 82.5). From Talkeetna jet-boat tours let fishermen access the middle section of the Susitna above Talkeetna and also the **Talkeetna River**. Most fishing from Talkeetna and along the length of the Susitna is in the clear-water rivers that run into the silty Susitna and Talkeetna.

Farther north you might want to try the **Chulitna River** (Mile 133) for grayling, **Troublesome Creek** (Mile 137) for grayling, rainbows and salmon (king fishing not allowed), or **Byers Lake** at Mile 147 for lake trout.

### Boating, Rafting, Canoeing, and Kayaking

**Big Lake**, located in the Mat-Su Valley is probably Anchorage's favorite water-sports destination. It's a large shallow lake that gets plenty warm enough for swimming. Several other nearby lakes are also popular but access isn't as easy for folks who do not have cabins and the lakes aren't as large.

The **Nancy Lake State Recreation Area**, accessible from Mile 67 of the Parks Highway via a 6.6-mile gravel road is a favorite canoeing area. There's a circular 16-mile canoe trail through 14 lakes and a longer one than connects with the Little Susitna River. Lakes offer fishing and there are quite a few black bears and other wildlife in the area. The South Rolly Campground is near the starting point of the canoe trail and makes a good base, there are also designated back-country camping sites along the canoe trail.

The **Little Susitna River** also makes a good canoe route. It is 56 miles from the Parks Highway bridge at Mile 57 to a takeout at the end of the Little Susitna Access Road off Knik Road. You can connect into the Nancy Lakes canoe trails using a portage 14 miles below the Parks Highway put-in point. The Little Susitna River is a very popular fishing river, there are so many power boats that restrictions on their use have been initiated in the interests of safety. Two weekends a month, the first and third, are designated as nonmotorized The second and fourth weekends are for power boats only.

The **Nenana River** runs right by the entrance to Denali National Park, floating this white-water river in rafts has become extremely popular as more and more people visit the park. Operators are based near the park entrance and are easy to find. You can make arrangements at your campground if you are staying at one of the commercial ones outside the park. This is a good way to spend a day while waiting for a seat on a bus into the park.

### Hiking and Mountain Biking

Hatcher Pass presents some of the best hiking opportunities north of Anchorage. The **Little Susitna Trail** climbs 8 miles along the upper Little Susitna River to the foot of the Mint Glacier from about Mile 14 of the Fishhook-Willow Road. The **Reed Lakes Trail** climbs 4 miles to Lower and Upper Reed Lakes with branches to the Snowbird Mine and Snowbird Glacier. This trail starts at Mile 2.4 of the Archangel Road which leaves the Fishhook-Willow Road at about Mile 14.5. From the **Independence Mine Historical Park** there are several short day hikes, the park is near Mile 17 of the Fishhook-Willow road. Mountain bikers will find the Fishhook-Willow Road to be a decent ride but automobile traffic can be a problem, particularly on weekends.

The Nancy Lakes Recreation Area is known for its canoe trails but also has a good hiking trail. There is a 3-mile **trail to Red Shirt Lake** with an 8-site tent-camping area at the lake. The trail runs along the tops of gravel ridges so it isn't as wet as most of the ground in the area. The trailhead is at the entrance of the South Rolly Lake Campground.

Denali State Park has several hiking possibilities. Most are on the mountain to the east of the highway, it's known as Kesugi Ridge. The **Kesugi Ridge Trail** (also sometimes called the Curry Ridge Trail) starts at the Upper Troublesome Creek Trailhead at Mile 138 of the Parks Highway. It climbs to the top of the ridge and runs 36 miles north before descending to the Little Coal Creek Trailhead at Mile 164 of the Parks Highway. An intermediate access points is a 3.5-mile trail from Byers Lake at Mile 147 of the Parks Highway. For shorter hikes you could do Troublesome Creek to Byers Lake (15 Miles) or Byers Lake to Little Coal Creek (27 Miles). A complicating factor is that during salmon season (middle of July to early September here) the Troublesome Creek portion of the trail is closed because there are too many bears for safety.

At **Byers Lake** there is also a pleasant trail around the lake, a distance of 4.1 miles. There's a walk-in tent campground on the east side of the lake, a distance of 1.8 miles from the trailhead at Byers Lake Campground.

Also in Denali State Park is the **Lower Troublesome Creek Trail** leading from the road at the Lower Troublesome Creek Recreation Site (Mile 137, Parks Highway) to the Chulitna River, a distance of only half a mile.

Denali National Park really offers three kinds of hiking. First, there's the kind where you climb Mt. McKinley, definitely outside the scope of this book. Second, there's hiking in the high country north of the Alaska Range near the access road, see Chapter 14 - Camping Away From the Road System for this. Finally, Denali National Park has several miles of trails near the park entrance. These are easy to access and do not require riding one of the park busses for access. The **Horseshoe Lake Trail** is .7 miles long and starts near the railroad tracks about 1.2 miles from the park entrance. **Mount Healy Overlook Trail** is 2.5 miles long and starts at the Denali Park Hotel which is near the park entrance. The **Rock Creek Trail, Taiga Loop Trail**, and **Morino Loop Trail** are all trails in the entrance area connecting the Denali Park Hotel with nearby facilities.

The 91-mile long **Park Road** makes a wonderful mountain bike ride. Vehicle traffic on the road is restricted largely to tour busses. A bicycle frees you to some degree from reliance on the busses for transportation yet you can use the special camper busses to transport your bicycle so you don't have to ride the whole road. Bicycles are not allowed off the road but campgrounds have bicycle racks where you can leave yours when you want to hike.

### Wildlife Viewing

The **Nancy Lake Recreation Area**, particularly away from the roads on the canoe routes, is an excellent place to see loons (each lake has a pair), beaver, moose, and black bears.

Driving north on the Parks Highway you will pass through **Broad Pass** at about Mile 200. Watch for caribou, stop occasionally and glass the wide-open hillsides on each side of the road.

**Denali National Park** is definitely the easiest place to see wildlife in Alaska. Grab a window seat on one of the busses that go as far as Eielson Visitor Center, better yet, go all the way to Wonder Lake. No guarantees, but on an average trip you might see a moose or two, caribou, Dall sheep, and probably several grizzly bears. See the Denali National Park section of this chapter for more information.

# THE ROUTES, TOWNS, AND CAMPGROUNDS

### WASILLA, THE MAT-SU VALLEY, AND THE HATCHER PASS ROAD
Wasilla Population 5,000, Elevation 330

The Matanuska-Susitna (Mat-Su) Valley is a huge mostly-flat area north of Anchorage. In the east (the Matanuska portion) the valley is oriented toward farming with Palmer the focal point of settlement (See Chapter 7 - The Glenn Highway). To the west is Wasilla which has grown rapidly since the Parks Highway was completed. Even farther west, in the Susitna Valley, there is less settlement with large areas west of the Parks highway and on the far side of the Susitna River having no road access at all.

The **Matanuska-Susitna Valley Visitor's Center** (HC01, Box 6166J21, Palmer, Alaska 99645; 907 746 5000) is located near the intersection of the Parks and Glenn Highways. From the Parks about .2 west of the intersection turn up the hill to the north on Welcome Way. This is a good place to educate yourself about the valley's attractions and ask questions. The Best View RV Park is right next door.

Wasilla is a spread out town. As real estate prices have increased in the Anchorage area many people have moved to the "valley" , and many of them are in or around Wasilla. There are large stores including Wal-Mart, Safeway, and Carrs. All of these stores are strung along several miles of the Parks Highway east of the town center.

Wasilla does have a town center. It is located north of the Parks Highway at about Mile 42. The **Dorothy G. Page Museum** includes the **Old Wasilla Town Site Park** with historical buildings. There's also a **farmers market** on Wednesdays.

From Wasilla at Mile 42.2 of the Parks Highway you can drive south on the **Knik Road** a distance of 29 miles to the **Susitna Flats State Game Refuge**. There is a 65-site state campground there as well as a launch ramp for access to the Little Susitna River. You drive on pavement to Mile 17 and then follow the gravel Goose Bay Point Road for another 12 miles.

Most visitors to Alaska are very familiar with the Iditarod Sled Dog Race. Held in March each year this 1,150-mile race from Anchorage to Nome attracts entrants from all over the world. The Anchorage to Wasilla portion of the race is ceremonial, the race really starts in Wasilla. You'll find the **Iditarod Trail Sled Dog Race Headquarters** and visitor's center (907 376-5155) near Wasilla at about Mile 2 of the Knik Road. The Lake Lucille Campground is right next door.

The Wasilla area has a good 18-hole course, the **Settler's Bay Golf Course** (907 376-5466 for tee times), located at Mile 8 on Knik Road.

From the intersection in Wasilla at Mile 42.2 of the Parks Highway you can also drive north to reach the **Hatcher Pass Road** and **Independence Mine State Historical Park**. There is also access from Mile 49 of the Glenn Highway on the Fishhook-Willow Road. The road from the Glenn Highway and the road from Wasilla meet about 9 miles north of Wasilla to form the Hatcher Pass Road which runs another 42 miles to meet the Parks Highway at Mile 71 near Willow. This road soon becomes gravel and climbs up into the very scenic Talkeetna Mountains. At Mile 17 of the Hatcher Pass Road a side road leads to the **Independence Mine State Historical Park** (907 745-2827). The park has old mining buildings and a visitors center, you can take guided tours of the buildings. There are several short hiking trails in the vicinity. The Hatcher Pass Road is not suitable for large RVs.

## Campgrounds
## Wasilla, the Mat-Su Valley, and the Hatcher Pass Road

✦ BEST VIEW RV PARK
   Address: P.O. Box 872001, Wasilla, AK 99687
   Telephone: (907) 745-7400 or (800) 478-6600
   Price: Medium

*GPS Location: N 61° 33' 41.1", W 149° 15' 19.5"*

The Best View is also located right next to the Mat-Su Visitor Center so it makes a convenient place to spend your first night if you plan to settle into the Mat-Su area for

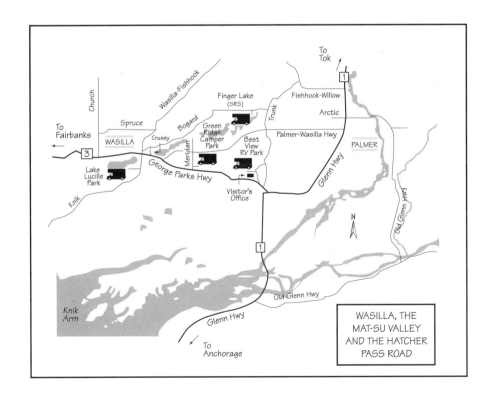

WASILLA, THE
MAT-SU VALLEY
AND THE HATCHER
PASS ROAD

a while. The campground sits on a ridge so there are excellent views of the surrounding mountains.

There are 64 spaces for transient RVs at this campground. There are also quite a few permanently located rigs but they are parked in separate areas nearby. The transient spaces have 30-amp electricity, sewer and water hookups. A few spaces even offer 50-amp power. There is also a tent-camping area. Many of the spaces are pull-throughs and almost all will accept large rigs. This campground is pretty much clear-cut, there aren't a lot of trees. The restrooms have free hot showers and there is a coin-operated laundromat. An unusual feature for a commercial campground is the fire pits at every space.

The campground is just off the Parks Highway very near its intersection with the Glenn. From the intersection drive only .2 mile and turn right on Welcome Way. Both the visitor center and the RV park are a short distance up this road.

✦ GREEN RIDGE CAMPER PARK
    Address: 1130 Vicki Way, Wasilla, AK 99687
    Telephone: (907) 376-5899
    Price: Medium

*GPS Location: N 61° 34' 16.4", W 149° 21' 25.1"*

This is a small, simple campground in a very convenient location. It sits on a corner along the Parks Highway near Wasilla across the street from the local Wal-Mart. We wouldn't be surprised if the free-campers across the street were tempted to come on over for hook-ups and hot showers.

The campground has 35 back-in or pull-in sites arranged off a large circular driveway. They all have full hookups with 30-amp power. In the center is the services building and well-trimmed grass sets everything off. The services building houses the office, a coin-op laundromat, and restrooms with free hot showers. Some sites have barbecues, they all have picnic tables. There is also a children's play area.

The campground is on the northeast quadrant of the intersection of the Parks Highway and the Seward Meridian Parkway. This is near Mile 39 of the Parks Highway, about 4 miles from its intersection with the Glenn and 3 miles from central Wasilla.

✦ FINGER LAKE STATE RECREATION SITE
    (STATE OF ALASKA)
        Location: Off Bogard Road
        Price: Low

*GPS Location:  N 61° 36' 37.7", W149° 15' 53.6"*

This state recreation site on Finger Lake is a popular fishing destination since the lake has rainbows, grayling, and silver salmon. There's a boat ramp at the campground, only boats without motors are allowed on the lake.

There are about 40 camping sites at this campground, most are smaller back-in wooded sites while the remainder are just back-in slots in a gravel parking lot. All sites have picnic tables and fire rings and many are near the lake. There are outhouses and a hand-operated water pump. This campground has a host and firewood is on sale. Stays are limited to seven days.

The campground is off Bogard Road, not exactly a major highway but still a fairly major arterial through the valley. You can reach the campground from many directions and via many routes. The one below is the most scenic. From about Mile 36 of the Parks Highway turn north on Trunk Road. Trunk meanders up past the University of Alaska's experimental farm, it intersects with the Palmer-Wasilla Highway after 3.1 miles. Drive straight across the intersection and continue to an intersection with Bogard Road after 1.1 miles. Turn left on Bogard and you will see the campground entrance road on your left in another .8 miles.

✦   LAKE LUCILLE PARK (CITY OF WASILLA)
        Location: Mile 2 Knik Road
        Price: Low

*GPS Location:  N 61° 34' 01.2", W 149° 28' 47.2"*

This small public campground was empty and in need of maintenance last time we visited. The Iditarod Sled Dog Race Headquarters located right at the entrance may bring you here so take a quick look, you may decide to spend the night.

There are now only about 18 sites at this campground. These are back-in public-campground sites set in natural vegetation with pretty good separation. There are picnic tables, fire pits, and outhouses. The campground is not really next to the lake which is just as well since this side of Lake Lucille is very swampy and has plenty of mosquitoes. Fishing for land-locked silver salmon is possible in the lake.

If you follow the Knik Road south from central Wasilla (near Mile 42 of the Parks Highway) you'll see the Iditarod Sled Dog Race Headquarters at about 2 miles on the right and the entrance to the park just beyond.

## FROM THE MAT-SU JUNCTION WITH THE GLENN HIGHWAY TO DENALI PARK
### (202 miles)

Almost immediately after leaving the Glenn Highway at Mile 35, in just .2 miles, a road leads up the hill to the right to the **Mat-Su Visitor's Center** (HC01 Box 6166 J21, Palmer, AK 99645; 907 746-5000). If you are planning to spend any time in the valley you will probably find a quick visit quite useful.

Continuing westward, the highway soon enters the outskirts of Wasilla. At Mile 42 the Knik Road goes south. Follow it for 2 miles and you'll see the Iditarod Museum on the right.

After passing through Wasilla watch for the **Big Lake** road at Mile 52. This large lake and many smaller surrounding ones attract large numbers of visitors. Because they're shallow they get warm enough for swimming and water sports in the summer. Many Alaskans have cabins here, there are also two state campgrounds on the lake and another on a small lake nearby.

From Mile 57 to Mile 97 the Parks Highway crosses many **streams that are popular destinations for Alaskan fishermen**. These streams include: the Little Susitna at Mile 57, Lower Willow Creek at Mile 71, Little Willow Creek at Mile 75, the Kashwitna River at Mile 83, Caswell Creek at Mile 84, Sheep Creek at Mile 89, and Montana Creek at Mile 97. There are many camping areas along this stretch of road, expect them to be very full on weekends during the salmon runs.

At Mile 67 you'll find an access road to another popular lake area, the **Nancy Lake State Recreation Area**. Nancy Lake and many nearby lakes form a popular canoeing area complete with a 16-mile canoe trail. There's also a large state campground here.

The small town of **Willow**, not long ago a candidate to be Alaska's capitol, appears at Mile 69. Almost in the middle of the somewhat spread-out area known as Willow, at Mile 71, is the junction for the gravel **Hatcher Pass Road**. This 42-mile road climbs into a scenic mountainous region before dropping into the Matanuska Valley near Wasilla. It is not suitable for large vehicles.

At Mile 99 a paved road leads north from the Parks Highway for 14 miles to **Talkeetna**. Talkeetna is a friendly little country town that is accustomed to lots of visitors. There are two big reasons for this. Talkeetna serves as the base for air taxi operators specializing in flying Mt. McKinley climbers up to the Kahiltna Glacier. Most of this activity takes place during the summer, the town is a beehive of activity during the climbing season. You can book a sightseeing flight with one of them too.

Talkeetna also serves as the base for charter riverboats taking fishermen up the Susitna River and Talkeetna Rivers to catch salmon. This is one of the most popular fishing charters in the state. Before driving in to Talkeetna stop and visit the **Talkeetna Visitor Center** located right at the junction with the Parks Highway (Box 985, Talkeetna, AK 99676; 907 733-2295 or 800 660-2688).

After passing the Talkeetna junction the highway curves west and crosses the Susitna River. Then is heads north again, up the Chulitna River and into high country at the foothills of the Alaska Range. You enter **Denali State Park** at Mile 133. It is largely undeveloped but offers great views of the Alaska Range. At Mile 135 there is an excellent viewpoint for looking at the south face of Mt. McKinley. Also visible are Mt. Foraker (17,400 ft.) and Mt. Hunter (14,573 ft.). There are trails along the ridges to the east of the highway, they are accessible at Troublesome Creek at Mile 138, Byers Lake at Mile 147, and at Little Coal Creek at Mile 164.

The highway soon enters **Broad Pass**. The name is accurate. You can often see caribou on the hillsides visible from the highway.

The junction with the **Denali Highway**, connecting with the Richardson Highway, is at Mile 210. The Denali Highway is unpaved but quite scenic. There are 113 miles of gravel and 21 miles of paved road before you reach Paxson on the Richardson Highway. Before the construction of the Parks Highway this was the access road for Denali

MOUNT MCKINLEY FROM PARK ROAD

National Park (then called McKinley National Park).

After passing the junction with the Denali Highway the Parks enters a much narrower pass, Windy Pass, and follows the Nenana River north to the Denali National Park access road at Mile 237.

## Campgrounds
## Mat-Su Junction with the Glenn Highway to Denali Park

✦ ROCKY LAKE STATE RECREATION SITE (STATE OF ALASKA)
        Location: Near Mile 3 of the Big Lake Road
        Price: Low

*GPS Location:  N 61° 33' 26.5", W 149° 49' 19.5"*

Rocky Lake is a small but pleasant state campground, a good place to stop during the week when the area isn't full of Anchorage residents. The lake is stocked and offers small landlocked salmon and a few rainbows.

There are 11 sites, most are right next to the lake. These are back-in sites set in a grove of trees, the 1996 Big Lake forest fire didn't touch this immediate area. The campground has picnic tables, fire pits, outhouses, a hand-operated water pump, a boat ramp, and an overflow parking area. The camping limit here is 7 days.

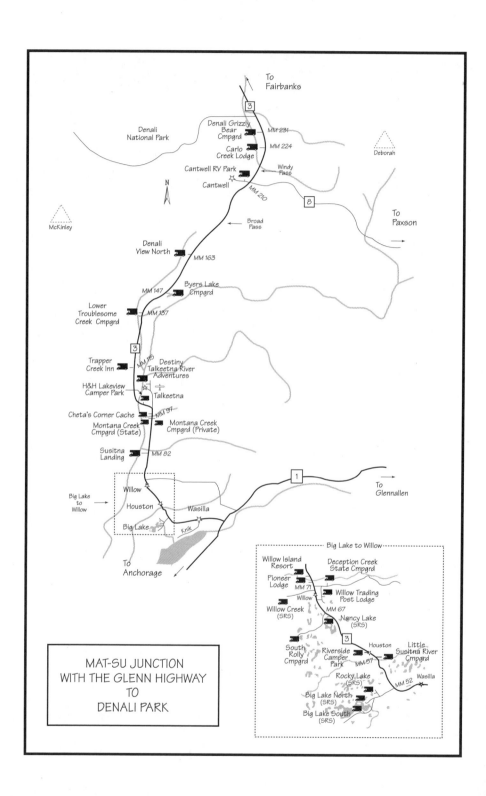

To find the campground drive south on Big Lake Road from the intersection at about Mile 52 of the Parks Highway. Turn right on Beaver Lake Road at about 3 miles and then left on Rocky Lake Road after .5 mile, the campground entrance will be on your left.

✦   BIG LAKE NORTH STATE RECREATION SITE
     (STATE OF ALASKA)
          Location: End of North Shore Drive off Big Lake Road
          Price: Low

*GPS Location: N 61° 32' 43.9", W 149° 51' 15.8"*

Big Lake is one of the most popular summer and winter destinations for Anchorage residents. The lake is large and shallow with many coves and islands, many cabins line the shore and even occupy some of the islands. The lake is plenty warm enough for swimming and is very popular with owners of recreational vehicles of all kinds, including those that float in the summer and snow machines in the winter.

If you don't own a cabin here then you can use two state recreation sites for access to the lake. The largest of the two is Big Lake North. Camping at Big Lake North means parking in a large gravel lot, there must be room for over 100 rigs. The campground offers picnic tables, fire pits, outhouses, a boat ramp, a designated swimming area, and a covered picnic area. There is a walk-in area for tent campers. The campground has a 7 day limit. Fishing in Big Lake is for rainbows, arctic char, and burbot.

To reach Big Lake North follow the Big Lake Road from Mile 52 of the Parks Highway. At 3.5 miles you will come to a fork in the road known as Fisher's Y. Take the right fork (North Shore Drive) and in another 1.5 miles you will come to the end of the road and the campground. The entire route is paved.

✦   BIG LAKE SOUTH STATE RECREATION SITE
     (STATE OF ALASKA)
          Location: Near Mile 5 of the Big Lake Road
          Price: Low

*GPS Location: N 61° 31' 56.8", W 149° 49' 57.6"*

Big Lake South is much smaller than Big Lake North but offers much the same features. There is room for about 15 campers here, some sites are arranged along the lake shore. This campground also has picnic tables, fire pits, outhouses, and a boat launch.

To reach the campground just follow the Big Lake Road from about Mile 52 of the Parks Highway. Take the left fork at Fisher's Y at Mile 3.5. The campground is on the right at about 5 miles.

◆ Little Susitna River Campground
  (City of Houston)
      Location: Mile 57 of the Parks Highway
      Price: Low

*GPS Location: N 61° 37' 50.2", W 149° 48' 12.0"*

This campground is a popular place when the salmon are running in the "Little Su". The river gets runs of kings, silvers, chums, reds, and pinks during May through August. The runs aren't totally predictable but you can tell when the fish are in, just watch for large numbers of fishermen. If there are no fish the campground will probably be almost deserted. This is also a put in point for boating on the Little Susitna River.

The Little Susitna River Campground is much like other government campgrounds in Alaska. This one might be considered just a little more rustic, the location isn't very scenic. The river and fishing are the draw here, the campground sits in the middle of a fairly unattractive stand of small bedraggled spruce trees. There are over 80 camping sites arranged off a maze of gravel roads, most sites are fairly short. Picnic tables and fire pits are provided. Toilets are the outhouse-type. There is a hand-operated water pump, a playground, and a covered picnic pavilion. There's a 10- day limit.

This campground is located north of the Parks Highway just west of the Little Susitna bridge at about Mile 57. There is also a large parking area and river access on the other side of the highway.

◆ Riverside Camper Park
      Address: Box 87, Houston, AK 99694
      Telephone: (907) 892-9020
      Price: Medium

*GPS Location: N 61° 37' 44.8", W 149° 48' 42.1"*

Just a short distance down the road from the Little Susitna Campground is a good commercial alternative. The Riverside offers a good selection of amenities and also access to the Little Susitna River.

The Riverside Camper Park has 56 back-in sites arranged in an open field next to the Little Susitna River. Each site has 30-amp electricity, sewer, water and a picnic table. There are also several dry camp or tent sites on grass with fire pits. The campground offers restrooms with hot showers and a coin-op laundromat. There is also a boat ramp. Next door is Miller Landing which also offers camping, as well as a small store with supplies.

The Riverside is on the south side of the Parks Highway near Mile 59. This is in the commercial center of the "city" of Houston.

✦ NANCY LAKE STATE RECREATION SITE
    (STATE OF ALASKA)
        Location: Near Mile 67 of the Parks Highway
        Price: Low

*GPS Location: N 61°42' 09.4", W 150° 00' 16.5"*

This state campground has a pleasant location atop a small ridge next to Nancy Lake. It is close to the highway and often almost empty, a good place to spend the night. The lake has rainbows, Dollies, burbot, and northern pike.

The campground has 30 back-in sites arranged around three circles. These are decently-separated sites surrounded by natural vegetation and trees, they have picnic tables and fire pits. There is a host at this campground and firewood is available for purchase. Interior roads are gravel as are parking pads. The campground has outhouses and a hand-operated water pump. There is also a boat ramp.

Watch carefully for the entrance road, it is well-marked but pretty small. The campground is near Mile 67 of the Parks Highway on the south side of the highway.

✦ SOUTH ROLLY CAMPGROUND (STATE OF ALASKA)
        Location: Nancy Lake Recreation Area, 6.6 miles
        south From Mile 67 of the Parks Highway
        Price: Low

*GPS Location: N 61° 40' 01.4", W 150° 08' 27.0"*

The Nancy Lakes Recreation area is a huge area of popular lakes, most accessible only by canoe trail. The largest formal campground for vehicle campers in the recreation area is the South Rolly Lake Campground.

This is a large and fairly new campground, there are about 100 sites overlooking the lake. Many of these camp sites are pull-throughs. The sites have the traditional picnic tables and outhouses. Interior roads and parking pads are gravel. These campsites are widely spaced and surrounded by trees, some are along the lake. The campground has a host so firewood is available for purchase, there are outhouses and a hand-operated water pump. Canoes are sometimes available for rent and there is a boat launch (electric motors only).

The disadvantage to this campground is that it is located well off the highway. An extremely wide gravel access road, 6 miles in length, provides access. Unfortunately the surface is usually washboarded. The road leaves the Parks Highway at about Mile 67, the campground is at its end, a distance of about 6.5 miles.

✦  WILLOW CREEK STATE RECREATION AREA
    (STATE OF ALASKA)
       Location: At the end of access road
       from Mile 71 of Parks Highway
       Price: Low

*GPS Location: N 61° 46' 24.4", W 150° 09' 41.0"*

The Willow Creek campground is another popular fishing destination. It offers access to the Susitna River at the mouth of Willow Creek. Willow Creek gets runs of kings, silvers, and pinks and also rainbows, dollies, and grayling.

The campground is relatively new, it is one of the big gravel parking lot type with back-in parking for about 130 rigs. Picnic tables, fire pits, and outhouses are provided. Walking trails lead to the river and bank fishing. Rafters from upstream use this facility as a take-out point.

Access to this campground is via a good but sometimes muddy 4-mile-long dirt and gravel road heading west from near Mile 71 of the Parks Highway.

✦  PIONEER LODGE
       Address: P.O. Box 1028, Willow, AK 99688
       Telephone: (907) 495-1000, Fax: (907) 495-6884
       Price: Medium

*GPS Location: N 61° 45' 55.2", W 150° 04' 00.2"*

The old Pioneer Lodge is one of two campgrounds facing each other across Willow Creek. This is one of the most popular and easily accessible streams in the state for fishermen after kings, chums, pinks, and silvers. From early June until well into August you can expect this place to be hopping on weekends and active during the week. You can fish from the bank in front of your rig or book a guided trip from the lodge.

There are some 25 camping slots with electric and water hookups at this campground including 10 that also have sewer hookups. Many additional campsites are available for tenters and self-contained rigs. The lodge has a dump station although you must back into it, not always an easy task in some rigs. The restrooms require coins for hot showers and there is a coin-op laundry. The lodge also offers a restaurant, bar, and liquor store. Fishing tackle and camping supplies are available.

The lodge is on the west side of the highway near Mile 71 of the Parks Highway. Just watch for the bridge over Willow Creek.

✦  WILLOW ISLAND RESORT
       Address: P.O. Box 85, Willow, AK 99688
       Telephone: (907) 495-6343
       Price: Medium

*GPS Location: N 61° 46' 04.0", W 150° 04' 04.5"*

Just like the Pioneer Lodge across the creek this campground caters to salmon fishermen. This place, however, is more campground and less lodge.

The campground has about 37 spaces with utility hookups. The 12 located right on the bank of the creek have electricity and water only, the remaining 25 are pull-throughs with 30-amp electricity, sewer, and water. There are also many dry sites. There is plenty of maneuvering room for big rigs in this open gravel surfaced lot. There is also an easy-to-access dump station. The modern services building has restrooms, free hot showers, and a coin-op laundry. A small store offers supplies, fishing tackle and expresso. Guided fishing trips are available or you can fish from the bank in front of the campground.

The Willow Island Resort is located near Mile 71 of the Parks Highway, on the west side of the road and the north bank of Willow Creek.

✦ DECEPTION CREEK STATE CAMPGROUND
   (STATE OF ALASKA)
      Location: One mile east of Mile 71 of the
      Parks Highway on the Hatcher Pass Road
      Price: Low

*GPS Location: N 61° 45' 45.4", W 150° 02' 28.8"*

This small state campground is really split into two locations. They lie about .2 mile apart. The farthest east campground has 7 small back-in sites surrounded by natural vegetation and has tables and fire pits. On the opposite side of Deception Creek is a parking area with about 8 walk-in tent sites. There is parking for 14 vehicles and the campsites have tables and fire pits. Both locations have outhouses. Unfortunately, neither campground is within sight of the creek.

This is an easy campground to find. Just drive east on the Hatcher Pass Road from Mile 71 of the Parks Highway near Willow for a mile. There is an entrance on either side of Deception Creek which is reported to have Dollies, rainbows, and grayling.

✦ WILLOW TRADING POST LODGE
      Address: P.O. Box 49, Willow, Alaska 99688
      Telephone: (907) 495-6457
      Price: Medium

*GPS Location: N 61° 44' 50.2", W 150° 02' 25.3"*

The Willow Trading Post Lodge is located in Willow but off the main highway. Many people whiz by and don't even know it's there.

The lodge has 8 back-in spaces in a secluded area behind the main lodge near a small lake. There are clean restrooms, hot showers, a laundromat, a restaurant and bar, and even horseshoes and a sauna. The lodge also has a liquor store and gift shop.

To find the lodge turn east at Mile 69.5 of the Parks Highway following signs to the post office. Turn left at .2 miles after crossing the RR tracks. The lodge will be on your right in another .2 miles.

◆  Susitna Landing
      Address: P.O. Box 871706, Wasilla, AK 99687
      Telephone: (907) 495-7700 or (907) 373-6700
      Internet: http://www.matnet.com/ron
      Price: Medium

*GPS Location: N 61° 54' 46.4", W 150° 05' 53.1"*

If you have a jet boat you probably know about Susitna Landing. If not you will probably enjoy watching the action as fishermen use this launch site at the mouth of the Kashwitna River on the Susitna River to embark and return from successful fishing trips.

The landing has 30 camping sites set on the gravel bar downstream from the launch site. Five of these have 30-amp electricity hook-ups. There is plenty of room for big rigs. Most camp sites have fire pits. Sanitary facilities are limited to outhouses but there is an expresso bar to compensate. Fishing tackle is available, as are guided fishing trips, float trips, and scenic river boat tours.

To reach Susitna Landing follow the good gravel road west 1 mile from about Mile 82.5 of the Parks Highway.

◆  Montana Creek Campgrounds
      Location: Mile 97 of the Parks Highway
      Price: Low

*GPS Location:  N 62° 06' 11.5", W 150° 03' 32.0"*

Montana Creek is another of the popular salmon fishing streams that cross the Parks Highway in this area. Montana Creek actually has three different campgrounds occupying quadrants formed by the crossing of the highway and the stream. Bank fishing for salmon is extremely popular at Montana Creek.

In the southwest quadrant is the State of Alaska owned Montana Creek Campground. It is actually managed by the same folks who operate the campground located across the highway. This campground is a big gravel parking lot with some picnic tables and fire pits. There are outhouses and a hand-operated water pump.

In the southeast quadrant is a privately owned operation also known as the Montana Creek Campground. There are two types of camp sites here. Toward the highway are a number of open back-in sites suitable for large rigs and surrounded by grass. Plans are in the works to provide electricity to these sites. Farther back from the road are many smaller well-separated back-in campsites surrounded by natural vegetation. Most of the sites at this campground have picnic tables and fire pits. Chemical toilets are provided and there is also a small store out front selling fishing tackle.

Finally, in the northwest quadrant is a third campground called Cheta's Corner Cache with approximately 45 smaller back-in sites surrounded by natural vegetation. There are picnic tables, fire pits, chemical toilets and some newly constructed outhouse buildings.

You'll find Montana Creek at Mile 97 of the Parks Highway.

♦  DESTINY - TALKEETNA RIVER
    ADVENTURES CAMPGROUND
        Address: P.O. Box 473, Talkeetna, AK 99676
        Telephone: (907) 733-2604
        Price: Medium

*GPS Location: N 62° 19' 32.1", W 150° 06' 28.6"*

Talkeetna has long needed an alternative to the somewhat informal camping/parking area down by the river just west of town. This new campground has controlled access and is located near the boat launch.

There are now about 40 camping sites arranged in a wooded area with gravel interior roads. There are no hook-ups but each campsite has a picnic table and fire ring and there are outhouses. At the entrance gate is a small store and tackle shop which offers showers. Next door is the Swiss-Alaska Inn which has a restaurant and there is a short trail leading to central Talkeetna.

As you enter Talkeetna watch for signs marking a road to the right leading to the airport. Take this road, cross the RR tracks, and turn left just on the far side of the tracks. Drive .7 mile, the campground entrance will be on your left.

♦  H & H LAKEVIEW CAMPER PARK
        Address: HC 89 Box 616, Willow, AK 99688
        Telephone: (907) 733-2415
        Price: Medium

*GPS Location: N 62° 08' 27.2", W 150° 03' 20.1"*

The H & H is a traditional-style roadhouse offering gas, a good restaurant, rooms and an RV park out back along the shores of a pleasant little lake.

The campground has 10 sites with 30-amp electricity on a gravel surface with plenty of room to maneuver big rigs. There is also lots of room for dry campers and a tent-camping area. There is a wash house with showers and a coin-op laundry. Use of a dump station and water fill-up are available for an extra charge.

The H & H is located near Mile 100 of the Parks Highway.

♦  TRAPPER CREEK INN
        Address: P.O. Box 13209, Trapper Creek, AK 99683
        Telephone: (907) 733-2302
        Price: Medium

*GPS Location: N 62° 18' 51.9", W 150° 13' 59.1"*

The Trapper Creek Inn is a roadhouse-style facility. They offer gas, groceries, gifts, rooms, a delicatessen, a laundromat, a cash machine and an RV campground. There's even a small airstrip out back and scenic flights are available.

The campground here has 32 spaces, some are pull-throughs. 18 of the spaces have full-hookups with 20-amp electricity. There is a covered gazebo at the center of the campground and the sites are separated by trees and natural vegetation. The inn offers hot showers and a laundromat. There's also a dump station.

The Trapper Creek Inn is located in Trapper Creek at about Mile 115 of the Parks Highway.

✦ LOWER TROUBLESOME CREEK CAMPGROUND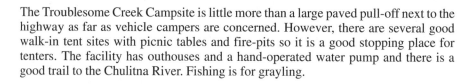
   (DENALI STATE PARK)
   Location: Mile 137 of the Parks Highway
   Price: Low

*GPS Location: N 62° 37' 30.8", W 150° 13' 40.5"*

The Troublesome Creek Campsite is little more than a large paved pull-off next to the highway as far as vehicle campers are concerned. However, there are several good walk-in tent sites with picnic tables and fire-pits so it is a good stopping place for tenters. The facility has outhouses and a hand-operated water pump and there is a good trail to the Chulitna River. Fishing is for grayling.

✦ BYERS LAKE CAMPGROUND (DENALI STATE PARK)
   Location: Mile 147 of the Parks Highway
   Price: Medium

*GPS Location:  N 62° 44' 37.6", W 150° 07' 31.0"*

One of our favorite state campgrounds for big rigs is Byers Lake. It is well-wooded, has plenty of pull-throughs, and is seldom crowded. There are boats for rent to explore the lake (only electric motors are allowed) and several good hiking trails.

The campground has 62 campsites. Interior roads are gravel as are parking pads. The sites are well-separated and surrounded by trees and natural vegetation. There are picnic tables and fire-pits at the sites, a hand-operated water pump, and outhouses. This campground has a host on site and firewood can be purchased.

The campground is located well off the highway. The entrance road is on the east side of the highway at about the 147 Mile marker of the Parks Highway.

✦ DENALI VIEW NORTH (DENALI STATE PARK)
   Location: Mile 163 of the Parks Highway
   Price: Low

*GPS Location: N 62° 53' 23.9", W 149° 46' 47.1"*

The outstanding feature of this campground is the fantastic view of Denali and the Alaska Range. The camping area itself is nothing more than a large paved parking lot shared with tour busses and other highway travelers. There are about 20 back-in sites available for camping with picnic tables and fire pits. The wayside has outhouses, a hand-operated water pump, and a telescope. There is also a park host.

✦ CANTWELL RV PARK
    Address: P.O. Box 210, Cantwell, AK 99279
    Telephone: (907) 768-2210 or (800) 940-2210
    Fax: (907) 262-5149
    Internet: http://www.alaskaone.com/cantwellrv
    Price: Medium

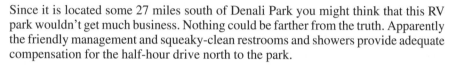

*GPS Location: N 63° 23' 33.3", W 148° 54' 33.9"*

Since it is located some 27 miles south of Denali Park you might think that this RV park wouldn't get much business. Nothing could be farther from the truth. Apparently the friendly management and squeaky-clean restrooms and showers provide adequate compensation for the half-hour drive north to the park.

The Cantwell is a large campground with 79 spaces, 68 of them are large pull-throughs. Each site has 30-amp electricity. This campground is basically a very large leveled gravel field so big rigs can easily maneuver. The campground has a dump station and water fill hose. The services building houses the office, a small gift shop with a few supplies, hot showers costing $2, clean restrooms, and a laundromat. There is one community fire ring.

This campground is located on the spur road to Cantwell. Turn west at the junction of the Denali and Parks Highways (about Mile 210 of the Parks), the campground is on the right after a short distance.

✦ CARLO CREEK LODGE
    Address: HC2 Box 1530, Healy, AK 99743
    Telephone: (907) 683-2576 or (907) 683-2573
    Price: Medium

*GPS Location: N 63° 33' 49.9", W 148° 49' 12.2"*

The Carlo Creek Lodge campground is nice. The sites are unique, complete with covered picnic table areas and moveable fire grills that actually work, and they are well separated by trees. There are 25 sites at this small campground/lodge. 13 of them have 20-amp electric hookups. Some sites are situated along Carlo Creek near the Nenana River. Most of the sites at this campground are fairly small and maneuvering room is limited. The campground also has a shower house, restrooms, some very cute outhouses, a dump station, a water fill station, and a gift shop and general store. There's a restaurant within walking distance.

The campground is located at about Mile 224 of the Parks Highway, 12 miles south of the Denali Park entrance.

◆ DENALI GRIZZLY BEAR CABINS & CAMPGROUNDS
   Address: P.O. Box 7, Denali National Park,
   AK 99755
   Telephone: (907) 683-2696 (Summer) or
   (907) 683-1337 (Winter)
   Internet: http://www.alaskaone.com/dengrzly/index.htm
   Price: High

*GPS Location: N 63° 39' 16.0", W 148° 50' 02.8"*

For a campground that can handle big rigs (and small ones, and tents) near Denali Park our choice would have to be the Denali Grizzly. It is located just south of the park, just across the Nenana River.

This campground has about 80 sites, the majority of them are dry camping sites but some 30 have water and electricity hookups. Many of these are back-in sites long enough for larger rigs. Each site has a picnic table and fire pit, restrooms have flush toilets and coin-operated hot showers. There is a dump station and also a store with supplies, gifts, and a good selection of micro-brews. A restaurant is located nearby. Reservations are recommended.

The campground is located about 6 miles south of the Denali Park entrance near Mile 231 of the Parks Highway.

## DENALI NATIONAL PARK

Denali Park is one of Alaska's prime attractions and is not to be missed. If you have come north to see wildlife, this is the place. The 6 million plus acre park encompasses the highest portion of the Alaska Range including Mt. McKinley, at 20,320 feet the highest peak in the northern hemisphere. It also includes a huge, mostly treeless alpine region of foothills to the north of the range that is prime habitat for grizzlies, caribou, wolves, and other wildlife.

The park does contain several campgrounds. These are Riley Creek, Morino Backpacker (tents), Savage River, Sanctuary River (tents only), Teklanika River, Igloo Creek (tents only) and Wonder Lake (tents only). These campgrounds are popular, especially the one at Teklanika because it allows you to drive quite a distance into the park to get to your campsite.

One of the reasons for the abundant wildlife in the park is that the Park Service severely limits access. Very few vehicles travel the one road that leads far into the park. Most visitors entering must do so in busses. The difficult access is the price you pay to see wildlife. Don't let the restrictions frustrate you. Instead plan ahead and relax, the park is well worth the effort you will expend to visit it.

A somewhat complicated reservation system is used to ensure that most visitors are able to enjoy Denali. The procedures seem to change slightly each year but these are the rules for 1998 according to the park web site (see address below). A similar system is used for bus and campground reservations. About forty percent of both bus and

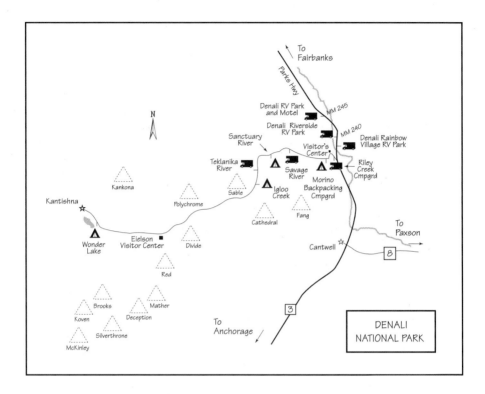

campground spaces can be reserved in advance. This can be done by mail, fax, or phone. Mail reservations must be received at least 30 days prior to the planned visit. Fax and phone reservations are accepted up to two days in advance of the planned visit (actually one day for busses by phone) but should be made as far in advance as possible since the available slots are likely to have been claimed by the time you call if you delay. The remaining 60% of bus and camping slots are parceled out on a first-come, first-served basis at the park where you can make reservations up to two days in advance. Since 60% of the spaces are reserved for in-person purchase you are probably going to be able to get a park campsite and bus space within two days. Your best plan is to reserve far in advance for both bus and campground slots. Failing that, arrive early in the day and hope for the best. Keep in mind that June and July are the most popular months for visiting the park. The crowds begin to taper off by the middle of August. You can stay in a campground just outside the park entrance if you are not able to get a site in the park.

Phone numbers for reservations are 800 622-7275 in the U.S. except Alaska, and 907 272-7275 for international and Alaska calls. The lines are open from the third Monday in February through August 31, from 7 AM to 5 PM Alaska time. Fax and mail reservation service begins December 1 and continues until August 31. The address is Denali Park Resorts Visitor Transportation System, 241 West Ship Creek Ave., Anchorage, AK 99501. The fax number is 907 264-4684. It is easiest to pay by credit card; Visa, Master Card, and Discover Card are accepted. To insure that you enclose all the necessary information you can download a form from the internet at http://www.nps.gov/dena. This net site is also a good source of other information about the park.

There are private bus operators with tours into the park. You may have better luck using one of these. You can book reservations to join one of these tours in the park area or even depart from Fairbanks. Check with the office at one of the commercial campgrounds.

There are also many private campgrounds near the park entrance. Most visitors to the park will find that these are much more convenient than facilities inside the park.

## Denali National Park Campgrounds

✦ RILEY CREEK CAMPGROUND
(DENALI NATIONAL PARK)
    Location: Inside the park near the entrance
    Price: Medium

*GPS Location: N 63° 44' 07.9", W 148° 53' 47.5"*

Riley Creek is the largest of the park's campgrounds and one of the easiest to actually get into. The campground has 100 campsites off two large loops, some are pull-throughs. Each site has a picnic table and fire pit. A maximum of 8 people (2 tents) is allowed at each site. Interior roads are paved, parking pads are gravel. There is a central food locker area where you can store food that might attract bears. The restrooms have no showers but they do have flush toilets. About a mile from the campground is McKinley Mercantile which has limited supplies and where it is also possible to get a shower or buy firewood. There's a restaurant at the Denali Park Hotel, also about a mile from the campground. This campground has a host and there is a campfire circle. Reservations are recommended, sign-in at the visitor center is required, see reservation information above.

✦ MORINO BACKPACKING CAMPGROUND
(DENALI NATIONAL PARK)
    Location: Mile 1.5 of the park road near the hotel and railroad depot
    Price: Low

Morino Campground is a 60-site campground for backpackers near the facilities at the park entrance. Telephones, a small store with showers, and the hotel restaurant are located nearby. There are no vehicle parking spaces. Fires are not allowed. There are chemical toilets and food storage lockers. Campers can self-register at this campground if they find room, often there is some because sites are not delineated and people really crowd in. No reservations are taken.

✦ SAVAGE RIVER CAMPGROUND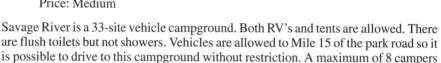
    Location: Mile 13 of park road
    Price: Medium

Savage River is a 33-site vehicle campground. Both RV's and tents are allowed. There
are flush toilets but not showers. Vehicles are allowed to Mile 15 of the park road so it
is possible to drive to this campground without restriction. A maximum of 8 campers
(2 tents) are allowed in each space. Reservations are recommended, sign-in at the
visitor center is required, see information about reservations above.

✦ SANCTUARY RIVER CAMPGROUND
    Location: Mile 22 of the park road
    Price: Low

Sanctuary River is a very small 3-site tent campground. There is a chemical toilet and
bear-proof food storage lockers. No campfires are allowed, only stoves. No reservations are taken for this campground, sign-in at the visitor center is required, see information about reservations above.

✦ TEKLANIKA RIVER CAMPGROUND
    Location: Mile 29 of the park road
    Price: Medium

Teklanika River Campground is a large vehicle campground with 53 sites. Each has a
fire pit and picnic table. There are flush toilets but no showers. A maximum of 8
campers (2 tents) are allowed in each site. The location of this campground inside the
park on limited access road beyond the 15-mile checkpoint makes it popular but im-
poses restrictions. Campers are given special permits to drive in and return, vehicles
can not be used otherwise. In addition, campers must stay 3 days at the campground to
limit road traffic. Reservations are recommended, sign-in at the visitor center is required, see information about reservations above.

✦ IGLOO CREEK CAMPGROUND
    Location: Mile 34 of the park road
    Price: Low

Igloo Creek is a 7-site tent-only campground. There are chemical toilets and no fires
are allowed, only stoves. Food is stored in lockers. No reservations are taken for this
campground, sign-in at the visitor center is required, see information about reservations above.

✦ WONDER LAKE CAMPGROUND
    Location: Mile 85 of the park road
    Price: Medium

The 28-site tent-only campground at Wonder Lake has a choice location with great views of the mountain, when it's out. Food is stored in lockers. No campfires are allowed, only stoves. A maximum of 4 campers (1 tent) are allowed in each site. Reservations are recommended, sign-in at the visitor center is required, see information about reservations above. There are lake trout in Wonder Lake.

✦ DENALI RAINBOW VILLAGE RV PARK
    Address: P.O. Box 777, Denali, AK 99755
    Telephone: (907) 683-3362, Fax (907) 683-7275
    Price: High

*GPS Location: N 63° 44' 48.1", W 148° 53' 53.4"*

The Denali Rainbow Village is the closest RV park to Denali Park. It is new, but there is so much building going on around it and the land apparently so valuable that there is some question in our minds about how long it will last.

For the present, however, there are 26 pull-through sites located on a flat gravel bench outside the park entrance and down the road a bit. Each site has electricity and there is a dump station and water fill station. There is also lots of room for dry camping. The park has restrooms with hot showers, and a laundry house. Restaurants and a small store are located in the immediate vicinity

GRIZZLY BEARS AT DENALI NATIONAL PARK

The Denali Rainbow Village and RV Park are located on the east side of the Parks Highway near the 239 mile mark, about 1.3 miles north of the Denali Park entrance.

✦ DENALI RIVERSIDE RV PARK
    Address: P.O. Box 194, Healy, AK 99743
    Telephone: (888) 778-7700
    Price: High

*GPS Location: N 63° 46' 07.0" , W 148' 54' 48.7"*

This huge new campground not far north of the Denali Park entrance road sits right where dozens of free-campers parked in years past. It overlooks the Nenana River.

The Riverside has 96 campsites with room for more. 73 of them offer electricity and water hookups. Each site has a picnic table and fire pit. There is a dump station and water fill station. Restrooms have flush toilets and coin-op hot showers, there's also a coin-op laundry and gift shop. A shuttle bus to the park is available.

The campground is located near Mile 240 of the Parks Highway. It is about 3 miles north of the park entrance road.

✦ DENALI RV PARK AND MOTEL
    Address: P.O. Box 155, Denali Park, AK 99755
    Telephone: (907) 683-1500 or (800) 478-1501
    Price: High

*GPS Location: N 63° 49' 17.0", W 148° 59' 13.2"*

Not far north of the Denali Park entrance is a large well-established RV park and motel, the Denali. It seems to be the closest park to Denali that offers full hookups.

This campground has some 90 sites, 21 have full hookups with 30-amp electricity, 52 more have water and electricity, and 17 are electricity only. Sites have picnic tables and are separated by grass. The campground also has a dump station. The restrooms have flush toilets and coin-op showers, they are individual rooms with both toilet and shower. There's also a gift shop and a laundromat is promised for next year (1998).

The campground is on the west side of the Parks Highway near Mile 245. It is 7.8 miles north of the Denali entrance road.

## FROM DENALI PARK TO FAIRBANKS
### (121 miles)

After passing the Denali Park Entrance the Parks Highway continues through the Nenana Canyon and soon passes Healy. **Healy** is the location of Alaska's largest open pit coal mine, you can often see the huge drag line stripping overburden on the hilltop to the east of the highway.

As the road descends out of the mountains you will begin to notice the dips and heaves that indicated that it was built on permafrost. This section of road from the mountains to Nenana on the Tanana River was one of the most difficult sections of the entire highway to build, even though the terrain is flat. At Mile 283 you pass the access road to **Clear**, a huge radar site that is part of the ballistic missile early warning system.

At Mile 304 you will enter **Nenana** (population 400). Today this small village of 400 people serves largely as a transfer point for fuel and other goods from the railroad to river barges headed for villages on the Tanana and Yukon Rivers. It is best known as the site of the **Nenana Ice Classic**, an annual betting pool where hundreds of thousands of dollars are wagered by people trying to guess the exact time in the spring when the river ice will go out. The **Nenana Visitor Center** (907 832-9953) is at the corner at Mile 304 where the A Street goes into Nenana. When the Alaska Railroad was completed in 1923 President Harding drove a golden spike in Nenana, today the **Alaska Railroad Museum** is in the renovated original **Nenana Railroad Depot** which is on the National Register of Historic Places.

After leaving Nenana the highway crosses the Tanana River and makes its ways across rolling hills for 54 miles before descending into Fairbanks.

## Campgrounds
## Denali Park to Fairbanks

✦ OTTO LAKE RV PARK
   Address: P.O. Box 195, Healy, AK 99743
   Telephone: (907) 683-2100
   Price: Medium

*GPS Location: N 63° 50' 55.4", W 149° 01' 58.5"*

This campground has an atmosphere much like one of the state campgrounds but also offers the benefits of a commercial one.

Otto Lake is a primitive campground, there are no hookups. There are 49 sites, mostly back-ins. About half sit along the shore of little Otto Lake. Some sites have picnic tables and fire pits. The sites are mostly well separated and there is natural vegetation between them. The campground has outhouses but does offer a dump station and water fill station. There are several nice tent sites and also a boat launch. Canoes and paddle boats are available for rent.

The campground is located about 10 miles north of the Denali entrance road. From about Mile 247 of the Parks Highway follow Otto Lake Road west for .5 miles, the campground is on the left.

✦  McKINLEY RV AND CAMPGROUND
      Address: P.O. Box 340, Healy, AK 99743
      Telephone: (907) 683-2379 or (800) 478-2562,
      Fax (907) 683-2281
      Price: High

*GPS Location: N 63° 51' 57.7", W 149° 01' 06.8"*

Until recently this campground was a KOA. After (or before, if you're heading south) the high-country gravel campgrounds to the south you'll appreciate the grass at this campground.

There are 89 sites at the McKinley. Full-hookup and pull-throughs are offered as well as sites with only water and electric, electric only, and dry. There's also a tent camping area. The campground has flush toilets, free hot showers, a coin-op laundromat, a gift and supplies shop, mini golf, and a playground. There was even an expresso kiosk when we visited.

The campground is located in Healy, on the east side of the Parks Highway at Mile 248.5. This is 11 miles north of the Denali Park entrance road.

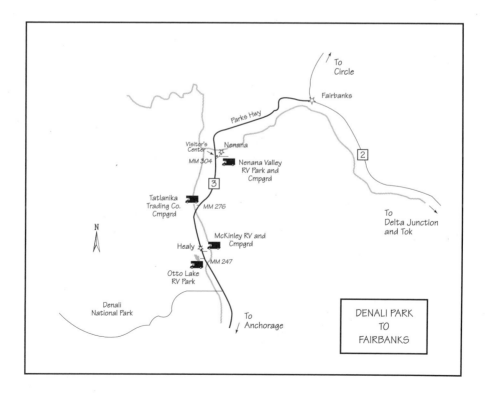

✦ TATLANIKA TRADING CO. CAMPGROUND
   Address: Mile 276 Parks Highway
   (P.O. Box 40179), Clear, AK 99704
   Telephone: (907) 582-2341
   Price: Medium

*GPS Location: N 64° 12' 54.8", W 149° 16' 05.2"*

One of the nicer places to stop along the Parks Highway and one of the best deals is the Tatlanika Trading Post.

The place is best known for its great gift shop but the Tatlanika also has 11 camping sites, some are suitable for large rigs. Many of them are situated along the Nenana River. The sites have electricity and water with picnic tables and a fire pit. They are well separated with natural vegetation. The campground has a dump station and flush toilets, showers are also available for $2.

The Tatlanika Trading Post is located at Mile 276 of the Parks Highway, just north of a bridge over the Nenana River.

✦ NENANA VALLEY RV PARK AND CAMPGROUND
   Address: P.O. Box 207, Nenana, AK 99760
   Telephone: (907) 832-5230
   Price: Medium

*GPS Location: N 64° 33' 44.1", W 149° 05' 26.4"*

Located right in the friendly little town of Nenana many travelers on the Parks consider this campground to be a must stop. You can easily stroll around town, or rent a bicycle to go farther afield.

The campground is a large well-clipped grassy field with 40 spaces. 30 have electricity and are pull-throughs with plenty of room for big rigs. There's also a nice grassy tent area. There are clean restrooms with free hot showers and a coin-op laundromat. The campground has a water fill station and a dump station.

To reach the campground take the road to central Nenana (A Street) from the Y at the visitor center. Turn right on 4th in just a short distance and then drive two blocks, the campground will be on your right between B and C Street.

## PARKS HIGHWAY DUMP STATIONS

Many of the campgrounds in this chapter have dump stations or sewer hookups, see the individual entries for these. There is generally a fee charged for using them, particularly if you are not staying at the campground. Here are some additional possibilities.

In the **Wasilla** area try the MAPCO Express at 255 North Boundary, Wash Day Laundry & Dry Cleaning at 754 Westpoint Drive, Wasilla Chevron at Mile 43 of the Parks

Highway or Big Lake Texaco at Mile 3.5 of the Big Lake Road.

In **Trapper Creek** the Petracache at Mile 115 has a dump station.

In **Talkeetna** there is a dump station at Three Rivers Tesoro on Main Street.

Near **Denali National Park** in Healy is Teklanika Trading Post at Mile 276 of the Parks Highway. There is also a dump station inside the park near the Riley Creek Campground entrance which is not far from the highway.

In **Nenana** there's a dump station at the Nenana Information Center at Mile 303.5 of the Parks Highway.

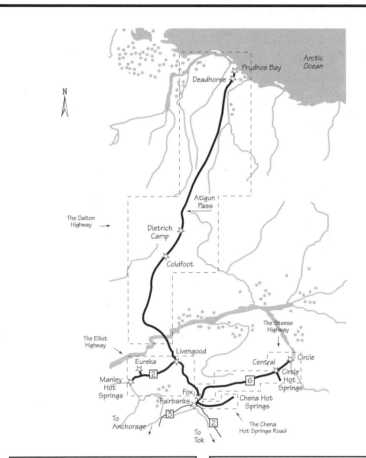

N

Arctic Ocean

Prudhoe Bay

Deadhorse

Atigun Pass

The Dalton Highway →

Dietrich Camp

Coldfoot

The Steese Highway

The Elliot Highway →

Livengood

Eureka

Central

Circle

2

6

Circle Hot Springs

Manley Hot Springs

Fox

Chena Hot Springs

Fairbanks

To Anchorage

3

2

To Tok

The Chena Hot Springs Road

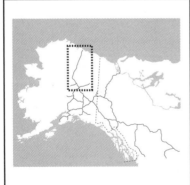

# NORTH OF FAIRBANKS

# INTRODUCTION

There are a surprising number of roads giving access to the country north of Fairbanks. Both RVers and tent campers will find much to interest them in this region.

Fairbanks and the area north to the Brooks Range have some of the best summer weather in the state. On many summer days you can expect blue skies with cumulous clouds building in the afternoon to produce a few showers that disperse in the evening. Daytime temperatures approaching 70° are not uncommon. During the middle of the summer you can also expect long days, in fact it will never get really dark during June and July.

The region is definitely uncrowded. For a short time before the growth of Dawson City, Circle City was the largest city in a very large. The city served the Birch Creek mining district in the hills to the South. There were also many other mining areas along these roads. When the mining pretty much shut down in the 1940's most people left the area leaving interesting ghost towns and mining relics, and the roads to reach them.

### Highlights

There are three developed and easy to reach hot springs north of Fairbanks. Closest and easiest with a paved road all the way, is **Chena Hot Springs** on the Chena Hot Springs Road. The largest pool is at **Circle Hot Springs** near Central on the Steese Highway. There is also a hot springs at **Manley Hot Springs** at the end of the Taylor Highway.

The entire region was a mining area. Important strikes include Pedro Creek on the Circle Hot Springs Road; Upper Goldstream Creek near Fox, Cleary Creek, Chatanika, Nome Creek, Birch Creek and Circle-Mastodon Creek on the Steese Highway; Tolovana (Livengood), Eureka and Tofty on the Elliott Highway; and Ruby (Wiseman) and Coldfoot on the Dalton Highway. Many relics of these gold rushes remain within easy walking distance of the highways.

The 414-mile long **Dalton Highway**, also long known as the pipeline haul road, is a major destination in its own right. You'll find an entire section about this formidable but rewarding route below.

### Fishing

Fishing in the interior is primarily for grayling, whitefish, and northern pike. King, silver, and chum (also known as calico or dog) salmon do get far into the interior, but by the time they get this far up the river they are quite red and often no good for eating. Local fishermen do enjoy catching and releasing them, however.

The **Chena River**, which runs through Fairbanks, was a very good grayling stream at one time but the fish population crashed in the 80's. The upper reaches in the Chena River State Recreation Area are clear and fun to fish. The grayling are coming back, all grayling fishing in the Chena is catch-and-release. You might want to give it a try. There's easy access off the Chena Hot Springs Road in many places.

The **Chatanika River** is another clear-water river that has seen heavy fishing pressure for grayling. From April 1 to May 31 the Chatanika is catch-and-release for grayling, the rest of the year only fish at least 12 inches long can be kept. Access to the Chatanika is from the Steese Highway at Mile 35 and 39 and from the Elliott Highway at Mile 11. The best access is by canoe, see below.

On the Steese Highway there are several **small lakes in the tailing piles at Chatanika** that are stocked with grayling. They're between Mile 29 to Mile 40 and are marked with signs on the road.

**Beaver and Birch Creeks** run north into the Yukon River, both have good grayling fishing. Access to Beaver Creek is very limited and along most of the river requires either a hike or airplane ride. The hedwaters are road-accessible from Mile 57 of the Steese Highway on the Nome Creek Road. Access to Birch Creek is at Mile 94 and Mile 147 of the Steese Highway. Both of these rivers are popular canoe routes, they're designated Wild and Scenic Rivers, see below.

The **Tolovana River** joins the Chatanika River near Minto. The upper reaches provide good grayling fishing, access is from bridges on the Elliott Highway at Mile 57 and Mile 75. Other creeks to try on the Elliott Highway are **Tatalina Creek** (Mile 45), **Hutlinana Creek** (Mile 129), and **Baker Creek** (Mile 137).

The **Dalton Highway** remains a wilderness road and fishing in the creeks it crosses can be good. These are mostly grayling streams but swampy areas with slow-moving water have northern pike. Try **Hess Creek** (Mile 24), the **Ray River** (Mile 70), **No Name Creek** (Mile 79), the **Kanuti River** (Mile 106), **Fish Creek** (Mile 114), **South Fork of Bonanza Creek** (Mile 125), the **North Fork of Bonanza Creek** (Mile 126), **Prospect Creek** (Mile 135), the **Jim River** (Mile 140, 141), **Grayling Lake** (Mile 151), the **South Fork of the Koyukuk River** (Mile 156), **Minnie Creek** (Mile 187), and the **Dietrich River** (Mile 207).

### Boating, Rafting, Canoeing, and Kayaking

There are four popular canoe routes north of Fairbanks and accissible from the road. These are the Chena River, the Chatanika River, Beaver Creek, and Birch Creek.

The **Chena River** has excellent road access. The upper river is in the Chena River State Recreation Area. Short or long floats are available, from a few hours to almost 80 hours (all the way to Fairbanks) of float time. Tent camping on gravel bars along the river is allowed within the Recreation Area. Access points along the Chena Hot Springs Road are at Mile 48.9, Mile 44.0, Mile 39.5, Mile 37.8, Mile 31.6, Mile 28.6, Mile 28, Mile 27, and off the Grange Hill Road at Mile 20.8. There's also access from Nordale Road and at several places in Fairbanks. The river is rated as Class II and has sweepers and log jams so exercise caution. Lower sections of the river are slower and easier to negotiate.

The **Chatanika River** is navigable a distance of about 130 miles but most canoers float no more than the 60 river miles between Sourdough Creek and the Elliott Highway which takes three to four days. This is a Class I and Class II river with log jams and sweepers so exercise caution. Access points are from the Steese Highway at Sourdough Creek (Mile 60), Cripple Creek (Mile 53), Long Creek (Mile 45), the Chatanika River Bridge (Mile 39), and on the Elliott Highway at Mile 11.

**Birch Creek** is a National Wild and Scenic River with road-accessible put-in and take-out points. The put-in is at Twelve Mile Creek on the Steese Highway (Mile 94), the take-out is at the Birch Creek Bridge at Mile 147 of the Steese Highway. Between the two are 126 river miles for a 7 to 10 day float. Birch Creek does not run along the road, this is a wilderness float. The water is rated Class I and II with some Class III rapids so exercise caution. Much of the river is within the Steese National Conservation Area.

**Beaver Creek** is the most remote of these rivers. There is road access to the put-in point but it is necessary to arrange for an aircraft for take-out. This river is a National Wild and Scenic River. The put-in point is on Nome Creek which is accessible from via the U.S. Creek Road from Mile 57 of the Steese Highway. From the put-in to take-out at a gravel bar at Victoria Creek is 127 river miles and takes 7 or 8 days. The first two days are likely to be slow going as you line your canoe or raft for six miles through shallow water as far as Beaver Creek. This is a Class I river in remote country with log jams and sweepers, exercise caution.

## Hiking and Mountain Biking

The high country north of Fairbanks is excellent hiking terrain with many designated trails. Most trails are within the Chena River State Recreation Area, the White Mountains National Recreation Area, the Steese National Conservation Area, or the Trans-Alaska Pipeline Utility Corridor.

The **Chena River State Recreation Area** has a good selection of trails. The **Granite Tors Trail** is a 15-mile loop trail up a ridge on one side of Rock Creek to a region of rocky pillars in high treeless country, and then back to the starting point along the other side of Rock Creek. The trail has an elevation gain of 2,500 feet and takes from 4 to 8 hours. Access is from the Tors Trail Campground at Mile 39 of the Chena Hot Spring Road. An easier trail is the **Angel Rocks Trail,** a 3.5-mile (round trip) hike to rock outcroppings above the river. Access is from a parking lot at Mile 48.9 of the Chena Hot Springs Road. Finally, the challenging **Chena Dome Trail** is a 30-mile loop through high country following a chain of rock cairns that mark the trail. Altitude gain is over 3,000 feet. Plan on 2 to 4 days to make the loop. Access is from Mile 50.5 of the Chena Hot Springs Road. Of these three trails only the last is open to mountain bikes.

The White Mountains National Recreation Area has lots of trails, unfortunately almost all of them are designed for winter use, they are too wet to make good summer hiking trails. The **Summit Trail** is an exception. This ridge trail from Mile 28 of the Elliot Highway is a one-way day hike of 3.5 miles to the north side of Wickersham Dome, a climb of 900 feet. It is also possible to follow this trail much farther to Birch Creek. The one-way distance to the creek is 20 miles.

A popular trail along the Steese Highway is the **Pinnell Mountain Trail**. It connects Eagle Summit at Mile 107 and Twelvemile Summit at Mile 85. The trail is 27 miles long and follows mountain ridges with wonderful views in all directions. There are basic shelters at Mile 10 and Mile 17.5 as measured from the Eagle Summit trailhead, the BLM recommends walking the trail from Eagle Summit to Twelvemile Summit because it is slightly easier in that direction. Plan on two to four days to finish this hike. Water can be a problem, don't pass up a source. You may have to descend from the ridgeline to find it. Some sections of the trail are marked with cairns. Visiting the summits and walking the trail at the summer solstice has become very popular. From June 18 to June 24 the sun doesn't dip below the horizon at all from higher points on the trail, the solstice is June 20 or 21.

On the Elliott Highway near Manley Hot Springs is the trail to **Hutlinana Warm Springs**. The 8-mile trail follows Hutlinana Creek north from near the bridge at Mile 139.

Along the **Dalton Highway** hiking options are limited except in the high country. Check at the triagency visitor's center at Mile 175 for suggested routes. Try the trail up Gold Creek from Mile 197 to **Bob Johnson Lake**. The distance is 13 miles and the lake is known for its fishing (grayling, lake trout, and northern pike). Really ambitious hikers can also climb Sukakpak Mountain near Mile 204 for great views.

### Wildlife Viewing

You are likely to run into a moose almost anywhere along the roads north of Fairbanks and there are often grouse and ptarmigan feeding along the sides of the roads. The **Dalton Highway** is in another class entirely. From Atigun Pass (Mile 245) to Galbraith Lake (Mile 275) you are almost sure to see Dall sheep. Also watch for caribou, arctic fox, muskoxen, and a long list of birds. The BLM even prints a booklet that serves as a checklist titled *Birds Along the Dalton Highway*.

ARCTIC TERN NESTING ON A GRAVEL BAR

# THE ROUTES, TOWNS, AND CAMPGROUNDS

## STEESE HIGHWAY
### (162 miles)

The Steese Highway was the first of the roads north of Fairbanks. Today it is not the busiest, the Dalton Highway claims that honor, but it is the only one of the roads that begins in Fairbanks. The others all branch off the Steese.

For the first 44 miles the Steese Highway is paved. Then for another 83 miles to Central the road is wide and generally in good shape but not paved. The remaining 35 miles to Circle City on the banks of the Yukon River are not as wide or well-maintained but still easily good enough for even the largest RVs.

The Steese Highway starts as the Steese Expressway running just east of downtown Fairbanks. At Mile 5 the Chena Hot Springs Road cuts off to the east. There's a **pipeline viewing area** at Mile 7 and at Mile 11 the expressway reaches the Fox junction.

Fox is in the middle of an area of tailing piles from gold dredges that worked the region until WW II. There is a dredge located near Fox (**Gold Dredge #8**) that is open to the public and another on private land at Mile 29 in Chatanika.

At Fox junction the Steese Highway goes right while the Eliott Highway continues straight. After turning right you'll soon see the **Pedro Monument** on the left at Mile 16. Felix Pedro discovered gold near here, this was the strike that caused the founding of the city of Fairbanks.

The road climbs over the first of three summits, 2,233 foot **Cleary Summit**, at Mile 21 and descends into the **Chatanika River Valley**. This valley was another gold mining area, there are lots more tailing piles. The second Steese Highway dredge is near the road at Mile 29. The Chatanika Valley had two gold mining towns, Cleary and Chatanika. It also has the beautifully clear Chatanika River.

As the road continues northwest up the Chatanika Valley you may notice a large pipeline to the left. This is the **Davidson Ditch**, a system of ditches on the mountaintops and inverted siphons in the valleys that delivered water to the mining operations downstream. It is no longer in use but was only closed down after the 1967 Fairbanks flood.

The road eventually climbs up out of the trees to 2,982 foot **Twelvemile Summit** The Pinnell Mountain National Recreation Trail, leading 24 miles to Eagle Summit, leaves the road here. Note the scattered shiny pieces of airplanes that didn't quite make it over the summit.

The road takes a slightly lower route than the Pinnell trail to **Eagle Summit** at Mile 108. From there it descends to Central at Mile 127.

**Central** is a small town with a population of about 400 dating from the days of the Birch Creek strike in the early 1890's. Today there's a post office, an airstrip, a museum, and a couple of roadhouses. Gas is available.

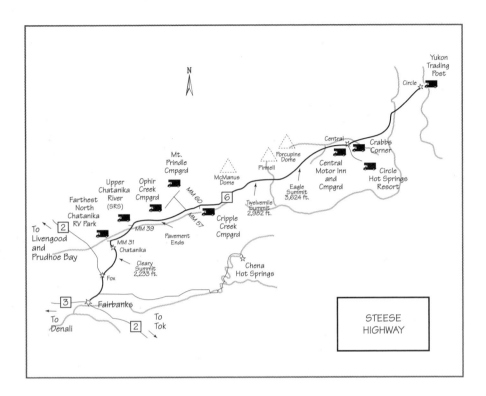

In the middle of town is the junction with a gravel road that leads 8 miles to Circle Hot Springs Resort.

From Central the Steese Highway is narrower and not as straight. It continues another 35 miles to **Circle City** on the Yukon river. Circle also dates from the Birch Creek Strike. It was known as the Paris of the north in the few short years before gold was found at Dawson City. Once that happened the miners abandoned Circle and headed upstream. Today you'll find a town with a population of about 100 people. Despite the name Circle is well south of the Arctic Circle, to cross it you'll have to drive up the Dalton Highway. Services in Circle include a small store, gas, a laundromat, and a campground on the bank of the river.

## Steese Highway Campgrounds

✦ FARTHEST NORTH CHATANIKA RV PARK
    Address: P.O. Box 10574, Fairbanks, AK 99710
    Telephone: (907) 389-8000
    Price: Medium

*GPS Location: N 65° 08' 01.7", W 147° 27' 41.2"*

This campground is indeed the farthest north campground with RV hookups, at least on the Steese Highway. Coldfoot Services on the Dalton does have electrical hookups so you might include it in the competition.

This new campground has about 35 full-hookup RV sites (30-amp plugs) and also some dry sites sitting in a large gravel area with some trees. Other amenities are lacking, there are no toilets or showers although there is a dump station.

Look for the campground on the west side of the Steese Highway near Chatanika at about Mile 31.

◆ UPPER CHATANIKA RIVER STATE RECREATION SITE
(STATE OF ALASKA)
    Location: Mile 39 Steese Highway
    Price: Low
        *GPS Location: N 65° 11' 33.6", W 147° 15' 23.9"*

The Upper Chatanika campground is one of the nicest in this area. It offers some sites right on this beautifully clear wilderness river. This is a popular put-in point for canoeing the river.

There are 24 vehicle camping sites at this campground. They are well-separated by trees and natural vegetation and have picnic tables and fire pits. This campground has a host and firewood is offered for purchase. There are outhouses and a hand-operated water pump.

The campground is on the Steese Highway to Circle at Mile 39.

◆ WHITE MOUNTAINS GATEWAY CAMPGROUNDS (BLM) -
MT. PRINDLE CAMPGROUND AND OPHIR CREEK CAMPGROUND
    Location: Both are off U.S. Creek Road off Mile 57
    of the Steese Highway
    Price: Low

The BLM is constructing two new campgrounds and planning to open them in May, 1998. Both are off the Nome Creek Road which is the access route to the Beaver Creek National Wild River and the White Mountains. The route has been named the White Mountains Gateway.

Mt. Prindle Campground will have 13 wheelchair-accessible campsites with picnic tables and fire rings. These are separated back-in sites. The campground has outhouses and water. There will be a new hiking trail to upper Nome Creek. To reach the campground turn north on the U.S. Creek Road at Mile 57 of the Steese Highway. Drive 6 miles to the Nome Creek Road, turn right and drive another four miles to the campground.

Ophir Creek Campground will have nineteen wheelchair-accessible campsites off two loops. These are also separated back-in sites. Outhouses and a hand-operated water pump will be provided. This campground provides access to Nome Creek which is used by floaters to reach Birch Creek. To reach the campground turn north on the U.S. Creek Road at Mile 57 of the Steese Highway. Drive 6 miles to the Nome Creek Road, turn left and drive another 12 miles to the campground.

✦ CRIPPLE CREEK CAMPGROUND (BLM)
    Location: Mile 60 of Steese Highway
    Price: Low

*GPS Location: N 65° 16' 34.1", W 146° 39' 13.4"*

This small campground is the last one before Central. There are 12 back-in vehicle sites in a grove of mixed spruce and birch. Picnic tables and fire pits are provided. There is also a tent camping area. Unfortunately none of the sites are located along the river. There are outhouses and a hand-operated water pump. The BLM also operates a recreational rental cabin at this campground. You must pre-register to use it, see our section about rental recreational cabins in Chapter 14 - Camping Away From the Road System.

You will find this campground on the north side of the road near Mile 60.

✦ CRABB'S CORNER
    Address: P.O. Box 30109, Central, AK 99730
    Telephone: (907) 520-5599
    Price: Low

*GPS Location: N 65° 34' 18.4", W 144° 48' 13.3"*

Crabb's sits right on the corner where the spur road out to Circle Hot Springs leaves the Steese Highway in the tiny town of Central. They offer camping in a nice little shaded park across the road with picnic tables and barbecues. There are no hookups but there is an outhouse and showers are available. Crabb's also has a cafe and sells groceries and gas.

Watch for Crabb's in "downtown" Central at about Mile 128 of the Steese Highway.

✦ CENTRAL MOTOR INN AND CAMPGROUND
    Address: Box 24, Central, AK 99730
    Telephone: (907) 520-5228, Fax (907) 520-5230
    Price: Low

*GPS Location: N 65° 34' 16.1", W 144° 48' 47.7"*

The Central Motor Inn offers motel rooms, a restaurant, and a bar. They also will let RVs park in their parking lot or nearby and have some grassy areas suitable for tent camping. Showers are included in the price of a campsite. There are no hookups but there is a dump station.

The Central Motor Inn is at about Mile 127 of the Steese Highway in the town of Central, it is south of the spur road to Circle Hot Springs.

✦ CIRCLE HOT SPRINGS RESORT
    Address: Central, AK 99730
    Telephone: (907) 520-5113, Fax (907) 520-5442
    Price: Low

*GPS Location: N 65° 29' 03.4", W 144° 38' 23.8"*

Circle Hot Springs has always been a favorite destination for northern residents. The beautiful drive from Fairbanks now only takes about 3 hours since even the gravel portion of the road lets you drive at fairly high speeds.

The resort has 6 no-hookup sites with room for lots more rigs in the parking lot and also some decent tent sites. Campers use the toilets and showers at the pool. The resort features a huge swimming pool that is maintained at a temperature of about 100° F. The resort also has a restaurant and hiking trails.

To reach Circle Hot Springs follow the Steese Highway to Central, turn right at about Mile 128 in the middle of town and proceed 8 miles on the Circle Hot Springs road to the resort.

CIRCLE HOT SPRINGS

◆ YUKON TRADING POST
    Address: Circle, Alaska, 99733
    Telephone: (907) 773-1217
    Price: Free

*GPS Location: N 65° 49' 32.7", W 144° 03' 46.7"*

The town of Circle provides parking for RVs at the boat ramp which forms the very end of the Steese Highway. There are back-in spaces for about 10 rigs with picnic tables and barbecues. An outhouse is nearby and just across the road is the Yukon Trading Post with groceries, gifts, and a cafe. Behind the trading post is a laundry which has hot showers.

To find this campground just follow the Steese Highway to its end at the Yukon River, about Mile 162.

## CHENA HOT SPRINGS ROAD
### (57 Miles)

The Chena Hot Springs Road is the most civilized of the routes north of Fairbanks. The road leads almost directly east from a junction at Mile 5 of the Steese Highway. The Chena Hot Springs Road is 57 miles long and paved for its entire length. It generally leads up the valley of the Chena River. Along the way there are several campgrounds and access points for fishing or floating the Chena and also access to several good hiking trails into the surrounding hills.

### Chena Hots Springs Road Campgrounds

◆ PLEASANT VALLEY RV PARK
    Address: P.O. Box 16019, Two Rivers, AK 99716
    Telephone: (907) 488-8198, Fax (907) 490-29
    Price: Medium

*GPS Location: N 64° 52' 57.3", W 146° 51' 48.0"*

Looking for a campground near Fairbanks in a wilderness setting but with the conveniences of hookups and flush toilets? This campground fills the bill, it is only 27 miles northeast of Fairbanks and convenient to the Chena River State Recreation Area for fishing and float trips.

This new campground is set in a grove of birch trees. There are 16 long pull-throughs, separated by trees, with fire pits and free firewood. Sites have electric (20 and 30-amp) and water hookups. There are also several tent sites. The campground has flush toilets and showers and a dump station. There is a small store with groceries and RV supplies and across the road is a restaurant and another store. This campground is a Coast to Coast Good Neighbor Park and also a Passport America park. You can rent canoes at the campground for floating the Chena.

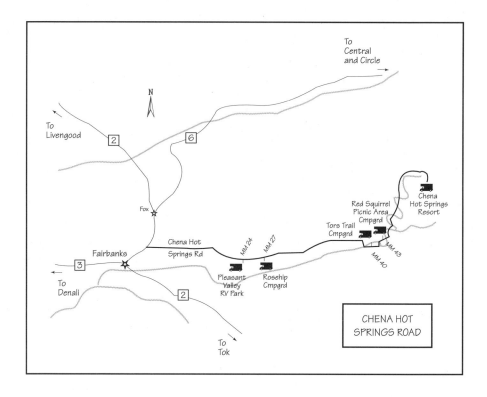

To find the campground drive north on the Steese Highway 5 miles to the Chena Hot Springs Road. Turn toward Chena Hot Springs and drive 24 miles, you'll see the RV park on the right. The office is in the nearby tool-rental center.

✦  ROSEHIP CAMPGROUND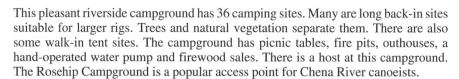
   (CHENA RIVER STATE RECREATION AREA)
      Location: Mile 27 Chena Hot Springs Road
      Price: Low

*GPS Location: N 64° 52' 38.2", W 146° 45' 58.4"*

This pleasant riverside campground has 36 camping sites. Many are long back-in sites suitable for larger rigs. Trees and natural vegetation separate them. There are also some walk-in tent sites. The campground has picnic tables, fire pits, outhouses, a hand-operated water pump and firewood sales. There is a host at this campground. The Rosehip Campground is a popular access point for Chena River canoeists.

The campground is located on the south side of the Chena Hot Springs Road at about Mile 27.

✦ GRANITE TORS TRAIL CAMPGROUND
    (CHENA RIVER STATE RECREATION AREA)
        Location: Mile 40 Chena Hot Springs Road
        Price: Low

*GPS Location: N 64° 54' 12.2", W 146° 21' 52.9"*

One of the most popular hikes in the Fairbanks area is to the Granite Tors, large granite rocks projecting from rounded hilltops. This campground makes a good base camp since it is where the trail starts.

The campground is located near the North Fork of the Chena River. There are 24 long back-in sites. They are well separated with spruces and other natural vegetation and have picnic tables and fire pits. This campground has outhouses, a hand-operated water pump, a canoe launching area, and a host.

You can't miss this campground since it sits on the north side of the highway near Mile 40 of the Chena Hot Springs Road. A bridge over the North Fork of the Chena helps mark the location.

✦ RED SQUIRREL PICNIC AREA CAMPGROUND
        Location: Mile 43 Chena Hot Springs Road
        Price: Low

*GPS Location: N 64° 56' 09.1", W 146° 17' 06.0"*

This is really just a picnic area with two covered picnic kiosks but camping is allowed in the large parking areas. The place is attractive and overlooks a small lake. There are picnic tables, fire rings, outhouses, and a hand-operated water pump.

The campground is located on the north side of the Chena Hot Springs Road at about Mile 43.

✦ CHENA HOT SPRINGS RESORT
        Address: P.O. Box 73440, Fairbanks, AK 99707
        Telephone: (907) 452-7867 or (800) 478-4681
        Price: Medium

*GPS Location: N 65° 03' 13.1", W 146° 03' 28.2"*

At the end of a 57-mile paved highway Chena Hot Springs is the easiest to reach of the three hot springs north of Fairbanks. The springs here were discovered in 1904, the water comes out of the ground at 165° F.

Chena Hot Springs is a small resort offering, campsites, hotel rooms, a restaurant and bar, a small enclosed swimming pool and hot tubs, and an aircraft landing strip. There are three camping areas. Ten parallel sites have 20, 30, and 50-amp electrical service. These sites are close together and have little to offer in the way of scenic beauty, but they do have an unobstructed view of the airstrip.

A second area, called the Upper Campground, has 13 sites suitable for RVs. There are no hookups but the sites are separated by trees and natural vegetation. There are conveniently located outhouses.

The lower campground is really suitable only for very small rigs and tent campers. There are 19 sites here including a grassy tent area and nearby outhouses. Walk the roads of this area before trying it in a rig.

The resort also has a dump station and a laundromat. Nearby cross-country skiing trails can be used as hiking trails in the summer.

Chena Hot Springs Resort is located at the very end of the Chena Hot Spring Road near Mile 57.

## ELLIOT HIGHWAY
### (152 miles)

If the Chena Hot Springs road is the most civilized of these routes north of Fairbanks the Elliot Highway is the quietest, at least once you pass the Dalton Highway Junction. The Elliot Highway leaves the Steese Highway at Mile 11 at the Fox junction. From there it leads northeast to Livengood. Just past Livengood the Dalton Highway turns north to the Arctic Ocean while the Elliot Highway heads westward to Manley Hot Springs.

THE TRANS-ALASKA OIL PIPELINE

The Elliot Highway is paved only as far as Mile 28. From there to the Dalton junction at Mile 73 the road is gravel but good, there is quite a bit of truck traffic bound for the North Slope. After the Dalton junction the road is much narrower and often rough but still suitable for all rigs.

At Mile 71 the road reaches **Livengood**, a historic gold-mining town. The Livengood strike was in 1914, today the town has about 100 inhabitants.

Just after Livengood the Dalton Highway (see below) and pipeline head north leaving a much smaller Elliot Highway. The Elliott follows ridgetops west with vistas to the south across the extensive Minto Flats. Many people camp at an unofficial camp-ground at Mile 75 at the Tolovana River Bridge. A side road at Mile 110 leads 10 miles south to **Minto**, an Athapaskan Indian village. Another side road at Mile 131 leads north to the gold-mining district of **Eureka**.

Finally at Mile 152 the highway reaches **Manley Hot Springs**. The hot springs and town were developed in the early 1900's to service nearby gold fields at Tofty and Eureka. Access to the Tanana River made the town a supply center. Today there are some 100 residents. Dry camping is allowed at the small city park in town just south of the slough. There are fire pits, picnic tables, and an outhouse. The Manley Hot Springs Resort has RV parking, a swimming pool, laundromat, showers, a dump station, and restaurant.

From Manley Hot Springs an access road leads 16 miles into the **Tofty** mining area. Mining continues in the district.

## Elliot Highway Campgrounds

✦ NORTHERN EXPOSURES RV PARK AND CAMPGROUND
    Address: P.O. Box 83517, Fairbanks, AK 99708
    Telephone: (907) 474-8088 or (800) 428-8303
    Price: Medium

*GPS Location: N 64° 57' 42.7", W 147° 37' 19.6"*

This campground is located in the spread-out old gold-mining community of Fox, about 10 miles north of Fairbanks on the Elliot Highway. There are several nearby attractions including a Trans-Alaska Pipeline viewing area, the Goldstream Dredge #8, the El Dorado Gold Mine, the NOAA Satellite Tracking Station, and several well-known restaurants. The campground is also only three miles from the place where gold was discovered by Felix Pedro in 1902 leading to the settlement of Fairbanks.

The new campground has 31 RV sites and additional tent sites. They are arranged on a gently sloping south-facing hillside overlooking the valley. Many sites are full-utility pull-throughs with 30 and 50-amp electricity. There is also a dump station. The central services building houses the reception desk, a lounge area, restrooms, free showers, and a laundromat.

To reach the campground follow the Steese Highway north from Fairbanks for 11 miles, then go straight ahead past the State of Alaska truck weighing station. You're now on the Elliot Highway and the campground is on your right just past the weighing station.

♦ OLNES POND CAMPGROUND
   (LOWER CHATANIKA STATE RECREATION AREA)
      Location: Mile 11 Elliot Highway
      Price: Low

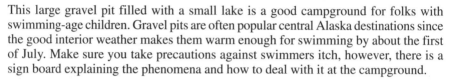

*GPS Location: N 65° 04' 36.4", W 147° 44' 47.6"*

This large gravel pit filled with a small lake is a good campground for folks with swimming-age children. Gravel pits are often popular central Alaska destinations since the good interior weather makes them warm enough for swimming by about the first of July. Make sure you take precautions against swimmers itch, however, there is a sign board explaining the phenomena and how to deal with it at the campground.

This is a popular day trip destination as well as a campground so there are large parking lots that can also be used for camping. There are dedicated campsites dotted around the lake along the surrounding tree line, we counted 15 of them with picnic tables and fire pits. There are outhouses and a hand-operated water pump.

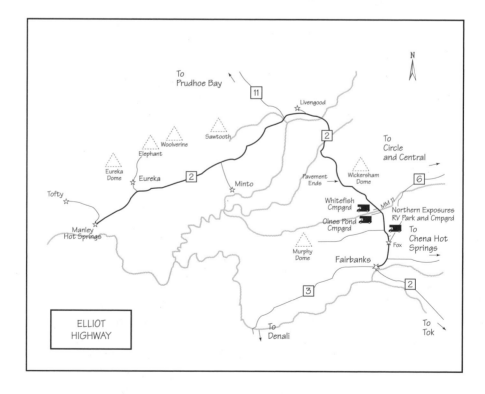

To reach the campground follow the road south from the Elliot Highway at about Mile 11. The good entry road is about 1.1 miles long and there is a dry creek crossing just before the campground that might give rigs with limited ground clearance a problem.

✦ WHITEFISH CAMPGROUND
  (LOWER CHATANIKA STATE RECREATION AREA)
    Location: Mile 11 Elliot Highway
    Price: Low

*GPS Location: N 65° 05' 10.2", W 147° 43' 53.0"*

This campground along the Chatanika River is a popular place to spear fish for whitefish in the fall, it is also the take-out point for canoers on the Chatanika River.

The campground has about 27 camping spots. Some are individual back-in slots surrounded by vegetation, some are parallel parking spaces along an access road, and some are just parking lot sites. There are many picnic tables and fire pits including a covered picnic area. There are also outhouses, a hand-operated water pump, and a boat launching ramp.

The campground is located about a half-mile past the turnoff to Olnes Pond on the Elliott Highway at Mile 11. If you are coming from Fairbanks turn left just after crossing the bridge.

## DALTON HIGHWAY
### (414 miles)

The North Slope Haul Road, now called the Dalton Highway, is one of the few remaining highways in the U.S. through really remote country. It is now open to tourist traffic all the way to Deadhorse. Along the highway you will find lots of opportunities for fishing, hiking, wildlife viewing, and just plain experiencing really empty country. Often you'll have nothing but the road and the pipeline to keep you company.

The Dalton Highway demands preparation. The road surface is gravel and often in poor condition. Travelers should carry at least two spare tires and any equipment necessary to change them. Your vehicle must be in excellent mechanical condition. Gasoline stops are few and far between, as are service facilities. If you do break down be prepared to pay a hefty price for tow service. Heavy trucks commonly travel the highway so tourists should exercise caution. In the event of a breakdown the truckers can relay messages, the commonly used CB channel is 19.

Mileages on the Dalton start at the southern end where the highway leaves the Elliott Highway at Mile 73. Gasoline and services are available at three locations: the **Yukon Crossing** at Mile 56, **Coldfoot** at Mile 175, and **Deadhorse** at Mile 414. Note the 239-mile gap between Coldfoot and Deadhorse.

Much of the land that the Dalton Highway crosses is public lands. From the Yukon

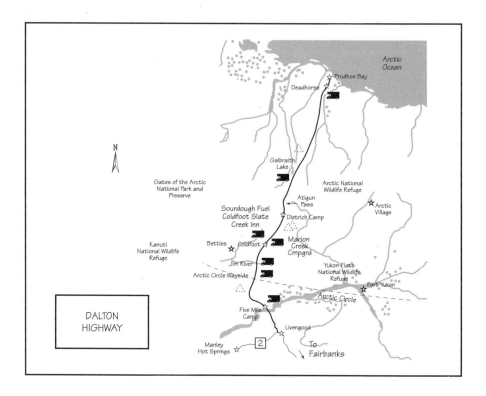

River crossing north to Mile 301 there is a 24-mile-wide utility corridor that is administered by the BLM. To the east along the Yukon River is the **Yukon Flats National Wildlife Refuge**. West of the highway at about Mile 115 is the **Kanuti National Wildlife Refuge**. West of the highway, this time in the Brooks Range, is the **Gates of the Arctic National Park and Preserve**. Finally, east of the highway through the Brooks Range and north to the ocean is the **Arctic National Wildlife Refuge**. Information and administrative offices are at the Yukon River Crossing Visitor Contact Station at Mile 56 and the Coldfoot Interagency Visitor Center at Mile 175. Both can provide lots of information about the road, the surrounding country, and recreational opportunities.

There is a historic gold mining area on the Dalton too. The strike at Coldfoot was in 1900, everyone later moved to a new strike at Wiseman. You'll still find some mining activity there.

Once you get to Prudhoe Bay you will find that you can not enter the oil fields and can not drive to the Arctic Ocean. The only access is through an authorized tour company. Check with the Arctic Caribou Inn (907 659-2368) or the Prudhoe Bay Hotel for tours and overnight parking. You should call the Alaska Department of Transportation at (907) 456-7623 to check on road conditions before heading north.

## Dalton Highway Camping Facilities

Formal camping facilities along the Dalton Highway are extremely limited. The only commercial campground is in Coldfoot at Mile 175. **Sourdough Fuel, Coldfoot Slate Creek Inn** has electrical hookups, water, showers, and a dump station for campers staying there. The BLM has a camping area near **Arctic Circle Wayside** in a gravel pit at Mile 115 with outhouses. The BLM also has a formal campground near Coldfoot at Mile 180. This is called **Marion Creek Campground** and has picnic tables, fire pits, and outhouses. Less formal camping sites are at Sixty-Mile Site (also called **Five-Mile Camp**) just north of the Yukon River, **Jim River** at Mile 136, and **Galbraith Lake** at Mile 275. RVers tend to camp pretty much anywhere that looks good, make sure not to block the pipeline maintenance access roads. Camping at Deadhorse is in parking lots. The BLM will undoubtedly develop more formal campsites as money becomes available and the number of travelers increases.

## NORTH OF FAIRBANKS DUMP STATIONS

There's a definite shortage of dump stations north of Fairbanks. A few private campgrounds have them but there are no government facilities. Be sure to empty your tanks in Fairbanks before you head north.

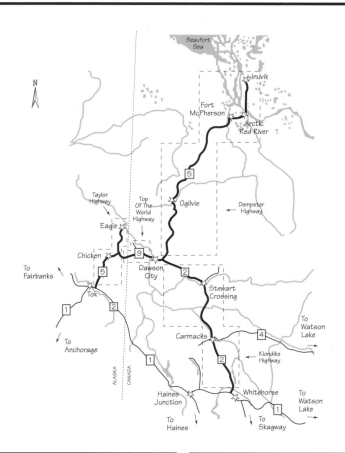

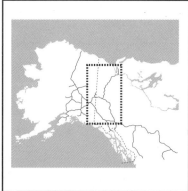

THE KLONDIKE LOOP

# CHAPTER

· · · · · · · · · · II

# THE KLONDIKE LOOP

## INTRODUCTION

A series of three different highways form a half-loop north of the Alaska Highway from Whitehorse to Tok. They are a not-to-be-missed alternate to the Alaska Highway. We recommend that travelers from the Lower 48 plan to drive the Klondike Loop one way and the Alaska Highway between Whitehorse and Tok the other.

The Klondike Loop is really three highways. From Whitehorse north to Dawson City in the Yukon you follow the Klondike Highway, the distance is 527 km (327 miles). Then, from Dawson City west for 127 km (79 miles) and across the Alaska - Canada border there is the Top of the World Highway. Finally, in Alaska, the route follows a portion of the Taylor Highway 155 kilometers (96 miles) south. The Taylor really runs from the Alaska Highway near Tok north to Eagle, in this chapter we'll cover that entire highway since Eagle in an interesting destination in its own right.

The Klondike Loop visits true gold rush country. The 1896 Klondike strike was made in the creeks near Dawson City. Many of the Klondike Argonauts traveled on the Yukon River from Whitehorse to Dawson City, the Klondike Highway from Whitehorse to Dawson City follows this general route, although it follows the much straighter route that was a winter trail and gets you there much faster.

### Highlights

Gold and the gold rushes are a big part of Alaska, past and present. There was no bigger rush than Dawson's Klondike rush. Even though the town is really in Canada no visit to Alaska would be complete without a visit to **Dawson City**.

A trip along the **Top of the World Highway** isn't to be missed. Now that the Canadian portion is hard surfaced the trip is even better. It comes complete with a ferry crossing of the Yukon River.

**Eagle**, Alaska is like no other small town in the state. Eagle is truly at the end of the road, but at one time it was in the center of the action. There's lots of history to see and friendly folks to show it to you.

The 460-mile **Dempster Highway** heads north from a junction near Dawson City. This is one of only two opportunities in the Yukon and Alaska to drive north of the Arctic Circle and approach the arctic coast. The Dempster ends at Inuvik, from there you can easily fly to other arctic destinations in the area.

### Fishing

Along the Klondike Highway between Whitehorse and Dawson give these waters a try: **Lake Laberge** (Km 225) for lake trout, grayling, and northern pike; **Fox Creek** (Km 229) for grayling, **Fox Lake** (Km 248) for lake trout, grayling and northern pike; **Little Fox Lake** (Km 259) for lake trout, grayling, and northern pike; **Braeburn Lake** (Km 282) for lake trout, grayling, and northern pike; **Twin Lakes** (Km 308) for lake trout, grayling, northern pike; **Nordenskiold River** (Km 355) for grayling; **Tatchun Creek** (Km 381) for grayling; **Tatchun Lake** (take four-mile road at Km 382) for northern pike; **Crooked Creek** (Km 525) for grayling; **Moose Creek** (Km 562) for grayling, **McQuesten River** (Km 584) for grayling; **Klondike River** (Km 700) for grayling; and finally, the **Yukon River** at Dawson City for grayling.

In Alaska the **Fortymile River** has grayling, try Mile 43, Mile 64, Mile 75, and Mile 81.of the Taylor Highway. Also try **Four Mile Lake** at Mile 4 of the Taylor Highway for rainbows, it is reached along a 1-mile trail.

### Boating, Rafting, Canoeing, and Kayaking

The **Yukon River** was the original highway in this country and it continues to be an excellent float trip. It is actually possible to travel the river from the upper end of the Chilkoot Trail at Lake Bennett downstream all the way to the mouth of the river in far western Alaska. Most people limit their trip to the section from Marsh Lake or Whitehorse to Dawson City or Eagle. Access to the river and the logistics of the drop-off and pick-up are easiest on this route. The Whitehorse to Dawson City section is easily done in a canoe, they can be rented in Whitehorse and arrangements made for a pick-up in Dawson City. Plan on about 2 weeks to make the trip to allow plenty of time to explore old gold rush settlements and relics along the way. The river has little in the way of challenges other than a 51-kilometer crossing of Lake Laberge where it is best to stay near the west shore. See chapter 14 for more about this.

The **Fortymile River** is a designated National Wild and Scenic River. It is rated Class

II to Class III with rapids to Class IV. Experienced paddlers can float this river in canoes but inflatables are probably best. Put-in points are the four bridges along the Taylor Highway with the take-out at Clinton which is near the Yukon at the end of a 25-mile road from Km 59 (Mile 37) of the Top Of The World Highway.

## Hiking and Mountain Biking

There is a hiking trail from the south end of the Yukon River bridge at Km 357 of the Klondike Highway near Carmacks. It follows the river east to **Coal Mine Lake**. Across the river is Tantalus Butte, known for its coal seams that were mined for riverboat fuel.

From an overlook at Km 379 there is a first-class trail down the bluff to the **Five-Finger Rapids** of the Yukon River. Stairs and boardwalks make this an easy hike.

Around Dawson City there are several interesting walks. The **sternwheeler graveyard** is on the west bank of the Yukon River. The trail begins at the Yukon River Campground. Follow the campground loop road as far downstream as possible, then the trail next to the river. You'll find three abandoned riverboats pulled up on the bank.

There's a trail to the top of **Midnight Dome** where you will find excellent views over Dawson City and the Yukon River. The trail is on the left just after you start up the Old Dome Road at the east end of King Street. You'll see a trail to Moosehide, but see below about this. It is also possible to drive to the top of Midnight Dome.

The virtually abandoned Han village called **Moosehide** is located downstream from Dawson City on the east side of the river. This village is private property and visitors should get permission from the Han Band office on Second Avenue next to the bank before hiking there. The trail starts at the bottom of the Old Dome Road at the east end of King Street.

The "creeks" make an interesting place to explore on foot or mountain bike. Two long gravel loop roads (one off the other) and several access roads leading off them let you explore **Eldorado Creek, Sulphur Creek, Dominion Creek, and Hunker Creek**; all very historic ground although much of it has been dredged in the years since the original 98 rush. A hiking route called the **Ridge Road Trail** is being developed.

# THE ROUTES, TOWNS, AND CAMPGROUNDS

## KLONDIKE HIGHWAY
### (527 km, 327 miles)

About 13 km (8 miles) north of Whitehorse Alaska-bound travelers have a choice. They can continue north on the Alaska Highway or turn right and head for Dawson City along what is called the Klondike Loop. If the road has been cleared of snow and is open you should consider visiting Dawson City on your way north, early fall snows could make a trip on the Top of the World Highway a real trial in September. On the other hand, if you plan to return south before September you can wait until then to visit Dawson.

The Klondike Highway (Yukon Highway 2) is an excellent paved highway. It is not difficult to drive the entire distance from Whitehorse to Dawson in one day in any rig. On the other hand, this is a historic route and there are some good places to do some exploring.

Because the Klondike Highway is in Canada it is marked in kilometers. The highway really starts in Skagway, so the kilometer marker at the beginning of this route near Whitehorse is the 192 km marker.

The first junction, at Km 198, will take you west to **Takhini Hot Springs**. The campground at the hot springs is listed under Whitehorse campgrounds because it is not far from that city. The hot springs is worth a stop even if you decide not to camp there.

After passing the Takhini Hot Springs Cutoff the highway passes along the west side of **Lake Laberge**. You will probably recognize this lake as Lake Lebarge from Robert Service's poem "The Cremation of Sam McGee". Unfortunately the big lake isn't really visible from the road. You can drive down to the lake and take a look at Lake Laberge Campground at Km 225. Lake Laberge was well-known to Klondike travelers since the big lake was the last part of the water route from Whitehorse to Dawson to thaw in the spring.

Like the Richardson Highway in Alaska the Klondike highway had a series of road houses to serve travelers in early days. The **Montague House** at Km 322 was one of these.

**Carmacks** at Km 357 was the location of a trading post founded by one of the three men who made the first gold discovery on the Klondike. George Carmack settled in Carmacks in 1892. Now there's a campground at Carmacks, not to mention other services. It is possible to take a boat tour from there through Five Finger Rapids.

A large pull-off at Km 380 gives a great view of **Five Finger Rapids** far below. These rapids were run by huge sternwheelers. The riverboats didn't have enough power to pass through going upstream so they were winched up on a cable. There are trails with boardwalks over wet areas leading from the overlook down to the rapids.

Silver was also mined in this part of the world. Follow the **Silver Trail** east from Km

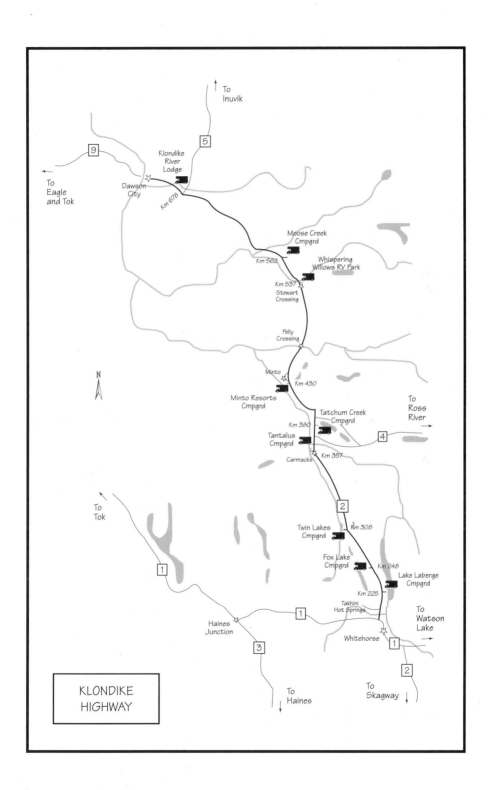

To
Inuvik

9

Klondike
River
Lodge

To
Eagle
and Tok

Dawson
City

Km 678

Moose Creek
Cmpgrd

Km 562

Whispering
Willows RV Park

Km 537
Stewart
Crossing

Pelly
Crossing

Minto

Km 430

Minto Resorts
Cmpgrd

Tatchum Creek
Cmpgrd

Km 380

To
Ross
River

Tantalus
Cmpgrd

Km 357

4

Carmacks

N

2

To
Tok

Twin Lakes
Cmpgrd

Km 308

Fox Lake
Cmpgrd

Km 248

Lake Laberge
Cmpgrd

1

Km 225

Takhini
Hot Springs

1

To
Watson
Lake

Haines
Junction

Whitehorse

1

3

2

To
Haines

To
Skagway

KLONDIKE
HIGHWAY

538 at Stewart Crossing. It will take you to Mayo, Elsa and Keno City, a distance of 61 km (38 miles). The first 52 km (32 miles), to Mayo, are paved, and there's a campground.

At Km 678 you'll reach the junction with the **Dempster Highway**. It is described below. Then, in just 37 more kilometers (23 miles) you'll reach the outskirts of Dawson City.

## Klondike Highway Campgrounds

✦ LAKE LABERGE CAMPGROUND (YUKON GOV.)
   Location: Km 225 Northern Klondike Highway
   Price: Low

*GPS Location: N 61° 04' 37.5", W 135° 11' 56.0"*

The campground has 22 vehicle sites and additional tent sites. Some are back-ins and others are around a gravel area near the lake adjoining a boat launch. Sites have picnic tables and fire pits. The campground also offers outhouses, a kitchen shelter and picnic area and drinking water.

✦ FOX LAKE CAMPGROUND (YUKON GOV.)
   Location: Km 248 of the Northern Klondike
   Highway
   Price: Low

*GPS Location: N 61° 14' 39.4", W 135° 27' 43.5"*

This popular campground has 33 sites, 3 are tent sites and the rest are separated vehicle sites. These are mostly back-ins, some are along the lake shore. All sites have picnic tables and fire pits. The campground also offers pit toilets, a playground, a covered kitchen and picnic area, a boat ramp, and a water faucet.

✦ TWIN LAKES CAMPGROUND (YUKON GOV.)
   Location: Km. 308 Northern Klondike Highway
   Price: Low

*GPS Location: N 61° 42' 19.9", W 135° 56' 21.9"*

Twin Lake Campground offers two different camping areas. The first has 10 back-in sites. They are well separated by trees and vegetation. Another 8 sites are arranged around a gravel parking lot near the lake. All have picnic tables and fire pits. The campground also offers a covered kitchen and picnic area, a hand-operated water pump, a boat ramp, and a small dock.

✦ TANTALUS CAMPGROUND
    Address: Box 113, Carmacks, Yukon Y0B 1C0
    Telephone: (867) 863-6271, Fax: (867) 863-6606
    Price: Low

*GPS Location: N 62° 16' 57.8", W 136° 18' 18.1"*

The Tantalus is operated by the Village of Carmacks but it appears to have been a normal Yukon Government campground with the same facilities. It sits next to the Yukon, a real attraction is the 2-kilometer boardwalk along the river, great for a stroll.

The campground has 15 dry vehicle sites, most are pull-throughs. There is also a tent camping area next to the river. Sites have picnic tables and fire pits and free firewood is provided. The campground also offers outhouses, a covered kitchen and picnic area, and a boat launch.

The campground is in Carmacks. Take the exit toward the river at Km 357 of the North Klondike Highway. Turn right when you reach the river in .1 mile and you'll come to the campground in another .3 miles.

✦ TATCHUN CREEK CAMPGROUND (YUKON GOV.)
    Location: Km 382 of the North Klondike Highway
    Price: Low

*GPS Location: N 62° 16' 57.8", W 136° 18' 18.1"*

The campground has 15 spaces, some are pull-throughs and there are several tent sites near the river. Trees and natural vegetation separate the spaces. Each space has a picnic table and fire pit, there are outhouses, a hand-operated water pump, a covered kitchen/picnic area, and free firewood.

✦ MINTO RESORTS CAMPGROUND
    Address: 4 - 12th Avenue, Whitehorse,
    Yukon Y1A 4J4 (res.)
    Telephone: (867) 633-5251 (res.)
    Price: Low

*GPS Location: N 62° 35' 00.7", W 136° 51' 08.3"*

Minto Resorts Campground has a very pleasant location along the bank of the Yukon River. You can relax on benches in a grassy area overlooking the river. There are also hot showers and flush toilets. This seems to be a popular tour bus stop since it is about half-way between Whitehorse and Dawson City.

Camping sites are located away from the river overlook in a tree-covered area. There are 27 sites with no hookups, most are pull-throughs. Picnic tables and half-barrel-type fire pits are provided. The campground has coin-op hot showers, a laundromat, a dump station and potable water fill.

Look for the paved half-mile driveway near Km 430 of the North Klondike Highway.

◆  WHISPERING WILLOWS RV PARK
        Address: Box 195, Mayo, Yukon
        Telephone: (867) 996-2123
        Price: Low

        *GPS Location: N 63° 22' 38.3", W 136° 40' 46.0"*

This is one of the few campgrounds with hookups between Whitehorse and the Dawson City.

The Whispering Willows has 32 sites with water and electric hookups on a gravel lot with some grass. There are also dry sites. There are flush toilets, hot showers (extra fee), a coin-op laundry, and a dump station (extra fee).

The campground is located at Km 537 of the North Klondike Highway.

◆  MOOSE CREEK CAMPGROUND (YUKON GOV.)
        Location: Km 562 of the North Klondike Highway
        Price: Low

        *GPS Location: N 63° 30' 35.5", W 137° 01' 42.9"*

The campground has 36 spaces. Six are tent sites, 3 are pull-throughs, and the remainder are back-in spaces. Aspens and natural vegetation separate the spaces. Each space has a picnic table and fire pit, there are outhouses, a hand-operated water pump, a children's playground, and free firewood. A trail leads to fishing at Moose Creek.

◆  KLONDIKE RIVER LODGE
        Address: Box 69, Dawson City, Yukon Y0B 1G0
        Telephone: (867) 993-6892
        Price: Medium

        *GPS Location: N 63° 59' 29.1", W 138° 45' 03.8"*

The Klondike River Lodge is a roadhouse with a cafe, motel, and gas sales. They also have about 15 back-in RV sites, some with full-hookups, some partial, and some dry, located in a gravel lot next to the main building. They offer free hot showers, a dump station, and a coin-op pressure vehicle wash.

The Lodge is located at the junction of the North Klondike Highway and the Dempster Highway. This is at Km 678 of the Klondike, about 26 miles from Dawson City.

## DAWSON CITY
### Population 2,000, Elevation 1,050 feet

There's lots to see and do in Dawson. You could reasonably say that the whole place is devoted to providing entertainment for visitors. This wasn't always the case, of course. When Skookum Jim, Tagish Charlie and George Carmack discovered gold on nearby Rabbit Creek in 1896 the Klondike River was best known as a good place to catch salmon. Two years later there was a population of 30,000 people in Dawson City and the surrounding creeks. A year later most of these prospectors had gone home or moved on to other places like Nome and Dawson City settled into a long decline. When the Alaska Highway was built through Whitehorse, Dawson eventually became a virtual ghost town.

Today the population of Dawson City explodes in the summer when the tourists arrive and the Top of the World Highway opens.

While you're in Dawson there will be lots to keep you busy. The **Gaslight Follies** are performed in the reconstructed **Palace Grand Theater. At Diamond Tooth Gertie's** you can gamble in a saloon much like those of 1898. There are also many interesting historical sites to visit. You can get full information at the **Dawson Visitor Reception Centre** (P.O. Box 389C, Dawson City, Yukon Y0B 1G0, Canada; 867 993-5566) on Front Street, they also have walking tours. Places you'll probably want to see are the **cabins of both Jack London and Robert Service**, the **Dawson City Museum** in the old Territorial Administration Building and the old **sternwheeler Keno** down by the waterfront.

If you find the Keno interesting you might want to visit Dawson's **sternwheeler graveyard**, it's on the far side of the river just downstream from the campground. You can

FERRY CROSSING YUKON AT DAWSON CITY

walk along the river to get there. If you really get intrigued by Yukon river travel there's also a tour boat operated by Westours (not a sternwheeler) that runs all the way to **Eagle.**

The gold didn't really come from Dawson, it came from the "creeks" located to the southwest. You can drive through the mining area by taking the **Bonanza Creek Road** at Km 715 of the Klondike Highway, just a mile or so from town. Twelve kilometers (8 miles) out this road is **Dredge #4** and at Km 15 (Mile 9) is the **Original Discovery Claim** on Rabbit (now Eldorado) Creek. Smaller vehicles or mountain bikers can make a 96-kilometer (60-mile) loop that takes them along Upper Bonanza Creek Road past **King Solomon Dome** and back down Hunker Creek back to the Klondike Highway. There's also an additional loop for the truly adventurous who want to see Sulphur and Dominion Creeks. The total of the two loops is 164 kilometers (102 miles). While you're out exploring the creeks you might want to stop and see **Bear Creek Historical Site** at Km 707 of the Klondike Highway. The Canadian park service operates this Klondike National Historical Site that shows the way of life during the industrial era of the gold fields from 1905 to 1966 when the dredges were used to mine gold.

Also just outside town is the 8-kilometer (5-mile) road up to **Discovery Dome** for a view over the town.

## Dawson City Campgrounds

✦ YUKON RIVER CAMPGROUND (YUKON GOV.)
    Location: Directly across Yukon River from Dawson City
    Price: Low

*GPS Location: N 64° 04' 23.5", W 139° 26' 18.7"*

This is a nice Dawson City campground with only one problem, it is a ferry ride away from the town. If you don't mind a short stroll there's no real problem. The ferry runs very frequently, it's free, and there should be no wait for walk-on passengers. From the campground you can easily walk down river a short distance to the sternwheeler graveyard.

The campground has almost 100 spaces, about 75 vehicle spaces and the remainder tent sites. Many of the spaces are pull-throughs and some spaces are right along the river. Trees and natural vegetation separate the spaces. Each one has a picnic table and fire pit, there are outhouses, hand-operated water pumps, a children's playground, a boat launch, and free firewood.

The campground is located about .3 kilometers (.2 miles) up the hill from the ferry landing area on the north side of the road.

✦ GOLD RUSH CAMPGROUND RV PARK
    Address: P.O. Box 198, Dawson City,
    Yukon Y0B 1G0
    Telephone: (867) 993-5247
    Price: Medium

*GPS Location: N 64° 03' 45.2", W 139° 25' 39.1"*

The Gold Rush is the only campground located conveniently right in Dawson City. We'll describe the campground we found in 1997 but major changes are planned for next year so it should be similar but much better.

There are about 75 sites of all kinds including tent sites. The campground is a large gravel park with the hookup sites arranged as back-ins around the border. There are hot showers (extra charge), a laundromat, and a dump and water station. Reservations are recommended.

Some of the changes planned for next year are landscaping between sites, a second dump station, and probably elimination of individual sewer drains (they are a real maintenance problem in far-north campgrounds).

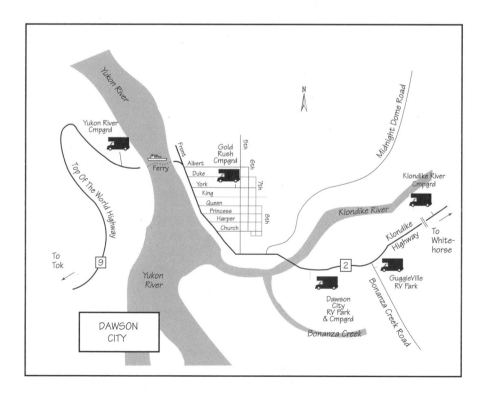

The campground is located at the corner of Fifth Ave. and York, about two blocks from Diamond Tooth Gertie's and near most other popular city destinations.

✦  Dawson City RV Park and Campground
      Address: Box 750, Dawson City, Yukon Y0B 1G0
      Telephone and Fax: (867) 993-5142
      Price: Low

*GPS Location: N 64° 02' 29.9", W 139° 24' 18.1"*

The second closest campground to town is this one (assuming you don't want to take the ferry). It is located on the dredge tailing piles just outside town.

The campground has 54 sites with electricity (15-amp) and water and many more dry vehicle sites and tent sites. There's a modern washroom building with individual shower rooms (extra fee). Other services include dump station, laundromat, coin-operated car wash, a service station, and a small grocery store. You can even pan for gold.

Dawson City RV Park is located at Km 715 of the North Klondike Highway, about 2.5 kilometers (1.5 miles) outside the city.

✦  GuggieVille R.V. Park
      Address: Box 311, Dawson City, Yukon Y0B 1G0
      Telephone: (867) 993-5008 or
      Winter Phone and Fax: (250) 558-3334
      Price: Medium

*GPS Location: N 64° 02' 22.6", W 139° 24' 02.6"*

Sure, this is the farthest commercial campground from central Dawson City, but not by much. At the time of our last visit in 1997 it was also the nicest. The gift shop is so good that tour busses stop here.

The campground has about 100 sites, 72 of them have water and 15-amp electricity hookups, the remainder are unserviced. Many of the sites have landscaping to separate them and there are picnic tables and some fire pits. There's a nice washhouse with individual shower rooms (extra fee), a laundromat, a coin-op pressure vehicle wash, bike rentals, gold panning, free firewood, a grocery and gift store, and a dump station.

The campground is located at Km 714 of the North Klondike Highway, about 2.3 miles outside the city.

✦  Klondike River Campground (Yukon Gov.)
      Location: Km 700 of the North Klondike Highway,
      about 12 miles from Dawson City
      Price: Low

*GPS Location: N 64° 02' 56.4", W 139° 06' 50.5"*

This government campground is close enough to Dawson City to use as a base for visiting the city and there is no ferry to worry about like there is for the other nearby government campground, the Yukon River Campground.

The campground has about 38 spaces. Some of the spaces are pull-throughs. Trees and natural vegetation separate the spaces. Each space has a picnic table and fire pit, there are outhouses, a hand-operated water pump, a children's playground, and free firewood. A half-mile trail will take you to the river.

From Dawson City drive to Km 700 of the North Klondike Highway, a distance of 12 miles.

## DEMPSTER HIGHWAY
### (460 miles)

The Dempster is Canada's road to the arctic north of the Arctic Circle. In length it is similar to Alaska's Dalton Highway, but the Dempster is a wider and better road and somewhat easier to drive. It is gravel, however, and has a reputation as being especially hard on tires. You can get lots of information about the Dempster at **the North-**

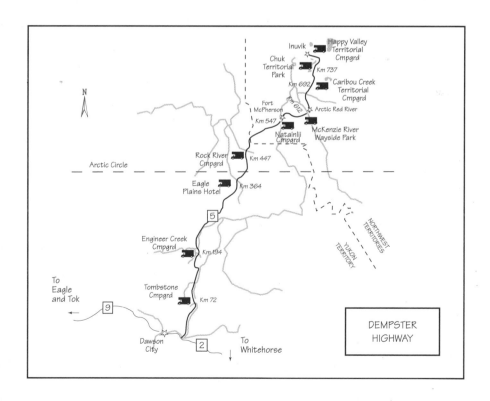

west **Territories Information Center** (867 993-6167) in Dawson City, it is just across Front Street from the Dawson Visitor Center. By mail contact: Western Arctic Tourism, P.O. Box 26002, Inuvik, N.T. X0E 0T0, Canada; 867 979-4321 or 800 661-0788. No one should attempt the Dempster without a visit there for first hand information about road conditions and ferry schedules (there are two of them along the route).

Kilometer markers start at the junction with the Klondike Highway, but they restart at 0 at the Northwest Territories border at Km 471. This can be confusing, references here are distance from the junction with the Klondike Highway near Dawson City. Services are very limited along the highway. Gas is available at Eagle Plains (Km 364), Fort McPherson (Km 557), and at Inuvik (Km 740). Your vehicle should be in good condition with good tires and at least one spare, two would be much better. Flying rocks can be hard on windshields so slow way down and pull over when you meet someone or when someone comes up behind you. RVers, especially those pulling trailers, should take precautions to protect their rigs from flying gravel. These should include protection of protruding plumbing fixtures on the bottom of the rig. See Chapter 2 - Details, Details, Details about doing this.

There are 8 government campgrounds along the highway: **Tombstone Campground** at Km 72, **Engineer Creek Campground** at Km 194, **Rock River Campground** at Km 447, **Natainlii Campground** at Km 547, **Mackenzie River Wayside Park** at Km 612, **Caribou Creek Territorial Campground** at Km 692, **Chuk Territorial Park** at Km 737, and the **Happy Valley Territorial Campground** in Inuvik which has a dump station. Additionally, there is a commercial RV campground at the Eagle Plains Hotel at Km 364 with electrical hookups and a dump station.

There's no question that driving the Dempster is something you'll never forget. Even more than on the Alaska Highway there's "miles and miles of miles and miles". The highway crosses true wilderness, also the Arctic Circle, the Yukon – NW Territories border, and two mountain ranges. You'll find lots of opportunities to see wildlife, particularly birds, and spectacular scenery but more than anything you'll probably be impressed by the sheer size of the country and the solitude.

Once you reach Inuvik (population 3,000) you may find little to do in this rainbow-colored but modern town. Inuvik was built only in 1955 when Aklavik, then the administrative center of the region, was flooded out. Inuvik's **Visitor Center** doubles as a museum for the Inuvialuit (Eskimo) and Gwich'in (Indian) cultures that share this region. The thing to do in Inuvik is to take an air-taxi or boat trip to one of several available destinations on the Mackenzie Delta or the Arctic Coast. Check at the Northwest Territories Information Center in Dawson for possibilities.

## TOP OF THE WORLD HIGHWAY
### (78 miles)

The 78-mile Top of the World Highway connects Dawson City with the Taylor Highway. The section from Dawson to the border customs stations, 65 miles (105 km), is now paved. The remaining 13 miles to the Taylor Highway and the Taylor itself are unpaved but usually in good shape. Kilometer marking start at the Yukon River and run to the border at Boundary. They then turn to mile markers and count up from 0 at the border. Fuel is usually available in Boundary, 69 miles from Dawson City, but the best plan is to buy it before leaving either Dawson or Tok. This highway is only open when the Yukon Ferry operates and snow allows, from May to October.

Virtually all of the Top of the World Highway runs above the timber line with great views in all directions. The only civilization is at the border stations and at nearby Boundary where there is a historic roadhouse. At Km 57 an unpaved side road runs 25 miles to **Clinton Creek**, an abandoned trading post and mining town near the mouth of the Fortymile River. Floaters on the Fortymile often use this as a take-out point.

Travelers on the highway should be aware that the customs stations are only open from 9 AM to 9 PM. You won't be able to pass if they aren't open. Also note that the ferry crossing the Yukon at Dawson City only runs during the day. Lines to cross on the ferry can get long at the height of the season.

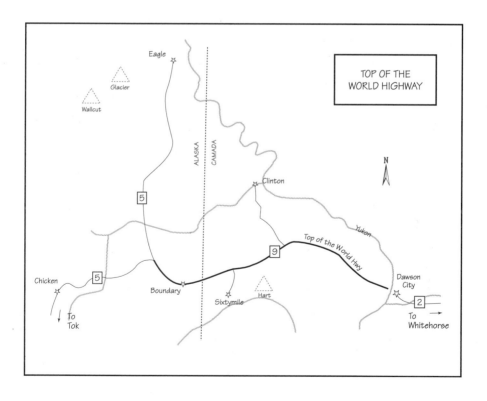

## Taylor Highway
### (160 miles)

The Taylor Highway, also called Alaska Route 5, runs 160 miles through high rolling hills to Eagle, Alaska on the Yukon River. En route the gravel highway passes through the Fortymile mining district and also provides a connection to the Top of the World Highway to Dawson City in the Yukon. Mileposts along the Taylor start at the Tetlin Junction at the southern end of the highway. The Tetlin Junction is on the Alaska Highway 10 miles east of Tok. The Taylor Highway is a gravel road. The section from the Tetlin Junction to the Jack Wade Junction at Mile 96 has been upgraded in recent years and is good for a gravel road. The section from Jack Wade Junction to Eagle, a distance of 65 miles, is not as good. Large vehicles (RVs) should drive cautiously. Large tour busses drive this route so you shouldn't have problems if you do. The Taylor Highway is closed during the winter.

Services are very limited along the Taylor so start with a full tank and watch your gas gauge. You can get gas at Chicken near Mile 67 and also in Eagle at Mile 160.

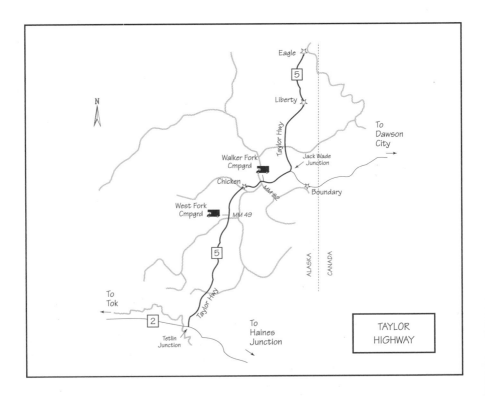

For much of its length the highway passes near the **Fortymile National Wild, Scenic, and Recreational River**. For information contact: BLM, Tok Field Office, P.O. Box 309, Tok, Alaska 99780; 907 883-5121. There are many popular floats along this river, also lots of gold rush history. This was the interior's first large gold rush area, miners already working the Fortymile were the first to reach the Klondike near Dawson when word of the strike there got out. Float trips on the Fortymile can be challenging and depend upon having adequate water. Check ahead if you plan to do one. For information contact the Bureau of Land Management at (907) 474-2350 in Fairbanks. The town of Eagle and large portions of the Yukon River valley to the east and west are inside the **Yukon–Charley Rivers National Preserve**. The preserve headquarters are in Eagle and can be reached by telephone at (907) 547-2233.

As you head up the Taylor Highway the first point of interest is a trail leading in to Four Mile Lake at Mile 4. The lake offers good rainbow fishing, the trail is a little less than a mile long. The road soon begins climbing to its first summit on Mt. Fairplay at Mile 33.

The first campground is the BLM's West Fork Campground at Mile 49, it is in the valley of the West Fork of the Fortymile River. The nearby bridge is a popular put-in point for floating the river. Another popular access point is the bridge at Mile 64.

Historic **Chicken** is near Mile 67, unfortunately it is on private property. Visit the Chicken Creek Café for gas, souvenirs, and possibly a guided tour of the ghost town. There's also a dredge nearby, ask about the location at the BLM's Chicken Field Station at Mile 68.

Another Fortymile River access point is the bridge over the South Fork at Mile 75. The BLM has another campground, the Walker Fork Campground, at Mile 82. Nearby, at Mile 86 you'll see the **Jack Wade Dredge** (actually the Butte Creek Dredge) next to the road.

At Mile 96 is the **Jack Wade Junction**. The Top of the World Highway swings east from here to Dawson City. The Taylor Highway goes left and continues to Eagle.

Continuing north the highway crosses Polly Summit and then descends to cross the Fortymile at Mile 113. This is a good put-in for floating the lower river out to where it meets the Yukon near Clinton Creek. The road continues, following O'Brien Creek and then ascends to cross American Summit. You'll get excellent views across the high country before the road descends along American Creek into Eagle.

## Taylor Highway Campgrounds

✦ WEST FORK CAMPGROUND (BLM)
    Location: Mile 49 of the Taylor Highway
    Price: Low

*GPS Location: N 63° 53' 14.5", W 142° 14' 15.1"*

There are few campgrounds in the Fortymile Country but this one is excellent. There are 18 vehicle camping sites and additional tent sites. Eight of the sites are actually

JACK WADE DREDGE

pull-throughs with room for big rigs. All sites are separated by natural vegetation and trees. There are picnic tables, fire pits, outhouses, and a hand-operated water pump. This campground also has a host.

Watch for the West Fork Campground on the west side of the road near Mile 49 of the Taylor Highway.

✦    WALKER FORK CAMPGROUND (BLM)
        Location: Mile 82 of the Taylor Highway
        Price: Low

        *GPS Location: N 64° 04' 38.3", W 141° 37' 50.1"*

This is another excellent BLM campground. It offers 18 campsites, some are short pull-throughs. Sites are separated by trees and shrubs. There are picnic tables, fire pits, outhouses and a hand-operated water pump. There is also a host at this campground.

The campground is on the west side of the Taylor Highway near Mile 82.

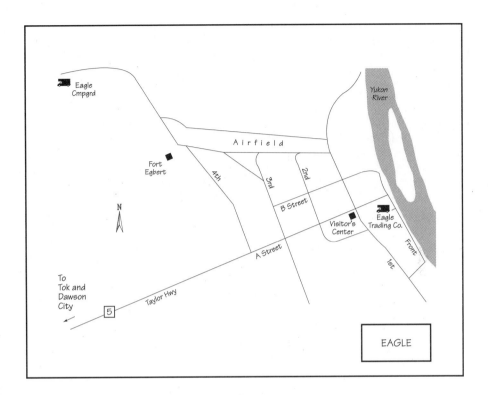

## EAGLE
### Population 150, Elevation 300 feet

During the gold rush period Eagle was, for a short time, an important litle place. Once the border between Alaska and Canada was established it became apparent that the U.S. government needed a presence near the gold fields. After all, the majority of the gold seekers were Americans.

Founded in about 1880 as Belle Isle, Eagle had a population of only thirty or so miners in 1897 but after the big influx of miners to Dawson City in 1898 some 1,700 people lived there. The first push toward growth was reaction against the control and tax collection activities of the Mounties on the other side of the border. Eagle soon became the American trading center for the gold-seekers. This activity inevietably attracted the U.S. government and the government activity definitely helped the town grow. As the first river town west of the border Eagle was a great place to collect customs duties and was the port of entry into Alaska for many miners as they abandoned Dawson City and headed for Nome and Fairbanks. Fort Egbert was established in 1889. A telegraph line, known as the WAMCATS line and running from Valdez to Eagle was finished in 1902. The Third Judical District and Judge Wickersham set up shop in Eagle in 1900 although he soon threw it over for Fairbanks.

Interesting structures from those days survive. The **Eagle Historical Society** serves as the town visitor information source (P.O. Box 23, Eagle City, Alaska 99738; 907 547-2325) and runs daily tours. They meet at **Judge Wickersham's courthouse** each morning during the summer. The courthouse serves as a museum and gift/book store. There are several other interesting sights in Eagle visited by the tour. The **Customs House** down by the river is also a museum. **Ft. Egbert**, the northern terminus of the WAMCATS telegraph line, has recently been restored and also has worth-while exhibits.

Eagle also has the headquarters for the **Yukon-Charley Rivers National Preserve** (P.O. Box 167, Eagle, Alaska 99738; 907 547-2233. The 2,260,000-acre preserve borders much of the Yukon River downstream almost as far as Circle. It also includes the waters of the remote Charley River which flows into the Yukon from the south about half way between Eagle and Circle. Many people float the Yukon from Dawson City or from Eagle to Circle City. Canoes are available for rent both in Dawson and in Eagle.

## Eagle Campgrounds

✦ EAGLE TRADING CO.
   Address: Box 36, Eagle, AK 99738
   Telephone: (907) 547-2220, Fax: (907 547-2202
   Price: Medium

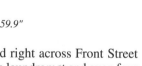

*GPS Location: N 64° 47' 21.2", W 141° 11' 59.9"*

The Eagle Trading Co. is a multi-faceted concern located right across Front Street from the banks of the Yukon. They have groceries, a cafe, a laundromat and even four full-hookup RV sites. These sites are nothing fancy and they are located right on the corner of Amundson and Front Streets, seemingly right in the center of all activities in town. However, when we stayed there (a Friday night) things were quiet enough. The view through the front window was great. Hot showers are included in the price.

As you come into Eagle just stay on the main road until you reach the river, turn right and you'll find the sites and Trading Co. on your right on the corner.

✦ EAGLE CAMPGROUND (BLM)
   Location: Just northwest of the Eagle town site
   Price: Low

*GPS Location: N 64° 47' 32.3", W 141° 13' 48.5"*

The government alternative while camping in Eagle is very nice. You're a ways from town but in a very pleasant woodland location. Town is an easy hike along the road or the old water pipeline trail.

The campground has 16 sites. They're set in spruce and are well-separated. Sites have picnic tables and fire pits and there are outhouses. There's also an interesting old cemetery near the entrance.

As you enter Eagle turn left on 4th. After .2 miles you'll pass Fort Egbert and the town's grass landing strip. Forge ahead and in another .5 mile you'll come to the campground entrance.

## KLONDIKE LOOP DUMP STATIONS

There are a very limited number of dump stations along this route, all located in campgrounds. See the individual campground entries for information. Make sure you empty your tanks before leaving Whitehorse or Tok.

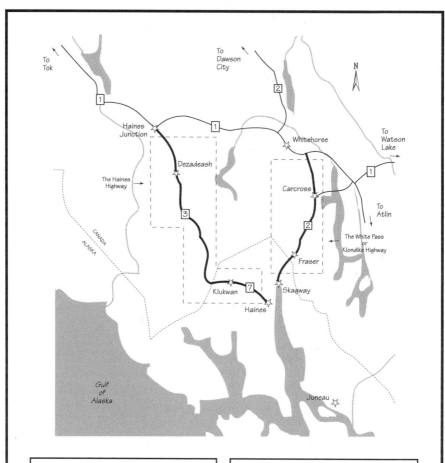

To Tok

To Dawson City

N

Haines Junction

1

Whitehorse

To Watson Lake

Dezadeash

The Haines Highway

Carcross

To Atlin

CANADA
ALASKA

3

2

The White Pass or Klondike Highway

Fraser

Klukwan

7

Skagway

Haines

Gulf of Alaska

Juneau

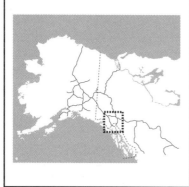

# SKAGWAY AND HAINES

# CHAPTER
. . . . . . . . . 12

# SKAGWAY AND HAINES

## INTRODUCTION

Skagway and Haines, located at the far north end of southeast Alaska and the inside passage, have always been gateways to the interior. In the early days the passes leading up and over the coastal mountains behind these two towns were used as trading routes between the coastal Tlingits and the Indians of the interior. Explorers and prospectors also used Skagway's White and Chilkoot Passes and Haines' Chilkat Pass. Today there are paved highways leading into the interior from both towns, they are now gateways to the Yukon and Alaska for ferry travelers and cruise ship passengers. There's also another little-known attraction to these towns, they receive far less rain than most of Southeast Alaska.

### Highlights

When the prospectors headed for the Klondike most of them traveled through **Skagway** or nearby Dyea and then passed over either the **White Pass** or the **Chilkoot Pass**. Today Skagway attracts huge numbers of tourists. From there you can ride a historic railroad over the White Pass or hike the famous **Chilkoot Trail**.

Many Alaska Highway travelers, those who do not plan to travel on the ferries, will appreciate the opportunity to see part of **Southeast Alaska.** In Skagway and Haines you will see steep mountains dropping into deep fiords with glaciers hanging above. You can easily get out on the water, there are tours, fishing charters, and even a walk-on ferry between the two towns. You can also use Haines as a base for an air-taxi flight over nearby **Glacier Bay**.

## Fishing

Skagway and Highway 2 to the north offer a few fishing opportunities. In Skagway there is a salmon hatchery, you can fish **Pullen Creek or the harbor** for kings in June, pinks in July and August, and silvers in September. Near Dyea the **Taiya River** has Dolly Varden in the spring and fall, also silvers and chum salmon in the fall. The **Dewey Lakes** (see hiking section), both upper and lower, have brook trout. The upper lake has smaller fish but they are easier to catch. In the salt water try **Taiya Inlet** for kings, silvers, pinks, dogs, Dollies and halibut. Charters are available.

Along Highway 2 the large lakes - **Tutshi, Tagish and Bennett** - all have lake trout and grayling, be aware that all or parts of some of these lakes are in British Columbia, not the Yukon, and a British Columbia fishing license is required. Farther north **Lewes Lake** (on a one-mile road from Km 136) has lake trout, grayling and northern pike.

Haines and the Haines Highway have more to offer. The salt water of **Chilkat Inlet**, **Chilkoot Inlet** and **Lutak Inlet** have all species of salmon as well as sea-run Dollies and halibut. It is possible to catch Dollies and pinks from the shore in many places. The top fresh-water fishing spot has got to be the short (about a mile long) section of the **Chilkoot River** between Chilkoot Lake and Lutak Inlet. It is known for Dolly Varden in April and May, two runs of reds (June/July and August), pinks during the second half of August, and silvers in early October. Fishing is also possible in the lake, particularly for Dollies. On the other side of town the **Chilkat River** also has fish, but silty conditions in the summer limit fishing to clear water tributary lakes and streams. In the fall it is possible to catch chum and silvers in this river near the airport. **Mosquito Lake** (Mile 27 Haines Highway) is known for both cutthroat trout and Dolly Varden.

Heading north on the Haines Highway try the **Takhanne River** (Mile 96) for grayling, Dollies, rainbows, and salmon below the falls; **Klukshu Lake** (Mile 112 ) for lake trout, rainbows, and reds; **Dezadeash Lake** (Mile 119) for lake trout, grayling, and northern pike; **Kathleen Lake** (Mile 135) for lake trout, grayling, and rainbows; and **Kathleen River** (Mile 136) for catch-and-release rainbows, lake trout, and grayling. Be aware of where you are fishing, separate licenses are required for Alaska, British Columbia, the Yukon Territory, and Kluane National Park.

## Boating, Rafting, Canoeing, and Kayaking

In Skagway the local float trip is down the **Taiya River** near Dyea and the Chilkoot Trail. Kayaks can be rented in Skagway for salt water exploration.

In Haines commercial float trips and jet boat tours are offered on the **Chilkat River**. It is also possible to book trips here for extended trips to float the famous **Tatshenshini**

**and Alsek Rivers**. Haines is also a good place to go ocean kayaking, guided trips and kayak rentals are available.

### Hiking and Mountain Biking

In Skagway the top hiking route has to be the **Chilkoot Trail**. See Chapter 14 - Camping Away From the Road System for information about this hike.

Much closer to town and less strenuous is the **Yakutania Point and Smuggler's Cove** waterfront trails. Just walk to the west end of 1ˢᵗ Avenue and cross the footbridge over the Skagway River.

From the east end of Third Avenue in Skagway cross the railroad tracks and you'll find the trail to the **Dewey Lake Trail System**. Destinations along the trails are Lower Dewey Lake (.7 mile), Icy Lake (2.5 miles), Upper Reid Falls (3.5 miles), Sturgill's Landing (4.5 miles), Upper Dewey Lake (3.5 miles) and the Devil's Punch Bowl (4.2 miles). There are some developed tent-camping sites along the trails as well as solitude and excellent views.

Another worthwhile hike in the Skagway area is really much more of a climb. The **Skyline Trail to AB Mountain** begins at Mile 3 of the Dyea Road. The climb and return should take four to five hours.

Haines also has a selection of trails. The **Seduction Point** trail starts at a trailhead parking lot at Chilkat State Park near the campground there. The trail leads 7 miles south to the point at the end of the Chilkat Peninsula called Seduction Point. In several places the trail actually runs along the beach and is not passable at high tide so plan accordingly. There are several tent-camping sites along the way and near the point. Some do not have drinking water including the one at the point.

Another hike not far away is the trail to the top of **Mt. Riley**. This is a good place to head for on clear days for views of Haines, the Lynn Canal, and the surrounding glaciers. There are actually two routes to the top of Mt. Riley. From Mile 3 of the Mud Bay Road (the road out to Chilkat State Park) there is a 2.8-mile trail that gains 1,500 feet to get to the top. From the end of Beach Road (the road that passes Portage Cove Campground) a four-mile trail climbs 1,600 feet to the same summit. Of course you can treat this as a traverse if you can arrange for a pick-up at the end.

A tougher trail in the Haines area is the **Mt. Ripinsky** trail. The mountain is an especially good place for views on a clear day, it tops out at 3,560 feet! You don't have to climb all the way to the summit for good views, however. This is fortunate since there is likely to be snow on the trail well into the summer. There are actually a north and south peak, the round-trip hike to the farther north peak is 8 miles, expect a hike that far to take a good six hours. To find the trail, head north on 2ⁿᵈ Ave. or Lutak Road.

When Lutak goes right continue on Young Street. Follow Young up the hill and then follow the road along a buried water pipeline for another mile to the trailhead.

### Wildlife Viewing

Haines is home to the **Alaska Chilkat Bald Eagle Preserve**. The area is unique in southeast Alaska because the Chilkat River here stays ice-free and affords bald eagles from far and wide the best place to find a meal. At the time of their peak numbers in November there can be 4,000 bald eagles in the area. A few eagles can be see year-round but the real viewing season is October to February. The preserve encompasses a49,000 acres, but the viewing area is between Mile 18 and Mile 22 of the Haines Highway. This area is known as the "council grounds". The only facilities are some newly completed restrooms, some parking slots, and limited walking paths. Observers and photographers can conflict with the traffic along the highway, both drivers and those on foot should exercise caution. For information call (907) 766-2202.

# THE ROUTES, TOWNS, AND CAMPGROUNDS

## SKAGWAY
### Population 700, Elevation sea level

Today's Skagway is something of a shock to someone who hasn't seen it in a few years. Visits by over 300 cruise ships each year have turned a picturesque but sleepy historic gold rush town into a true tourist destination. Much of downtown Skagway is now part of the **Klondike Gold Rush National Historical Park** and the streets are lined with restored buildings housing restaurants, souvenir stores, and hotels. Today's Skagway has become a fascinating place to visit and it's especially convenient since there are several RV parks within just blocks of the center of town.

The large number of cruise boat tourists have given rise to an active tourism infra-structure. A good place to start is the **Klondike Gold Rush Historical Park Visitor Center** (P.O. Box 517, Skagway, Alaska 99840; 907 983-2921, Fax 907 983-2046). It is located near the waterfront end of central Broadway Street in the old White Pass Railroad Depot. They have exhibits, films, and information about the Chilkoot Trail, Skagway, and the gold rush. They also have guided walking tours of Skagway. The **Skagway Convention and Visitor's Bureau Visitor Center** (P.O. Box 415, Skagway, Alaska 99840; 907 983-2854; web site: www.skagway.org) is temporarily located on Fifth Avenue but will eventually move back to the old Arctic Brotherhood Hall at Second and Broadway when McCabe College Exhibits move from the A. B. Hall to restored digs at McCabe College. Also worth a visit are the city's **Trail of 98' Skagway Museum, Alaska Wildlife Adventure & Museum**, the **Corrington Museum of Alaskan History**, **Pullen House**, and the **Gold Rush Cemetery**.

The historic **White Pass and Yukon Route** narrow-gauge railroad was finished in 1902. It was considered an engineering marvel as it climbed the precipitous White Pass and then continued on to Whitehorse. After the Klondike Highway to Whitehorse was opened in 1982 the railroad eventually shut down. Today it is running again, but only along the first section up through the pass. On tour ship visit days you can ride from Skagway up to Fraser, there are also some runs up to Lake Bennett to pick up hikers who have hiked the Chilkoot Trail. Busses connect with the train to go on to Whitehorse.

The **Chilkoot Trail** is once again very popular, although not quite as heavily traveled as during the gold rush. It is now part of the Klondike Gold Rush National Historical Park. So many people want to hike the 33-mile trail over 3,739 foot Chilkoot Pass that access has been limited because there are not enough camping sites. See the information in our Chapter 14 - Camping Away From the Road System.

## Skagway Campgrounds

✦ PULLEN CREEK RV PARK
   Address: P.O. Box 324, Skagway, AK 99840
   Telephone: (907) 983-2768 or (800) 936-3731
   Price: Medium

*GPS Location: N 59° 27' 23.3", W 135° 18' 54.3"*

This is a city-owned campground managed by a subcontractor. It has an excellent location near the boat harbor and within easy walking distance of town.

There are 32 back-in vehicle spaces with electricity (15 and 30-amp) and water. There are also a few tent sites. Spaces are surrounded by grass and a few trees. The restroom buildings are adequate but not great, they have coin-op showers and flush toilets. There is a dump station.

To find the park follow 2nd Ave. east from State Street. It crosses the RR tracks and curves right, you will see the campground on your right.

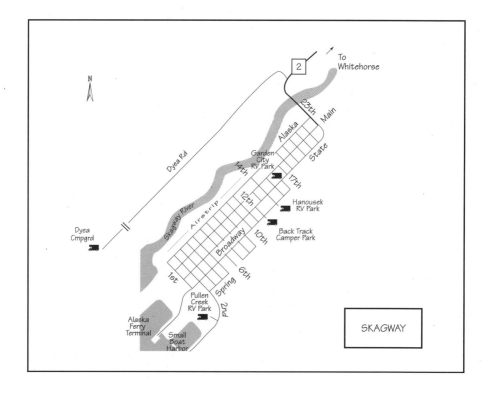

✦ BACK TRACK CAMPER PARK
   Address: P.O. Box 375, Skagway, AK 99840
   Telephone: (907) 983-3333, Fax: (907) 983-2444
   Price: Medium

*GPS Location: N 59° 27' 32.0", W 135° 18' 31.8"*

Our personal favorite of the Skagway private RV parks is the Back Track. It is located within easy walking distance of the central area of town yet is away from all of the noise except the railroad running right along the border of the campground. This doesn't seem to get any use at night so it's no problem.

The campground has about 30 spaces with both 20 and 30-amp electricity and water hookups. Most are back-ins but a couple are pull-throughs. There are also two areas with more trees that have back-in dry vehicle spaces or tent sites. All sites have picnic tables and some have fire pits. The main building houses the office, restrooms, individual shower rooms (coin-op), and a laundromat. Cable TV hook-ups are available and there is an RV wash. There is also a dump station.

From State Street, the main north-south arterial in Skagway, head east on 12th. You'll find the campground at the end of the avenue.

✦ HANOUSEK RV PARK
   Address: 14th and Broadway, Skagway, AK
   Price: Low

*GPS Location: N 59° 27' 38.7", W 135° 18' 22.9"*

Hanousek RV Park is a city-owned operation with a private manager. In 1997 that manager was the Garden City RV Park but that may not be so in coming years. In fact, there is some talk that the campground will be sold and may disappear.

Currently the campground seems to be used more by semi-permanent summer residents than by travelers. There are about 10 full hook-up back-in sites, most with rigs that have been there a while. There are also about 25 small dry vehicle sites and additional tent sites. Restrooms are in decent shape with individual shower rooms (coin-op).

From State Street, the main north-south arterial in Skagway, head east on 14th. You'll find the campground at the end of the avenue. It is just north of the Back Track RV Camper Park.

✦ GARDEN CITY RV PARK
   Address: P.O. Box 228, Skagway, AK 99840
   Telephone: (907) 983-2378, Fax (907) 983-3378
   Price: Medium

*GPS Location: N 59° 27' 40.5", W 135° 18' 15.0"*

The Garden City is a fairly new RV park. Construction is complete and has been for some time, but improvements are a continuing project as the owners strive to turn the park into a real showpiece.

The park has about 100 spaces, most have full-hookups (30-amp). Some pull-throughs are available. Parking is on good gravel with grass strips between sites. There are also tent sites. New modern restrooms have hot showers (extra cost) and there is a laundromat, a gift shop, and miniature golf.

The campground is located at the corner of State Street and 15th, right on your way in to or out of town. The walk to central Skagway takes only a few minutes.

✦  DYEA CAMPGROUND (NATIONAL PARK SERVICE)
    Location: Mile 6.6 of Dyea Road
    Price: Free

*GPS Location: N 59° 30' 18.7", W 135° 20' 50.5"*

The Dyea Campground is some distance from Skagway on a minor dirt road so it is not really recommended for large RVs. It is located close to the beginning of the Chilkoot Trail so hikers like to use it as a base camp. There is a parking area for the trail located at the campground.

This campground has 30 sites. They are set in an area of alders and cottonwoods near the Taiya River. Most are back-ins and they are well separated. Each site has a picnic table and a fire pit. There are outhouses and the campground does have a host.

To get to the campground follow the Dyea Road. It leaves the Klondike Highway just outside Skagway at Mile 2. The first 1.7 miles are paved, then the road narrows and becomes dirt. Smaller vehicles should have no problems. The campground is at 6.6 miles.

## WHITE PASS OR KLONDIKE HIGHWAY
### (99 miles)

The South Klondike Highway, Yukon Highway 2, is the southern portion of the same Klondike Highway that runs from Whitehorse to Dawson City. This portion of the highway was completed in 1982 and runs from Skagway up the famous White Pass and then north along several long lakes to Whitehorse. The excellent highway is paved for the entire distance, mile markers run north from Skagway to the border, then they change to kilometer markers and continue north. This short road actually passes through parts of Alaska, British Columbia, and the Yukon. We'll cover the road from south to north.

After leaving Skagway the road passes the junction for the 8-mile gravel road to **Dyea** at Mile 1.6 and begins climbing almost immediately. There are several places to pull off and look across the valley at the old gold rush trails and the railroad. The top of the pass is at Mile 14, the altitude is 3,292 feet. U.S. Customs is at Mile 6.7, the border at Mile 15, but Canadian Customs is located at Km 36 (Mile 22) at **Fraser**. This is the

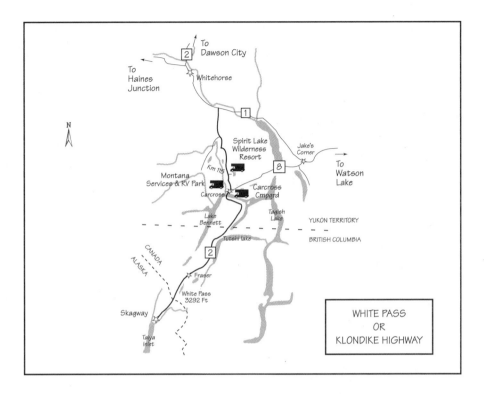

N

To Dawson City

To Haines Junction

Whitehorse

To Watson Lake

Spirit Lake Wilderness Resort

Jake's Corner

Km 115

Montana Services & RV Park

Carcross

Carcross Cmpgrd

Lake Bennett

Tagish Lake

YUKON TERRITORY

Tutshi lake

BRITISH COLUMBIA

CANADA

ALASKA

Fraser

White Pass 3292 Ft

Skagway

Taiya Inlet

WHITE PASS
OR
KLONDIKE HIGHWAY

turn-around for most White Pass railroad excursions from Skagway. A few miles farther along is **Log Cabin** where the Chilkoot Hiking Trail connects with the road. A few trains also continue on to the south end of Lake Bennett to pick up Chilkoot Trail hikers. The countryside around Fraser and Log Cabin is mostly glacier-scrubbed rock, very forbidding but beautiful.

Continuing north, the highway passes along the shores of Tutshi and Tagish Lake to **Carcross** at Km 105 (Mile 66). The name Carcross is a shortened form of Caribou Crossing. The town is located at a point long used by Indians for caribou hunting. During the gold rush, especially after the railroad was built, the town grew. It became a supply center for riverboat accessible destinations on Tagish and Atlin Lake. A fleet of sternwheelers serviced these lakes for many years. There's a **Visitor Reception Centre** (403 821-4431) located in the old railway station. The town's cemetery has the graves of two of the men who made the original Klondike strike and the wife of the third: Tagish Charlie, Skookum Jim and Kate Carmack.

Just north of Carcross at Km 106 (Mile 66) is another junction, this one for the Tagish Road (Yukon Highway 8) which leads east to the Alaska Highway at Jake's Corner. Just north of the intersection is a pull-off for the **Carcross Desert**. Here a small region of sand dunes will make you do a double-take and probably stop for a photo.

As the highway runs north it passes several lakes including Spirit, Emerald, Rat, Bear and Kookatsoon until meeting the Alaska Highway at Km 158 (Mile 99). From there the Klondike and Alaska highways are the same road as they pass through Whitehorse and then split north of town as the Klondike Highway heads for Dawson City.

## Campgrounds
## White Pass or Klondike Highway

◆ MONTANA SERVICES & RV PARK
    Address: Box 75, Carcross, YT Y0B 1B0
    Telephone: (867) 821-3708, Fax: (867) 821-3503
    Price: Low

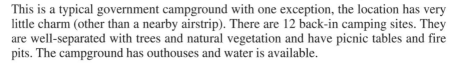

*GPS Location: N 60° 10' 04.8", W 134° 42' 13.0"*

This is a gas station and grocery store with 28 back-in camping slots with electricity in a gravel lot behind the main structure. There's lots of maneuvering room. Also available are flush toilets, showers, a laundromat, a grocery store, a dump station, and a restaurant. We found the staff to be very friendly.

Montana Services is located on the west side of the highway near Km 106 (Mile 66).

◆ CARCROSS CAMPGROUND (YUKON GOV.)
    Location: Km 107 Klondike Highway
    Price: Low

*GPS Location: N 60° 10' 20.5", W 134° 42' 03.2"*

This is a typical government campground with one exception, the location has very little charm (other than a nearby airstrip). There are 12 back-in camping sites. They are well-separated with trees and natural vegetation and have picnic tables and fire pits. The campground has outhouses and water is available.

Head east from the Klondike Highway at Km 106 (Mile 66) just north of Carcross next to the airstrip, you'll soon see the campground entrance.

◆ SPIRIT LAKE WILDERNESS RESORT
    Address: Mile 72.3 Klondike Highway,
    Carcross, Yukon
    Telephone and Fax: (867) 821-4337
    Price: Medium

*GPS Location: N 60° 14' 58.6", W 134° 44' 46.7"*

This small campground make a convenient overnight stop. It also makes a good base for canoe trips on the Wheaton River to Lake Bennett, they provide drop-off and pick-up services.

The campground has 6 back-in spaces with 30-amp electric hookups in an open gravel lot behind the main buildings. Farther back are about 15 more dry spaces in pine trees

A WHITE PASS AND YUKON RAILWAY STEAM ENGINE

near the lake for small rigs and tenters that have picnic tables and fire pits. A restroom building provides flush toilets and hot showers. Other services include a dump station and water fill point, hiking trails, canoe rentals, and a restaurant and bar.

The campground is located at Km 115 (Mile 72) of the Klondike Highway.

## HAINES
### Population 1,400, Elevation sea level

Haines is the "other" southeast town with a connection to the road system. In fact, Haines has had such a connection for many years. The Haines Road, now called the Haines Highway, was built in 1943 to connect with the Alaska Highway. The pass through the Coastal Mountains at Haines has been in use for centuries, first as a native trading route into the interior, then by Jack Dalton who pioneered a route here just before the Gold Rush and operated a toll road that was used to drive cattle into the Klondike.

Like Skagway, Haines gets its share of cruise ships so there are some tourist oriented attractions in town. The helpful **Visitor Information Center** (Second Avenue, Haines, AK; 907 766-2234, fax 907 766-3155, internet site: www.haines.ak.us) is just down the hill from Main St. Many of the attractions in town are related to old **Fort William Henry Seward**. It was active from 1904 to 1946 and is now privately owned. Many of the structures are in use as hotels, bed and breakfasts and restaurants, and shops. There is also a traditional Chilkat plank house and totem poles on the old parade grounds. The **Alaska Indian Arts Workshop** (766-2160) is a place where artists work on totem poles and other items. The **Chilkat Dancers** often perform at the **Chilkat Center for the Arts** (766-2160). A salmon bake is sometimes held at the Fort.

Haines is home to the **Chilkat Bald Eagle Preserve** which is discussed in detail under Wildlife Viewing at the beginning of this chapter. A related destination is the **American Bald Eagle Foundation** (907 766-3094) at the intersection of Second Avenue and the Haines Highway. They have a huge diorama showing local wildlife and also an eagle display as well as a gift shop.

Haines has an outstanding museum, the **Sheldon Museum** (907 766-2366). It's located just above the small boat harbor in the old Presbyterian mission location. There you'll find displays about the local Chilkat Indian culture, local transportation including the ferry system and highway, and even a movie about the nearby eagle preserve.

There are two excellent state parks near Haines. **Chilkat State Park** is south of town a few miles, take Mud Bay Road. This shoreline park offers hiking trails and beach walking. North of town on Chilkoot Lake is **Chilkoot Lake State Recreation Site** with a campground located on the shore of Chilkoot Lake. A short river runs from the lake to tidewater.

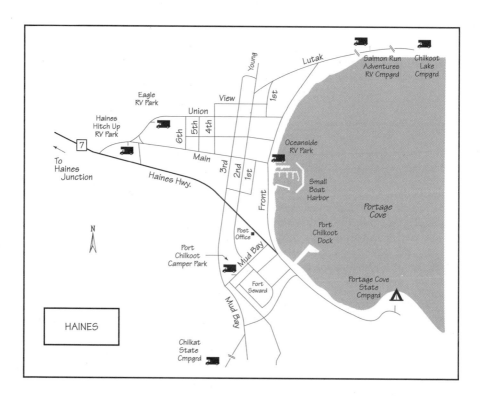

## Haines Campgrounds

✦ CHILKOOT LAKE STATE CAMPGROUND
   (STATE OF ALASKA)
   Location: 9.8 miles from Haines on the Lutak Rd.
   Price: Low

   *GPS Location: N 59° 20' 18.8", W 135° 33' 41.1"*

This is a beautiful state campground sitting in huge evergreens trees at the end of Chilkoot Lake. The short Chilkoot River runs nearby and may be open for salmon fishing during your stay.

There are 32 sites, a few are pull-throughs. Sites are well separated by huge trees and vegetation, the most popular ones are near the lake. All sites have picnic tables and fire pits. The campground has outhouses, a hand-operated water pump, and a boat ramp. There is also a host. This popular campground has a 7-day limit.

From downtown Haines follow 2nd Ave. north and zero your odometer at the Y where Young Road goes straight and the paved Lutak Road goes right. Follow Lutak Rd. (and ferry signs). At 3.9 miles you'll pass the Alaska State Ferries terminal, and at 8.7 miles come to the Chilkoot River Bridge. Just before the bridge the unpaved campground access road goes left, follow it for .5 miles to the campground.

✦ SALMON RUN ADVENTURES RV CAMPGROUND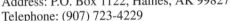
   Address: P.O. Box 1122, Haines, AK 99827-1122
   Telephone: (907) 723-4229
   Price: Medium

   *GPS Location: N 59° 18' 03.1", W 135° 30' 57.2"*

This unusual commercial campground sits on a steep heavily wooded hillside over-looking Chilkoot Inlet. The property extends down across the highway to the salt water, fishing is possible from the beach. Fishing charters are also offered.

There are 32 back-in spaces set under huge trees. These are well separated flat spaces off a steep but fairly wide circular access road. We think that the campground is suitable for rigs up to about 32 feet but you should take a look for yourself before pulling in. There are no hookups, power is currently supplied by generator but hydro power is a definite possibility in the near future. Sites have picnic tables, fire pits, and free firewood. There are flush toilets and hot showers (extra cost). There is no dump station and no water for fill-ups available although both are readily available in town. This campground is open all year round, a plus for RVers using the ferry in the winter.

Head out from central Haines on 2nd Ave. to the north and zero your odometer at the Y where Young road goes straight and Lutak goes right. The ferry terminal will be at Mile 3.9 and you'll see Salmon Run Adventures on the left at 6.2 miles.

✦ CHILKAT STATE PARK (STATE OF ALASKA)
   Location: Mile 6.8 of Mud Bay Road
   southwest of Haines
   Price: Low

*GPS Location: N 59° 08' 40.8", W 135° 22' 32.5"*

This campground is out of the way and usually not too crowded. An excellent hiking route, the Seduction Point beach trail (12 to 14 miles round trip) leaves from this campground. Big rigs need to be aware that the entrance road, while very wide, is also very steep, reportedly over ten percent. If your rig lacks climbing power you might want to avoid it.

The campground has 32 vehicle camping sites, 17 are large pull-throughs. Each site has a picnic table and fire pit. There are outhouses, a hand-operated water pump, and, downhill from the camp, a boat ramp and a dock on a pretty beach.

To reach the campground start at the Post Office near the end of the Haines Highway (see map). Drive southeast on the Haines Highway and take the first road to the right heading up the hill. This is Mud Bay Road. From there follow frequent signs for both Mud Bay Road and Chilkat State Park approximately 6.7 miles to the park entrance. The road is paved this entire distance. Turn right into the park and drive about .5 mile down a wide but steeply winding entrance road to the campground.

✦ EAGLE RV PARK
   Address: P.O. Box 43, Haines, AK 99827
   Telephone: (907) 766-2335 or (888) 306-z7521
   Price: Medium

*GPS Location: N 59° 14' 14.4", W 135° 27' 16.0"*

The Eagle is a medium-sized and pleasantly relaxed park. There are about 60 back-in sites with utilities, both full and partial hook-up, arranged around the perimeter of the property. Parking is on grass and electricity is both 20 and 30-amp. Cable TV is available. Many tent sites occupy the interior of the large circle on grass under trees. There's lots of maneuvering room. There are clean restrooms with flush toilets and showers in their own separate rooms. The campground also has a laundromat and a dump station. It is within easy walking distance of central Haines.

As you enter Haines bear left at the Welcome to Haines sign at the first Y. Bear left also at the second Y onto Union Street. You'll soon see the campground on your right. The physical address is 755 Union Street.

✦ HAINES HITCH-UP RV PARK
   Address: P.O. Box 383, Haines, AK 99827
   Telephone and Fax: (907) 766-2882
   Price: High

*GPS Location: N 59° 14' 09.4", W 135° 27' 35.2"*

The Hitch-Up is the largest and most polished campground in town. It will probably be the first you see when you arrive and you'll probably turn right into the entrance.

There are 92 large sites with full hookups (30-amp electricity). Many are pull-throughs and cable TV is available. All parking is on well-clipped very green grass. The modern central services building houses the office with gift shop and tour booking assistance, restrooms with free hot showers, and a laundromat. Across the street are a small restaurant and a liquor store, central Haines is within easy walking distance on city sidewalks. The physical address is 851 Main Street.

✦ OCEANSIDE RV PARK
    Address: P.O. Box 149, Haines, AK 99827
    Telephone: (907) 766-2444
    Price: Medium

*GPS Location: N 59° 14' 08.4", W 135° 26' 26.4"*

Centrally located at the foot of Main Street and right on the water the Oceanside has a lot going for it - a central location and a water view. There are 24 long back-in RV slots with full-hookups including cable. Picnic tables sit out front above the beach. Unfortunately there are no restrooms or showers so only self-contained rigs tend to stay here. The office is in the Harbor Bar just up the street. There's a nearby laundromat where you can get a shower if needed. Stores and restaurants are also close.

To reach the campground take the left fork at the Welcome to Haines sign as you enter town. Take a right at the next Y and you'll drive right into central Haines on Main Street. Drive all the way to the waterfront, take a jog to the left, and you're at the Oceanside RV Park.

✦ PORT CHILKOOT CAMPER PARK
    Address: P.O. Box 1589, Haines, Alaska 99827
    Telephone: (907) 766-2000 or (800) 542-6363 (U.S)
    (800) 478-2525 Yukon/BC
    Internet: http://www.haines.ak.us/hatsingland
    Price: Medium

*GPS Location: N 59° 13' 35.8", W 135° 26' 38.8"*

The Port Chilkoot offers something a little different. This campground sits under huge Sitka Spruces on the hillside near Fort Seward. Even so it's within walking distance of town.

The campground has about 90 spaces. Most are partial or dry spaces under the spruces but there are also some full-hookup spaces nearby with plenty of maneuvering room. Most spaces have picnic tables. There is also lots of room to tent camp. Restrooms are OK but not great, they have flush toilets and coin-op showers. There's also a laundromat and dump station.

To reach the campground just head uphill on Mud Bay Road from the Haines Highway near the post office. You'll see it almost immediately on your right.

◆ PORTAGE COVE STATE CAMPGROUND
   Location: On coast just past Port Chilkoot Dock
   Price: Low

*GPS Location: N59° 13' 32.5", W 135° 25' 32.4"*

Conveniently located about a mile from downtown Haines is a grass-covered tent campground. it is located right along the shore of Portage Cove. The campground has 9 sites with fire pits and picnic tables and there is water and outhouses.

## HAINES HIGHWAY
### (152 miles)

The Haines Highway has as long a history as any highway in this part of the world. Originally this pass through the Coastal Range was an Indian "kleena" or "grease trail" trading route. Coastal Indians carried trading goods, including fish oil from candlefish (also called eulachon, smelt, or hooligan), inland to trade for products of that area. Later, when the Russians arrived it was a fur-trade route. Anticipating an interior gold rush Jack Dalton scouted a route from Haines to Stewart Landing on the Yukon River. This route, which became a toll road, wasn't popular with gold seekers but was used during the Klondike Gold Rush to drive cattle inland. Gradually updated, the route became a gravel road during World War II and was connected to the new Alaska Highway. For many years this road was the only northern access to the Inside Passage and Alaskan ferry system in the Southeast. It was heavily used by Alaskans who didn't want to drive the entire Alaska Highway when traveling to and from Alaska.

The Haines Highway is now paved for its entire 152 miles from Haines to Haines Junction at Km 1,635 (Mile 985) of the Alaska Highway. The road is marked with mileposts starting in Haines and running to the border. There they change to kilometer posts for the Canadian section of the road. The Haines Highway starts in Haines and follows the Chilkat River north. Border stations are at Mile 40. It then climbs to cross Three Guardsmen Pass (3,215 feet) and Chilkat Pass (3,493 feet). It then descends to follow the Tatshenshini River into the lower lake country and finally hooks up with the Alaska Highway. As the road travels north it passes through or alongside several park areas: the **Alaska Chilkat Bald Eagle Preserve**, the **Tatshenshini-Alsek Wilderness Provincial Park, and Kluane National Park Preserve.**

### Haines Highway Campgrounds

◆ MOSQUITO LAKE STATE RECREATION SITE (STATE OF ALASKA)
   Location: Mile 2.4 of Mosquito Lake Rd, Junction at
   Mile 27 of Haines Highway
   Price: Low

*GPS Location: N 59° 27' 06.9", W 136° 01' 38.1"*

This is a very small state campground sitting next to little Mosquito Lake. Despite the name we found few mosquitoes when we visited. There are perhaps 5 poorly-defined small sites sitting under large trees at the lakeshore. The campground is not really suitable for large rigs. Picnic tables, fire pits, outhouses, and a small dock are provided.

Access is via a gravel road leaving the Haines Highway at Mile 27. At 2.2 miles there is a Y, go right. The campground is at 2.4 miles.

✦ SWAN'S REST RV PARK
    Address: HCR 60, Box 2860, Haines, AK 99827
    Telephone: (907) 767-5662
    Price: Medium

        *GPS Location: N 59° 27' 31.9", W 136° 01' 26.6"*

The Swan's Rest is a small RV park in a very pleasant setting well outside Haines but within easy driving distance. It is also near the Chilkat Bald Eagle Preserve and overlooks a quiet lake. The operators of the campground report that this lake is the southern-most nesting area for trumpeter swans in Alaska.

FISHWHEEL NEAR HAINES

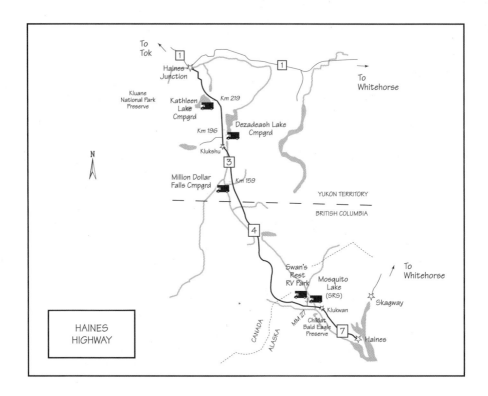

The campground has 12 back-in RV sites with full hookups including sewer. The parking surface is mowed grass and all of the sites overlook the lake. There is a restroom with hot shower (extra cost) and a coin-op laundry.

Access is via a gravel road leaving the Haines Highway at Mile 27. At 2.2 miles there is a Y, go right. The campground is at 2.9 miles, past the Mosquito Lake state campground.

✦   MILLION DOLLAR FALLS CAMPGROUND (YUKON GOV.)
      Location: Km 159 of the Haines Highway
      Price: Low

*GPS Location: N 60° 06' 24.1", W 136° 56' 40.9"*

This nice government campground has lots of room for big rigs although all 28 vehicle spaces are back-ins. There are also 6 tent sites. Spaces are well separated with trees and natural vegetation, there are picnic tables and fire pits at each space. The campground also has outhouses, two picnic and cooking shelters, a hand-operated water pump, and a playground. There's an interesting half-mile trail into a rocky ravine to an overlook above Million Dollar Falls.

✦ DEZADEASH LAKE CAMPGROUND (YUKON GOV.)
   Location: Km 196 of the Haines Highway, 32 miles from
   the Haines Junction.
   Price: Low

*GPS Location: N 60° 23' 53.2", W 137° 02' 33.5"*

This Yukon government campground occupies a small gravel point projection into Dezadeash Lake. It is very pleasant if the wind isn't blowing. Several of the 20 back-in sites are along the shore. The area is wooded but the sites tend to be closer together than in some government campgrounds. There are picnic tables and fire pits and the campground has a cooking and picnic shelter and boat launching ramp.

✦ KATHLEEN LAKE CAMPGROUND
   (CANADIAN NATIONAL GOV.)
      Location: Km 219 of the Haines Highway,
      27 km (17 miles) from Haines Junction.
      Price: Low

*GPS Location: N 60° 34' 43.3", W 137° 13' 02.6"*

Kathleen Lake Campground is located in Kluane National Park so you will notice some differences from the Yukon Government campgrounds you've been staying in, but the differences are small. This campground has 39 very large sites (good for RVs although all are back-ins) arranged on a small knoll in cottonwood and spruce. Sites have picnic tables and fire pits and, since this is Canada, free firewood. There are outhouses and a hand-operated water pump. Near the campground in a day-use area on the lake are a dock, a boat launch and a big fully enclosed cooking and picnic area. Fishing in the lake is said to be good and there is even a beach for a short stroll.

## SKAGWAY AND HAINES DUMP STATIONS

Most dump stations in the area covered by this chapter are at campgrounds. There are also stations in **Haines** at Charlie's Repair on Second Avenue and at Petro Express (Mile 0 Haines Highway).

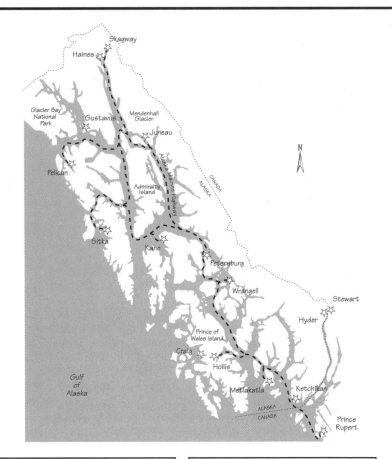

Skagway
Haines
Glacier Bay
National
Park
Gustavus
Mendenhall
Glacier
Juneau
Pelican
Admiralty
Island
Sitka
Kane
Petersburg
Wrangell
Stewart
Hyder
Prince of
Wales Island
Craig
Hollis
Metlakatla
Ketchikan
Gulf
of
Alaska
Prince
Rupert
N
CANADA
ALASKA
Alaska Marine Highway
ALASKA
CANADA

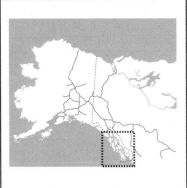

# SOUTHEAST ALASKA

# CHAPTER ......... 13

# SOUTHEAST ALASKA

## INTRODUCTION

Southeast Alaska, also called the Panhandle, is a different world from the other regions covered in this book. It's a land of water: deep fjords, green shorelines, glaciers, and rain. Travel in Southeast is almost entirely by boat or by air, there are very few roads.

Fortunately, there is a perfect answer to Southeast's transportation difficulties. The Alaska Ferry System turns the water barriers into highways. The state's six (soon to be seven) ferries dedicated to Southeast run frequently, and they can carry any RV. With proper planning you can travel through the panhandle conveniently and comfortably, stopping occasionally to see the sights.

The Alaska panhandle is famous for its weather, more specifically, its rain. However, it doesn't really rain in Southeast every day. The monthly rainfall statistics show an interesting pattern. First, it rains much more in the southern panhandle than in the northern part. Ketchikan in the far south averages about 7 ¾ inches in June while Juneau averages under 4 inches. Second, the summer is much drier than the winter. The best month is June, followed by July and then May. Be aware - Juneau averages twice as much rain in August as it does in June! In truth, there are many summer days when there is no rain, but luck has a lot to do with it.

Southeast, like the rest of the state, is sparsely populated. There are just seven towns of any size. These are Juneau, the largest and the state's capital, Ketchikan, Petersburg, Wrangell, Sitka, Skagway, and Haines. We've already talked about Skagway and Haines in Chapter 12. Another town, Prince Rupert in British Columbia, is also an important part of most visits to Southeastern Alaska. There are also some smaller towns and islands that are not on the mainline ferry route that make interesting stopping points, many are connected by smaller ferries.

## Highlights

The real highlight of Southeast Alaska is the scenery. As your ferry glides along the shorelines and through the passages you'll probably find yourself spending a lot of time either on deck or in the observation lounge watching both the wildlife and the traffic along the "Inside Passage" marine highway. You're sure to see many bald eagles, as well as the occasional whale or porpoise and perhaps even a bear.

Southeast Alaska has become cruise ship country. Some towns receive over 300 visits by the huge ships during the five-month-long May to September season. The **cruise ships** are themselves an interesting spectacle as they ghost through the fjords and pause to disgorge thousands of passengers for brief day-long visits to each port. A side benefit to the cruise industry is that most cities in Southeast offer a large number of tourist-oriented diversions and services. These include day-tours, stage shows, scenic flights, museums, shops, and restaurants. A good place to explore each town's offerings is the ubiquitous visitor's center sure to be located near the cruise ship docks. The most popular cruise ship destinations are **Ketchikan, Sitka, Juneau, Skagway**, and of course **Glacier Bay**. Some of the most popular sights include Juneau's **Mendenhall Glacier, Ketchikan's totem poles**, and **Sitka's Russian buildings and heritage**.

Those wanting to get away from civilization will find large areas of Southeast easily accessible. Kayakers, hikers, and assorted tent campers will enjoy **Misty Fiords National Monument Wilderness** near Ketchikan and **Glacier Bay National Park** near Juneau. For a place that is easier to access, even with a car or RV, try **Prince of Wales Island**. A ferry runs daily from Ketchikan to Hollis on the island.

## The Marine Highway

Since 1962 the State of Alaska has maintained a system of large ferries in lieu of a highway system in Southeastern Alaska. There have been six ships in the fleet but a new one will join in June 1998. The following information is from the 1988 schedule. It applies to the summer schedule, winter sailings are similar but reduced.

The ferry system is very popular and reservations must be made far ahead for the summer season. Don't cast your plans in concrete until you have your reservations, you might be disappointed. You will need reservations for both your vehicle and each passenger. Staterooms are optional, many people travel the entire passage without one and sleep in airline-style recliners or in the solarium areas. If you want a stateroom make sure to reserve one. You can save approximately 50% on a ticket through Southeast by driving to or from Prince Rupert instead of Bellingham. Many people do this, note the high frequency of sailings from Prince Rupert discussed below.

A word here about the cost of traveling on the ferry. For two people and a 21 foot RV to travel between Be

llingham and Haines costs approximately $1,350. Between Prince Rupert and Haines the cost would be approximately $650. A stateroom would add about $200 between Bellingham and Haines or $100 between Prince Rupert and Haines. These costs would vary somewhat with the type of stateroom and your stopovers. Larger rigs pay much more. You can see that driving the highway is the cheaper way to go even in a small RV, if you only consider gas. On the other hand, if you factor in wear and tear, the ferry may not be such a bad deal.

The *Columbia*, 418 feet long, runs between Bellingham, Washington and Haines with stops in Ketchikan, Wrangell, Petersburg, Juneau, Haines and Skagway. Southbound only the ferry also stops in Sitka. The Columbia leaves Bellingham each Friday evening and returns each Friday morning having turned around in Haines early Tuesday morning.

A new ferry, the *Kennicott*, is scheduled to join the fleet in June 1988. It is 380 feet long and is designed with open water capabilities that will allow it to run across the Gulf of Alaska. It will provide service between Bellingham and Skagway with departures on Tuesday evening. The *Kennicott* makes the same stops as the *Columbia* except that it stops in Sitka on the way north and not on the way south. Once each month in the summer the *Kennicott* will make a trip between Juneau and Seward with a stop in Valdez in each direction. During the weeks that the *Kennicott* makes this run it will also make a Prince Rupert to Skagway run, no ferry will make the second (Tuesday) Bellingham to Skagway run that week.

Two other mainline ferries each make two round trips each week running from Prince Rupert to Juneau with stops in Ketchikan, Wrangell, Petersburg and Sitka. Every second trip each ferry skips Sitka and adds Skagway and Haines to the run. These ships are the *Matanuska* (408 feet) and the *Taku* (352 feet). The four departures each week from Prince Rupert are at different times, schedules have to be juggled so that there are not two boats in the same port at the same time.

New for 1988 will be a daily round trip run from Juneau to Haines and Skagway by the *Malaspina* (408 feet) which was used on the Prince Rupert to Skagway run before the *Kennicott* joined the fleet.

Two additional southeast ferries make feeder trips to smaller ports. The *Aurora* (235 feet) works the southern panhandle out of Ketchikan with stops at Hollis on Prince of Wales Island, Metlakatla, and Stewart/Hyder. The *LeConte* (235 feet) works the northern panhandle out of Juneau with stops at Hoonah, Tenakee, Angoon, Sitka and Petersburg. Not all of these ports are visited each trip.

The ferries are nice but they aren't cruise ships. They have lounge areas, cafeterias, shower rooms, restaurants, and often a bar and excellent sit-down restaurant. During the summer most ferries have a U.S. Forest Service interpreter on board to provide information about the area and the wildlife. This makes sense because most of Southeast is inside the Tongass National Forest. Most of the ferries, the larger ones, have staterooms, but many people do not use them. You can save a lot of money by sleeping either in reclining seats or spreading a sleeping bag in the solarium. The solariums are partially glassed-in areas on upper decks. They have overhead heat lamps but are open to the weather at the aft end. Many people actually pitch tents in them and they are popular and often crowded and noisy. Passengers are not allowed to stay on the auto decks while the ferries are underway so sleeping in your rig is not an option. Our advice is to book a stateroom on overnight runs if possible, but don't panic if there isn't one available. Occasionally while underway and also while in port you will be allowed to visit your vehicle. Pets must stay on the vehicle deck. Propane must be turned off and sealed while on the ferry so you will not be able to keep your refrigerator and freezer running in your RV.

When the ferries dock it is often possible to get off and take a walk. Sometimes the stop will be for several hours. Layover time will be announced before docking and if the time of day is right there might be a bus into town or a tour available so that you can look around. Unfortunately it is not really possible to plan ahead for these layovers, if the ferry is running late the layover is likely to be shorter than expected.

It is possible to make reservations including stops at each port. There is a small extra cost for these stopovers and they must be planned and reserved in advance. It is well worth your time to sit down with a ferry schedule (see below for ordering address) and work out a schedule that will let you see and do all of the things you want.

During the 1997 season there was a major disruption in the ferry schedules when fishermen in Prince Rupert blocked an Alaska ferry as part of an international dispute over fishing rights. Ferry service to Prince Rupert was stopped for several months. This caused a lot of confusion and inconvenience. Businessmen in that city say the interruption cost them over $10,000 in business each day. As of this writing in the early spring of 1998 service to Prince Rupert has resumed. Hopefully this will continue without interruption.

We recommend that if you plan to use the ferry one way and drive the other you drive north and take the ferry south. Going north you will be fresh and each day's drive full of adventure. Heading south you'll have driven many miles and be ready to sit back and let the captain do the driving.

For information about schedules and rates you can contact the Alaska Marine Highway, P.O. Box 25535, Juneau, AK 99802-5535. Their toll free telephone number is (800) 642-0066 or fax (907) 277-4829 and their excellent web site is at http://

wwwdot.state.ak.us/external/amhs/home.html.

British Columbia has its own system with a ferry that runs between Port Hardy on Vancouver Island and Prince Rupert. You might want to drive the length of Vancouver Island from Victoria or Nanaimo to Port Hardy, catch the *Queen of the North* to Prince Rupert, and then use the Alaska Marine Highway to travel the rest of the way north. The ferry only runs during daylight hours, north one day and south the next. The route is very scenic and this is the best way to see it since the Alaska state ferries run much of it after dark. For information about schedules and rates contact BC Ferries, 1112 Fort St., Victoria, BC V8V 4V2, Canada. Their telephone number is (250) 386-3431, their fax number is (250) 381-5452, and their internet site address is http://bcferries.bc.ca/ferries.

# THE ROUTES, TOWNS, AND CAMPGROUNDS

## BELLINGHAM, WASHINGTON
### Population 130,000, Elevation sea level

It may seem strange to include information about a town in Washington in a book about Alaska. You might consider Bellingham an honorary Alaskan town. After all, Bellingham is closer to Ketchikan than Anchorage is. Many people start their Alaska trip in Bellingham.

At one time the southern terminal of the ferry system was in Seattle, 90 miles south of Bellingham. Moving to Bellingham cut several hours from the run north, a significant savings. Bellingham is also a lot less intimidating for RVers driving big rigs.

Bellingham has lots of good stores and is an excellent place to stock up on everything except perishables. Ferry rules require that you turn off the propane in your rig so if you depend upon a propane refrigerator you will want to make sure your freezer is empty. You may be able to keep the refrigerator cool by putting a block of ice in it.

### Bellingham to Ketchikan (37 hours)

The ferry usually leaves Bellingham about 6 PM so you won't have much of an opportunity to sightsee until first thing the following morning. By then the ship will probably be passing through Johnstone Strait well up the east side of Vancouver Island. Most of the route north is in protected waters, the ferry is usually rock steady. There are a few places where the inside passage is open to the Pacific waves, and the run across Smith Sound to the north of Vancouver Island is one of the longest. You should get there in the early afternoon, the open passage shouldn't take more than two hours.

Once across Smith Sound you'll be in true inside passage country. The passages narrow and you'll see little civilization. Two towns, Namu and Bella Bella will pass by but you will probably see little other than perhaps some lights in the distance. During the night you may notice the ferry do a little rolling and pitching, that is your signal that it is crossing Dixon Entrance near Prince Rupert and entering Alaska. You must set your watch back an hour to Alaska Time and get ready to dock in Ketchikan about 6 AM.

## PRINCE RUPERT
### Population 17,500, Elevation sea level

The northwest British Columbian city of Prince Rupert is the real gateway to Southeast Alaska. Prince Rupert is at the end of a good paved road and is much-closer to Alaska than Bellingham. Even Alaskans living in Southeast use the city as a gateway,

BC FERRY IN PRINCE RUPERT

many think it well worth the effort to drive 900 or so miles through Canada to reach the Lower 48. Incidentally, you can't get to Prince Rupert on the ferry from Bellingham, that boat doesn't stop here.

Prince Rupert is a very clean and well-organized little town with full services. It is the western terminus for one of Canada's few rail lines to the Pacific Ocean and dates from the early 1900's. Today the town continues to be an important port.

The town's **visitor center** is located at 100 1ˢᵗ Ave (Box 669 Prince Rupert, B.C. V8J 3S1, Canada; 250 624-5637 and 800 667-1994). Probably the most interesting area of Prince Rupert for visitors is **Cow Bay**. This small waterfront area has historical buildings now housing restaurants, pubs, and gift shops. Also interesting is the **Museum of Northern British Columbia** at First and McBride overlooking the water. Other sights include the **Kwinitsa Railway Museum**, and our favorite, the **North Pacific Cannery Village and Museum** with displays about the salmon canning industry that was the lifeblood of Southeast for many years.

## Prince Rupert Camping Facilities

✦ PARK AVENUE CAMPGROUND
  Address: Box 612, Prince Rupert, B.C.
  V8J 3R5, Canada
  Telephone: (250) 624-5861, Fax (250) 627-8009
  Price: Medium

This is the place to stay in Prince Rupert. It couldn't be more convenient for ferry passengers since it is just a kilometer (half mile) or so up the road from the docks for both the B.C. and Alaska ferries. It can get full on ferry days since almost everyone uses it. They have a somewhat remote overflow area for those who arrive after it fills. The office also serves as a local information office.

The campground has spacious gravel drives and camping sites spread down a gentle slope below the office. Some are drive-throughs. There are full hookups as well as firepits and picnic tables. Spaces are separated by wide grassy areas. Restrooms are newish frame buildings and have hot showers. There are also a coin-op laundry and a dump station. Reservations are recommended.

To find the campground just follow the signs toward the ferry. You'll find yourself on a wide highway called Park Avenue. The campground is well signed on the right, if you find yourself reaching the ferry parking area you've gone too far. The physical address is 1750 Park Avenue. The campground office stays open late for the convenience of ferry travelers.

✦ PRUDHOMME LAKE PROVINCIAL PARK
    Location: 20 km (12 miles) east of Prince Rupert on Highway 16
    Price: Low

*GPS Location: N 54° 14' 30.8", W 130° 08' 00.0"*

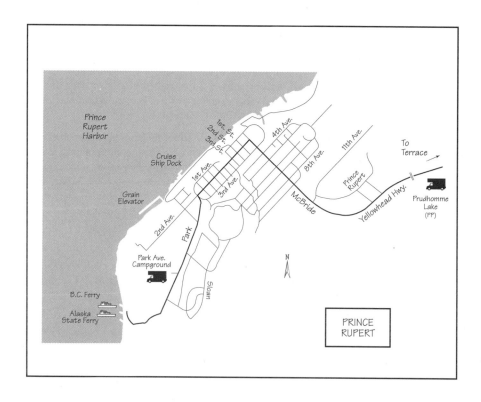

If you prefer a government campground for your visit to Prince Rupert the closest one is at Prudhomme Lake, about 20 km (12 miles) from town but just off the main highway. There are 24 medium-length spaces with the normal British Columbian campground amenities: picnic table, fire pit, free firewood, and outhouses. The adjacent Prudhomme Lake is said to have decent fishing for Dolly Varden and rainbows.

## Prince Rupert to Ketchikan (6 hours)

The ferries leave Prince Rupert at widely varying times. The run up to Ketchikan is relatively short. It runs across Dixon Entrance so a couple of hours of somewhat rough water are possible.

## KETCHIKAN
### Population 15,000, Elevation sea level

The ferry from Bellingham doesn't usually stop long in Ketchikan. Since the ferry dock is 2.5 miles north of town you aren't likely to have enough time to see much of the city except from the deck as you pass by.

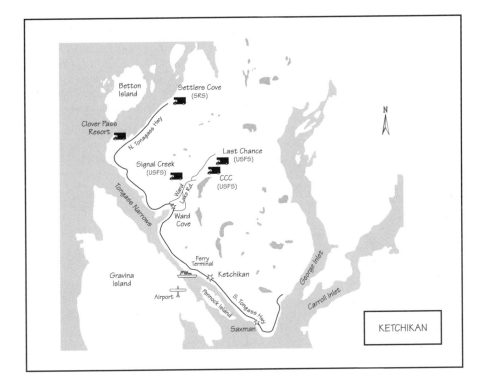

Since Ketchikan is Alaska's fourth largest city it is a good place to pause for a while and look around. The town stretches for several miles along the waterfront, it's long and skinny because there isn't much flat building space. A lot of the central downtown area is actually built on pilings. The airport for Ketchikan is located on the far side of the Tongass Narrows, you have to take a short ferry ride to get there. The Tongass Narrows are also used as a landing strip by the local float plane operators and there are several small boat harbors. All of this makes the waterfront an interesting and active place to explore.

Ketchikan's history is long and varied. The site was first an Indian fishing village, then a cannery town, a mining town, a cannery town for a second time, a timber town, and now something of a tourist town. As the largest town in the southern panhandle Ketchikan is also a transportation hub and a supply center. If you plan to visit either **Misty Fjords National Monument** or Prince of Wales Island (see below) you'll be passing through Ketchikan or using it as a base. There is a special **U.S. Forest Service** office for Misty Fjords and the Ketchikan Ranger District at 3031 Tongass Ave (907 225-2148).

Ketchikan has one of four **Alaska Public Lands Information Centers** placed in gateways to Alaska. This one, the **Southeast Alaska Visitor Center**, (50 Main Street, Ketchikan, Alaska 99901; 907 228-6214) is near the cruise ship docks. Others are in Tok, Fairbanks, and Anchorage. This is the first place to go for information about any government-owned lands you are interested in, including state parks, national forests, monuments, and national parks.

There's one more visitor center in Ketchikan, the **Ketchikan Visitors Bureau** (131 Front St., Ketchikan 99901; 907 225-6166 or 800 770-2200) very near the Southeast Alaska Visitor Center. This one specializes in information about Ketchikan itself. **Creek Street**, the towns former red light district seems to be the top attraction for cruise ship passengers. There are shops and a museum with wooden walkways built over a salmon spawning stream. Nearby is a tramway up to a hotel, the **Cape Fox Westmark**. Go on up to see the view and to take a look at some modern totem poles.

Ketchikan is known for its totem poles. The **Totem Heritage Center** is near the downtown area and has 33 of them. The **Saxman Totem Park**, located 2.5 miles south of town has another 28 of them and the **Totem Bight State Historical Park** 9.9 miles north of town has 14 totems and a model of a Tlingit community house. Along with all those totem poles you'll want to see the **Tongass Historical Museum** (629 Dock Street; 907 225-5600) to gain some perspective and see displays of Tlingit baskets and blankets.

## Ketchikan Camping Facilities

Ketchikan is pretty well equipped for campers. There are five campground: one is private, three are USFS campgrounds, and one is a state campground. All of the campgrounds are north of town on either the North Tongass Highway or the Ward Lake Road which branches off this highway about 6.5 miles north of central Ketchikan. There is a **dump station** in town at the Ketchikan Public Works Office (3291 Tongass Ave.) two blocks north of the ferry terminal.

Driving north from central Ketchikan on the North Tongass Highway the ferry docks are at about Mile 2. The Ward Lake Road Junction is at Mile 7. See below for information about the three USFS campgrounds on this road.

Continuing on the North Tongass Highway the entrance road for the **Clover Pass Resort** is on the left at Mile 14. This commercial campground has 35 RV sites with electric, sewer and water hookups. There is also a laundromat and a dump station. Call 1-800-410-2324 for reservations.

The **Settlers Cove State Recreation Site** is near the end of the North Tongass Highway at Mile 18. This waterfront campground has 13 sites with picnic tables, firepits, and outhouses.

There are three USFS campgrounds on the Ward Lake Road. The **Signal Creek USFS Campground** on Ward Lake at Mile 1 has 25 sites with tables, fire pits, and outhouses. For reservations call 1-800-280-2267. Nearby is the **CCC (Three C's ) USFS Campground** with four more sites. Finally, at Mile 3 is the **Last Chance USFS Campground** with 19 spaces, picnic tables, fire pits, and outhouses.

## Side Trip to Prince of Wales Island from Ketchikan (2 hours, 45 minutes)

The short run over to Hollis from Ketchikan on the state ferry Aurora has become quite popular. Make sure to secure reservations in advance if you plan to visit Prince of Wales Island.

## PRINCE OF WALES ISLAND

Prince of Wales Island offers the best opportunity to explore an undeveloped region of Southeast in your rig. The island has been logged, most of the roads were built for that purpose. Now there are some 2,000 miles of roads, mostly unpaved logging roads but also some paved miles between Hollis, Craig, and Klawock. This is a good place to go to see black bears, there are also many excellent fishing opportunities.

Hollis is near the ferry landing, there is little else there. Klawock (population 900), is 24 miles west of Hollis on a paved road and has a good totem pole collection. The service center of the island is Craig, 5 paved miles south of Klawock. Craig (population 1,500) has supermarkets, gas, laundromat, and restaurants. All of these towns are in the central portion of the island.

South of the Klawock/Craig/Hollis axis is Hydaburg (population 500). This town of mostly Haida Indians has many totem poles and is an excellent departure point for kayaking the protected west coast of Prince of Wales Island.

To the north of the Klawock/Craig/Hollis axis are most of the logging roads and several smaller communities. Thorne Bay is back across on the east side of the island, it

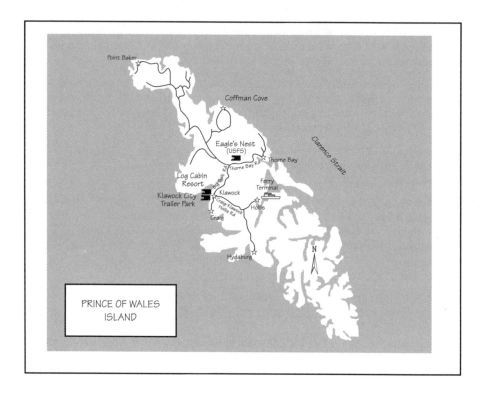

PRINCE OF WALES
ISLAND

is a former logging town. There are several USFS campgrounds and cabins scattered around this part of the island.

For information about the Tongass National Forest (most of Southeast) and Prince of Wales Island contact the Forest Service Information Center at 101 Egan Drive, Juneau, AK 99801 (907 586-8751).

## Prince of Wales Island Camping Facilities

Camping facilities on Prince of Wales include one commercial campground, a city campground, a developed USFS campground, and quite a few small USFS campgrounds with limited facilities. There are many spots on the miles of logging roads where you can free camp without services. Respect private land ownership. There is a dump station in Craig, contact the police department for directions and to get a key. There is also one in Thorne Bay.

The **Log Cabin Resort** in Klawock is the island's commercial campground and has 10 RV spots with full hookups. There are hot showers, flush toilets, and a laundry. They also offer meals and boat rentals. Call 907 775-2205 or 800 544-2205 for reservations. Nearby is the **Klawock City Trailer Park** which may have some room for travelers, check with the city clerk.

The **USFS Eagle's Nest Campground** has 12 campsites with picnic tables, firepits, a hand-operated water pump and outhouses. A boardwalk trail from the campground accesses fishing at Ball's Lake. It is located on the Thorne Bay road about 19 miles from Klawock. Drive north on Big Salt Road and then turn east on the Thorne Bay Road at Mile 17.

## Ketchikan to Wrangell (6 hours)

The relatively short run up Clarence Straight to Wrangell offers views of Prince of Wales Island, third largest island in the U.S., to the west along much of the route. The ferry docks right in Wrangell. The layover is generally short but occasionally there are delays due to tide conditions in the Wrangell Narrows to the north which give time for a look around town.

## WRANGELL
### Population 2,500, Elevation sea level

Wrangell is strategically located near the mouth of the Stikine River. The Stikine has long been a highway into the interior of British Columbia, at one time the swift-

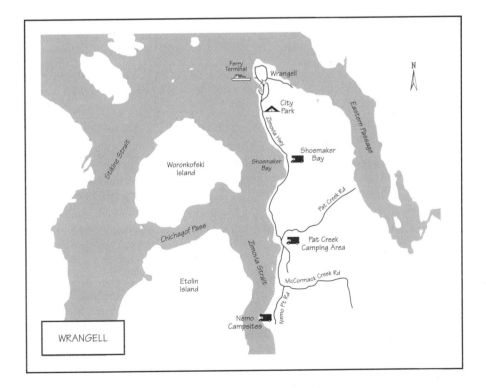

flowing river was home to several steamboats. The Russians and British used the river as a fur-trading base and later Wrangell was a supply base for the Stikine (1861), Cassiar, and even the Klondike gold rushes. Today the economy is based on fishing, timber, and tourism, but the Stikine still provides access to mines in the interior.

Wrangell doesn't get nearly as many cruise ships as Ketchikan, Juneau or Skagway so the tourism here is oriented more toward ferry travelers. Sights open when the ferry is in town, especially if the stopover is going to be long enough for passengers to spend some time ashore. There's a **Visitor's Information Center** (Box 49, Wrangell, Alaska 99929; 907 874-3901 or 800 367-9745) near the cruise ship dock and ferry terminal. In town you'll want to visit **Shakes Island** which has totem poles and a tribal house built by the CCC. **Petroglyphs** along the beach north of town are visible at low tide.

If you decide to stay for a while you'll find that **Wrangell Island**, like Prince of Wales Island, has lots of logging roads giving access to some interesting country. The U.S. Forest Service office at 525 Bennett St. (907 874-2323) has information about attractions, campgrounds, trails, and roads.

The **Stikine-LeConte Wilderness** Area is easily reached by boat from Wrangell. The Stikine is a popular float river, particularly the upper reaches near Telegraph Creek. The LeConte tidewater glacier to the north of the Stikine is probably more easily reached from Petersburg which is slightly closer. There are many Forest Service rental cabins along the Stikine as well as two hot springs. For information contact the Tongass National Forest Wrangell Ranger District at P.O. Box 51, Wrangell, AK 99929; (907) 874-2323.

## Wrangell Camping Facilities

In or near Wrangell you'll find one city campground for RV's, a city campground for tents only, and a USFS campground. There are dump stations at the city RV campground and also in town at the corner of Front Street and Case Avenue.

South of town on the Zimovia Highway is the **City Park**. This tent-only campground has firepits and restrooms. It is located at Mile 2.

The city RV campground is called **Shoemaker Bay**. There are tent sites and RV sites in several locations, some with electrical hookups, a dump station and restrooms with showers as well as a pool. It is located at Mile 5 of the Zimovia Highway south of town.

The **Pat Creek Camping Area** at Mile 11 of the Zimovia Highway is run by local civic organizations and has limited services. There is parking for several rigs but don't count on much else.

The **Nemo Campsites** are off USFS Road 6267 from Mile 14 and have picnic tables, fire rings and outhouses.

## Wrangell to Petersburg (3 hours)

The ferry trip from Wrangell to Petersburg is one of the most interesting of the entire

Inside Passage. Much of the route is through the **Wrangell Narrows** between Kuprenof and Mitkof Islands. This 21-mile passage is often as narrow as 300 feet and quite shallow, there is a string of range markers showing the crew where to steer. The passage through the narrows is very impressive, you'll like the lights at night and the chance to see the intricate passage better during daylight passages. The ferries can only pass through at high tide and this is a big factor in scheduling the ferries. Most cruise ships don't get to go through the narrows because they're too big.

## PETERSBURG
### Population 3,500, Elevation sea level

Petersburg may be only a few miles from Wrangell but the atmosphere is entirely different. Petersburg is scrubbed and neat and shows its Norwegian heritage. Petersburg is a fishing town with just a little logging thrown in. Like Wrangell, few cruise ships stop in Petersburg.

Also like Wrangell, Petersburg has a local **Visitor Information Office** (P.O. Box 649, Petersburg 99833; 907 772-3646) and a **U.S. Forest Service Office** (Box 1328, Petersburg, AK 99833; 907 772-4636). They're located together at 1$^{St}$ and Fram and have information and maps of roads, trails, and campgrounds on **Mitkof Island** and

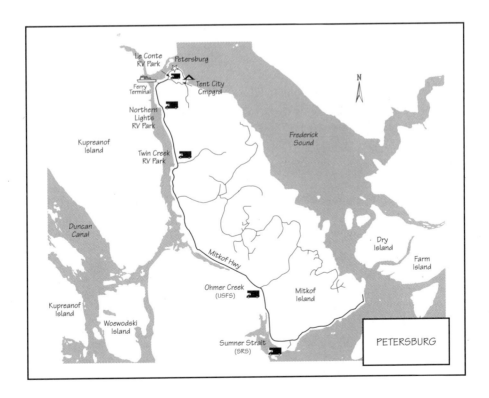

other islands nearby.

Sights in Petersburg are limited and show off the town's Norwegian heritage. Wander around town and admire the trim lawns and decorated buildings including the **Sons of Norway Hall**. A Viking boat, the **Valhalla**, sits next to the hall. There's also the **Clausen Museum** (907 772-3598) with some excellent commercial fishing exhibits.

Petersburg, like Wrangell, is used as an access point for the nearby **Stikine-LeConte Wilderness**. There are tours out to see the **Le Conte Glacier** about 25 miles east. You can also take jet boat tours up the Stikine.

## Petersburg Camping Facilities

Petersburg is surprisingly well supplied with campgrounds. The town has three commercial ones with hookups, a city tent campground, and several USFS campgrounds. Eight hour RV parking is also allowed in the ferry staging area near the south boat harbor. This is handy for ferry arrivals late at night.

**Le Conte RV Park** is in town at 4th and Haugen. They have hookups, showers, a laundromat, and a dump station. Call 907 772-4680 for reservations.

Also in town is the **Tent City Campground** which is operated by the city. It is primarily a tent campground with wood platforms and is heavily used by cannery workers. The campground has a cooking area and restrooms with showers.

The remainder of the camping areas are south of town along the Mitkof Highway. The **Northern Lights RV Park** at Mile 3 has 12 sites with full hookups but no restrooms. Call 907 772-3345 for reservations.

The **Twin Creek RV Park** is at Mile 7.5. They have hookups, a store, laundromat, hot showers, and a dump station. Call (907) 772-3244 for reservations.

At Mile 22 on the Mitkof Highway is the **USFS Ohmer Creek Campground**. It has 10 sites, picnic tables, firepits, and outhouses.

There is also a state campground at Mile 26. The **Sumner Strait State Recreation Area** is undeveloped but provides space for camping in both tents and RVs.

## Petersburg to Sitka (10 hours)

If you look at your map you'll see that unlike other Southeast towns Sitka isn't really located along the Inside Passage. The town sits on the west side of Baranof and is quite remote from the normal protected shipping routes. To get to Sitka the ferry must negotiate the narrow and aptly named **Peril Strait**. This must be done at slack water so the ferry is often delayed in Sitka giving visitors a chance to look around. Peril Strait is probably the best place along the entire ferry route to watch for wildlife, particularly bald eagles.

Not all ferries stop at Sitka when passing between Petersburg and Juneau. Those that don't go directly up Stephens Passage on the east side of Admiralty Island. The trip takes 8 hours and 45 minutes. You'll probably want to make sure yours is a Sitka ferry, even if you don't plan to stop over in Sitka the cost is the same and you have the opportunity to see Peril Strait and perhaps take a quick tour of Sitka while the ferry is in port.

## SITKA
### Population 9,100, Elevation sea level

Sitka was the capital of Russian America. Long an Indian settlement, the Russians moved in in 1799, were kicked out by the Indians a few years later, and then re-established themselves after a major battle. Sitka is a popular cruise ship port so there are quite a few things to see. The **Visitor's Information Center** (P.O. Box 1226, Sitka, AK 99835; 907 747-5940) is located downtown near the Pioneer's Home.

The **Centennial Building**, located at the harbor's edge, is the center of cruise ship activities. Since there is no dock for them in Sitka tourists come ashore in small boats. The **New Archangel Dancers** perform traditional Russian dances and various tours leave from the Centennial Building. The building also houses the **Isabel Miller Museum** the town's historical museum.

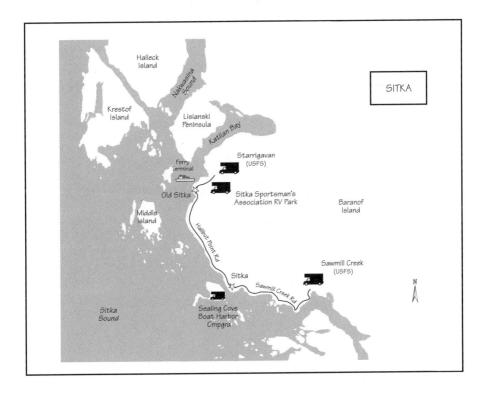

Many of the sights in Sitka are Russian and are located near each other. They include the reconstructed **St. Michael's Cathedral**. The original burned down in 1966 but the irreplaceable icons were saved and are in the new church. There's also the painstakingly restored **Russian Bishop's House**, a reconstructed **Russian blockhouse**, **Castle Hill** where Baranov's Castle was located before it burned in 1894, and a **Russian Orthodox cemetery** with graves dating from long before the U.S. purchase of Alaska.

The Russian and Indian cultures come together forcefully at the **Sitka National Historical Park**. It is located just southeast of town at the mouth of the Indian River. This is the site of the 1804 Tlingit-Russian battle. There is a Tlingit cultural museum and workshop and several totem poles along pleasant trails. Nearby **Sheldon Jackson Museum** has an excellent museum with artifacts representing many of Alaska's native cultures.

## Sitka Camping Facilities

Sitka has four campgrounds, one is commercial, one is a city campground with hookups, and the other two are USFS campgrounds. Dump stations are available at the wastewater treatment plant on Japonski Island, and at the City Maintenance Shop 2.5 miles north of town on Halibut Point Road.

The ferry terminal in Sitka is 7 miles north of town on Halibut Point Road. The **USFS Starrigavan Campground** is north of the ferry terminal at Mile 7.8 of the Halibut Point Road. It has 24 sites with picnic tables, fire pits and outhouses.

Also near the ferry terminal is the **Sitka Sportsman's Association RV Park**. This commercial campground has 16 sites with electrical and water hookups, restrooms, and showers. Call 907 747-6033 for reservations.

In Sitka on Japonski Island is the city's **Sealing Cove Boat Harbor Campground**. It has 26 sites with electrical and water hookups and restrooms with flush toilets.

Finally, 5 miles south of town on Sawmill Creek Road then 1.4 miles on Blue Lake Road is the **USFS Sawmill Creek Campground** with 8 RV sites and additional tent sites. There are outhouses at the campground.

## Sitka to Juneau (8 hours, 45 minutes)

The ferries leave Sitka the way they arrive, through Peril Straight. They then travel up Chatham Straight with Admiralty Island to the east and Chichagof Island to the west. At the north end of Admiralty Island the ferry rounds the Mansfield Peninsula and docks at Auke Bay, 13 miles north of downtown Juneau. If the stop is long enough (it often is) you can take a quick bus tour of Juneau even if you don't schedule a stopover.

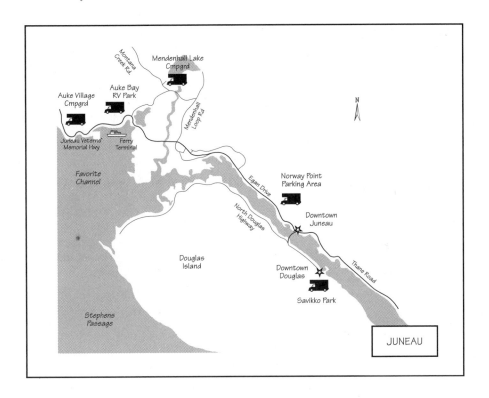

## JUNEAU
### Population 30,000, Elevation sea level

Alaska's capital city is one of the most popular tourist destinations in Southeast, almost all of the cruise ships stop here. There are quite a few things to see and do in Juneau. The big business in this state capital is government however, not tourism. That makes it an interesting place to visit since not everything is tourist oriented.

Juneau actually spreads over quite a large area for a Southeastern city. The downtown area is cramped, the buildings climb up the side of Mt. Juneau and Gastineau Peak. The population has spread out over neighboring Douglas Island which is connected by a bridge and north into the Mendenhall Valley where there is lots more room.

The **Visitor Information Center** (134 Third St., Juneau, AK 99801; 907 586-2201) in Juneau is in the Davis Log Cabin located downtown at the corner of 3rd and Seward. There's also a small one at the ferry dock. RVers will appreciate an **RVer information booth** at the Nugget Mall in the Mendenhall Valley south of the ferry dock. It is staffed by the local Good Sam chapter. There are two places to go for outdoor-oriented information in Juneau, both operated by the U.S. Forest Service. There is an information office in Centennial Hall downtown and also the **Forest Service District Office** at 8465 Old Dairy Road (907 789-3111). Juneau is the usual jumping off point for both Glacier Bay National Park and Admiralty Island's Pack Creek Bear Observatory, see Chapter 14 for more about both of these destinations.

Visitor-oriented sights and activities in Juneau include the **Alaska State Museum** (907 465-2901) and the **Juneau-Douglas City Museum** (907 586-3572) downtown. State buildings including the **Governor's Mansion**, **State Office Building** (SOB), **State Capitol Building**, and **House of Wickersham** are worth a look. The downtown area is interesting to explore, you can get walking tour maps at the visitor information center. A new attraction in Juneau is the **Mt. Roberts Tramway and Observatory**. You can ride up for the views, to visit the restaurant, or to hike.

Probably the most-visited sight in Juneau is the **Mendenhall Glacier**. The huge glacier is actually inside the city limits, you can drive to the Mendenhall Visitor Center. There are hiking trails in the area.

## Juneau Camping Facilities

Juneau gets a lot of camping visitors and has the facilities to handle them. There are five campgrounds in town: there is one commercial RV park, two USFS campgrounds, and two city-operated parking areas. Downtown Juneau is quite cramped and parking difficult. Try leaving your RV outside town and using the Capital Transit Bus System.

The **Auke Bay RV Park** is the commercial campground. It is located about 1.5 miles east toward town from the ferry terminal at Auke Bay. The RV park has 25 large sites with electricity, sewer, and water hookups. There are also restrooms with showers and laundry facilities. There is an overflow area. Reservations can be made by calling 907 789-9467.

The USFS also operates a campground near the ferry terminal. The **Auke Village Campground** is also 1.5 miles from the ferry terminal, but toward the west in the direction away from town. This campground has 12 sites for smaller rigs and is near the beach. There are picnic tables and firepits as well a flush toilet.

A second USFS campground is located about 5 miles from the ferry terminal near the Mendenhall Glacier. The **Mendenhall Lake Campground** has 60 sites but they are mostly tent-camping sites. Only 16 of them are large enough for vehicles over 20 feet long. The campground has picnic tables and fire pits as well as flush toilets and a dump station. Reservations can be made here by calling 800 280-CAMP. To drive to the campground from the ferry terminal turn right when you leave the terminal and drive 1.7 miles to Loop Road. Turn left and drive 3.2 miles to Montana Creek Road. Turn left on Montana Creek Road and drive .8 miles to the campground.

CRUISE SHIPS AT SKAGWAY

The city allows RV parking in lots near two boat harbors. The first is at the **Norway Point Parking Area** near the Aurora Boat Basin where there is room for ten RVs. Facilities consist of portable toilets. There is no fee. The second is **Savikko Park** in Douglas where there is room for four RVs. Facilities consist of a dump station and public restrooms. There is a $5 fee.

## Juneau to Haines (4 hours, 30 minutes) and Skagway (1 hour)

From Juneau ferries travel north up the Lynn Canal to Haines and then Skagway. Almost all of the ferries make both stops. Both town provide access to the Alaska Highway in Canada and eventually to Alaska.

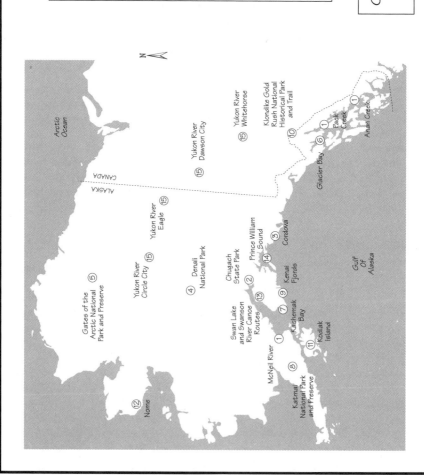

# CAMPING AWAY FROM THE ROAD SYSTEM

# CAMPING AWAY FROM THE ROAD SYSTEM

## INTRODUCTION

A quick look at a map of Alaska will show you that highways reach only a small portion of the huge land area. In the west, the north, the southwest, and even in the central part of the state where the few roads are located there are thousands of square miles with tiny populations only assessable using air or water transportation. No visit to Alaska can really be considered complete if you don't make at least one trip into the true wilderness. It's the only way you can appreciate one of Alaska's truly outstanding features: miles and miles of country with no people.

There are several ways to get away from the highways. The least expensive is no doubt hiking. Several areas have excellent trail systems. But for quick access to really remote country there is no substitute for an aircraft. Alaska has an air transportation system like nowhere else, don't hesitate to use it. In a few areas boats provide the best access whether they are the State Ferries of Southeast, Southcentral, and Southwest or a riverboat, kayak, raft or canoe.

### Preparation for an Off Highway Trip

Your first step should be thorough **research** of the planned trip. You need to know all about the destination, how to get there, what kind of weather to expect, and much more. The more information you have the more enjoyable and safer your trip will be. You can find a lot of information in books, magazines, and on the internet. Alaska's Public Lands Information Centers are also a great place to start. Contact the one in Anchorage at: Alaska Public Lands Information Center, 605 W. 4th Ave., Suite 105,

Anchorage, AK 99501; 907 271-2737.

Many Alaska off-road camping destinations will be on government lands with a managing agency. Most specialize in providing information to interested visitors. A letter and follow-up phone call can net you a lot of information including the names of some possible guides and transportation options.

It is important to have good maps of the area you will visit. These should be USGS maps with good detail including terrain data. They're a great planning tool and will be a big help once you are in the woods. Never go into the wilderness without good maps.

## Gear for an Off Highway Trip

We'll assume that you are an experienced wilderness camper. If not, you should not consider venturing far into the wilderness without an experienced guide. You should outfit yourself for an Alaska trip much like you would elsewhere. The following information and ideas cover areas that may be unfamiliar to you because they are specific to Alaska.

You should, of course, carry good maps and a compass. Alaska is unusual, however, in that some areas have few useful features to allow you to place yourself on a map. Huge flat regions have no mountains for triangulation, and from the ground it is difficult to see the bodies of water that are the only real way of placing yourself. On some river floats it is very difficult to tell how far you have come and therefore to adjust the schedule of your trip. One oxbow bend looks much like another on the map. You may arrive days before your pick up or days late. Consider carrying a **GPS** (global positioning satellite) receiver. It will give you a lot of peace of mind.

Alaska camping requires a good **tent**. It must be waterproof and bug proof. It must also be very durable. High winds can tear a cheap tent apart and leave you with no protection from the weather and the bugs. Many people like to have a dark-colored tent in Alaska, it helps them to sleep when the sun continues to shine all night. Finally, a tent that can stand without stakes is very useful, particularly when you are camping on gravel bars or moss tussocks where pegs just don't hold well.

Even in the middle of the summer it is a good idea to have a **sleeping bag** that will keep you warm down into the low 30's (Fahrenheit) . If it gets colder you can wear clothes in the bag to stay warm. The bag should be a synthetic so that it will be warm when wet and so that you can get it dry if it does get wet. You will need a **foam pad**, the ground can be cold when permafrost is just a few inches beneath the surface.

A **stove** of some kind is essential for camping in Alaska. Many areas do not even have firewood available since they are beyond the timber line. Others have only very wet wood. Many parks do not allow campfires at all. We like the kind that will burn on a wide variety of fuels since it may be hard to find exactly what you need in a remote location. You can almost always find gasoline.

You will need some means of **water purification**. Giardia lamblia (the protozoan that causes beaver fever) is widespread throughout the state. Boiling water for 5 minutes will kill it, but boiling uses fuel and leaves hot water—OK for cooking but not great when you are thirsty. We like a backpacker's water filter. If you start with water that isn't stagnant and smelly you don't need a really expensive one designed for removing viruses and bacteria, in fact a filter with a really small pore size will quickly become unusable when used to filter silty water. A pore size of 2 microns (yes 2, not .2) is small enough to filter out giardia and other protozoans. When you must use silty water you should let it sit in a pan until the suspended material has had a chance to settle, that will extend the life of your filter.

Normal **hiking boots** often don't work well in Alaska. They're fine in high well-drained terrain, but many Alaskan trails are very wet. If you think that your hiking area might be wet make sure to have some kind of rubber boots that will provide enough support to let you hike comfortably. Many hikes require repeated river crossings. These rivers can be cold, many come directly from glaciers. You will need some kind of easy-drying shoe to wear across them, many people bring canvas tennis shoes along. Another alternative is neoprene booties like scuba divers wear. They keep your feet warmer than tennis shoes but aren't very good for wearing around camp.

When around the water in Alaska the footwear of choice is often **hip boots**. When you wear them in a boat never tie them to your belt, if you fall overboard they can kill you. Make sure you can kick out of them in an emergency. Chest waders are a real no-no in a boat unless they are the neoprene type that actually help you float.

When crossing rivers you will need a **hiking stick** or pole. Since such a stick can be hard to find above the tree line you may want to carry poles. The new collapsible walking poles can also be a big help when crossing moss tussocks and other unstable ground with a pack on your back.

**Clothing** must be warm and capable of keeping you warm when wet. This means wool or synthetics. Cotton is useless unless it is a dry sunny day. Why carry it along? Clothing that can be layered so that you are always comfortably dressed is best. Bring three changes of clothes: one that you will probably have gotten wet, one to wear, and a backup. You'll want synthetic long underwear, even in the summer bring at least one light pair for top and bottom. For rain gear forget ponchos, you want a durable coat and pant combination that will keep you dry. A waterproof hat with a brim will really be appreciated if the rain keeps coming and coming. A wool stocking cap is also very useful, it is light and will keep you warm in cooler temperatures and when sleeping. Finally, bring a mosquito head net that will fit over that wide-brimmed hat. You may not need it but when you do you will love it. Also bring gloves, they'll protect you from the weather and from the bugs.

**Insect repellant** is essential. See Chapter 2 for a discussion of this.

Many Alaska wilderness trips are float trips on rivers or remote kayak expeditions.

Many of those require that you use a small aircraft for transportation. That means you can't use a hard-shell canoe or kayak since it is not legal to fly an aircraft with such a load tied to the float struts when passengers are being carried. Even with no passengers a special permit is required. Folding kayaks and canoes and inflatable rafts are very popular in Alaska. If you plan to do a lot of this type of travel and you want to purchase an expensive piece of gear for Alaska, these are just the ticket. On the other hand, rafts are often available for rent from air-taxi operators. Before allowing yourself to be dropped in the wilderness with a rental raft make sure that you know it is in excellent condition. Also make sure you have a repair kit in your gear.

## Safety

There are some safety issues that are unique to Alaska. Even if you have extensive camping experience elsewhere you should be aware of them.

When traveling in the wilderness it is essential that a **reliable person** back home knows where you are. That person should know your exact planned route and schedule and the name of the charter operator responsible for picking you up, if there is one. If you don't show up at the expected time your reliable friend can raise the alarm. We do not feel that having an air taxi or charter boat operator know your plans is enough. Better to have someone who knows you well and who will not drop the ball. Actually, better to have two such people.

**Never travel alone** in the wilderness. If something happens—you break a leg, an axe slips—you will need help. Also never travel on an isolated river in only one raft or boat. You don't want to be stuck if your only boat is damaged beyond repair.

Almost all Alaskan wilderness areas are home to lots of **bears**. There are very few bear attacks, but there are some. Both black and brown bears are dangerous. It is absolutely essential that you use proper camping techniques in bear country. Pamphlets are distributed from many sources in the state with information about how to camp in bear country and how to react if you meet a bear. There is also a lot of information available about bear habits. The best way to stay safe is to know a lot about the subject.

Here are some of the essentials. Do not set your tent up on a game trail or in an area with bear sign like tracks and droppings. If a bear is attracted to your campsite and then leaves you should pack up and leave immediately, it may return. Bears are attracted by food odors and also by the smell of cosmetics and perfume. Cook well away from your tent. Store food well away from your tent (300 feet minimum) and suspend it high in a tree if there is one. You can throw a rope over a limb to do this. Wrap food in double plastic and seal it. Never cook or eat in your tent. If you ever have cooked in the tent it must be washed thoroughly or replaced. Garbage will attract bears. Double bag garbage in sealed plastic and keep it far from your tent. Clean fish well away from camp, preferably in the water and downstream. Don't wear your cooking or fish-cleaning clothes to bed, store them in a sealed double plastic bag away from your tent. Wash yourself before going to bed to remove food and fish odors.

When hiking it is important not to surprise a bear. This is easy to do, particularly when traveling up wind. Make noise, perhaps by talking or even the use of bells attached to your equipment or tin cans filled with pebbles. Most bears will get out of your way if they hear you coming. Mountain bikers should be particularly cautious, they travel quickly and can easily come up on a bear with little warning. Hikers must be alert and watch the trail ahead at all times. Be particularly cautious if your view is obstructed by underbrush or a turn in the trail.

If you do happen to meet a bear on the trail do not approach for a better look. Do not run. Any bear can outrun you over any terrain. Stay calm. Bears seldom attack unless threatened or provoked. Sows with cubs are particularly dangerous because they tend to be very protective. Slowly back away and leave the area. If the bear follows try dropping an item of clothing or even your pack to distract it. Again, do not run. If it continues to come talk in a calm but firm voice. You may try climbing a tree but be aware that bears are quick and can also climb trees, a tree-climbing strategy is not always successful.

If you are attacked try to protect your vital organs. Drop to the ground with your face down, knees drawn up to your chest and hand clasped tightly over the back of your neck. In most cases you want to keep still and not present a threat to the bear, hopefully he will soon leave.

Some experts, including the Yukon Government's bear pamphlet, advise fighting back if the attacking bear is a black bear without cubs. The pamphlet says to yell and fight back as hard as you can, with a rock, a tree branch, or your bare hands.

Many Alaskans carry weapons in the wilderness. This is not allowed in some park areas but it is allowed in many others. Experts say that nothing less than a 30-06 rifle or shotgun is really useful and these are inconvenient and heavy. An alternative is pepper spray—the big bottles of it designed specifically for bears. The judge is still out on these. They are sometimes ineffective and even if driven off with spray bears often return. Definitely do not spray pepper spray on something as a repellent, bears may actually be attracted. A favorite story in the North is the one about the cheechako who sprayed himself with bear spray as he would have done with insect repellent. There have been cases of airplanes, rafts, and tents that have been chewed by bears attracted by the taste of the pepper.

Many people do not carry any bear protection, they rely on the statistics that show actual bear attacks are unusual.

**Hypothermia** can be a real danger in Alaska because temperatures are often in a range that is dangerous. Long days of even 40° to 50° temperatures can cause hypothermia, especially if there is moisture involved. Be aware and don't let yourself get chilled. Most rivers and lakes in the north are very cold, immersion even for minutes is life-threatening. Stay near shore and always wear a life preserver.

There may be lots of wildlife in Alaska but it is foolish to think that you will be able to feed yourself with it during a camping trip. Most game is protected unless it is hunting season. The fish probably won't bite if you are depending upon them. Always **bring enough food** for your planned trip, plus several days extra rations for if you get lost or injured. If you are expecting pick up by a boat or airplane it is not at all unusual for weather to cause delays of up to a week in some areas. Plan accordingly.

## Low Impact Camping

Responsible camping in the wilderness means low-impact camping. Try to leave as little sign of your passing as possible.

While you are on the move try to stay on existing trails. Wear boots with shallow treads. Hike single file to keep from widening the trail. When there is no trail try to stay on rocks and creek beds, stay off loose or wet terrain. If you must walk over delicate terrain like a meadow spread out and do not walk single file.

When camping find a place that won't be damaged by your campsite. Gravel is best. Don't cut trees and brush. Wear light shoes instead of heavy boots in camp and avoid making paths. Avoid campfires if there is not a suitable site, use a stove instead. Gravel bars along rivers are good campfire sites since high water in the spring generally scours them. Carry out all garbage. Drain dishwater into a small hole well away from streams and lakes and cover with earth. Use only biodegradable soap and wash well away from lakes and streams. Dispose of human waste by digging a shallow hole well away from streams and lakes and then covering it with earth when you are done, burn or carry out toilet paper.

## Air Transportation

Small aircraft are often used for transportation in Alaska. Even small villages usually have an airport and at least weekly scheduled service. It is usually less expensive to travel on a scheduled carrier than to charter your own aircraft so check into this if you are heading into the bush. Travel to a transportation hub that is close to your final destination before you charter.

The final leg of your trip may require the actual charter of an aircraft. Most transportation hubs have several different outfits so rates are usually competitive. Before shopping you need to know exactly how much your gear weighs. The cost to you will depend upon several factors: the size aircraft required, type of aircraft required (floats or wheels), the flight time, and how busy the air taxi operator is. Check with several outfits and make sure that the one you choose is familiar with your destination. Many off-runway landing sites are not easy to use, actual experience in flying to the place you want to go is important.

Weather can greatly restrict a small aircraft. Depend upon your pilot to make weather

SMALL AIRCRAFT ARE OFTEN USED TO REACH REMOTE PARTS OF ALASKA

decisions. Do not pressure a pilot to fly in questionable weather, that is the cause of many accidents. Weather may delay your departure or pick up. Always have enough food with you on a trip to allow you to comfortably wait out an extended period of bad weather.

Waiting for a pick up can be a stressful experience. Sometimes weather en route is impassable even though the weather you can see seems just fine for flying. You will feel much better about it if you know that someone other than the air taxi operator knows you are out there. Make sure a reliable friend knows when you are to return and who you have contracted for your pickup. There have been a few cases where parties have been dropped off and not picked up as scheduled. There have even been fatal cases where people chartered into the wilderness and didn't set up any pick up at all. Make sure your pick up arrangements are clear and unambiguous. You and the charter operator must know the exact location. It must be easy to identify from the ground and also from the air.

### The Public-Use Cabins

One of the best ways to get out into the wilderness in Alaska is to rent a cabin from the government. Several different management agencies, both Federal and State, have a considerable number of cabins scattered around the state. These cabins are a good deal, many are available for around $25 per night and most are in very desirable locations. Unfortunately each of the organizations has its own reservation system. Here's a quick rundown of what is available and where you can get further information.

**US Forest Service in Tongass National Forest** - About 150 cabins, almost all require boat, aircraft, or hiking access. All have wood or oil stove, table, chairs, beds without mattresses and outhouses. Some cabins have boats. Cost is $25 per night. For more information contact the Alaska Public Lands Information Center, 605 W. Fourth Ave, Suite 105, Anchorage, AK 99501; 907 271-2599 or the Forest Service Information Center, 101 Egan Drive, Juneau, AK; 907 586-8751.

**US Forest Service in Chugach National Forest** - About 45 cabins in the Kenai Mountains and Prince William Sound. All except one require boat, aircraft, or hiking access. All have wood or oil stove, table, chairs, beds without mattresses and outhouses. Some cabins have boats. Cost is $25 per night. For more information contact the Alaska Public Lands Information Center, 605 W. Fourth Ave, Suite 105, Anchorage, AK 99501; 907 271-2599 or the Forest Service Information Center, 101 Egan Drive, Juneau, AK; 907 586-8751. There is a nice pamphlet about these cabins.

**Alaska Dept. of Natural Resources** - They have 35 cabins in the Interior, Southcentral, and Southeast Alaska. A few are accessible by road, most require a boat, aircraft, or hiking. Cabins are similar to Forest Service cabins. Fees vary from $15 to $50 per night. For information contact DNR Public Information Center, 3601 C St., Suite 200, Anchorage, AK 99503; 907 269-8400. There is also a good internet site with information about the cabins: http://www.dnr.state.ak.us/parks/directory.htm.

**Bureau of Land Management** - The BLM has several cabins near Fairbanks. For information contact the BLM Fairbanks Support Center, 1541 Gaffney Road, Fairbanks, AK 99703; 907 356-5345.

**Fish and Wildlife Service** - The USF&W Service has several cabins on Kodiak Island. For information contact the Refuge Manager, Kodiak National Wildlife Refuge, 1390 Buskin River Road, Kodiak, AK 99615; 907 487-2600.

The cabins are nothing luxurious, really just a glorified form of camping. They do provide a roof over your head for protection from the weather, heat, and some protection from bears. Most require that you bring everything you will need: bedding, kitchen utensils, lanterns, and so on. You also must arrange your own transportation, most air and boat charter operators in the region will be familiar with the cabins and how best to access them.

# A SELECTION OF OFF-HIGHWAY DESTINATIONS

In this section you'll find a quick summary of just some of the smorgasbord of off the road offerings available around the state. Each summary has information about location, attractions, and how best to get there. Since there is no room in this book for the many maps that would be necessary to show all of these places you should read them with a supplementary map in hand. The best would probably be the Alaska Atlas & Gazetteer, see the Travel Library in Chapter 2 for more information.

## BEAR-VIEWING HOTSPOTS
## McNEIL RIVER, PACK CREEK, ANAN CREEK, AND OTHERS

When the salmon start running the bears soon appear. Coastal brown bears are the same animal as the smaller inland grizzlies, they just eat better. Several places in Alaska have become known as the best places to see bears, lots of bears.

**McNeil River** is the best of the bunch, and the hardest to get into. The river is located on the west side of Cook Inlet and flows into Kamishak Bay. Literally dozens (often over 50 at one time) of brown bears fish for salmon in the falls near viewing platforms. The presence of observers seems to make little difference to the bears, they just go ahead and mind their own business. Only 10 people are allowed to be there at one time. The season is from June through the middle of August. The best access is by float plane from Homer or Kenai. Tent sites are designated and are located away from the river. Access is limited, visitors are selected by lottery, applications must be in by March 1. For more information contact the Alaska Department of Fish and Game, Division of Wildlife Conservation, 333 Raspberry Road, Anchorage, AK 99518; (907) 267-2179.

**Pack Creek** is located on the east side of Admiralty Island, about 25 miles from Juneau. Admiralty Island is known for its brown bears, there are thought to be some 1,700 of them on the island. Pack Creek is the easiest place to see them, there is a viewing platform but no overnight camping is allowed. Usually viewers see only a few bears at a time. The season lasts from the middle of July to the last part of August. Access is by boat or float plane from Juneau. Twenty-four people each day are allowed to visit, permits are handed out on a first-come, first-served basis. For information contact the Admiralty Island National Monument, 8461 Old Dairy Road, Juneau, AK 99801; (907) 586-8790.

**Anan Creek Bear Observatory** is another Southeast location. This is primarily a viewing spot for black bears although a few browns do show up. The observatory is located about thirty miles southeast of Wrangell near the mouth of Bradfield Canal. There is a viewing platform here also, usually several bears are visible. No camping is permitted in the area although there is a Forest Service rental cabin about a mile away. The season at Anan Creek runs from the first part of July through the first part of September while the pink salmon are running. Self-guided visitors are not limited although tour operators are. Groups are limited to eight people. For information contact the U.S. Forest Service , Wrangell Ranger District, P.O. Box 51, Wrangell, Alaska;

(907) 874-2323.

Two other good bear-viewing areas are mentioned in other places in this book: Fish Creek near Hyder, Alaska is covered in Chapter 5 and the Brooks River in Katmai National Park is discussed below.

## CHUGACH STATE PARK

490,000-acre Chugach State Park is a mountainous area that directly adjoins Anchorage to the east. Most of the park, in fact, is technically within the boundaries of the Municipality of Anchorage. Anchorage residents can literally be in the wilderness within minutes of leaving their homes. The park is popular with almost everyone interested in the outdoors and offers opportunities to hike, camp, climb rocks or mountains, mountain bike, kayak, fish, hunt, snow-machine, ski, float rivers, and even hang-glide. Accommodating all these uses means that the park has zones and restricted areas to keep incompatible uses separated. There is wildlife in this park even though it is part of the largest city in the state; you may see black and brown bears, mountain goats, Dall sheep, moose, wolves, bald eagles, and even beluga whales.

There are about 50 miles of maintained trails within the park, and many more miles of excellent alpine hiking although alder thickets can be a problem. Popular hikes include **Flattop Mountain** (1.5 miles one way), **Williwaw Lakes** (5 miles one way), **Wolverine Peak** (6 miles one way), **McHugh and Rabbit Lakes Trail** (7 miles one way) and **Crow Pass** (26 miles one way). There are also good trails from the Eklutna Lake Campground.

Camping is the park is mostly unrestricted. The park has a formal campground, Eklutna Lake, which is covered in Chapter 7 of this book. Fires are not allowed in the park except in the fire pits at the few formal campsites. Use camp stoves instead.

Access to the park is from many points including the Seward Highway along Turnagain Arm, the upper hillside area of Anchorage, the Arctic Valley Road (from Mile 6 of the Glenn Highway), the Eagle River Road (from Mile 13 of the Glenn Highway) and the Eklutna Road (from Mile 26 of the Glenn Highway). Visitor centers are located at the end of the Eagle River Road and at the Potter Section House at Mile 115 of the Seward Highway near Potter Marsh and Turnagain Arm. For information contact Chugach State Park, Potter Section House, HC 52, Box 8999, Indian, AK 99540; (907) 345-5014. The Eagle River Visitor Center phone is (907) 694-2108.

## CORDOVA AND THE COPPER RIVER DELTA

Cordova is one of two destinations in this chapter that is perfectly suitable for RVs. The other is Kodiak, see below. Access to this small southcentral Alaska town is quite easy. The Alaska Marine Highway system connects Cordova frequently with both Whittier and Valdez. Cordova is a pleasant little town, but the town isn't the only attraction here. The **Copper River Highway** leads out of town to the east, crossing the **Copper River Delta**, one of Alaska's premier bird migration and nesting areas, and then turns northeast to dead end after 48 miles at the collapsed **Million Dollar Bridge** and **Child's Glacier**.

Cordova (population 2,600) today is primarily a fishing town but has good tourist facilities. It was originally the salt-water terminus of the Copper River and Northwestern Railway, which was built to transport copper ore from the Kennicott Mine and operated until 1938. For visitor information go to either the **Chamber of Commerce** on first street (P.O. Box 99, Cordova, AK 99574; 907 424-7260) or the **Cordova Museum and Library** at 622 1$^{st}$ Street. The museum is also an excellent place to start your tour of the area, it has historical and art exhibits. Another important information site is the **USFS Cordova Area District Office** at 612 2$^{nd}$ St. (Chugach National Forest, Cordova Ranger District, P.O. Box 280, Cordova, AK 99574; 907 424-7661) which has an interpretive center and information about local hikes, attractions, and wildlife viewing areas. Cordova hosts the **Copper River Shorebird Festival** during May and a **silver salmon derby** in August.

An important attraction is the Copper River Highway and its sights. Wildlife often seen along the road includes trumpeter swans, dusky geese, ducks, moose, bears and beavers. There are also several good fishing holes and viewpoints to watch spawning salmon. The road is paved as far as the airport at Mile 12, then turns to gravel. There is a bird viewing boardwalk and picnic area at the end of a 3-mile road from Mile 17 known as **Alaganik Slough**. There is also a formal viewing area for **Childs Glacier** at

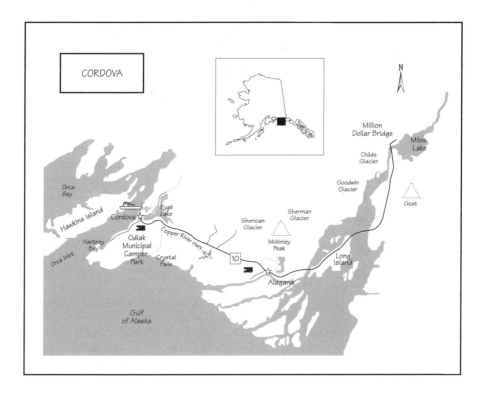

Mile 48 just before you reach the **Million Dollar Bridge**. Be careful here, we know a woman who ended up in the hospital after a huge wave caused by ice falling from the nearby glacier swept over her—keep your eyes open! The bridge at the end of the road is open to traffic although it was severely damaged in the Good Friday Earthquake in 1964, crossing it is not recommended. The road beyond only goes a short distance.

Cordova has a municipal campground, the **Odiak Municipal Camper Park** with 24 sites, electrical hookups, a dump station, and showers. Reservations are recommended, call 907 424-6200. It is located at Mile .5 of the Whitsed Road to Hartney Bay which leaves the Copper River Highway at Mile 1.5. Sign in at City Hall. RVers also camp at **Alaganik Slough** at Mile 17 of the Copper River Highway.

## DENALI NATIONAL PARK - ON FOOT

Denali National Park is one of the most popular destinations in Alaska. We've described the basics of a visit in Chapter 9—the way most people do it. Denali National Park is also an excellent place to wander around the backcountry. The alpine terrain along both sides of the park access road is relatively easy to hike, even without trails.

Backcountry camping in the park is closely regulated. The park is divided into 43 zones. Overnight camping in each is limited, you have to have a permit for the zone in order to overnight there. During the entire summer season most zones are full. Permits are only available at the Visitor's Center in the park, it is not unusual to wait for 2 to 4 days before you can get a permit. The most popular zones are 8, 9, 10, 11, 12, 13, 15, 18, and 27; largely because they are easily accessible and have good terrain for hiking.

To get your permit go to the Visitor Center. There you watch a video about backcountry traveling in the park including information about bear safety. You then can see what is available in the way of backcountry openings and apply for your permit. Some zones are occasionally closed due to problems with curious or aggressive bears. Many people take a permit for an easy to access zone for the first days of their stay and permits for harder to get zones for later in their stay. Once you have your permit you will be issued a bear-proof food container for stays in most zones. Once you have your permit you can reserve space on a bus into the park.

## GATES OF THE ARCTIC NATIONAL PARK AND PRESERVE

This park covers 8,090,000 acres of the Brooks Range to the west of the Dalton Highway and north of the Arctic Circle. The area encompassed is largely tundra-covered foothills and mountains to over 7,000 feet and including the Frigid Crags and Boreal Mountain for which the park is named. There are six national wild and scenic rivers in the park: the **Alatna, John, Kobuk, Noatak, North Fork Koyukuk and Tinayguk**. This is completely undeveloped wild and empty country with wildlife including caribou, moose, grizzly and black bears, wolves, Dall sheep and a host of smaller animals and many birds.

Access to the park is usually by small float aircraft charter from Bettles which gets scheduled air service from Fairbanks. Pick up supplies in Fairbanks since Bettles has little to offer. There is also some access for hikers and river travelers from the Dalton Highway near Wiseman and to the north.

Unrestricted camping is allowed throughout the park although there are no formal campsites. Firewood can be hard to find in treeless areas so bring along a camp stove. Fishing and guns are both allowed. Mosquitoes can be bad. Hiking in the park can be very slow and tedious, even areas free of trees have hard-to-penetrate alder thickets. One of the most popular activities is floating the many rivers in the park with occasional hikes away from the river.

The park is managed by the National Park Service. The Coldfoot Interagency Visitor Center at Mile 175 of the Dalton Highway has information for travelers using that access route. For information contact Superintendent, Gates of the Arctic National Park and Preserve, P.O. Box 74680, Fairbanks, AK 99707; (907) 456-0281.

## GLACIER BAY NATIONAL PARK AND PRESERVE

This 3,234,000-acre national park is located at the far north end of the inside passage and extends out along the open Gulf Coast as far as Dry Bay. Most visitor interest is in the southern portion of the park, the huge glacial inlets. These inlets—**Glacier Bay**, **Muir Inlet**, **Reid Inlet**, **Tarr Inlet** and others—have to be the best place in the world to see the effects of glaciation and the re-vegetation process. That is because this entire region was covered by glaciers in 1794 when visited by Captain Vancouver, today the glaciers have retreated as far as 65 miles. There are 12 tidewater glaciers in the park. The park is also an excellent place to view whales: there are minkes, humpbacks, and orcas. There are also black and brown bears, moose, mountain goats, harbor seals, sea lions and wolves. Whale watching is also very good in Icy Strait, just outside the entrance to Icy Bay.

There are no roads to the park. Access, however, is not difficult. **Gustavus** (pop. 400) is a gateway to the park. It has a good airport, stores, restaurants, and scheduled jet service. From Gustavus a 10-mile road leads into the park terminating at **Bartlett Cove** where park headquarters are located as well as a lodge, a tent campground, and a dock for boats making excursions into the park. Taxis and busses run between Gustavus and Bartlett Cover. From Bartlett Cove an excursion boat runs into the park and up Muir Inlet, they will drop kayakers and hiking parties and pick them up at an agreed time. Charter boats from Gustavus will do the same thing. You can also arrange for drop off and pick up with a float plane. Kayak rentals are available. Glacier Bay is also heavily visited by cruise ships, they tour the fjords but do not stop

Campers are offered an orientation at the park headquarters at Bartlett Cove. There is a nearby tent 25-site **campground** that is free but has a 14-day limit. Firewood is available. At Bartlett Cover there are several miles of nature trails. Away from Bartlett Cove camping is not restricted. It is recommended that you fill out a backcountry use

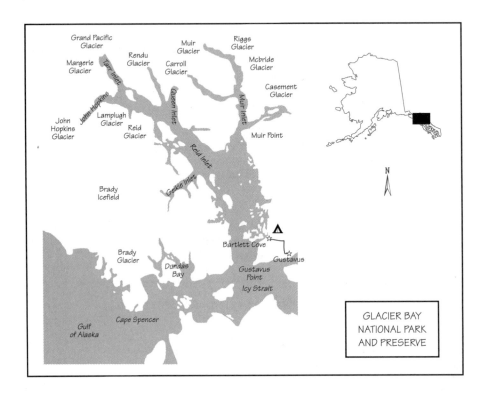

GLACIER BAY
NATIONAL PARK
AND PRESERVE

permit at Bartlett Cove before heading out. In the park expect lots of rain and be prepared with wet weather gear. Campfires are only allowed below the high tide line, bring a stove. There are no formal trails but hiking is good along beaches and in open areas where the glaciers have recently retreated. Kayaking is very popular. Firearms are not allowed in the park, fishing is permitted.

There is a visitor's center located at the lodge at Bartlett Cove. Glacier Bay National Park is managed by the National Park Service. For more information contact the park headquarters at: Glacier Bay National Park Headquarters, P.O. Box 140, Gustavus, AK 99826; (907) 697-2232 or (907) 697-2230.

## KACHEMAK BAY STATE PARK AND WILDERNESS PARK

A large part of the view that you see across Kachemak Bay from Homer is part of the 380,000-acre Kachemak Bay State Park. Encompassing much of the south side of Kachemak Bay, the park also stretches across the peninsula to take in the fjord country to the west of Kenai Fjords National Park. Across from Homer **Halibut Cove** is the center of activities. There is a ranger station there as well as trail heads giving access to about 30 miles of trails to mountain overlooks, glaciers, and lakes. There are also several campsites. Camping is unrestricted, campfires are permitted, as are hunting and fishing. The remote Gulf of Alaska side of the park is much less developed but is popular with kayakers and other boat-oriented visitors.

There is no road access to the park, most visitors catch a daily ferry to Halibut Cover. It swings by **Gull Island**, one of he best places in southcentral Alaska for viewing sea birds including puffins. Float planes from Homer are also used to access the park, particularly the southern Gulf Coast portion.

For information about the park contact the Division of Parks & Outdoor Recreation, Kenai Area Office, P.O. Box 1247, Soldotna, AK 99669: 907 262-5581 or the Kenai Area South District Office, M.P. 168.5 Sterling Highway, Homer, AK; 907 235-7024.

## KATMAI NATIONAL PARK AND PRESERVE

One of the oldest federal park areas in Alaska is 3,955,000-acre Katmai National Park and Preserve. It is also one of the most expensive to access since the location is fairly remote. There are many attractions in the park. **Brooks Camp** and the **Brooks River** are the most popular, many tourists visit on day trips to view brown bears fishing for red salmon from viewing platforms constructed for the purpose. The **Valley of Ten Thousand Smokes** is a ash-covered volcanic landscape with good hiking possibilities accessible along a 24-mile road by daily van from Brooks Camp. Fishing is also extremely popular in the park, Brooks Camp was originally a fishing camp, today fishing there is limited but there are many other destinations in the park for fishermen. A national wild and scenic river, the **Alagnak**, and also the **Nonvianuk River**, are popular floats for fishermen. Kayakers and canoers will find many routes on the huge lakes of the park including a 40-mile round trip paddle from Brooks Camp to the **Bay of Islands** on Naknek Lake and a longer 75-mile **circular trip on Naknek Lake, Lake Grosvenor, the Savonoski River and Iliuk Arm**.

The access gateway to the park is King Salmon which gets jet service from Anchorage. From King Salmon access into the park is usually by amphibian or float aircraft.

There is a 30-site tent campground at Brooks Camp with cooking shelters and bear-proof food-storage caches, reservations are required. Brooks Camp also has other facilities including a ranger station, lodge, dining room, convenience store, and canoe rentals. Camping throughout the rest of the park is allowed although permits are required. Campfires are discouraged since wood is scarce and wet, bring a stove. Weather can be very wet. Grizzly bears can be thick and caution is required. Firearms are not allowed within the park although hunting is allowed in the preserve section in the far north at Kukaklek and Nonvianuk Lakes.

The park is managed by the National Parks Service, for information contact Katmai National Park and Preserve, P.O. Box 7, King Salmon, AK 99613; (907) 246-3305.

WESTERN ALASKA KING SALMON

## KENAI FJORDS NATIONAL PARK

Kenai Fjords National Park covers 588,000 acres of the southern coast and the ice-covered interior of the Kenai Peninsula near Seward. The **Harding Icefield** overlooks four major fjords and several offshore rookery islands in the park. The rough coastal waters at the mouth of the fjords and the hostile weather has kept development in the fjords to a minimum. This is great place to see glaciers, marine mammals, and sea birds. Visitors often see orcas, minke whales, humpback whales, gray whales, Dall porpoises, harbor seals, sea lions, sea otters, and sea birds including horned and tufted puffins, rhinoceros auklets, common murres, and marbled murrelets. Land mammals include black bears, mountain goats, and moose. Grizzly (brown) bears are uncommon except in Resurrection Bay near Seward.

One of the best features of the park is that access is not difficult. The town of Seward is near, there is actually road access to **Exit Glacier** just outside town. Access to the fjords is by charter boat or float plane from Seward or float plane from Homer. Most park visitors are day trippers on tour boats from Seward. Kayakers sometimes paddle into the park from Seward but it is a long paddle, it is easier to arrange for drop off and pick up by a charter boat.

There is a small tent-only **campground** at the Exit Glacier. Otherwise camping in the park is mostly unrestricted but there are no formal campsites. Hiking along the glacial fjords is very difficult and even for kayakers camping sites can be hard to find. Kayaking is popular, but only the experienced should venture into the park because the waters are open and often rough. Come prepared for wet weather. Campfires are allowed but bring a stove, wood is often wet. Fishing and firearms are allowed. Much of the shore-line in the park has recently been selected by the Port Graham Corp., a native corpo-ration. Check at the Seward visitor center before venturing into the park on a wilder-ness trip to see how this will affect your visit.

The park visitor's center is located in Seward near the small boat harbor. The park is managed by the National Park Service. For information contact the park headquarters at P.O. Box 1727, Seward, Alaska 99664; 907 224-3175.

## KLONDIKE GOLD RUSH NATIONAL HISTORICAL PARK AND TRAIL

The Klondike Gold Rush National Historical Park celebrates the 1897-1898 gold rush to Dawson City. Park units include the Chilkoot Trail, the White Pass Trail, much of downtown Skagway, Dyea, and even a visitor center in Seattle. The Chilkoot Trail is a 33-mile-long hiking trail that starts at Dyea and ends at Lake Bennett in the Yukon Territory. It is jointly administered by Parks Canada and the National Park Service. The trail is extremely interesting to anyone with an interest in the gold rush, it is a sort of museum with ruins and hardware cast aside by the stampeders.

Some parts of the trail are difficult and the weather can turn on you so it is important to be prepared for cold weather, particularly along the alpine section between Sheep Camp and Deep Lake (about 10 miles). Snow in the pass means that it is not usually possible to do the hike except between late June and early September. The Chilkoot is a three to five day hike with designated camping areas. Most people walk it from south to north but it is perfectly acceptable to do it in the opposite direction. The trail starts near the Taiya River bridge near the Dyea town site about 8 miles outside Skagway. Campgrounds are **Canyon City** at Mile 7.5, **Pleasant Camp** at Mile 10.5, **Sheep Camp** at Mile 11.5, **Happy Camp** at Mile 20.5, **Deep Lake** at Mile 23, **Lake Lindeman** at Mile 26, **Bare Loon Lake** at Mile 29, and **Lake Bennett** at Mile 33. From the Taiya River bridge the trail follows the Taiya River valley and then a canyon to Sheep Camp. From there the trail climbs across boulders (the golden stairs) to the top of the pass and the Canadian border. From the border the trail gradually descends to Lake Bennett. Once at Bennett hikers can sometimes catch a train back to Skagway

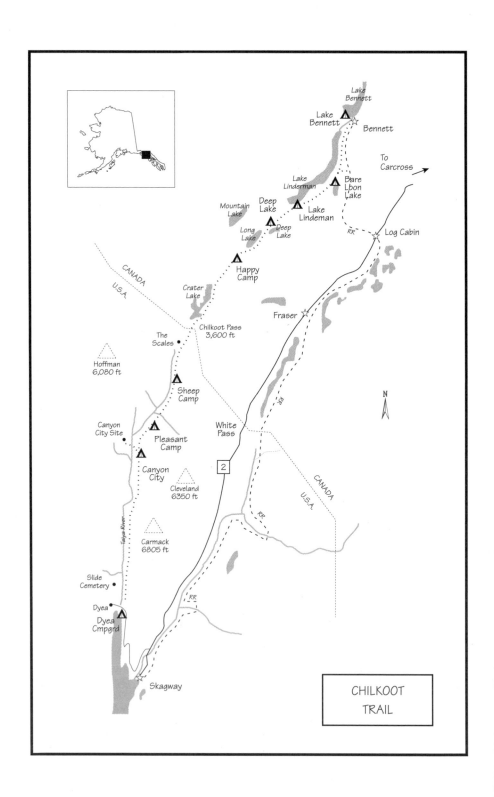

Lake
Bennett

Lake
Bennett                    Bennett

To
Carcross

Lake
Linderman        Bare
                 Lbon
                 Lake

Mountain      Deep
Lake          Lake        Lake
                          Lindeman

Long          Deep
Lake          Lake                      RR      Log Cabin

                    Happy
                    Camp

CANADA
U.S.A.

Crater
Lake
                              Fraser
Chilkoot Pass
3,600 ft

The
Scales

Hoffman
6,080 ft                                RR

            Sheep
            Camp

Canyon                                  White
City Site                               Pass

            Pleasant
            Camp                                    N

Canyon
City                                    2           CANADA
                                                    U.S.A.
Cleveland
6350 ft

Talya River                  RR

Carmack
6805 ft

Slide
Cemetery

Dyea                    RR

Dyea
Cmpgrd

            Skagway

CHILKOOT
TRAIL

or a boat to Carcross. It is also possible to walk out to Log Cabin which is at about Mile 22 of the Klondike Highway from Skagway. A daily shuttle bus returns to Skagway from Log Cabin.

The trail has become very popular and overcrowding has meant that new rules have recently been imposed by the trail's managers. Only fifty hikers per day are now allowed to cross. A hiking permit is required. Reservations are highly recommended since 42 of the 50 slots are reserved leaving space for only 8 walk-ins each day. Call (867) 667-3910 or (800) 661-0486 for reservations. When you call be prepared with a credit card number, mailing address, number of people and names, preferred starting date and two alternates, and your itinerary. There is a $10 reservation fee per hiker and

YES, YOU REALLY CAN WEAR SHORTS IN ALASKA

a $35 per hiker backcountry permit fee ($17.50 for youths). Detailed information will be mailed to you when you apply for your reservation. These rules were in effect for 1997, they may change. Some of the campgrounds may also be closed. The White Pass Railroad's plans for servicing Bennett are also uncertain. Hopefully all of this will get sorted out in the next few years, but don't wait. Just call and see what the present rules are.

## KODIAK ISLAND

Kodiak Island is a very interesting destination for RV campers. It is connected to the road system by the Alaska Marine Highway. Service is from both Homer and Seward by the ferry *Tustumena*. This ferry can not take vehicles over 40 feet long. Kodiak is a very active fishing and fish processing port, but also has good tourist facilities. The island is probably best known for its huge population of very large brown bears.

The town of Kodiak (population 7,000) has a visitor center at 100 Marine Way. (Kodiak Island Visitors Bureau, 100 Marine Way, Kodiak, AK 99615; 907 486-4782). Sights in town are limited, you may want to visit the **Baranov Museum** near the visitor

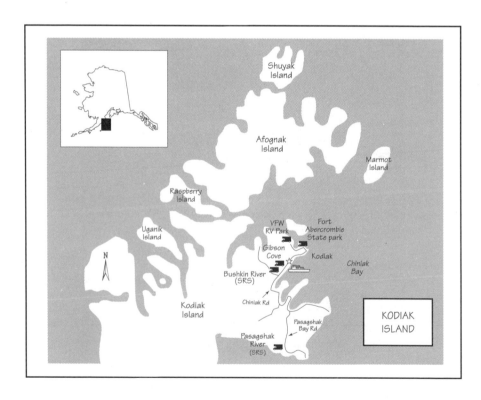

center which is located in a Russian-built structure and is a designated National Historic Landmark. It covers the Russian period of Alaska's history. Another museum in town is the **Alutiiq Museum Archaeological Repository Center** which has articles from sites all around the island. You'll also want to visit the **Kodiak National Wildlife Refuge Visitor's Center** at Mile 4 of the Chiniak Road near the Bushkin River Campground (139 Buskin River road, Kodiak, AK 99615; 907 487-2600).

The Kodiak Area has several roads leading to quiet beaches and scenic outlooks. There are also many hiking trails in the area and fishing holes. Rezanof-Monashka Bay Road runs north from town for 11 miles to Monashka Bay. En route it passes **Fort Abercrombie State Park**. Chiniak Road goes south for 43 miles.

The road system really only reaches a small part of the island, many area attractions are accessible only by boat or aircraft. Shuyak Island is about 50 miles to the north, it is a State Park known for its kayaking waters, there are several rental cabins in the park. **The Kodiak National Wildlife Refuge** covers almost all of Kodiak Island itself. If you want to see bears it is best to get out into it. The air-taxi and tour operators in Kodiak know the places to go, many maintain cabins or campsites for bear-viewing trips.

Campgrounds are not difficult to find in Kodiak. Fort Abercrombie State Park at Mile 4 of the Rezanof-Monashka Bay Road has a 13-site campground with the normal state campground facilities. Farther out on the same road is the VFW RV Park (Mile 7) which has electricity, water, and sewer hookups.

On Chiniak Road there are two campgrounds. At mile 2 is the Gibson Cove Municipal Campground which has toilets and showers. At Mile 4 near the National Wildlife Refuge Headquarters is the Bushkin River State Recreation Site which has 15 sites, normal state campground facilities, and also a dump station.

Finally, there is the Pasagshak River State Recreation Site with 7 sites. This campground is located at Mile 9 of the Pasagshak Bay Road which leaves the Chiniak Road at Mile 30.

## NOME

Nome is the access point for another extensive Alaska road system that in not connected to the main highway system. You can't bring your RV here, there is no ferry connection, but it is possible to fly in to Nome and then rent a car or bicycle.

Nome (population 4,000) is a very important town in Alaska's history. The Nome gold rush of 1899 was the state's largest (Dawson City, of course, is in Canada). Mining in Nome during the gold rush was largely on the beaches, but later the area around Nome was heavily dredged, over 40 dredges remain near Nome, some occasionally active, and there are said to be about 100 of them on the Seward Peninsula. Nome is nationally known as the destination for the **Iditarod Sled Dog Race** and is also the center for an unusual industry, growing reindeer.

Despite its remote location Nome does get a lot of tourists. Most are traveling as part

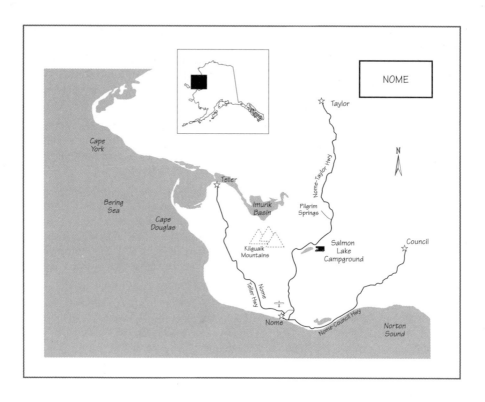

of a package tour included as part of their cruise, bus, train, and air tour of the state. The Visitor Center is on Front Street (Nome Convention & Visitors Bureau, Box 240, Nome, AK 99762; 907 443-5535). Nome has lots of gift shops courtesy of the many tourists, ivory carvings are the hot item. Be sure to visit the **Carrie McLain Museum** in the library basement to se the gold rush exhibits.

Three different gravel roads lead out of Nome like the forks of a trident. They make excellent bike or driving trips. It is probably best to bring your own mountain bike to Nome because you can cover a lot of miles here and will appreciate a good bike. Temperatures can be cool and there is often wind so come prepared.

The **Teller Road** is the left hand fork, it leads 73 miles north to Teller. Along the way it passes King Island fish camp and through an area that is home to a 25,000 animal reindeer herd. The coast is often within view. Teller is a village with a population of about 300 people, you can stay at the school if you don't want to camp. Teller was the place where the dirigible Norge landed after the first crossing of the North Pole.

The center fork leading out of Nome is the **Kougarok** or **Taylor Road** which leads 86 miles northeast past the eastern edge of the **Kigluaik Mountains**. The Kigluaik Mountains are managed by the Bureau of Land Management and are in interesting hiking area. There is a BLM campground, the **Salmon Lake Campground**, at Mile 38. Hike-in destinations in the area include the Wild Goose Pipeline, Crater Lake, and the Mosquito Pass area. For information contact the BLM Kobuk District Office, 1150 University Avenue, Fairbanks, AK 99709; 907 474-2330 or the BLM Nome Field Office, P.O. Box 925, Nome, AK 99762; 907 443-2177. Another point of interest is **Pilgrim Hot Springs**, located on an eight-mile road leaving the Kougarok Road 13 miles north of Salmon Lake Campground. This place was a resort of sorts during the gold rush, later is was a Catholic orphanage. Today it is on the National Register of Historic Places.

The third fork is the **Council Road** which leads 72 miles east. Much of the road is along the coast. Sights along the way are Safety Sound at Mile 25 with a bird-watching boardwalk and the Last Train to Nowhere at Mile 33. You have to ford the Bear River to reach Council, it is not recommended unless you have local knowledge.

## PRINCE WILLIAM SOUND

Prince William Sound (PWS) has become a well-known Alaskan place name. Bruised but not beaten by the Exxon Valdez oil spill PWS remains a jewel. A huge jewel, but a jewel. The Sound covers some 25,000 square miles and has an estimated 2,500 miles of shoreline. This shoreline is almost all wilderness, the only towns are Whittier, Valdez, Cordova, and Tatitlik. The entire sound with the exception of Port Valdez is within the boundaries of the Chugach National Forest which is administered by the U.S. Forest Service. For information contact USFS, Chugach National Forest, 201 E. 9th Ave., Suite 206, Anchorage, AK 99501; 907 271-2500.

Wildlife viewing opportunities in the Sound are very good. Marine mammals include orcas, gray whales, humpback whales, sea lions, sea otters, and harbor seals. On shore you'll find black and brown bears, mountain sheep, moose, and Sitka black-tailed deer. Over 3,000 bald eagles are said to frequent the Sound, as well as marine seabirds and shorebirds.

Many of the visitors to the Sound travel on cruise ships, ferries, or excursion boats. Many cruise ship schedules now include a visit to **College Fjord**, an excellent place to see a lot of glaciers all in one place. Many excursion cruises also visit College Fjord, usually from Whittier. Excursions from Valdez generally visit **Columbia Glacier** instead, this largest of Alaskan glaciers was the source of the ice that caused the Exxon Valdez to shift course and go aground. State of Alaska Marine Highway ferries also run across the Sound; from Seward to Valdez, from Valdez to Cordova, from Whittier to Cordova, and from Whittier to Valdez. The ferries don't get really close to the glaciers but there are plenty of great views from their decks anyway.

A sailboat, power boat, or a kayak gives you the freedom to really explore Prince William Sound. Access is from Whittier, Valdez, Cordova, or Seward. It is also perfectly feasible to charter a boat or aircraft to deliver you pretty much anywhere in PWS. The State of Alaska has 14 marine parks in the Sound and 5 more near Seward with scenic anchorages, camping sites on shore, and recreational opportunities. Most

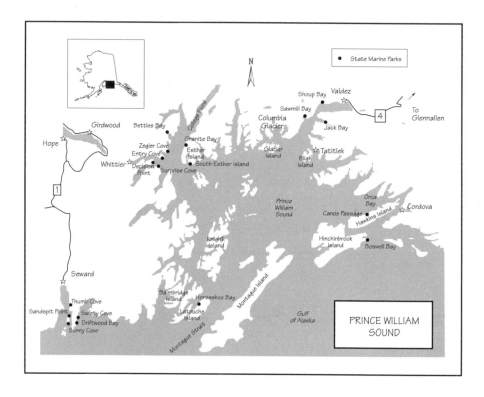

are clustered around Whittier, Valdez, or Cordova. For more information including individual maps contact Alaska State Marine Parks, Kenai Area Office, P.O. Box 1247, Soldotna, AK 99669; 907 262-5581. There are also many rental cabins located around the sound, managed by the USFS. Camping in Chugach National Forest is mostly unrestricted, campfires are allowed but dry firewood can be difficult to find. There are private lands throughout the Sound, particularly the eastern Sound, respect private property.

## SWAN LAKE AND SWANSON RIVER CANOE ROUTES

The Kenai National Wildlife Refuge has two excellent canoe routes. They are both accessed off the same road. Follow the Swanson River Road which becomes the Swan Lake Road at Mile 17—it leaves the Sterling Highway at Mile 83, just west of Sterling. Mileages given here are from the Sterling Highway. There are three small USF&W campgrounds along this road in addition to the canoe routes: **Dolly Varden Lake Campground** (Mile 14), **Rainbow Lake Campground** (Mile 16), and **Fish Lake Campground** (Mile 20). None are good for big rigs. The canoe routes run through an area that has many moose, beavers, loons, bald eagles, and swans. There are also a few black and brown bears, otters, and wolves. Fishing can be good for Dolly Varden, silver and red salmon, and rainbows. Registration at trail heads is required, parties are limited to 15 people. Camping is unrestricted but you should use established camp-sites if you find them. Fires are usually allowed but it can be difficult to find mineral soil to build one, bring a stove. The area is managed by the USF&W Service. For information contact Refuge Manager, Kenai National Wildlife Refuge, P.O. Box 2139, Soldotna, AK 99669; 907 262-7021.

The shortest and easiest of the two routes is the **Swan Lake Route**. It starts from either of two trailheads: the West Entrance at Canoe Lake (Mile 21), and the East Entrance at Portage Lake (Mile 27). From either entrance the routes pass through several lakes connected by portages and then reach the Moose River which flows into the Kenai near Sterling. These routes take about a week to complete and cover a distance of about 60 miles. Many additional lakes are accessible by making side trips from the main routes.

The **Swanson River Route** begins at Paddle Lake (Mile 30). You travel north through a series of lakes until reaching the Swanson River. You then travel down the Swanson with no portages to either a take-out at the Swanson River Landing (19 river miles) near Mile 17 or to a take-out at Captain Cook State Recreation Area (43 river miles) off the North Kenai Spur Highway. This trip also takes about a week.

## YUKON RIVER

The Yukon River is one of the longest navigable waterways on the North American Continent. It is actually possible to canoe or kayak from the headwaters near the head of the Chilkoot Pass all the way to the Bering Sea. En route you would have to make a portage at Whitehorse around a dam, run rapids at the outlet of Lake Lindeman and below Carmacks, and paddle across 5 rather large lakes, but otherwise your trip would be very uncomplicated.

As a practical matter most people travel the upper river from near Whitehorse to Circle City in Alaska. Distance and approximate time to complete are as follows: Whitehorse to Dawson City, 460 miles, 2 weeks; Dawson City to Eagle, 100 miles, 4 days; Eagle to Circle City, 150 miles, 1 week.

Canoes can be rented in Whitehorse, Dawson City, and Eagle. The rental companies can help you work out the logistics. Many people do this so some of the support structure is in place.

Below Eagle the river runs through the Yukon-Charlie Rivers National Preserve. For information contact: National Park Service, Yukon-Charlie Rivers National Preserve, P.O. Box 167, Eagle, AK; 907 547-2233.

# MAP INDEX

# CAMPGROUND INDEX

| | | | |
|---|---|---|---|
| Byers Lake Campground | Mat-Su Jct. to Denali Park | State of Ak. | 272 |
| Camp Run-A-Muck | Stewart and Hyder | Commercial | 129 |
| Campground Services | Watson Lake | Commercial | 89 |
| Cantwell RV Park | Mat-Su Jct. to Denali Park | Commercial | 273 |
| Carcross Campground | White Pass Highway | Yukon Ter. | 336 |
| Caribou Creek Territorial Campground | Dempster | NW Ter. | 318 |
| Carlo Creek Lodge | Mat-Su Jct. to Denali Park | Commercial | 273 |
| Cassiar RV Park | Yhd Hwy to Meziadin Lk | Commercial | 125 |
| CCC (Three C's) USFS Campground | Ketchikan | USFS | 357 |
| Centennial Camper Park | Anchorage | Local Gov. | 183 |
| Centennial Park Campground | Soldotna | Local Gov. | 234 |
| Central Motor Inn and Campground | Steese Highway | Commercial | 293 |
| Charlie Lake Provincial Park Campground | Taylor & Ft. St. John | B.C. Prov. | 75 |
| Chena Hot Springs Resort | Chena Hot Springs Road | Commercial | 297 |
| Chena Lakes Recreation Area | North Pole and Badger Rd | Local Gov. | 152 |
| Chena Marina RV Park | Fairbanks | Commercial | 146 |
| Chena River State Recreation Site | Fairbanks | State of Ak. | 146 |
| Chilkat State Park | Haines | State of Ak. | 340 |
| Chilkoot Lake State Campground | Haines | State of Ak. | 339 |
| Chistochina RV Park | Glennallen to Tok | Commercial | 198 |
| Chuk Territorial park | Dempster | NW Ter. | 318 |
| Circle Hot Springs Resort | Steese Highway | Commercial | 294 |
| City of Seward Waterfront Campground | Seward | Local Gov. | 221 |
| Clam Gulch State Recreation Area | Soldotna to Homer | State of Ak. | 242 |
| Clearwater State Recreation Site | Delta Junction | State of Ak. | 119 |
| Clover Pass Resort | Ketchikan | Commercial | 357 |
| Coal River Lodge | Ft. Nelson to Watson Lake | Commercial | 87 |
| Congdon Creek Campground | Whitehorse to Tok | Yukon Ter. | 107 |
| Cooper Creek Campground | Tern Lake to Soldotna | USFS | 226 |
| Copper River Campground | Wrangell-St Elias, McCarthy | State of Ak. | 162 |
| Cottonwood RV Park and Campground | Whitehorse to Tok | Commercial | 106 |
| Crabb's Corner | Steese Highway | Commercial | 293 |
| Crescent Creek Campground | Tern Lake to Soldotna | USFS | 225 |
| Cripple Creek Campground | Steese Highway | BLM | 293 |
| Crooked Creek RV Park | Soldotna to Homer | Commercial | 242 |
| Crooked Creek State Recreation Site | Soldotna to Homer | State of Ak. | 241 |
| Crow Creek Mine | Anchorage to Tern Lake | Commercial | 212 |
| Dalan Campground | Whitehorse to Tok | Commercial | 108 |
| Dawson City RV Park and Campground | Dawson City | Commercial | 316 |
| Dawson Peaks Resort & RV Park | Watson Lake to Whitehorse | Commercial | 94 |
| Deadman Lake Campground | Whitehorse to Tok | USF&W | 110 |
| Dease Lake R.V. Park | Meziadin Lk to Alaska Hwy | Commercial | 133 |
| Deception Creek State Campground | Mat-Su Jct. to Denali Park | Commercial | 269 |
| Deep Creek Beach Campground | Soldotna to Homer | State of Ak. | 245 |
| Deep Creek North & South Waysides | Soldotna to Homer | State of Ak. | 245 |
| Delta State Recreation Site | Delta Junction | State of Ak. | 119 |
| Denali Grizzly Bear | Mat-Su Jct. to Denali Park | Commercial | 274 |
| Denali Rainbow Village RV Park | Denali National Park | Commercial | 278 |
| Denali Riverside RV Park | Denali National Park | Commercial | 279 |
| Denali RV Park and Motel | Denali National Park | Commercial | 279 |
| Denali View North | Mat-Su Jct. to Denali Park | State of Ak. | 272 |
| Destiny - Talkeetna River | Mat-Su Jct. to Denali Park | Commercial | 271 |
| Dezadeash Lake Campground | Haines Highway | Yukon Ter. | 345 |
| Discovery Campground | North Kenai | State of Ak. | 238 |

| | | | |
|---|---|---|---|
| Hidden Lake Campground | Tern Lake to Soldotna | USF&W | 228 |
| Highlander Camper Park | Anchorage | Commercial | 181 |
| Hillside Motel and RV Park | Anchorage | Commercial | 181 |
| Historical Hicks Creek Roadhouse | Palmer to Glennallen | Commercial | 192 |
| Homer Spit Campground | Homer | Commercial | 249 |
| Husky 5th Wheel RV Park | Fort Nelson | Commercial | 79 |
| Hylen's Camper Park | Soldotna to Homer | Commercial | 244 |
| Igloo Creek Campground | Denali National Park | NPS | 277 |
| Iron Creek Lodge | Ft Nelson to Watson Lake | Commercial | 88 |
| Izaak Walton State Recreation Site | Tern Lake to Soldotna | State of Ak. | 229 |
| J&H Wilderness Resort | Ft. Nelson to Watson Lake | Commercial | 86 |
| Jade City Campground | Meziadin Lk to Alaska Hwy | Commercial | 135 |
| Jim River | Dalton Highway | BLM | 303 |
| John's Motel and RV Park | Anchorage | Commercial | 183 |
| Johnson Lake State Campground | Soldotna to Homer | State of Ak. | 240 |
| Johnson's Crossing Campground Services | Watson Lake to Whitehorse | Commercial | 95 |
| Junction 37 RV Park | Watson Lake to Whitehorse | Commercial | 93 |
| Kamping Resorts of Alaska (K.R.O.A.) | Palmer to Glennallen | Commercial | 194 |
| Karen A. Hornaday Hillside Park | Homer | Local Gov. | 250 |
| Kasilof River State Recreation Site | Soldotna to Homer | State of Ak. | 240 |
| Kasilof RV Park | Soldotna to Homer | Commercial | 241 |
| Kathleen Lake Campground | Haines Highway | Can Pk Ser | 345 |
| Kelly & Peterson Lake Campgrounds | Tern Lake to Soldotna | USF&W | 227 |
| Kenai Fjords RV Park | Seward | Commercial | 222 |
| Kenai Princess RV Park | Tern Lake to Soldotna | USFS | 225 |
| Kenai Riverbend Campground | Soldotna | Commercial | 235 |
| Kenai RV Park | Kenai | Commercial | 236 |
| Kenny Lake Mercantile & RV Park | Wrangell-St Elias, McCarthy | Commercial | 161 |
| Kinaskan Lake Provincial Park | Meziadin Lk to Alaska Hwy | B.C. Prov. | 132 |
| King Mountain State Recreation Site | Palmer to Glennallen | State of Ak. | 192 |
| Kiskatinaw Provincial Park CG | Dawson Crk to Ft. St. John | B.C. Prov. | 70 |
| Kitwanga Centennial Park | Yhd Hwy to Meziadin Lk | Local Gov. | 125 |
| Klawock City Trailer Park | Prince of Wales Island | Local Gov. | 358 |
| Klondike River Campground | Dawson City | Yukon Ter. | 316 |
| Klondike River Lodge | Klondike Highway | Commercial | 312 |
| Kluane RV Campground | Whitehorse to Tok | Commercial | 105 |
| Kluane Wilderness Village | Whitehorse to Tok | Commercial | 108 |
| Kyllonen's RV Park | Soldotna to Homer | Commercial | 247 |
| Lake Creek Campground | Whitehorse to Tok | Yukon Ter. | 108 |
| Lake Laberge Campground | Klondike Highway | Yukon Ter. | 310 |
| Lake Louise Recreation Area | Palmer to Glennallen | State of Ak. | 194 |
| Lake Lucille Park | Wasilla | Local Gov. | 261 |
| Lakeview Campground | Whitehorse to Tok | USF&W | 111 |
| Land's End RV Park | Homer | Commercial | 249 |
| Last Chance USFS Campground | Ketchikan | USFS | 357 |
| Le Conte RV Park | Petersburg | Commercial | 362 |
| Liard River Hotsprings Provincial Park | Ft. Nelson to Watson Lake | B.C. Prov. | 86 |
| Liard River Lodge | Ft. Nelson to Watson Lake | Commercial | 86 |
| Liberty Falls State Recreation Site | Wrangell-St Elias, McCarthy | State of Ak. | 162 |
| Lions Rainey Creek Municipal | Stewart and Hyder | Local Gov. | 128 |
| Little Nelchina State Recreation Site | Palmer to Glennallen | State of Ak. | 193 |
| Little Susitna River Campground | Mat-Su Jct. to Denali Park | Local Gov. | 266 |
| Little Tonsina River State Rec Site | S Glenn Jct. To Valdez | State of Ak. | 164 |
| Log Cabin Resort | Prince of Wales Island | Commercial | 358 |

| | | | |
|---|---|---|---|
| Lost Lake Campground | Delta Junction | State of Ak. | 121 |
| Lower Skilak Lake Campground | Tern Lake to Soldotna | USF&W | 229 |
| Lower Troublesome Creek Campground | Mat-Su Jct. to Denali Park | State of Ak. | 272 |
| Mackenzie River Wayside Park | Dempster | NW Ter. | 318 |
| MacKenzie's RV Park | Whitehorse | Commercial | 101 |
| Mackintosh Lodge | Whitehorse to Tok | Commercial | 105 |
| Marion Creek Campground | Dalton Highway | BLM | 303 |
| Marsh Lake Campground | Watson Lake to Whitehorse | Yukon Ter. | 96 |
| Matanuska Glacier State Rec Site | Palmer to Glennallen | State of Ak. | 192 |
| Matanuska River Park | Palmer | Local Gov. | 188 |
| McDonald Campground | Ft. Nelson to Watson Lake | B.C. Prov. | 85 |
| McKinley RV and Campground | Denali Park to Fairbanks | Commercial | 281 |
| Mendenhall Lake Campground | Juneau | USFS | 366 |
| Meziadin Junction Services | Yhd Hwy to Meziadin Lk | Commercial | 127 |
| Meziadin Lake Provincial Park | Yhd Hwy to Meziadin Lk | B.C. Prov. | 126 |
| Mile "0"RV Park and Campground | Dawson Creek | Commercial | 67 |
| Miller's Landing Campground | Seward | Commercial | 222 |
| Million Dollar Falls Campground | Haines Highway | Yukon Ter. | 344 |
| Minto Resorts Campground | Klondike Highway | Commercial | 311 |
| Montana Creek Campgrounds | Mat-Su Jct. to Denali Park | Commercial | 270 |
| Montana Services & RV Park | White Pass Highway | Commercial | 336 |
| Moon Lake State Recreation Site | Tok to Delta Junction | State of Ak. | 116 |
| Moose Creek Campground | Klondike Highway | Yukon Ter. | 312 |
| Moose Horn RV Park | Glennallen | Commercial | 196 |
| Moose Meadows Resort | Meziadin Lk to Alaska Hwy | Commercial | 134 |
| Moose Pass Alaska RV Park | Tern Lake to Seward | Commercial | 218 |
| Morgan's Landing State Recreation Area | Tern Lake to Soldotna | State of Ak. | 230 |
| Morino Backpacking Campground | Denali National Park | NPS | 276 |
| Morley River Lodge | Watson Lake to Whitehorse | Commercial | 94 |
| Mosquito Lake state Recreation Site | Haines Highway | State of Ak. | 342 |
| Mountain Ridge Motel and RV Park | Whitehorse | Commercial | 99 |
| Mountain Shadow RV Park and CG | Meziadin Lk to Alaska Hwy | Commercial | 133 |
| Mountain View RV Park | Palmer | Commercial | 188 |
| Mukluk Annie's Salmon Bake | Watson Lake to Whitehorse | Commercial | 95 |
| Muncho Lake Lodge | Ft. Nelson to Watson Lake | Commercial | 85 |
| Naabia Niign Campground | Whitehorse to Tok | Commercial | 111 |
| Nancy Lake State Recreation Site | Mat-Su Jct. to Denali Park | State of Ak. | 267 |
| Natainlii Campground | Dempster | NW Ter. | 318 |
| Nemo Campsites | Wrangell | USFS | 360 |
| Nenana Valley RV Park and Campground | Denali Park to Fairbanks | Commercial | 282 |
| Ninilchik Beach Campground | Soldotna to Homer | State of Ak. | 244 |
| Ninilchik River Campground | Soldotna to Homer | State of Ak. | 242 |
| Ninilchik River Scenic Overlook | Soldotna to Homer | State of Ak. | 243 |
| Ninilchik View Campground | Soldotna to Homer | State of Ak. | 245 |
| Norlite Campground & RV Park | Fairbanks | Commercial | 148 |
| North Country Service Center Ltd. | Whitehorse to Tok | Commercial | 105 |
| Northern Exposures RV Park and CG | Elliot Highway | Commercial | 299 |
| Northern Lights RV Park | Dawson Creek | Commercial | 67 |
| Northern Lights RV Park | Petersburg | Commercial | 362 |
| Northern Nights CG and RV Park | Glennallen | Commercial | 196 |
| Northern Rockies Highland Glen Lodge | Ft. Nelson to Watson Lake | Commercial | 85 |
| Northstar | Tok | Commercial | 113 |
| Norway Point Parking Area | Juneau | Local Gov. | 367 |
| Oceanside RV Park | Haines | Commercial | 341 |

| | | | |
|---|---|---|---|
| Oceanview RV Park | Homer | Commercial | 250 |
| Odiak Municipal Camper Park | Cordova | Local Gov. | 380 |
| Ohmer Creek Campground | Petersburg | USFS | 362 |
| Olnes Pond Campground | Elliot Highway | State of Ak. | 300 |
| Otter Falls Cutoff | Whitehorse to Tok | Commercial | 104 |
| Otto Lake RV Park | Denali Park to Fairbanks | Commercial | 280 |
| Overland RV Park | Kenai | Commercial | 235 |
| Park Avenue Campground | Prince Rupert | Commercial | 353 |
| Pasagshak River State Recreation Site | Kodiak | State of Ak. | 389 |
| Pat Creek Camping Area | Wrangell | Commercial | 360 |
| Paxson Lake BLM Campground | Delta Jct. to S. Glenn Jct. | BLM | 156 |
| Peace Island Park Campground | Taylor & Ft. St. John | Local Gov. | 71 |
| Peters Creek "petite" RV Park | Anchorage to Palmer | Commercial | 186 |
| Pine Lake Campground | Whitehorse to Tok | Yukon Ter. | 104 |
| Pine Valley Motel and Café | Whitehorse to Tok | Commercial | 108 |
| Pink Mountain Campsite and R.V. Park | Ft. St. John to Ft. Nelson | Commercial | 77 |
| Pink Mountain Motor Inn | Ft. St. John to Ft. Nelson | Commercial | 77 |
| Pioneer Lodge | Mat-Su Jct. to Denali Park | Commercial | 268 |
| Pioneer RV Park | Whitehorse | Commercial | 99 |
| Pleasant Valley RV Park | Chena Hot Springs Road | Commercial | 295 |
| Porcupine Campground | Anchorage to Tern Lake | USFS | 216 |
| Porcupine Creek State Recreation Site | Glennallen to Tok | State of Ak. | 200 |
| Port Chilkoot Camper park | Haines | Commercial | 341 |
| Portage Cove State Campground | Haines | State of Ak. | 342 |
| Primrose Campground | Tern Lake to Seward | USFS | 219 |
| Prophet River Provincial Park CG | Ft. St. John to Ft. Nelson | B.C. Prov. | 78 |
| Prudhomme Lake Provincial Park | Prince Rupert | B.C. Prov. | 354 |
| Ptarmigan Creek | Tern Lake to Seward | USFS | 219 |
| Pullen Creek RV Park | Skagway | Local Gov. | 332 |
| Quartz Creek Campground | Tern Lake to Soldotna | USFS | 225 |
| Quartz Lake Campground | Delta Junction | State of Ak. | 120 |
| Rainbow Lake Campground | Swanson River | USF&W | 391 |
| Rancheria RV Park | Watson Lake to Whitehorse | Commercial | 93 |
| Raven RV Park | Whitehorse to Tok | Commercial | 105 |
| Red Goat Lodge | Meziadin Lk to Alaska Hwy | Commercial | 132 |
| Red Squirrel Picnic Area Campground | Chena Hot Springs Road | State of Ak. | 297 |
| Resurrection Pass Trailhead | Anchorage to Tern Lake | USFS | 216 |
| Resurrection Trail Resort | Anchorage to Tern Lake | Commercial | 217 |
| Rika's Roadhouse | Delta Junction | State of Ak. | 120 |
| Riley Creek Campground | Denali National Park | NPS | 276 |
| Rita's Campground RV Park | Tok | Commercial | 115 |
| River Quest RV Park | Soldotna | Commercial | 234 |
| River Terrace RV Park | Soldotna | Commercial | 233 |
| Rivers Edge Recreation Park | Palmer to Glennallen | Commercial | 190 |
| Rivers Edge RV Park & Campground | Fairbanks | State of Ak. | 147 |
| Riverside Camper Park | Mat-Su Jct. to Denali Park | Commercial | 266 |
| Riverside House RV Park | Soldotna | Commercial | 233 |
| Riverview RV Park | North Pole and Badger Rd | Commercial | 149 |
| Road's End RV Park | North Pole and Badger Rd | Commercial | 149 |
| Robert Service Campground | Whitehorse | Local Gov. | 100 |
| Rock River Campground | Dempster | Yukon Ter. | 318 |
| Rocky Lake State Recreation Site | Mat-Su Jct. to Denali Park | State of Ak. | 263 |
| Ron's RV park | Taylor & Ft. St. John | Commercial | 75 |
| Rosehip Campground | Chena Hot Springs Road | State of Ak. | 296 |

| | | | |
|---|---|---|---|
| Rotary R.V. Park | Taylor & Ft. St. John | Commercial | 74 |
| Russian River Campground | Tern Lake to Soldotna | USFS | 227 |
| Salcha River State Recreation Site | Fairbanks to Delta Junction | State of Ak. | 153 |
| Salmon Lake Campground | Nome | BLM | 391 |
| Salmon Run Adventures RV CG | Haines | Commercial | 339 |
| Sanctuary River Campground | Denali National Park | NPS | 277 |
| Santaland RV Park & Campground | North Pole and Badger Rd | Commercial | 150 |
| Savage River Campground | Denali National Park | NPS | 277 |
| Savikko Park | Juneau | Local Gov. | 367 |
| Sawmill Creek Campground | Sitka | USFS | 364 |
| Scout Lake Recreation Site | Tern Lake to Soldotna | State of Ak. | 229 |
| Sea Otter R.V. Park | Valdez | Commercial | 168 |
| Sealing Cove Boat Harbor Campground | Sitka | Local Gov. | 364 |
| Seaview Bar, Café, Motel, and RV Park | Anchorage to Tern Lake | Commercial | 215 |
| Sehja Services and RV Park | Whitehorse to Tok | Commercial | 107 |
| Settlers Cove State Recreation Site | Ketchikan | State of Ak. | 357 |
| Sheep Mountain Lodge | Palmer to Glennallen | Commercial | 193 |
| Shepherd's Inn RV Park | Ft. St. John to Ft. Nelson | Commercial | 76 |
| Ship Creek Landings Downtown RV Park | Anchorage | Commercial | 184 |
| Shoemaker Bay | Wrangell | Local Gov. | 360 |
| Signal Creek USFS Campground | Ketchikan | USFS | 357 |
| Sikanni River RV Park | Ft. St. John to Ft. Nelson | Commercial | 77 |
| Sitka Sportsman's Association RV Park | Sitka | Commercial | 364 |
| Smith's Green Acres | Delta Junction | Commercial | 119 |
| Snag Junction Campground | Whitehorse to Tok | Yukon Ter. | 109 |
| Sourdough Campground | Tok | Commercial | 114 |
| Sourdough Country Campsite R.V. Park | Watson Lake to Whitehorse | Commercial | 96 |
| Sourdough Creek BLM Campground | Delta Jct. to S. Glenn Jct. | BLM | 157 |
| Sourdough Fuel, Coldfoot Slate Creek Inn | Dalton Highway | Commercial | 303 |
| Sourdough Pete's RV Park | Taylor & Ft. St. John | Commercial | 73 |
| South Rolly Campground | Mat-Su Jct. to Denali Park | State of Ak. | 267 |
| Spirit Lake Wilderness Resort | White Pass Highway | Commercial | 336 |
| Spit Dry Camping | Homer | Local Gov. | 249 |
| Sportsman's Lodge Russian River Ferry | Tern Lake to Soldotna | USF&W | 227 |
| Squanga Lake Campground | Watson Lake to Whitehorse | Yukon Ter. | 96 |
| Squirrel Creek State Recreation Site | S Glenn Jct. To Valdez | State of Ak. | 164 |
| Stariski State Recreation Site | Soldotna to Homer | State of Ak. | 246 |
| Starrigavan Campground | Sitka | USFS | 364 |
| Strawberry Flats Campground | Ft. Nelson to Watson Lake | B.C. Prov. | 84 |
| Summit Lake Provincial Campground | Ft. Nelson to Watson Lake | B.C. Prov. | 83 |
| Sumner Strait State Recreation Area | Petersburg | State of Ak. | 362 |
| Sunrise Inn RV Park | Tern Lake to Soldotna | Commercial | 223 |
| Susitna Landing | Mat-Su Jct. to Denali Park | Commercial | 270 |
| Swan's Rest RV Park | Haines Highway | Commercial | 343 |
| Swiftwater Park | Soldotna | Local Gov. | 232 |
| Takhini Hot Springs | Whitehorse | Commercial | 101 |
| Tanana Valley Campground | Fairbanks | Local Gov. | 148 |
| Tangle Lakes Campground | Denali Highway | BLM | 158 |
| Tangle River Campground | Denali Highway | BLM | 159 |
| Tantalus Campground | Klondike Highway | Commercial | 311 |
| Tatchun Creek Campground | Klondike Highway | Yukon Ter. | 311 |
| Tatlanika Trading Co. Campground | Denali Park to Fairbanks | Commercial | 282 |
| Tatogga Lake Resort | Meziadin Lk to Alaska Hwy | Commercial | 132 |
| Tazlina River RV Park | Wrangell-St Elias, McCarthy | Commercial | 160 |